C O N T E N T S.

Tables

CONTENTS.

ERRATUM.

Page 19. line 5. from foot, *for* 33° 45′ *read* 8° 15′

INTRODUCTION.

THE following Collection contains moſt of the Tables which are needed in teaching a Courſe of Mathematics, or which are uſeful in Surveying, Navigation, and the other practical arts depending upon that Science.

OF LOGARITHMS.

LOGARITHMS are artificial numbers, by the help of which arithmetical operations are performed with more diſpatch, and which have contributed much to facilitate mathematical calculation, and extend mathematical ſcience. They were invented by Baron Napier of Merchiſton, who publiſhed the firſt Tables in the year 1614.

If the Logarithms of two numbers be added, their ſum is the Logarithm of the product ariſing from the multiplication of the numbers.— This is the fundamental property of Logarithms, from which all the others are derived.

The firſt notion of Logarithms was ſuggeſted by comparing arithmetical and geometrical progreſſions.

A rank of numbers, whoſe differences are equal, is termed an arithmetical ſeries, or progreſſion, as 2, 4, 6, 8, where the common difference is 2; or 0, 3, 6, 9, where the common difference is 3.

A rank of numbers whoſe ratios are equal, that is, where each term is formed from the former by multiplying or dividing it by the ſame number, is called a geometrical ſeries or progreſſion, as 1, 2, 4, 8, where the common ratio is 2; or 1, 3, 9, 27, where the common ratio is 3.

If d denote the common difference of an arithmetical ſeries whoſe firſt term is 0, and r the common ratio of a geometrical ſeries whoſe firſt term is 1, the ſucceſſive terms of the ſeries will be repreſented by the algebraic ſymbols as under,

Arithmetical progreſſion, 0, d, 2d, 3d, 4d, 5d, 6d, 7d.
Geometrical progreſſion, 1, r, r^2, r^3, r^4, r^5, r^6, r^7.

Now if d be taken for 1, and r for 4, the foregoing progreſſions will become

Arithm. progr. 0, 1, 2, 3. 4, 5, 6, 7.
Geomet. progr. 1, 4, 16, 64, 256, 1024, 4096, 16384.

Let it be required to multiply 64 by 256. The term in the arithmetical progreſſion correſponding to 64 is 3, and therefore it may be repreſented by r^3; for the ſame reaſon 256, which ſtands under 4, may be repreſented by r^4; and their product, according to the rules of algebra,

b will

will be r^7, and will ftand under 7 in the arithmetical progreffion, where
we find 16384. Thus the numbers in the arithmetical progreffion ferve
as logarithms to thofe in the geometrical progreffion.

This inference is drawn from general principles, and may be applied to
to any progreffions of the kinds defcribed. In the common tables of Logarithms, the arithmetical progreffion 0, 1, 2, 3, &c. is chofen as the fimp-
left, and the geometrical progreffion 1, 10, 100, 1000, &c. as the moft
convenient. The correfponding terms of thefe progreffions are as follow.

Logarithms, 0, 1, 2,   3,   4.
Numbers,   1, 10, 100, 1000, 10000.

Hence it appears that the logarithm of 1 is 0, the logarithm of 10 is 1,
the logarithm of 100 is 2, the logarithm of 1000 is 3, and in general the
logarithm of 1 with cyphers annexed is the fame as the number of cyphers.
The logarithm of any number under 10, being lefs than 1, is a decimal fraction; the logarithm of any number between 10 and 100, is 1 with a decimal fraction annexed: the logarithm of any number between 100 and
1000 is 2 with a decimal fraction annexed. The integer of the logarithm is always lefs by one than the integer places of the correfponding
number, ; and it is called the index becaufe it points out the number of
integer places.

The logarithms of decimal fractions, have their index negative. If
there be no cypher between the decimal point and firft fignificant figure,
the index is — 1 ; if there one cypher between them the index is — 2 ;
if two cyphers the index is — 3, and fo on. Thefe indices muft be added and fubtracted according to the rules of algebra.

If numbers be expreffed by the fame fignificant figures, whether all the
figures be integers, or the whole or part of them decimals, and whether
there be cyphers annexed to the integers, or prefixed to the decimals,
their logarithms only differ in the index.

Inftead of negative indices, fome make ufe of the arithmetical complement, or the remainder obtained by fubtracting the negative index from
10. Thus, if there be no cypher before the fignificant figures the index
is 9; if there be one cypher, the index is 8; if two cyphers, 7. If a
logarithm of this fort be added, 10 muft be taken from the index of the
fum. If it be fubtracted, 10 muft be added to the index of the minuend.

EXAMPLES.

Number	Log.
365200, — —	5,562531
36520, — , —	4,562531
3652, — —	3,562531
365,2 — —	2,562531
36,52 — —	1,562531
3,652 — —	0,562531
,3652 —	— 1,562531 or, 9,562531
,03652	— 2,562531 or, 8,562531
,003652	— 3,562531 or, 7,562531

PROBLEM I. *To find the Logarithm of any number from the Tables.*

The index of the logarithm is not printed in the following tables, except for numbers under 100, but is eafily fupplied, being always lefs by
unity than the number of integers, as mentioned above.

If the number be under 100, feek it under N in the firft page of the
table, and directly againft it you have the logarithm.

If

If the number be between 100 and 1000, feek it in fome of the following pages in the marginal column intitled N, and againſt it, in the next column, intitled ⊙, you have the logarithm. The index, which is 2, muſt be fupplied, and as the two figures which immediately follow the index, are the fame for feveral lines, they are only printed in the firſt, and muſt be fupplied in the following ones where they are wanting.

If the number be between 1000 and 10000, look for the three firſt figures of the number on the marginal column intitled 0, and for the fourth on the top of the page; then directly under the laſt, and on the line with the former, you will find the four laſt figures of the logarithm. If the two firſt figures be marked in the firſt column of logarithms in that line, under 0, they are to be taken from it; and if not, from the firſt line above where they are marked, and the index, which is 3, prefixed.

It will be obferved that as the two firſt figures of the logarithm after the index, are the fame for feveral lines, they are only printed in the firſt line to fave room : But as they often change in the middle of a line, to prevent miſtakes, when that happens, the remainder of the line is left blank, and the remaining logarithms marked in a line below, at the beginning of which the proper initial figures are placed.

If the number be between 10000 and 100000. Find the logarithm of the firſt four figures as above, and take the number oppofite to the right hand column D, which is called the tabular difference ; multiply this by the laſt figure of the given number ; cut off the right hand figure of the product, and add the remaining figure to the logarithm already taken ; to this prefix the index 4, and you have the logarithm required.

Ex. Let the logarithm of 53724 be required.

Logarithm of 5372		730136
Tabular difference	81	
which multiplied by the unit place	4	
the product is	32,4	32
Logarithm of 53724		4,730168

For the logarithm of 53720 muſt be 4,730136
and the logarithm of 53730 4,730217
and their diff. which is marked in the col. D. 81

Now if $\frac{4}{10}$ of this difference, or 32, be added to the former logarithm, the fum will be the logarithm of 53724. If the figure cut off exceed 5, an unit ſhould be added to the preceding figure.

The logarithm of numbers between 100000 and 1000000 may be found nearly in the fame manner.

The logarithms of mixed numbers and decimal fractions are found by the fame rules, the index being determined by the number of integer places, as mentioned already.

If the logarithms of a vulgar fraction be required, from the logarithm of the numerator fubtract the logarithm of the denominator, the remainder is the logarithm of the fraction.

Thus, to find the logarithm of $\frac{5}{93}$.

From the logarithm of 5	0,698970
Subtract the logarithm of 93	1,968483
Logarithm of $\frac{5}{93}$	— 2,730487

The

The logarithms wanting the indices are decimal fractions, as has been observed already, and may be extended to any number of places. In some tables they are restricted to 5 places; in the following one, to 6 places; in others they extend to 7 or more places. In comparing logarithms from different tables, it is to be observed that if the places omitted in the shorter ones exceed 5, an unit ought to be added to the figure retained, that it may be as near the truth as possible. Thus the logarithm of 5388, extended to seven places, is 3,7314276, but restricted to six places is 3,731428, because 3,7314280 is nearer to the true logarithm than 3,7314270: for the same reason, the logarithm, if restricted to 5 places, is 3,73143.

When the last figure of a logarithm or decimal fraction is higher than the truth, we sometimes annex the character — to point out that something ought to be subtracted, and when the restricted logarithm or fraction is too low, we annex +, to signify that something ought to be added.

PROBLEM II.　*To find the number corresponding to any logarithm.*

Look for the logarithm next less than the given one, in some left hand column under o; then observe along that line, till you find either the given logarithm, or, if it cannot be exactly found, the logarithm next lower. Then you have the three first figures of the number required on the margin against the logarithm, and the fourth on the top of the column.

If the index be 3, the four figures thus found are integers. If the index be less than 3, the number of integer places is determined by the index, and the rest are decimals. If the index be o or 1, the corresponding integer may be found in the first page of the tables, and when the index is 2, the integer may be found on the margin, against the nearest logarithm in the column intitled o: but as it oftener happens that some decimal is annexed to the integer, it is better always to take out four figures according to the above directions, and, if the number required be an integer of less than four places, the figures cut off will be cyphers.

If the logarithm in the tables next higher than the given one be nearer to it than the next lower, we may take out the number corresponding thereto, which will be higher than the exact number required.

EXAMPLES.

Logarithm			Number
3,774006	—	—	5943
2,774006	—	—	594.3
1,930048	—	—	·85,12 +
0,930048	—	—	8,512 +
2,790132	—	—	616,8 —
1,591065	—	—	39,00

If the index be 4, the number consists of five integer places. Find the four higher places by the foregoing directions, and subtract the logarithm found in the tables from the given one; to the remainder annex a cypher, and divide that number by the tabular difference; the quotient is the fifth figure of the number required.

Ex.

Ex. ·Given Logarithm   4,514853
Neareſt in tables   4,514813   Number   33720

Tabular difference 133)   400(3

Number required — — · —   32723

In like manner the number correſponding to any logarithm may be found to five places, whereof ſome may be decimals as the index points out ; and the number may be found to ſix places if the Tabular diſference amounts to 100, by annexing two cyphers to the remainder, and continuing the quotient to two places.

PROBLEM III.   *To perform multiplication by logarithms.*

Add the logarithms of the factors, their ſum is the logarithm of the product.

Example 1.	*Example* 2.
Multiply 136 by 73	Multiply 15,48 by 6,12
136 Log. 2,133539	15,48 Log. 1,189771
73 Log. 1,863323	6,12 Log. 0,786751

Product 9928 Log. 3,996862   Product 94,73+ Log. 1,976522

If one or both factors be decimal fractions, the negative indices muſt be added according to the rules of algebra.

Otherwiſe :—Remove the decimal point to the right hand till each factor have one integer place at leaſt, and proceed as above ; then remove the decimal point of the product as many places to the left hand as it was removed before, in both factors together to the right hand.

Example

Multiply ,52 by ,08	*Otherwiſe*
,52 Log. —1,716003	5,2 Log. 0,716003
,08 Log. —2,903090	8 Log. 0,903090

Product ,0416 Log. —2,619393   Prod. ,0416 (41,6) Log. 1,619093

PROBLEM IV.   *To perform diviſion by logarithms.*

From the logarithm of the dividend ſubtract the logarithm of the diviſor, the remainder is the logarithm of the quotient.

Example 1.	*Example* 2.
Divide 1404 by 52.	Divide 21,08 by 6,2
1404 Log. 3,147367	21,08 Log. 1,323871
52 Log. 1,716003	6,2 Log. 0,792392

Quotient 27 Log. 1,431364   Quotient 3,4 Log. 0,531479

If either or both factors be decimals, or if the diviſor be greater than the dividend, the ſubtraction is to be performed according to the rules of algebra.

Otherwiſe.

Otherwise.—Remove the decimal points to the right hand till both factors contain an integer, and the dividend be greater than the divisor. Then if the dividend be more places removed than the divisor, remove the decimal point of the quotient as many places to the left hand ; but if the divisor be more places removed, then remove the decimal point of the quotient as many places to the right hand. If the divisor and dividend be equally removed, the quotient is not altered.

Example 1.

Divide ,01728 by ,12.   *Otherwise.*
,01728 Log. —2,237544   1,728 Log. 0,237544
,12   Log. —1,079181   1,2 Log. 0,079181

Quotient ,144   Log. —1,158363 Quot. ,144 (1,44) Log. 0,158363

Example 2.

Divide ,3588 by ,0023.   *Otherwise.*
,3588 Log. —1,554852   3,588 Log. 0,554852
,0023 Log. —3,361728   2,3   Log. 0,361728

Quotient 156,0 Log. 2,193124   Quot. 156 (1,56) Log. 0,193224

PROBLEM V. *To find a fourth proportional to three given numbers ; or to work the rule of three by logarithms.*

Add the logarithms of the second and third terms, from their sum subtract the logarithm of the first, the remainder is the logarithm of the number required.

Example. 2482 : 2774 :: 5491.

Second term, 2774	Log.	3,443106
Third term, 5491	Log.	3,739651
		7,182757
First term, 2482	Log.	3,394802
Fourth term, 6137	Log	3,787955

Another way is, to work by the arithmetical complement, or the number obtained by subtracting the logarithm from 10,000000. Add the arithmetical complement of the logarithm of the first term to the logarithms of the second and third ; subtract 10 from the index of the sum, and you have the logarithm of the fourth.——The above example, wrought in this manner, will stand thus,

First term, 2482	Arithm. comp. Log.	6,605198
Second term, 2774	Logarithm	3,443106
Third term, 5491	Logarithm	3,739651
Fourth term, 6137	Logarithm	3,787955

PROBLEM VI. *To raise powers; that is, to find the square, cube, &c. of any number, by logarithms.*

Multiply the logarithm of the number by the exponent of the power; the product is the logarithm of the power.

Example 1.	*Example 2.*
What is the cube of 18?	What is the fifth power of 7?
18 Log. 1,255273	7 Log. 0,845098
3	5

Cube 5832 Log. 3,765819   Fifth power 16807 Log. 4,225490

PROBLEM VII. *To extract roots by logarithms.*

Divide the logarithm of the given number by the exponent of the root; the quotient is the logarithm of the root.

Example 1.	*Example 2.*
What is the square root of 3249?	What is the cube root of 5832?
3249 Log. 3,511750	5832 Log. 3,765818
Sq. root 57 Log. ½ 1,755875	Cube root 18 Log. ⅓ 1,255273

LOGARITHMIC

SINES, TANGENTS. AND SECANTS.

THE Artificial, or Logarithmic Sines, Tangents and Secants, are the logarithms of the natural numbers which express the measure of the sine, tangent or secant of the corresponding arch, the radius being 10,000,000,000, the logarithm of which is 10.

To find, by the tables, the Logarithmic Sine, Tangent and Secant of an arch, or angle, of any number of degrees and minutes.

If the degrees be under 45, find them at the top of some page, and against the minutes on the left hand, under the word Sine, Tangent, or Secant at the top, you have the logarithm required. The Cosines, Cotangents and Cosecants are found in the same manner.

If the degrees be above 45, and less than 90, find them at the foot of some page, and above the word Sine, Tangent, or Secant at the foot, you have the logarithm.

If the degrees be 90, or upward, subtract the given degrees and minutes from 180°, the remainder is the supplement of the given arch or angle, and has the same Sine, Tangent and Secant.

Thus

Thus, the Sine of	37°	9′	is	9,780,968
the Sine of	53	12		9,903487
the Sine of	126	14		9,906667
the Tangent of	28	53		9,741664
the Tangent of	67	19		10,378858
the Secant of	0	59		10,000064
the Secant of	89	59		13,536274
the Cosine of	12	21		9,989832
the Cotangent of	62	45		9,711836

To find [nearly] the fine, tangent or fecant for any degrees, minutes and feconds propofed.

To facilitate this, there are columns, intitled D, placed betwen the Sines and Cofecants, between the Tangents and Cotangents, and between the Secants and Cofines, which contain the differences correfponding to 100 feconds; therefore, if the two laft figures be taken as decimals, we have the difference correfponding to one fecond.

Take out the logarithm for the given degree and minute, and alfo the difference from the column intitled D; multiply the difference by the given number of feconds; cut off two decimal places from the product, and add the remaining ones to the logarithm for the degrees and minutes; the fum is the logarithm for the degrees, minutes, and feconds required.

EXAMPLE.

Let the logarithmic fine of 36° 9′ 5″ be fought.

Log. Sine of 36° 9′	9,770779	Diff.	288
	14		5
Log. Sine of 36° 9′ 5″	9,770793		14,40

The differences for the Cofines are the fame as for the Secants; thofe for the Cotangents are the fame as for the Tangents, and thofe for the Co-fecants the fame as for the fines.

The logarithm of the Cotangent is the arithmetical complement of that of the tangent, their fum being 20,000000. The fame correfpondence takes place between the logarithms of the Sine and Cofecant, and alfo between thofe of the Cofine and Secant. By attending to this an indiftinct figure may fometimes be fupplied, or an error detected.

To find the degrees and minutes anfwering to any given logarithmic fine, tangent, or fecant.

Seek the neareft logarithm, either under or above its refpective title. If the title be at the top of the page, the degrees are taken from the top of the page, and the minutes from the left hand; but if the title bea at the foot of the column, the degrees are taken from the foot of the page, and the minutes from the right hand.

It may be noticed that if the logarithmic fine do not exceed 9,84985, if the index of the tangent be lefs thon 10, and if the fecant do not exceed 10,150515 it will be found in the column whofe title is at the top:

But

But if the index of the tangent be 10, or upwards, or if the fine or fe-cant exceed the number above mentioned, it will be found in the columns whose titles are at the foot.

Every fine, tangent and fecant anfwers to two angles, whereof one is the fupplement of the other. Thus,

the log. fine   9,601280 anfwers to 23° 32' or 156° 28'
the log. fine   9,948910 — — 62 45 or 117 15
the log. tangent 9,768703 — — 30 25 or 149 35
the log. tangent 10,372148 — — 67 0 or 113 0
the log. fecant 10,005521 — — 9 7 or 170 53
the log. fecant 10,199573 — — 50 50 or 129 10

To find the degrees, minutes, and feconds correfponding to any given loga-rithmic fine, tangent or fecant.

Take out the degrees and minutes correfponding to the next lower lo-garithm in the proper column, as directed above, and fubtract that loga-rithm from the given one; annex two cyphers to the remainder, and di-vide by the tabular difference: the quotient is the feconds to be annexed to the degrees and minutes already found.

Example. Let the angle correfponding to the log. fine 9,453498 be required.

Given logarithm   9,453498
Next lower in table 9,453342 = Sine 16° 30' 0"

Tabular difference 710) 15600(22

Angle required,   16   30   22

If the tabular difference exceed 100, the angle thus obtained is gene-rally true to a fecond. Otherwife it cannot be depended on within the number of feconds pointed out by dividing the 100 by the tabular dif-ference. Thus if the difference be 50, it may be depended on to 2 fe-conds; if 20, to 5 feconds.

Computations in Trigonometry are operations by the rule of three, in which fome or all of the terms are fines, tangents or fecants. They are generally wrought by logarithms, the terms being fought in the table of the logarithms of numbers, or of fines, tangents and fecants, according as the analogy directs.

Example 1. Given the legs of a plane right angled triangle, AB 375, AC 294, Sought the angle B.
The analogy for this cafe is, AB : AC : : R : T, B.

AC 294   Log.   2,468347
R.   Log.   10,

AB 375   Log.   12,468347
                 2,574031

T, B 38° 6' Log.   9,894316
          c

The Learner will readily perceive that the addition or subtraction of the logarithm of the radius may be performed without repeating the logarithm.

The method of working by the arithmetical complement of the fift term, already described, may be used, and is peculiarly convenient, when that term is a sine, tangent or secant; the arithmetical complement is obtained at once from the tables, the cosecant being the arithmetical complement of the sine; the cotangent that of the tangent; and the cosine, that of the secant.

Example 2. Given the angle A of an oblique plane triangle 42° 12' the angle B 73° 9' and side BC 4385. Sought the side AC.

The analogy for this case is

$$S, A : S, B : : BC : AC.$$

		Otherwise.
S, B 73° 9' = 9,980942		
BC 4385 = 3,641970	S, A ar. comp. ,172811	
	S, B = 9,980942	
13,622912	BC = 3,641970	
S, A 42° 12' = 9,827189		
AC 6248 = 3,795723	AC 6248 3,795723	

Example 3. Given the legs of a right angled spherical triangle AB 71° 49', AC 39° 42'. Sought the angle B.

The analogy for this case is,

$$S, AB : R : : T, AC : T, B$$

R + T, AC = 19,919191	S, AB ar. comp. ,022248
S, AB = 9977752	T, AC = 9,919191
T, B 41° 9' 9,941439	T, B 41° 9' 9,941439

Example 4. Given the side A B of a spherical triangle 63° 8', the side AC 45° 12', and the angle C 39° 21'. Sought the angle B.

The analogy for this case is,

$$S, AB : S, AC : : S, C : S, B.$$

		Otherwise.
S, AC 45° 12' = 9,850996		
S, C 39 21 = 9,802128	S, AB ar. comp. ,049606	
	S, AC = 9,850996	
19 653124	S, C = 9,802128	
S, A B 63 8 = 9,950394		
S, B 30 17 = 9,702730	S, B 30° 17' = 9,702730	

The following rules for small angles are more accurate than those already given.

To find the logarithmic fine, tangent or fecant of an angle under 2°

From the common logarithm of the number of feconds in the given angle, fubtract the logarithm of the feconds in the degree and minute next lower; add the remainder to the logarithmic fine, tangent or fecant of the degrees and minutes; the fum is the logarithmic fine, tangent or fecant required.

Example. What is the fine of 1° 15′ 12″?

$$
\begin{array}{llll}
1°\ 15′\ 12″ &=& 4512″ & \text{Log.}\quad 2{,}654369 \\
1\ \ 15\ \ \ 0 &=& 4500 & \phantom{\text{Log.}\quad} 2{,}653213 \\
\hline
& & & \phantom{\text{Log.}\quad} 1156 \\
1\ \ 15\ \ \ 0 & \text{Log. fine} & & 8{,}338753 \\
\hline
1\ \ 15\ \ 12 & \text{Log. fine} & & 8{,}339909
\end{array}
$$

By the former rule, the logarithmic fine would have been 8,339903.

To find the degrees, minutes and feconds correfponding to the Sine, &c. of an angle under 2°.

Take out the degrees and minutes correfponding to the next lower logarithm; fubtract that logarithm from the given one; add to the remainder the common logarithm of the number of feconds in the degrees and minutes found; this fum is the logarithm of the number of feconds in the angle required.

Example. What angle correfponds to the log. tangent 8,522460?

$$
\begin{array}{llll}
\text{Given Logarithm} & & & 8{,}522460 \\
\text{Neareft in the tables T, 1° 54′} & & & 8{,}520790 \\
\hline
& & & 1670 \\
1° 54′ &=& 6840″\ \text{Log.} & 3{,}835056 \\
\hline
\text{T, 1° 54′ 26″} &=& 6866\ \text{Log.} & 3{,}836726
\end{array}
$$

To find the logarithmic verfed fine of any angle.

Take the logarithmic fine of half the angle, multiply it by 2, and from the product fubtract the logarithm of half the radius, which is 9,698970, the remainder is the logarithmic verfed fine of the angle.

Example. Let the logarithmic verfed fine of 35° 46′ be required.

$$
\begin{array}{lll}
\text{Half 35° 46′} = 17° 53′\ \text{Log. fine} & & 9{,}487251 \\
\text{Multiplied by} & & 2 \\
\hline
\text{Product} & & 18{,}974502 \\
\text{Subtract} & & 9{,}698970 \\
\hline
\text{Log. verfed fine of 35° 46′} & & 9{,}275532
\end{array}
$$

OF

OF THE TABLE OF

DIFFERENCE of LATITUDE and DEPARTURE.

THE principal ufe of this table (called alfo, The Traverfe Table) is to facilitate the computation of a day's work in Navigation. It is drawn out in two parts; the firft for each degree of the Quadrant, and the fecond for each point and quarter-point of the Compafs. The degrees under 45, and points of the compafs under 4, are marked at the top of the pages; the degrees above 45, and points above 4, at the foot. The diftances from 1 to 100 miles, alfo the hundreds from 100 to 900 miles, are marked on the margin, and the tenths of a mile are added, for greater convenience, at the foot of the right hand pages.

The diftance and courfe in degrees or points being given, to find the difference of latitude and departure.

Seek the courfe at the top or foot of the pages, and the diftance on the margin; then under, or above the former, and againft the latter you have the difference of latitude and departure in the columns marked at the top or foot, according as the courfe was taken from the one or the other. If the diftance exceed 100, or contain a decimal, the feveral parts muft be collected, as in the following example.

Let the courfe be 35 degrees, and diftance 227,6 miles.

		diff lat.	dep.
200	Miles	163,8	114,7
27	Miles	22,1	15,5
,6	Miles	,5	,3
		186,4	130,5

OF THE TABLE OF

MERIDIONAL PARTS.

THIS table is ufed in computations in Mercator's failing, for obtaining the enlarged difference of latitude, when the true is given, or the true difference of latitude when the enlarged is given. The degrees are marked at the tops of the columns, and the minutes on the margin.

PROB-

PROBLEM I. *To find the enlarged difference of latitude, when both latitudes are given.*

Take out the meridional parts correfponding to the latitudes, their difference, if the latitudes be of the fame name; but their fum, if the names of the latitudes be oppofite, is the enlarged difference of latitude.

Example 1. Let the latitudes be 57° 9′ N, and 35° 1′ N.

57° 9′	M. P.	4199,2
35 1		2245,5
Enl. diff. lat,		1953,7

Example 2, Let the latitudes be 12° 45′ N, and 7° 19′ S,

12° 45′ N.	M. P.	771,4,
7 19 S.		440,2
Enl. diff. lat.		1211,6

PROBLEM II. *Given one latitude, and enlarged difference of latitude, fought the other latitude*

Cafe 1. If the voyage lead away from the equator, add the meridional parts correfponding to the given latitude, to the given enlarged difference of latitude; feek the fum in the table, and you have the degrees on the top of the column, and the minutes on the margin.

Example. A ship fails northerly from latitude 38° 17′ N, and the enlarged difference of latitude is 1052. Sought latitude arrived at.

38° 17′ N	M. P.	2489,9
		1052
50 43	Lat. fought,	3541,9

Cafe 2. If the voyage lead towards the equator, write the enlarged difference of latitude under the meridional parts correfponding to the given latitude, and fubtract the leffer from the greater. The degrees and minutes correfponding to the remainder, found as above, is the latitude required, and is of the fame name with the given latitude, if the meridional parts correfponding to that latitude be greater; but of an oppofite name, if the enlarged difference of latitude be greater.

Example 1. Latitude 15° 9′ N, enlarged difference of latitude 695,6 foutherly

15° 9′ N	M. P.	919,8
		695,6
Latitude fought 3 44 N,	—	224,2

Ex-

Example 2. Latitude 8° 17' N, enlarged difference of latitude 1238
foutherly

　　　　　　　8° 17' N, — — 498,7
　　　　　　　　　　　　　　　1238,

Latitude fought 12 14 S. — — 739,3

OF THE TABLE OF

THE SUN'S DECLINATION.

THIS table is extended in four parts, adapted to Leap year, and the firft, fecond, and third years after leap year. The months are marked at the top of the page, and the days on the margin; under the former and againft the latter, you have the fun's declination at noon, for the meridian at Greenwich, to the neareft fecond.

If this table fhould be ufed after the 28th of February 1800, it will be neceffary, on account of the omiffion of a leap year, to look for the day in the table which follows that on which the declination is required. The fame muft be done in the tables of right afcenfion, tranfit of the polar ftar, and equation of time.

If the Declination be required for any place whofe difference of longitude from Greenwich is given, the number of minutes from the table of the variation of the fun's declination, correfponding to the neareft day inferted in that table, and the neareft 10 degrees of longitude muft be applied to the declination of Greenwich. If the longitude be weft, that number muft be added, when the day falls between the equinox and the folftice (from 20th of March to 22d of June, and from 22d of September to 22d of December), but added, when the day falls between the folftice and equinox (from 22d of December to the 20th of March, and from 22d of June to 22d of September), but if the longitude be eaft, the number muft be fubtracted, between the equinox and folftice, but added between the folftice and equinox.

The Table of RFRACTION contains a correction to be fubtracted from the apparent altitude of the heavenly bodies, in order to obtain their true altitude. The rays of light, in paffing thro' the atmofphere are bent from their rectilineal direction, towards the perpendicular; in confequence of which the heavenly bodies, except when in the zenith, appear higher than they ought to do.—This table is in two parts, the former gives the refraction in minutes and feconds, the latter in minutes only. When the inftruments ufed only take the angles to minutes, it will be fufficient to take the correction from the fecond part of the table, and fubtract the minutes that ftand againft that altitude, in the table, which is neareft to the obferved altitude.

The Table of the DIP of the HORIZON contains the angle which a line drawn from the obferver's eye to the vifible horizon, or edge of the water, makes with a true horizontal line. This angle is greater, the higher the
　　　　　　　　　　　　　　　　　　　　　　　　　　ob-

observer is above the surface of the sea, and must be subtracted from all altitudes observed by Hadley's quadrant, or any similar instrument. This table is in two parts as the former, and to the second part there is annexed in a separate column, the distance of the visible horizon from the observer.

This table gives the dip, upon the supposition that the horizon is entirely open. But as observations may sometimes be taken when the sun is seen over land, and the ship nearer to the shore than the visible horizon would be if it were unconfined, another table is annexed, in which the distances of the ship from the shore are marked on the margin, and the observer's height at the top. Seafaring men can generally estimate with sufficient exactness, the distance of a ship from the shore, when it does not exceed six miles, which is the greatest distance of the visible horizon from an observer on the deck of any ship. Then, against that distance, and under the height of the observer, the dip corresponding to the observation will be found.

The principal use of these tables is to compute the latitude from an observation of the sun's meridional altitude.

RULE. From the observed altitude, let the refraction and dip corresponding to that altitude, be subtracted, and if the observation be taken on the sun's lower limb, let his semidiameter be added; by which means the true or corrected altitude of the sun's centre is obtained.

Let the corrected altitude be marked with its name, whether North or South, and let the complement of this be taken, which is the zenith distance, and of the opposite name from the altitude; under this write the declination with its name. The sum of the zenith distance and declination, if their names be the same, but their difference, if their names be opposite, is the latitude required, and is of the same name as the greater.

If the latitude be only required to the nearest minute, which is generally reckoned sufficiently accurate in navigation, and is all that can be obtained by the instruments in common use at sea, it will be sufficient to take the refraction and dip from the second part of the tables, and to estimate the sun's semi-diameter, always at 16'; but if the latitude be required to the nearest second, the refraction and dip must be taken from the former part of the tables, and the declination and sun's semi-diameter, from the nautical almanack, where they are given to seconds. The sun's parallax in altitude should also be added to the observed altitude.

Example. On the 13th of March 1791, under the longitude of Greenwich, the sun's altitude was observed, 43° 12' S, by Hadley's quadrant, the observer's height being 18 feet. Required the Latitude.

Observed altitude		43°	12' S
Refraction	—		1
Dip	—		4
Sun's semidiameter	+		16
Corrected altitude	—	43	23 S
Zenith distance		46	37 N
Declination		2	49 S
Latitude		43	48 N

More

More correctly,

Obferved altitude	43°	12'	"	S
Refraction	—	1	1	
Dip	—	4	3	
Semidiameter	+	16	8	
Parallax	+	—	7	
Corrected altitude	43	23	11	S
Zenith diftance	46	36	49	N
Declination	2	49	12	S
Latitude	43	47	37	N

The Table of difference between the APPARENT LEVEL, and the TRUE contains the number of feet, inches and decimals of an inch, to be fubtracted from the height of the mark to which a levelling inftrument is directed, in order to obtain the point that is really on a level with the inftrument. The caufe of this difference is the curvature of the earth.

The Table of LINKS to be fubtracted from *Gunter's* CHAIN, for reducing a flanting line to the horizontal, is in two parts: the firft for each degree of elevation as far as 30°, which is as much as commonly occurs in land meafuring; the fecond for thofe elevations which require an even number of links, and quarters of a link, to be fubtracted. This will be more ready in practice, and fufficiently accurate. In ufing it, we take that elevation which is neareft to the true one. In fome theodolites, the links and quarters to be deducted are marked on the vertical arch, by which the ufe of this table is fuperfeded.

The Table of the SUN's RIGHT ASCENSION is computed for the third year after leap year, but may be adapted to other years as follows: for the fecond year after leap year, add one minute; for the firft year after leap year add two minutes; for leap year in March and the following months, add three minutes, but in January and February fubtract one minute. Thus the right afcenfion is obtained to the neareft minute. If greater acuuracy be required, the right afcenfion muft be taken from the nautical almanack for the year, where it is computed to feconds.

In the Table of the FIXED STARS the right afcenfion is given to fecond of time, and the declination to feconds of a degree. As the table is fitted to the beginning of the year 1790; to find the right afcenfion and declination of a ftar at any other time, the annual variations (which are given in feconds, and decimals of a fecond) muft be multiplied by the number of years, and parts of a year elapfed fince 1790, and the product of the variation in declination, added, or fubtracted, according as it is marked + or — in the table.

Example Let the Right Afcenfion and Declination of Aldebaran on the firft of July 1795 be required,

	Right Afcenfion. h. m. f.	Declination. d. m. f.
Annual Variation,	— — 3,42	+ — — 8,26
	5	5
Variation in 5 Years,	— — 17,10	— — 41,30
in ¼ Year,	— — 1,71	— — 4,23
R. Afc. and Decl. 1790,	4 23 53,	16 4 25,
R. Afc. and Decl. required,	4 24 12	16 5 11

The Declination of the Fixed Stars is applied, in the fame manner as that of the Sun, for determining the latitude by an obfervation of the meridional altitude. The chief ufe of the tables of Right Afcenfion of the Stars is, to find the time when any ftar paffes the meridian; and confequently to find the hour, when a ftar is obferved, or determined by a computation founded on an obfervation of its altitude, to be, upon the meridian.

Rule. From the Right Afcenfion of the ftar fubtract that of the fun; the remainder is the time when the ftar paffes the meridian. If the Sun's Right Afcenfion be greater, add 24 hours to that of the ftar.

Ex. At what time will the ftar *Capella* pafs the meridian on the 10th of February 1790?

	h. m.
Right Afcenfion of Capella,	5 1
of the Sun,	21 38
Time of Tranfit, Evening.	7 23

In thefe computations, the hours are reckoned to 24, agreeably to the practice of Aftronomers, beginning at noon, and continuing to noon of the following day.

The Table of the TRANSIT of the POLAR STAR over the MERIDIAN is ufeful for afcertaining the meridian, in order to determine the Variation of the Compafs, and for other purpofes. It is adapted to Leap Year, and may be ufed for any year without material error; but for greater accuracy we may add one minute in the firft year after leap year, two minutes in the fecond, and three in the third; and in the months of January and February, take out the number for the day following the given one.

The Table of the EQUATION of TIME contains the number of minutes and feconds, which being added to, or fubtracted from, *mean time,* or the time fhown by a good clock, gives *apparent time,* or the time fhown by the fun on a dial. It is ufeful for regulating clocks, and for many other purpofes.

This Table, being computed for the third year after leap year, may be fitted for other years as follows. In the fecond year after leap year, take one fourth of the difference between the Equation for the given, and the following day; for the firft year after leap year, take one half of that difference, and for leap year take three fourths. The numbers thus taken are to be added to the numbers in the table, when the equation is increafing, and fubtracted, when it is diminifhing. Alfo in the months of January and February, in leap year, the number correfponding to the day following the given one muft be taken.

P. S.

P. S. SINCE the foregoing part of the Introduction, and the Tables, already described, were printed off; a few others, not originally intended, have been added, to render this Collection more complete.

A TABLE of the SUN's SEMIDIAMETER for every fixth day in the year, which is useful in computing the Latitude, with greater accuracy, from an obfervation of his meridional altitude, upon the principles already explained ; also in correcting the obferved diftances of the Moon from the Sun.

A Table of the LOGARITHMS of HALF ELAPSED TIME, MIDDLE TIME, and RISING, ufeful in computing the Latitude from two obfervations of the Sun's Altitude, and in feveral other nautical Problems.

The logarithm of half elapfed time is the arithmetical complement of that of the fine of the correfponding angle, or the logarithm of the Co-fecant of the fame, deducting 10 from the index. The logarithm of the middle time is the logarithmic fine of the correfponding angle diminifhed by 4,69897, the logarithm of 50000, or half the radius. The logarithm rifing is the logarithmic verfed fine of the correfponding angle, 5 being fubtracted from the index. Thefe tables are given in hours, minutes, and half minutes. The columns of half elapfed time, and middle time are only carried to fix hours, beyond which they are never wanted ; that of rifing is extended to nine hours.

To find the logarithm from this table to any fecond of time, Take out the logarithm correfponding to the time next lower, alfo the difference between the fame and the following logarithm ; multiply the difference by the number of feconds in the given time above the time in the tables, and divide the product by 30 ; the remainder is a proportional part to be fubtracted from the tabular logarithm of half elapfed time, but added to the tabular logarithms of middle time, and rifing.

Ex. What is the logarithm half elapfed time correfponding to 1 hour, 12 minutes, 37 feconds ?

h. ' "			
1 12 30	Log. ½ Elapfed Time	51002	Diff. 291
	Prop. part	68	Sec. 7
1 12 37	Log. ½ Elapfed Time	50934	30)2037
			68

To find the hour, minute, and feconds correfponding to any logarithm. Take out the hour, minute, and half minute next lower from the table, and write the difference between the logarithm taken out, and the given one, alfo the difference between the logarithm taken out, and that which immediately follows in the table ; multiply the former difference by 30, and divide the product by the latter. The quotient is a number of feconds which muft be added to the time already taken out to complete the time required. *Ex.*

Ex. What is the time corresponding to the logarithm 5,25260, middle time?

			h. ' "
Given logarithm	5,25260		
Next lower in table	5,25245	=	4 13 30
Next higher in table	5,25282		

Difference of 1st and 2d	25
	30

Difference of 2d and 3d	47)750(16	— — 16

Time required,   4 13 46

To find the logarithmic versed sine of any angle, Convert the degrees and minutes into time, at the rate of an hour for 15 degrees ; take out the logarithm rising corresponding to that time, and add 5 to the index.

A Table of NATURAL SINES. The arrangement and use of this table is obvious from that of logarithmic sines already explained. The natural versed sine may also be easily found from it.

To find the natural versed sine of an angle under 90° ; from the radius, or 100000, subtract the natural co-sine, the remainder is the natural versed sine required.

To find the natural versed sine of an angle above 90° ; add the natural sine of the excess above 90° to 100000, the sum is the natural versed sine required.

To find the angle corresponding to any given natural versed sine. If the versed sine be under 100000, subtract it from 100000, and find the angle whose natural sine is equal to the remainder, the complement of which is the angle required. If the versed sine be above 100000, subtract 100000 from it, find the angle whose natural sine answers to the remainder, and add 90° to it. The sum is the angle required.

A Table of CORRECTION of the MOON's ALTITUDE.—This correction is the difference between the moon's parallax and refraction, and must be added to the observed altitude, in order to give the true altitude. The moon's horizontal parallax in minutes, is marked on the top of the page, and its altitude, in degrees, on the margin. Under the former, and on the line with the latter, you have the correction required.

If the horizontal parallax be given in minutes and seconds, a proportional part must be allowed for the seconds. This allowance is always to be added. If the apparent altitude be given in degrees and minutes, a proportional part must also be allowed for the minutes. This allowance is to be added, when the apparent altitude is under 15° ; because so far the correction increases with the altitude ; but when the apparent altitude is above 15°, it must be subtracted, because the correction decreases above that altitude.

Ex. 1. What is the correction corresponding to 57' 24" horizontal parallax, and 8° 15' altitude ?

Correction hor par. 57' and alt. 8°		49 57
Prop. part for 24" hor. parallax	+	— 24
Prop. part for 15' altitude	+	— 8
Correction required. — — —		50 29

Ex.

Ex. 2. Let the horizontal parallax be 55′ 12″, and apparent altitude 41° 25′. Required the correction?

		′	″
Correction for hor. par. 55′ alt. 41°		40	25
Prop. part for 12″ hor. parallax	+	—	9
Prop part for 25′ alt.	—	—	15
Correction required, — — —	—	40	19

THE moſt uſeful Tables in COMPOUND INTEREST, PROBA-BILITIES of LIVES, and ANNUITIES for YEARS and LIVES are inſerted in the concluſion. Theſe, indeed, belong to a ſubjeƈt uncon-neƈted with the others. The Compiler, however, found it convenient to have all the Tables, to which he had occaſion to refer the Students who attended his Leƈtures, collected together ; and they may perhaps, accom-modate others in the ſame manner.

MARISCHAL COLLEGE,
    May 20, 1790.

A S great attention has been given to the Correction of the Preſs, it is hoped few or no errors have eſcaped notice, excepting thoſe mentioned in the annexed Table of

E R R A T A.

Page.
    4 againſt 200, for 1031 read 1030
    10 On margin, place 548 in the blank under 547.5.
        549 under 548 ; and a blank under 549
    28 Second line of third column, for 3316 r. 1326.
    48 Co-ſine 29° 11′ for 940046 read 941046
    62 At foot, for 56 Degrees read 46 Degrees
Of the two pages maked 80, the firſt ſhould be 79
    100 Under Sept. for m. d read h. m.
        Under Jan. and againſt 2 from top, for 6.6 read
        6.2
    100 The marginal figures in the left hand column
        from 21 to 31 are placed too low.
    102 In the column of names of ſtars, for *Caprella*,
        read *Capella*.
    109 Oppoſite 37′ 30″ in column of riſing, for 81441
        read 81141

A TABLE

A

TABLE

OF

LOGARITHMS

Of NUMBERS From, 1 to 10000.

And of Logarithmic SINES, TANGENTS, and SECANTS, to each Degree and Minute of the Quadrant.

Num.	Log.	Num.	Log.	Num.	Log.
1	0.000000	34	1.531479	67	1.826075
2	0.301030	35	1.544068	68	1.832509
3	0.477121	36	1.556302	69	1.838849
4	0.602060	37	1.568202	70	1.845098
5	0.698970	38	1.579784	71	1.851258
6	0.778151	39	1.591065	72	1.857332
7	0.845098	40	1.602060	73	1.863323
8	0.903090	41	1.612784	74	1.869232
9	0.954243	42	1.623249	75	1.875061
10	1.000000	43	1.633468	76	1.880814
11	1.041393	44	1.643453	77	1.886491
12	1.079181	45	1.653213	78	1.892095
13	1.113943	46	1.662758	79	1.897627
14	1.146128	47	1.672098	80	1.903090
15	1.176091	48	1.681241	81	1.908485
16	1.204120	49	1.690196	82	1.913814
17	1.230449	50	1.698970	83	1.919078
18	1.255273	51	1.707570	84	1.924279
19	1.278754	52	1.716003	85	1.929419
20	1.301030	53	1.724276	86	1.934498
21	1.322219	54	1.732394	87	1.939519
22	1.342423	55	1.740363	88	1.944483
23	1.361728	56	1.748188	89	1.949390
24	1.380211	57	1.755875	90	1.954243
25	1.397940	58	1.763428	91	1.959041
26	1.414973	59	1.770852	92	1.963788
27	1.431364	60	1.778151	93	1.968483
28	1.447158	61	1.785330	94	1.973128
29	1.462398	62	1.792392	95	1.977724
30	1.477121	63	1.799341	96	1.982271
31	1.491362	64	1.806180	97	1.986772
32	1.505150	65	1.812913	98	1.991226
93	1.518514	66	1.819544	99	1.995635

N·	0	1	2	3	4	5	6	7	8	9	D
100	000000	0434	0868	1301	1734	21 66	2598	3029	3460	3891	432
101	4321	4751	5180	5609	6038	6466	6894	7321	7748	8174	428
102	8600	9026	9451	9876							425
01					0300	0724	1147	1570	1993	2415	423
103	2837	3259	3680	4100	4520	4940	5360	5779	6197	6615	419
104	7033	7451	7863	8284	8700	9116	9532	9947			416
02									0361	0775	414
105	1189	1603	2016	2428	2841	3252	3664	4075	4486	4896	412
106	5306	5715	6124	6533	6942	7350	7757	8164	8571	8978	408
107	9384	9789									406
03			0195	0600	1004	1408	1812	2216	2619	3021	404
108	3424	3826	4227	4628	5029	5430	5830	6229	6629	7028	400
109	7426	7825	8223	8620	9017	9414	9811				397
04								0207	0602	0998	396
110	1393	1787	2182	2575	2969	3362	3755	4148	4540	4931	393
111	5323	5714	6105	6495	6885	7275	7664	8053	8442	8830	389
112	9218	9606	9993								387
05				0380	0766	1152	1538	1924	2309	2694	386
113	3078	3463	3846	4230	4613	4996	5378	5760	6142	6524	382
114	6905	7286	7666	8046	8426	8805	9185	9563	9942		379
06										0320	378
115	0698	1075	1452	1829	2206	2582	2958	3333	3709	4083	376
116	4458	4832	5206	5580	5953	6326	6699	7071	7443	7814	372
117	8186	8557	8928	9298	9668						370
07						0038	0407	0776	1145	1514	369
118	1882	2250	2617	2985	3352	3718	4085	4451	4816	5182	366
119	5547	5912	6276	6640	7004	7368	7731	8094	8457	8819	363
120	9181	9543	9904								361
08				0266	0626	0987	1347	1707	2067	2426	360
121	2785	3144	3503	3861	4219	4576	4934	5291	5647	6004	357
122	6360	6716	7071	7426	7781	8136	8490	8845	9198	9552	355
123	9905										353
09		0258	0611	0963	1315	1667	2018	2370	2721	3071	351
124	3422	3772	4122	4471	4820	5169	5518	5866	6215	6562	349
125	6910	7257	7604	7951	8297	8644	8990	9335	9681		346
10										0026	345
126	0370	0715	1059	1403	1747	2090	2434	2777	3119	3462	343
127	3804	4146	4487	4828	5169	5510	5851	6191	6531	6870	340
128	7210	7549	7888	8227	8565	8903	9241	9578	9916		338
11										0253	337
129	0590	0926	1262	1598	1934	2270	2605	2940	3275	3609	335
130	3943	4277	4611	4944	5278	5610	5943	6276	6608	6940	333
131	7271	7603	7934	8265	8595	8926	9256	9586	9915		330
12										0245	330
132	0574	0903	1231	1560	1888	2216	2543	2871	3198	3525	328
133	3852	4178	4504	4830	5156	5481	5806	6131	6456	6781	325
134	7105	7429	7752	8076	8399	8722	9045	9368	9690		323
13										0012	322
135	0334	0655	0977	1298	1619	1939	2260	2580	2900	3219	321
136	3539	3858	4177	4496	4814	5133	5451	5768	6086	6403	318
137	6721	7037	7354	7670	7987	8303	8618	8934	9249	9564	316
138	9879										315
14		0194	0508	0822	1136	1450	1763	2076	2389	2702	314
139	3015	3327	3639	3951	4263	4574	4885	5196	5507	5818	311
140	6128	6438	6748	7058	7367	7676	7985	8294	8603	8911	309
141	9219	9527	9835								308
15				0142	0449	0756	1063	1370	1676	1982	306
142	2288	2594	2900	3205	3510	3815	4119	4424	4728	5032	305
143	5386	5640	5943	6246	6549	6852	7154	7457	7759	8061	303
144	8362	8664	8965	9266	9567	9868					301
16							0168	0468	0769	1068	300

N	0	1	2	3	4	5	6	7	8	9	D
145	161368	1667	1967	2266	2564	2863	3161	3460	3757	4055	299
146	4353	4650	4947	5244	5541	5838	6134	6430	6726	7022	297
147	7317	7613	7908	8203	8497	8792	9086	9380	9674	9968	295
148	170262	0555	0848	1141	1434	1726	2019	2311	2603	2895	293
149	3186	3478	3769	4060	4351	4641	4932	5222	5512	5802	291
150	6091	6381	6670	6959	7248	7536	7825	8113	8401	8689	289
151	8977	9264	9552	9839							288
	18				0126	0413	0699	0986	1272	1558	287
152	1844	2129	2415	2700	2985	3270	3554	3839	4123	4407	285
153	4691	4975	5259	5542	5825	6108	6391	6674	6956	7239	283
154	7521	7803	8084	8366	8647	8928	9209	9490	9771		281
	19									0051	280
155	0332	0612	0892	1171	1451	1730	2010	2289	2567	2846	279
156	3125	3403	3681	3959	4237	4514	4792	5069	5346	5623	278
157	5900	6176	6452	6729	7005	7281	7556	7832	8107	8382	276
158	8657	8932	9206	9481	9755						275
	20					0029	0303	0577	0850	1124	274
159	1397	1670	1943	2216	2488	2761	3033	3305	3577	3848	272
160	4120	4391	4662	4933	5204	5475	5745	6016	6286	6556	271
161	6826	7095	7365	7634	7903	8172	8441	8710	8978	9247	269
162	9515	9783									268
	21		0051	0318	0586	0853	1120	1388	1654	1921	267
163	2188	2454	2720	2986	3252	3518	3783	4049	4314	4579	266
164	4844	5109	5373	5638	5902	6166	6430	6694	6957	7221	264
165	7484	7747	8010	8273	8535	8798	9060	9322	9584	9846	262
166	220108	0370	0631	0892	1153	1414	1675	1936	2196	2456	261
167	2716	2976	3236	3496	3755	4015	4274	4533	4792	5051	259
168	5309	5568	5826	6084	6342	6600	6858	7115	7372	7630	258
169	7887	8144	8400	8657	8913	9170	9426	9682	9938		256
	23									0193	255
170	0449	0704	0960	1215	1470	1724	1979	2233	2488	2742	254
171	2996	3250	3504	3757	4011	4264	4517	4770	5023	5276	253
172	5528	5781	6033	6285	6537	6789	7041	7292	7544	7795	252
173	8046	8297	8548	8799	9049	9299	9550	9800			250
	24								0050	0300	250
174	0549	0799	1048	1297	1546	1795	2044	2293	2541	2790	249
175	3038	3286	3534	3782	4030	4277	4524	4772	5019	5266	248
176	5513	5759	6006	6252	6499	6745	6991	7236	7482	7728	246
177	7973	8219	8464	8709	8954	9198	9443	9687	9932		245
	25									0176	244
178	0420	0664	0908	1151	1395	1638	1881	2125	2367	2610	243
179	2853	3096	3338	3580	3822	4064	4306	4548	4790	5031	242
180	5273	5514	5755	5996	6236	6477	6718	6958	7198	7439	241
181	7679	7918	8158	8398	8637	8877	9116	9355	9594	9833	239
182	260071	0310	0548	0787	1025	1263	1501	1738	1976	2214	238
183	2451	2688	2925	3162	3399	3636	3873	4109	4345	4582	237
184	4818	5054	5290	5525	5761	5996	6232	6467	6702	6937	235
185	7172	7406	7641	7875	8110	8344	8578	8812	9046	9279	234
186	9513	9746	9980								233
	27			0213	0446	0679	0912	1144	1377	1609	233
187	1842	2074	2306	2538	2770	3001	3233	3464	3696	3927	232
188	4158	4389	4620	4850	5081	5311	5542	5772	6002	6232	230
189	6462	6691	6921	7151	7380	7609	7838	8067	8296	8525	229
190	8754	8982	9210	9439	9667	9895					228
	28						0123	0351	0578	0806	228
191	1033	1261	1488	1715	1942	2169	2395	2622	2849	3075	227
192	3301	3527	3753	3979	4205	4431	4656	4882	5107	5332	226
193	5557	5782	6007	6232	6456	6681	6905	7130	7354	7578	225
194	7802	8025	8249	8473	8696	8920	9143	9366	9589	9812	223
195	290035	0257	0480	0702	0925	1147	1369	1591	1813	2034	222
196	2256	2478	2699	2920	3141	3363	3583	3804	4025	4246	221

N.	0	1	2	3	4	5	6	7	8	9	D.
197	294466	4687	4907	5127	5347	5567	5787	6007	6226	6446	220
198	6665	6884	7104	7323	7542	7761'	7979	8198	8416	8635	219
199	8853	9071	9289	9507	9725	9943					219
30							0161	0378	0595	0813	218
200	▮▮	1247	1464	1681	1898	2114	2331	2547	2764	2980	217
201	3196	3412	3628	3844	4059	4275	4491	4706	4921	5136	216
202	5351	5566	5781	5996	6211	6425	6639	6854	7068	7282	215
203	7496	7710	7924	8137	8351	8564	8778	8991	9204	9417	213
204	9630	9843									213
31			0056	0268	0481	0693	0906	1118	1330	1542	212
205	1754	1966	2177	2389	2600	2812	3023	3234	3445	3656	211
206	3867	4078	4289	4499.	4710	4920	5130	5340	5551	5760	210
207	5970	6180	6390	6599	6809	7018	7227	7436	7646	7854	209
208	8063	8272	8481	8689	8898	9106	9314	9522	9730	9938	208
209	320146	0354	0562	0769	0977	1184	1391	1598	1805	2012	207
210	2219	2426	2633	2839	3046	3252	3458	3665	3871	4077	206
211	4282	4488	4694	4899	5105	5310	5516	5721	5926	6131	205
212	6336	6541	6745	6950	7155	7359	7563	7767	7972	8176	204
213	8380	8583	8787	8991	9194	9398	9601	9805			204
33								0008	0211		203
214	0414	0617	0819	1022	1225	1427	1630	1832	2034	2236	202
215	2438	2640	2842	3044	3246	3447	3649	3850	4051	4253	202
216	4454	4655	4856	5056	5257	5458	5658	5859	6059	6260	201
217	6460	6660	6860	7060	7260	7459	7659	7858	8058	8257	200
218	8456	8656	8855	9054	9253	9451	9650	9849			200
34									9947	0246	199
219	0444	0642	0841	1039	1237	1435	1632	1830	2028	2225	198
220	2423	2620	2817	3014	3212	3409	3606	3802	3999	4196	197
221	4392	4589	4785	4981	5178	5374	5570	5766	5962	6157	196
222	6353	6549	6744	6939	7135	7330	7525	7720	7915	8110	195
223	8305	8500	8694	8889	9083	9278	9472	9666	9860		195
35										0054	194
224	0248	0442	0636	0829	1023	1216	1410	1603	1796	1989	193
225	2183	2375	2568	2761	2954	3147	3339	3532	3724	3916	193
226	4108	4301	4493	4685	4876	5068	5260	5452	5643	5834	192
227	6026	6217	6408	6599	6790	6981	7172	7363	7554	7744	191
228	7935	8125	8316	8506	8696	8886	9076	9266	9456	9646	190
229	9835										190
36		0025	0215	0404	0593	0783	0972	1161	1350	1539	189
230	1728	1917	2105	2294	2482	2671	2859	3048	3236	3424	188
231	3612	3800	3988	4176	4363	4551	4739	4926	5113	5301	188
232	5488	5675	5862	6049	6236	6423	6610	6796	6983	7169	187
233	7356	7542	7729	7915	8101	8287	8473	8659	8844	9030	186
234	9216	9401	9587	9772	9958						186
37						0143	0328	0513	0698	0883	185
235	1068	1253	1437	1622	1806	1991	2175	2360	2544	2728	184
236	2912	3096	3280	3464	3647	3831	4015	4198	4382	4565	184
237	4748	4932	5115	5298	5481	5664	5846	6029'	6212	6394	183
238	6577	6759	6942	7124	7306	7488	7670	7852	8034	8216	182
239	8398	8580	8761	8943	9124	9306	9487	9668	9849		182
240	38										181
	0211	0392	0573	0754	0934	1115	1296	1476	1656	1837	181
241	2017	2197	2377	2557	2737	2917	3097	3277	3456	3636	180
242	3815	3995	4174	4353	4533	4712	4891	5070	5249	5428	179
243	5606	5785	5964	6142	6321	6499	6677	6856	7034	7212	178
244	7390	7568	7746	7923	8101	8279	8456	8634	8811	8989	178
245	9166	9343	9520	9698	9875						178
39						0051	0228	0405	0582	0759	177
246	0935	1112	1288	1464	1641	1817	1993	2169	2345	2521	176
247	2697	2873	3048	3224	3400	3575	3751	3926	4101	4277	176
248	4452	4627	4802	4977	5152	5326	5501	5676	5850	6025	175

N.	0	1	2	3	4	5	6	7	8	9	D.
249	396199	6374	6548	6722	6896	7070	7245	7418	7592	7766	174
250	7940	8114	8287	8461	8634	8808	8981	9154	9327	9501	173
251	9674	9847									173
40			0020	0192	0365	0538	0711	0883	1056	1228	173
252	1400	1573	1745	1917	2089	2261	2433	2605	2777	2949	172
253	3120	3292	3464	3625	3807	3978	4149	4320	4492	4663	171
254	4834	5005	5175	5346	5517	5688	5858	6029	6199	6370	171
255	6540	6710	6881	7051	7221	7391	7561	7731	7900	8070	170
256	8240	8410	8579	8749	8918	9087	9257	9426	9595	9764	169
257	9933										169
41		0102	0271	0440	0608	0777	0946	1114	1283	1451	169
258	1620	1788	1956	2124	2292	2460	2628	2796	2964	3132	168
259	3300	3467	3635	3802	3970	4137	4305	4472	4639	4806	167
260	4973	5140	5307	5474	5641	5808	5974	6141	6308	6474	167
261	6640	6807	6973	7139	7306	7472	7638	7804	7970	8135	166
262	8301	8467	8633	8798	8964	9129	9295	9460	9625	9791	165
263	9956										165
42		0121	0286	0451	0616	0781	0945	1110	1275	1439	165
264	1604	1768	1933	2097	2261	2426	2590	2754	2918	3082	164
265	3246	3410	3573	3737	3901	4064	4228	4392	4555	4718	164
266	4882	5045	5208	5371	5534	5697	5860	6023	6186	6349	163
267	6511	6674	6836	6999	7161	7324	7486	7648	7811	7973	162
268	8135	8297	8459	8621	8782	8944	9106	9268	9429	9591	162
269	9752	9914									161
43		0075	0236	0398	0559	0720	0881	1042	1203		191
270	1364	1525	1685	1846	2007	2167	2328	2488	2649	2809	161
271	2969	3129	3290	3450	3610	3770	3930	4090	4249	4409	160
272	4569	4728	4888	5048	5207	5366	5526	5685	5844	6003	159
273	6163	6322	6481	6640	6798	6957	7116	7275	7433	7592	159
274	7751	7909	8067	8226	8384	8542	8700	8859	9017	9175	158
275	9333	9491	9648	9806	9964						158
44						0122	0279	0437	0594	0752	158
276	0909	1066	1224	1381	1538	1695	1852	2009	2166	2323	157
277	2480	2636	2793	2950	3106	3263	3419	3576	3732	3888	157
278	4045	4201	4357	4513	4669	4825	4981	5137	5293	5448	156
279	5604	5760	5915	6071	6226	6382	6537	6692	6848	7003	155
280	7158	7313	7468	7623	7778	7933	8088	8242	8397	8552	155
281	8706	8861	9015	9170	9324	9478	9633	9787	9941		155
45										0095	155
282	0249	0403	0557	0711	0865	1018	1172	1326	1479	1633	154
283	1786	1940	2093	2247	2400	2553	2706	2859	3012	3165	153
284	3318	3471	3624	3777	3930	4082	4235	4387	4540	4692	153
285	4845	4997	5149	5302	5454	5606	5758	5910	6062	6214	152
286	6366	6518	6670	6821	6973	7125	7276	7428	7579	7730	152
287	7882	8033	8184	8336	8487	8638	8789	8940	9091	9242	151
288	9392	9543	9694	9845	9995						151
46						0146	0296	0447	0597	0747	151
289	0898	1048	1198	1348	1498	1649	1799	1948	2098	2248	150
290	2398	2548	2697	2847	2997	3146	3296	3445	3594	3744	150
291	3893	4042	4191	4340	4489	4639	4787	4936	5085	5234	149
292	5383	5532	5680	5829	5977	6126	6274	6423	6571	6719	148
293	6868	7016	7164	7312	7460	7608	7756	7904	8052	8200	148
294	8347	8495	8643	8790	8938	9085	9233	9380	9527	9675	147
295	9822	9969									147
47			0116	0263	0410	0557	0704	0851	0998	1145	147
296	1292	1438	1585	1732	1878	2025	2171	2317	2464	2610	146
297	2756	2903	3049	3195	3341	3487	3633	3779	3925	4070	146
298	4216	4362	4508	4653	4799	4944	5090	5235	5381	5526	146
299	5671	5816	5962	6107	6252	6397	6542	6687	6832	6976	145
300	7121	7266	7411	7555	7700	7844	7989	8133	8278	8422	145
301	8566	8711	8855	8999	9143	9287	9431	9575	9719	9863	144

161

N.	0	1	2	3	4	5	6	7	8	9	D.
302	480007	0151	0294	0438	0582	0725	0869	1012	1156	1299	144
303	1443	1586	1729	1872	2016	2159	2302	2445	2588	2731	143
304	2874	3016	3159	3302	3445	3587	3730	3872	4015	4157	143
305	4200	4442	4584	4727	4869	5011	5153	5295	5437	5579	142
306	5721	5863	6005	6147	6289	6430	6572	6714	6855	6997	142
307	7138	7280	7421	7563	7704	7845	7986	8127	8269	8410	141
308	8551	8692	8833	8973	9114	9255	9396	9537	9677	9818	141
309	9958	**49** 0099	0239	0380	0520	0661	0801	0941	1081	1222	140
310	1362	1502	1642	1782	1922	2062	2201	2341	2481	2621	140
311	2760	2900	3040	3179	3319	3458	3597	3737	3876	4015	139
312	4155	4294	4433	4572	4711	4850	4989	5128	5267	5406	139
313	5544	5683	5822	5960	6099	6237	6376	6514	6653	6791	139
314	6930	7068	7206	7344	7482	7621	7759	7897	8035	8173	138
315	8311	8448	8586	8724	8862	8999	9137	9275	9412	9550	138
316	9687	9824	9962	**50** 0099	0236	0374	0511	0648	0785	0922	137
317	1059	1196	1333	1470	1607	1744	1880	2017	2154	2290	137
318	2427	2564	2700	2837	2973	3109	3246	3382	3518	3654	136
319	3791	3927	4063	4199	4335	4471	4607	4743	4878	5014	136
320	5150	5286	5421	5557	5692	5828	5963	6099	6234	6370	136
321	6505	6640	6775	6911	7046	7181	7316	7451	7586	7721	135
322	7856	7991	8125	8260	8395	8530	8664	8799	8933	9068	135
323	9202	9337	9471	9606	9740	9874	**51** 0008	0143	0277	0411	134
324	0545	0679	0813	0947	1081	1215	1348	1482	1616	1750	134
325	1883	2017	2150	2284	2417	2551	2684	2818	2951	3084	133
326	3218	3351	3484	3617	3750	3883	4016	4149	4282	4415	133
327	4548	4680	4813	4946	5079	5211	5344	5476	5609	5741	133
328	5874	6006	6139	6271	6403	6535	6668	6800	6932	7064	132
329	7196	7328	7460	7592	7724	7855	7987	8119	8251	8382	132
330	8514	8645	8777	8909	9040	9171	9303	9434	9565	9697	131
331	9828	9959	**52** 0090	0221	0352	0483	0614	0745	0876	1007	131
332	1138	1269	1400	1530	1661	1792	1922	2053	2183	2314	131
333	2444	2575	2705	2835	2966	3096	3226	3356	3486	3616	130
334	3746	3876	4006	4136	4266	4396	4526	4656	4785	4915	130
335	5045	5174	5304	5434	5563	5693	5822	5951	6081	6210	129
336	6339	6468	6598	6727	6856	6985	7114	7243	7372	7501	129
337	7630	7759	7888	8016	8145	8274	8402	8531	8660	8788	129
338	8917	9045	9174	9302	9430	9559	9687	9815	9943	**53** 0072	128
339	0200	0328	0456	0584	0712	0840	0968	1095	1223	1351	128
340	1479	1607	1734	1862	1990	2117	2245	2372	2500	2627	128
341	2754	2882	3009	3136	3263	3391	3518	3645	3772	3899	127
342	4026	4153	4280	4407	4534	4661	4787	4914	5041	5107	127
343	5294	5421	5547	5674	5800	5927	6053	6179	6306	6432	126
344	6558	6685	6811	6937	7063	7189	7315	7441	7567	7693	126
345	7819	7945	8071	8197	8322	8448	8574	8699	8825	8951	126
346	9076	9202	9327	9452	9578	9703	9829	9954	**54** 0079	0204	125
347	0329	0455	0580	0705	0830	0955	1080	1205	1330	1454	125
348	1579	1704	1829	1953	2078	2203	2327	2452	2576	2701	125
349	2825	2950	3074	3199	3323	3447	3571	3696	3820	3944	124
350	4068	4192	4316	4440	4564	4688	4812	4936	5060	5183	124
351	5307	5431	5554	5678	5802	5925	6049	6172	6296	6419	124
352	6543	6666	6789	6913	7036	7159	7282	7405	7529	7652	123
353	7775	7898	8021	8144	8266	8389	8512	8635	8758	8881	123
354	9003	9126	9249	9371	9494	9616	9739	9861	9984	**55** 0106	123
355	0228	0351	0473	0595	0717	0840	0962	1084	1206	1328	122

N.	0	1	2	3	4	5	6	7	8	9	D.
356	551450	1572	1694	1810	1938	2059	2181	2303	2425	2546	122
357	2668	2790	2911	3033	3155	3276	3398	3519	3640	3762	121
358	3883	4004	4126	4247	4368	4489	4610	4731	4852	4973	121
359	5094	5215	5336	5457	5578	5699	5820	5940	6061	6182	121
360	6302	6423	6544	6664	6785	6905	7026	7146	7267	7387	121
361	7507	7627	7748	7868	7988	8108	8228	8349	8469	8589	120
362	8709	8829	8948	9066	9188	9308	9428	9548	9667	9787	120
363	9907										120
	56	0026	0146	0265	0385	0504	0624	0743	0863	0982	120
364	1101	1221	1340	1459	1578	1698	1817	1936	2055	2174	119
365	2293	2412	2531	2650	2769	2887	3006	3125	3244	3362	119
366	3481	3600	3718	3837	3955	4074	4192	4311	4429	4548	119
367	4666	4784	4903	5021	5139	5257	5376	5494	5612	5730	116
368	5848	5966	6084	6202	6320	6437	6555	6673	6791	6909	118
369	7026	7144	7262	7379	7497	7614	7732	7849	7967	8084	118
370	8202	8319	8436	8554	8671	8788	8905	9023	9140	9257	117
371	9374	9491	9608	9725	9842	9959					117
	57						0076	0193	0309	0426	117
372	0543	0660	0776	0893	1010	1126	1243	1359	1476	1592	117
373	1709	1825	1942	2058	2174	2291	2407	2523	2639	2755	116
374	2872	2988	3104	3220	3336	3452	3568	3684	3800	3915	116
375	4031	4147	4263	4379	4494	4610	4726	4841	4957	5072	116
376	5188	5303	5419	5534	5650	5765	5880	5996	6111	6226	115
377	6341	6457	6572	6687	6802	6917	7032	7147	7262	7377	115
378	7492	7607	7721	7836	7951	8066	8181	8295	8410	8525	115
379	8639	8754	8868	8983	9097	9212	9326	9441	9555	9669	114
380	9784	9898									114
	58		0012	0126	0240	0355	0469	0583	0697	0811	114
381	0925	1039	1153	1267	1381	1494	1608	1722	1836	1950	114
382	2063	2177	2291	2404	2518	2631	2745	2858	2972	3085	114
383	3199	3312	3426	3539	3652	3765	3879	3992	4105	4218	113
384	4331	4444	4557	4670	4783	4896	5009	5122	5235	5348	113
385	5461	5574	5636	5799	5912	6024	6137	6250	6362	6475	113
386	6587	6700	6812	6925	7037	7149	7262	7374	7486	7599	112
387	7711	7823	7935	8047	8160	8272	8384	8496	8608	8720	112
388	8832	8944	9056	9167	9279	9391	9503	9615	9726	9838	112
389	9950										112
	59	0061	0173	0284	0396	0507	0619	0730	0842	0953	112
390	1065	1176	1287	1399	1510	1621	1732	1843	1955	2066	111
391	2177	2288	2399	2510	2621	2732	2843	2954	3064	3175	111
392	3286	3397	3508	3618	3729	3840	3950	4061	4171	4282	111
393	4393	4503	4614	4724	4834	4945	5055	5165	5276	5386	110
394	5496	5606	5717	5827	5937	6047	6157	6267	6377	6487	110
395	6597	6707	6817	6927	7037	7146	7256	7366	7476	7586	110
396	7695	7805	7914	8024	8134	8243	8353	8462	8572	8681	110
397	8791	8900	9009	9119	9228	9337	9446	9556	9665	9774	109
398	9883	9992									109
	60		0101	0210	0319	0428	0537	0646	0755	0864	109
399	0973	1082	1191	1299	1408	1517	1625	1734	1843	1951	109
400	2060	2169	2277	2386	2494	2603	2711	2819	2928	3036	108
401	3144	3253	3361	3469	3577	3686	3794	3902	4010	4118	108
402	4226	4334	4442	4550	4658	4766	4874	4982	5089	5197	108
403	5305	5413	5521	5628	5736	5844	5951	6059	6166	6274	108
404	6381	6489	6596	6704	6811	6919	7026	7133	7241	7348	107
405	7455	7562	7669	7777	7884	7991	8098	8205	8312	8419	107
406	8526	8633	8740	8847	8954	9061	9167	9274	9381	9488	107
407	9594	9701	9808	9914							107
	61				0021	0128	0234	0341	0447	0554	107
408	0660	0767	0873	0979	1086	1192	1298	1405	1511	1617	106
409	1723	1829	1936	2042	2148	2254	2360	2466	2572	2678	106
410	2784	2890	2996	3102	3207	3313	3419	3525	3630	3736	106

N.	0	1	2	3	4	5	6	7	8	9	D.
411	613842	3947	4053	4159	4264	4370	4475	4581	4686	4792	106
412	4897	5003	5108	5213	5319	5424	5529	5634	5740	5845	105
413	5950	6055	6160	6265	6370	6475	6580	6685	6790	6895	105
414	7000	7105	7210	7315	7420	7524	7629	7734	7839	7943	105
415	8048	8153	8257	8362	8466	8571	8675	8780	8884	8989	104
416	9093	9198	9302	9406	9511	9615	9719	9823	9928	0032	104
62											
417	0136	0240	0344	0448	0552	0656	0760	0864	0968	1072	104
418	1176	1280	1384	1488	1592	1695	1799	1903	2007	2110	104
419	2214	2318	2421	2525	2628	2732	2835	2939	3042	3146	104
420	3249	3353	3456	3559	3663	3765	3869	3972	4076	4179	104
421	4282	4385	4488	4591	4694	4793	4901	5004	5107	5209	103
422	5312	5415	5518	5621	5724	5827	5929	6032	6135	6238	103
423	6340	6443	6546	6648	6751	6853	6956	7058	7161	7263	103
424	7366	7468	7571	7673	7775	7873	7980	8082	8184	8287	102
425	8389	8491	8593	8695	8797	8900	9002	9104	9206	9308	102
426	9410	9511	9613	9715	9817	9919	0021	0123	0224	0326	102
63											
427	0428	0530	0631	0733	0834	0936	1037	1139	1241	1342	102
428	1444	1545	1647	1748	1849	1951	2052	2153	2255	2356	101
429	2457	2558	2660	2761	2862	2963	3064	3165	3266	3367	101
430	3468	3569	3670	3771	3872	3973	4074	4175	4276	4376	101
431	4477	4578	4679	4779	4880	4981	5081	5182	5283	5383	100
432	5484	5584	5685	5785	5886	5986	6087	6187	6287	6388	100
433	6488	6588	6688	6789	6889	6989	7089	7189	7289	7390	100
434	7490	7590	7690	7790	7890	7990	8090	8190	8289	8389	100
435	8489	8589	8689	8789	8885	8988	9084	9184	9287	9387	99
436	9486	9586	9686	9785	9885	9934	0084	0183	0283	0382	99
64											
437	0481	0581	0680	0779	0879	0978	1077	1176	1276	1375	99
438	1474	1573	1672	1771	1870	1970	2069	2168	2267	2366	99
439	2464	2563	2662	2761	2860	2952	3058	3156	3255	3354	99
440	3453	3551	3650	3749	3847	3946	4044	4143	4242	4340	98
441	4439	4537	4635	4734	4832	4931	5029	5127	5226	5324	98
442	5422	5520	5619	5717	5815	5913	6011	6109	6208	6306	98
443	6404	6502	6600	6698	6796	6894	6991	7089	7187	7285	98
444	7383	7481	7579	7676	7774	7872	7969	8067	8165	8262	98
445	8360	8458	8555	8653	8750	8848	8945	9043	9140	9237	97
446	9335	9432	9530	9627	9724	9821	9919	0016	0113	0210	97
65											
447	0307	0405	0502	0599	0696	0793	0890	0987	1084	1181	97
448	1278	1375	1472	1569	1666	1762	1859	1956	2053	2150	97
449	2246	2343	2440	2536	2633	2730	2826	2923	3019	3116	97
450	3213	3309	3405	3502	3598	3695	3791	3888	3984	4080	96
451	4176	4273	4369	4465	4562	4658	4754	4850	4946	5042	96
452	5138	5234	5331	5427	5523	5619	5714	5810	5906	6002	96
453	6098	6194	6290	6386	6481	6577	6673	6769	6864	6960	96
454	7056	7151	7247	7343	7438	7534	7629	7725	7820	7916	96
455	8011	8107	8202	8298	8393	8488	8584	8679	8774	8870	95
456	8965	9060	9155	9250	9346	9441	9536	9631	9726	9821	95
457	9916	0011	0106	0201	0296	0391	0486	0581	0676	0771	95
66											
458	0865	0960	1055	1150	1245	1339	1434	1529	1623	1718	95
459	1813	1907	2002	2096	2191	2285	2380	2474	2569	2663	95
460	2758	2852	2947	3041	3135	3230	3324	3418	3512	3607	94
461	3701	3795	3889	3983	4078	4172	4266	4360	4454	4548	94
462	4642	4736	4830	4924	5018	5112	5206	5299	5393	5487	94
463	5581	5675	5769	5862	5956	6050	6143	6237	6331	6424	94
464	6518	6612	6705	6799	6892	6986	7079	7173	7266	7359	94
465	7453	7546	7640	7733	7826	7920	8013	8106	8199	8293	93
466	8386	8479	8572	8665	8758	8852	8945	9038	9131	9224	93

N.	0	1	2	3	4	5	6	7	8	9	D.
467	669317	9410	9503	9596	9689	9782	9875	9967			93
67									0060	0153	93
468	0246	0339	0431	0524	0617	0710	0802	0895	0988	1080	93
469	1173	1265	1358	1451	1543	1636	1728	1821	1913	2005	92
470	2098	2190	2283	2375	2467	2560	2652	2744	2836	2929	92
471	3021	3113	3205	3297	3390	3482	3574	3666	3758	3850	92
472	3942	4034	4126	4218	4310	4402	4494	4586	4677	4769	92
473	4861	4953	5045	5137	5228	5320	5412	5503	5595	5687	92
474	5778	5870	5962	6053	6145	6236	6328	6419	6511	6602	91
475	6694	6785	6876	6968	7059	7151	7242	7333	7424	7516	91
476	7607	7698	7789	7881	7972	8063	8154	8245	8336	8427	91
477	8518	8609	8700	8791	8882	8973	9064	9155	9246	9337	91
478	9428	9519	9610	9700	9791	9882	9973				91
68								0063	0154	0245	91
479	0336	0426	0517	0607	0698	0789	0879	0970	1060	1151	90
480	1241	1332	1422	1513	1603	1693	1784	1874	1964	2055	90
481	2145	2235	2326	2416	2506	2596	2686	2777	2867	2957	90
482	3047	3137	3227	3317	3407	3497	3587	3677	3767	3857	90
483	3947	4037	4127	4217	4307	4396	4486	4576	4666	4756	90
484	4845	4935	5025	5114	5204	5294	5383	5473	5563	5652	89
485	5742	5831	5921	6010	6100	6189	6279	6368	6457	6547	89
486	6636	6726	6815	6904	6994	7083	7172	7261	7351	7440	89
487	7529	7618	7707	7796	7886	7975	8064	8153	8242	8331	89
488	8420	8509	8598	8687	8776	8865	8953	9042	9131	9220	89
489	9309	9398	9486	9575	9664	9753	9841	9930			89
69									0019	0107	89
490	0196	0285	0373	0462	0550	0639	0728	0816	0905	0993	89
491	1081	1170	1258	1347	1435	1524	1612	1700	1789	1877	88
492	1965	2053	2142	2230	2318	2406	2494	2583	2671	2759	88
493	2847	2935	3023	3111	3199	3287	3375	3463	3551	3639	88
494	3727	3815	3903	3991	4078	4166	4254	4342	4430	4517	88
495	4605	4693	4781	4868	4956	5044	5131	5219	5307	5394	88
496	5482	5569	5657	5744	5832	5919	6007	6094	6182	6269	87
497	6356	6444	6531	6618	6706	6793	6880	6968	7055	7142	87
498	7229	7317	7404	7491	7578	7665	7752	7839	7926	8014	87
499	8100	8188	8275	8362	8448	8535	8622	8709	8796	8883	87
500	8970	9057	9144	9231	9317	9404	9491	9578	9664	9751	87
501	9838	9924									87
70			0011	0098	0184	0271	0358	0444	0531	0617	87
502	0704	0790	0877	0963	1050	1136	1222	1309	1395	1482	86
503	1568	1654	1741	1827	1913	1999	2086	2172	2258	2344	86
504	2431	2517	2603	2689	2775	2861	2947	3033	3119	3205	86
505	3291	3377	3463	3549	3635	3721	3807	3893	3979	4065	86
506	4151	4236	4322	4408	4494	4579	4665	4751	4837	4922	86
507	5008	5094	5179	5265	5350	5436	5522	5607	5693	5778	86
508	5864	5949	6035	6120	6206	6291	6376	6462	6547	6632	85
509	6718	6803	6888	6974	7059	7144	7229	7315	7400	7485	85
510	7570	7655	7740	7826	7911	7996	8081	8166	8251	8336	85
511	8421	8506	8591	8676	8761	8846	8931	9015	9100	9185	85
512	9270	9355	9440	9524	9609	9694	9779	9863	9948		85
71										0033	85
513	0117	0202	0287	0371	0456	0540	0625	0710	0794	0879	85
514	0963	1048	1132	1217	1301	1385	1470	1554	1638	1723	84
515	1807	1892	1976	2060	2144	2229	2313	2397	2481	2566	84
516	2650	2734	2818	2902	2986	3070	3154	3238	3323	3406	84
517	3491	3575	3659	3742	3826	3910	3994	4078	4162	4246	84
518	4330	4414	4497	4581	4665	4749	4833	4916	5000	5084	84
519	5167	5251	5335	5418	5502	5586	5669	5753	5836	5920	84
520	6003	6087	6170	6254	6337	6421	6504	6588	6671	6754	83
521	6838	6921	7004	7088	7171	7254	7338	7421	7504	7587	83
522	7671	7754	7837	7920	8003	8086	8169	8253	8336	8419	83

N.	0	1	2	3	4	5	6	7	8	9	D.
523	718502	8585	8668	8751	8834	8917	9000	9083	9105	9248	83
524	9331	9414	9497	9580	9663	9745	9828	9911	9994		83
	72									0077	83
525	0159	0242	0325	0407	0490	0573	0655	0738	0821	0903	83
526	0986	1068	1151	1233	1316	1398	1481	1563	1646	1728	82
527	1811	1893	1975	2058	2140	2222	2305	2387	2467	2552	82
528	2634	2716	2798	2881	2963	3045	3127	3209	3291	3374	82
529	3456	3538	3620	3702	3784	3866	3948	4030	4112	4194	82
530	4276	4358	4440	4522	4604	4685	4767	4849	4931	5013	82
531	5095	5176	5258	5340	5422	5503	5585	5667	5748	5830	82
532	5912	5993	6075	6156	6238	6320	6401	6483	6564	6646	82
533	6727	6809	6890	6972	7053	7134	7216	7297	7379	7460	81
534	7541	7623	7704	7785	7866	7948	8029	8110	8191	8273	81
535	8354	8435	8516	8597	8678	8759	8841	8922	9003	9084	81
536	9165	9246	9327	9408	9489	9570	9651	9732	9813	9893	81
537	9974										81
	73	0055	0136	0217	0298	0378	0459	0540	0621	0701	81
538	0782	0863	0944	1024	1105	1186	1266	1347	1428	1508	81
539	1589	1669	1750	1830	1911	1991	2072	2152	2233	2313	81
540	2394	2474	2555	2635	2715	2796	2876	2956	3037	3117	80
541	3197	3278	3358	3438	3518	3598	3679	3759	3839	3919	80
542	3999	4079	4160	4240	4320	4400	4480	4560	4640	4720	80
543	4800	4880	4960	5040	5120	5199	5279	5359	5439	5519	80
544	5599	5679	5759	5838	5918	5998	6078	6157	6237	6317	80
545	6397	6476	6556	6635	6715	6795	6874	6954	7034	7113	80
546	7193	7272	7352	7431	7511	7590	7670	7749	7829	7908	79
547	7987	8067	8146	8225	8305	8384	8463	8543	8622	8701	79
548	8781	8860	8939	9018	9097	9177	9256	9335	9414	9493	79
549	9572	9651	9731	9810	9889	9968					79
	74						0047	0126	0205	0284	79
550	0363	0442	0521	0600	0678	0757	0836	0915	0994	1073	79
551	1152	1230	1309	1388	1467	1546	1624	1703	1782	1860	79
552	1939	2018	2096	2175	2254	2332	2411	2489	2568	2647	79
553	2725	2804	2882	2961	3039	3118	3196	3275	3353	3431	78
554	3510	3588	3667	3745	3823	3902	3980	4058	4136	4215	78
555	4293	4371	4449	4528	4606	4684	4762	4840	4919	4997	78
556	5075	5153	5231	5309	5387	5465	5543	5621	5699	5777	78
557	5855	5933	6011	6089	6167	6245	6323	6401	6478	6556	78
558	6634	6712	6790	6868	6945	7023	7101	7179	7256	7334	78
559	7412	7489	7567	7645	7722	7800	7878	7955	8033	8110	78
560	8188	8266	8343	8421	8498	8576	8653	8731	8808	8885	77
561	8963	9040	9118	9195	9272	9350	9427	9504	9582	9659	77
562	9736	9814	9891	9968							77
	75				0045	0123	0200	0277	0354	0431	77
563	0508	0586	0663	0740	0817	0894	0971	1048	1125	1202	77
564	1279	1356	1433	1510	1587	1664	1741	1818	1895	1972	77
565	2048	2125	2202	2279	2356	2433	2509	2586	2663	2740	77
566	2816	2893	2970	3047	3123	3200	3277	3353	3430	3506	77
567	3583	3660	3736	3813	3889	3966	4042	4119	4195	4272	77
568	4348	4425	4501	4578	4654	4730	4807	4883	4960	5036	76
569	5112	5189	5265	5341	5417	5494	5570	5646	5722	5799	76
570	5875	5951	6027	6103	6180	6256	6332	6408	6484	6560	76
571	6636	6712	6788	6864	6940	7016	7092	7168	7244	7320	76
572	7396	7472	7548	7624	7700	7775	7851	7927	8003	8079	76
573	8155	8230	8306	8382	8458	8533	8609	8685	8761	8836	76
574	8912	8988	9063	9139	9214	9290	9366	9441	9517	9592	76
575	9668	9743	9819	9894	9970						75
	76					0045	0121	0196	0272	0347	75
576	0422	0498	0573	0649	0724	0799	0875	0950	1025	1101	75
577	1176	1251	1326	1402	1477	1552	1627	1702	1778	1853	75
578	1928	2003	2078	2153	2228	2303	2378	2453	2529	2604	75

N.	0	1	2	3	4	5	6	7	8	9	D.
579	762679	2754	2829	2904	2978	3053	3128	3203	3278	3353	75
580	3428	3503	3578	3653	3727	3802	3877	3952	4027	4101	75
581	4176	4251	4326	4400	4475	4550	4624	4699	4774	4848	75
582	4923	4998	5072	5147	5221	5296	5370	5445	5520	5594	75
583	5669	5743	5818	5892	5966	6041	6115	6190	6264	6338	74
584	6413	6487	6562	6636	6710	6785	6859	6933	7007	7082	74
585	7156	7230	7304	7379	7453	7527	7601	7675	7749	7823	74
586	7898	7972	8046	8120	8194	8268	8342	8416	8490	8564	74
587	8638	8712	8786	8860	8934	9008	9082	9156	9230	9303	74
588	9377	9451	9525	9599	9673	9746	9820	9894	9968	0042	74
77											74
589	0115	0189	0263	0336	0410	0484	0557	0631	0705	0778	74
590	0852	0926	0999	1073	1146	1220	1293	1367	1440	1514	74
591	1587	1661	1734	1808	1881	1955	2028	2102	2175	2248	73
592	2322	2395	2468	2542	2615	2688	2762	2835	2908	2981	73
593	3055	3128	3201	3274	3348	3421	3494	3567	3640	3713	73
594	3786	3860	3933	4006	4079	4152	4225	4298	4371	4444	73
595	4517	4590	4663	4736	4809	4882	4955	5028	5100	5173	73
596	5246	5319	5392	5465	5538	5610	5683	5756	5829	5902	73
597	5974	6047	6120	6193	6265	6338	6411	6483	6556	6629	73
598	6701	6774	6846	6919	6992	7064	7137	7209	7282	7354	73
599	7427	7499	7572	7644	7717	7789	7862	7934	8006	8079	72
600	8151	8224	8296	8368	8441	8513	8585	8658	8730	8802	72
601	8874	8947	9019	9091	9163	9236	9308	9380	9452	9524	72
602	9596	9669	9741	9813	9885	9957					72
78							0029	0101	0173	0245	72
603	0317	0389	0461	0533	0605	0677	0749	0821	0893	0965	72
604	1037	1109	1181	1253	1324	1396	1468	1540	1612	1684	72
605	1755	1827	1899	1971	2042	2114	2186	2258	2329	2401	72
606	2473	2544	2616	2688	2759	2831	2902	2974	3046	3117	71
607	3189	3260	3332	3403	3475	3546	3618	3689	3761	3832	71
608	3904	3975	4046	4118	4189	4261	4332	4403	4475	4546	71
609	4617	4689	4760	4831	4902	4974	5045	5116	5187	5259	71
610	5330	5401	5472	5543	5615	5686	5757	5828	5899	5970	71
611	6041	6112	6183	6254	6325	6396	6467	6538	6609	6680	71
612	6751	6822	6893	6964	7035	7106	7177	7248	7319	7390	71
613	7460	7531	7602	7673	7744	7815	7885	7956	8027	8098	71
614	8168	8239	8310	8381	8451	8522	8593	8663	8734	8804	71
615	8875	8946	9016	9087	9157	9228	9299	9369	9440	9510	71
616	9581	9651	9722	9792	9863	9933					70
79							0004	0074	0144	0215	70
617	0285	0356	0426	0496	0567	0637	0707	0778	0848	0918	70
618	0988	1059	1129	1199	1269	1340	1410	1480	1550	1620	70
619	1691	1761	1831	1901	1971	2041	2111	2181	2252	2322	70
620	2392	2462	2532	2602	2672	2742	2812	2882	2952	3022	70
621	3092	3162	3231	3301	3371	3441	3511	3581	3651	3721	70
622	3790	3860	3930	4000	4070	4139	4209	4279	4349	4418	70
623	4488	4558	4627	4697	4767	4836	4906	4976	5045	5115	70
624	5185	5254	5324	5393	5463	5532	5602	5672	5741	5811	70
625	5880	5949	6019	6088	6158	6227	6297	6366	6436	6505	69
626	6574	6644	6713	6782	6852	6921	6990	7060	7129	7198	69
627	7268	7337	7406	7475	7545	7614	7683	7752	7821	7890	69
628	7960	8029	8098	8167	8236	8305	8374	8443	8513	8582	69
629	8651	8720	8789	8858	8927	8996	9065	9134	9203	9272	69
630	9341	9409	9478	9547	9616	9685	9754	9823	9892	9961	69
631	800029	0098	0167	0236	0305	0373	0442	0511	0580	0648	69
632	0717	0786	0854	0923	0992	1060	1129	1198	1266	1335	69
633	1404	1472	1541	1609	1678	1747	1815	1884	1952	2021	69
634	2089	2158	2226	2295	2363	2432	2500	2568	2637	2705	68
635	2774	2842	2910	2979	3047	3116	3184	3252	3321	3389	68
636	3457	3525	3594	3662	3730	3798	3867	3935	4003	4071	68

N.	0	1	2	3	4	5	6	7	8	9	D.
637	804139	4208	4276	4344	4412	4480	4548	4616	4685	4753	68
638	4821	4889	4957	5025	5093	5161	5229	5297	5365	5433	68
639	5501	5569	5637	5705	5773	5841	5908	5976	6044	6112	68
640	6180	6248	6316	6384	6451	6519	6587	6655	6723	6790	68
641	6858	6926	6994	7061	7129	7197	7264	7332	7400	˜467	68
642	7535	7603	7670	7738	7806	7873	7941	8008	8076	8143	68
643	8211	8279	8346	8414	8481	8549	8616	8684	8751	8818	68
644	8886	8953	9021	9088	9156	9223	9290	9358	9425	9492	67
645	9560	9627	9694	9762	9829	9896	9964	0031	0098	0165	67
81											
646	0233	0300	0367	0434	0501	0569	0636	0703	0770	0837	67
647	0904	0971	1039	1106	1173	1240	1307	1374	1441	1508	67
648	1575	1642	1709	1776	1843	1910	1977	2044	2111	2178	67
649	2245	2312	2378	2445	2512	2579	2646	2713	2780	2847	67
650	2913	2980	3047	3114	3181	3247	3314	3381	3448	3514	67
651	3581	3648	3714	3781	3848	3914	3981	4048	4114	4181	67
652	4248	4314	4381	4447	4514	4581	4647	4714	4780	4847	67
653	4913	4980	5046	5113	5179	5246	5312	5378	5445	5511	66
654	5578	5644	5711	5777	5843	5910	5976	6042	6109	6175	66
655	6241	6308	6374	6440	6506	6573	6639	6705	6771	6838	66
656	6904	6970	7036	7102	7169	7235	7301	7367	7433	7499	66
657	7565	7631	7698	7764	7830	7896	7962	8028	8094	8160	66
658	8226	8292	8358	8424	8490	8556	8622	8688	8754	8820	66
659	8885	8951	9017	9083	9149	9215	9281	9346	9412	9478	66
660	9544	9610	9676	9741	9807	9873	9939	0004	0070	0136	66
82											
661	0201	0267	0333	0399	0464	0530	0595	0661	0727	0792	66
662	0858	0924	0989	1055	1120	1186	1251	1317	1382	1448	66
663	1514	1579	1644	1710	1775	1841	1906	1972	2037	2103	65
664	2168	2233	2299	2364	2430	2495	2560	2626	2691	2756	65
665	2822	2887	2952	3018	3083	3148	3213	3279	3344	3409	65
666	3474	3539	3605	3670	3735	3800	3865	3930	3996	4061	65
667	4126	4191	4256	4321	4386	4451	4516	4581	4646	4711	65
668	4776	4841	4906	4971	5036	5101	5166	5231	5296	5361	65
669	5426	5491	5556	5621	5686	5751	5815	5880	5945	6010	65
670	6075	6140	6204	6269	6334	6399	6464	6528	6593	6658	65
671	6723	6787	6852	6917	6981	7046	7111	7175	7240	7305	65
672	7369	7434	7499	7563	7628	7692	7757	7821	7886	7951	64
673	8015	8080	8144	8209	8273	8338	8402	8467	8531	8595	64
674	8660	8724	8789	8853	8918	8982	9046	9111	9175	9239	64
675	9304	9368	9432	9497	9561	9625	9690	9754	9818	9882	64
676	9947	0011	0075	0139	0204	0268	0332	0396	0460	0525	64
83											
677	0589	0653	0717	0781	0845	0909	0973	1037	1102	1166	64
678	1230	1294	1358	1422	1486	1550	1614	1678	1742	1806	64
679	1870	1934	1998	2062	2126	2189	2253	2317	2381	2445	64
680	2509	2573	2637	2700	2764	2828	2892	2956	3020	3083	64
681	3147	3211	3275	3338	3402	3466	3530	3593	3657	3721	64
682	3784	3848	3912	3975	4039	4103	4166	4230	4294	4357	63
683	4421	4484	4548	4611	4675	4739	4802	4866	4929	4993	63
684	5056	5120	5183	5247	5310	5373	5437	5500	5564	5627	63
685	5691	5754	5817	5881	5944	6007	6071	6134	6197	6261	63
686	6324	6387	6451	6514	6577	6641	6704	6767	6830	6894	63
687	6957	7020	7083	7146	7210	7273	7336	7399	7462	7525	63
688	7583	7652	7715	7778	7841	7904	7967	8030	8093	8156	63
689	8219	8282	8345	8408	8471	8534	8597	8660	8723	8786	63
690	8849	8912	8975	9038	9101	9164	9227	9289	9352	9415	63
691	9478	9541	9604	9667	9729	9792	9855	9918	9981	0043	63
84											
692	0106	0169	0232	0294	0357	0420	0482	0545	0608	0671	63
693	0733	0796	0859	0921	0984	1046	1109	1172	1234	1297	63

N.	0	1	2	3	4	5	6	7	8	9	D.
694	841359	1422	1485	1547	1610	1672	1735	1797	1860	1922	63
695	1985	2047	2110	2172	2235	2297	2360	2422	2484	2547	62
696	2609	2672	2734	2796	2859	2921	2983	3046	3108	3170	62
697	3233	3295	3357	3420	3482	3544	3606	3669	3731	3793	62
698	3855	3918	3980	4042	4104	4166	4229	4291	4353	4415	62
699	4477	4539	4601	4664	4726	4788	4850	4912	4974	5036	62
700	5098	5160	5222	5284	5346	5408	5470	5532	5594	5656	62
701	5718	5780	5842	5904	5966	6028	6090	6151	6213	6275	62
702	6337	6399	6461	6523	6585	6646	6708	6770	6832	6894	62
703	6955	7017	7079	7141	7202	7264	7326	7388	7449	7511	62
704	7573	7634	7696	7758	7819	7881	7943	8004	8066	8128	62
705	8189	8251	8312	8374	8435	8497	8559	8620	8682	8743	62
706	8805	8866	8928	8989	9051	9112	9174	9235	9296	9358	61
707	9419	9481	9542	9604	9665	9726	9788	9849	9911	9972	61
708	850033	0095	0156	0217	0279	0340	0401	0462	0524	0585	61
709	0646	0707	0769	0830	0891	0952	1014	1075	1136	1197	61
710	1258	1320	1381	1442	1503	1564	1625	1686	1747	1809	61
711	1870	1931	1992	2053	2114	2175	2236	2297	2358	2419	61
712	2480	2541	2602	2663	2724	2785	2846	2907	2968	3029	61
713	3090	3150	3211	3272	3333	3394	3455	3516	3576	3637	61
714	3698	3759	3820	3881	3941	4002	4063	4124	4185	4245	61
715	4306	4367	4427	4488	4549	4610	4670	4731	4792	4852	61
716	4913	4974	5034	5095	5156	5216	5277	5337	5398	5459	61
717	5519	5580	5640	5701	5761	5822	5882	5943	6003	6064	61
718	6124	6185	6245	6306	6366	6427	6487	6548	6608	6668	61
719	6729	6789	6850	6910	6970	7031	7091	7151	7212	7272	60
720	7332	7393	7453	7513	7574	7634	7694	7754	7815	7875	60
721	7935	7995	8056	8116	8176	8236	8297	8357	8417	8477	60
722	8537	8597	8657	8718	8778	8838	8898	8958	9018	9078	60
723	9138	9198	9258	9318	9379	9439	9499	9559	9619	9679	60
724	9739	9799	9859	9918	9978	0038	0098	0158	0218	0278	60
					86						
725	0338	0398	0458	0518	0578	0637	0697	0757	0817	0877	60
726	0937	0996	1056	1116	1176	1236	1295	1355	1415	1475	60
727	1534	1594	1654	1714	1773	1833	1893	1952	2012	2072	60
728	2131	2191	2251	2310	2370	2430	2489	2549	2608	2668	60
729	2728	2787	2847	2906	2966	3025	3085	3144	3204	3263	60
730	3323	3382	3442	3501	3561	3620	3680	3739	3798	3858	59
731	3917	3977	4036	4096	4155	4214	4274	4333	4392	4452	59
732	4511	4570	4630	4689	4748	4808	4867	4926	4985	5045	59
733	5104	5163	5222	5282	5341	5400	5459	5518	5578	5637	59
734	5696	5755	5814	5874	5933	5992	6051	6110	6169	6228	59
735	6287	6346	6405	6465	6524	6583	6642	6701	6760	6819	59
736	6878	6937	6996	7055	7114	7173	7232	7291	7350	7409	59
737	7467	7526	7585	7644	7703	7762	7821	7880	7939	7998	59
738	8056	8115	8174	8233	8292	8350	8409	8468	8527	8586	59
739	8644	8703	8762	8821	8879	8938	8997	9055	9114	9173	59
740	9232	9290	9349	9408	9466	9525	9584	9642	9701	9760	59
741	9818	9877	9935	9994	0053	0111	0170	0228	0287	0345	59
				87							
742	0404	0462	0521	0579	0638	0696	0755	0813	0872	0930	58
743	0989	1047	1106	1164	1223	1281	1339	1398	1456	1515	58
744	1573	1631	1690	1748	1806	1865	1923	1981	2040	2098	58
745	2156	2215	2273	2331	2389	2448	2506	2564	2622	2681	58
746	2739	2797	2855	2913	2972	3030	3088	3146	3204	3262	58
747	3321	3379	3437	3495	3553	3611	3669	3727	3785	3844	58
748	3902	3960	4018	4076	4134	4192	4250	4308	4366	4424	58
749	4482	4540	4598	4656	4714	4772	4830	4888	4945	5003	58
750	5061	5119	5177	5235	5293	5351	5409	5466	5524	5582	58
751	5640	5698	5756	5813	5871	5929	5987	6045	6102	6160	58
752	6218	6276	6333	6391	6449	6507	6564	6622	6680	6737	58

N.	0	1	2	3	4	5	6	7	8	9	D.
753	876795	6853	6910	6968	7026	7083	7141	7199	7256	7314	58
754	7371	7429	7487	7544	7602	7659	7717	7774	7832	7889	58
755	7947	8004	8062	8119	8177	8234	8292	8349	8407	8464	57
756	8522	8579	8637	8694	8752	8809	8866	8924	8981	9039	57
757	9096	9153	9211	9268	9325	9383	9440	9497	9555	9612	57
758	9669	9726	9784	9841	9898	9956					57
88							0013	0070	0127	0185	57
759	0242	0299	0356	0413	0471	0528	0585	0642	0699	0756	57
760	0814	0871	0928	0985	1042	1099	1156	1213	1271	1328	57
761	1385	1442	1499	1556	1613	1670	1727	1784	1841	1898	57
762	1955	2012	2069	2126	2183	2240	2297	2354	2411	2468	57
763	2525	2581	2638	2695	2752	2809	2865	2923	2980	3037	57
764	3093	3150	3207	3264	3321	3377	3434	3491	3548	3605	57
765	3661	3718	3775	3832	3888	3945	4002	4059	4115	4172	57
766	4229	4285	4342	4399	4455	4512	4569	4625	4682	4739	57
767	4795	4852	4909	4965	5022	5078	5135	5192	5248	5305	57
768	5361	5418	5474	5531	5587	5644	5700	5757	5813	5870	57
769	5926	5983	6039	6096	6152	6209	6265	6321	6378	6434	56
770	6491	6547	6604	6660	6716	6773	6829	6885	6942	6998	56
771	7054	7111	7167	7223	7280	7336	7392	7448	7505	7561	56
772	7617	7674	7730	7786	7842	7898	7955	8011	8067	8123	56
773	8179	8236	8292	8348	8404	8460	8516	8573	8629	8685	56
774	8741	8797	8853	8909	8965	9021	9077	9134	9190	9246	56
775	9302	9358	9414	9470	9526	9581	9638	9694	9750	9806	56
776	9862	9918	9974								56
89				0030	0086	0141	0197	0253	0309	0365	56
777	0421	0477	0533	0589	0644	0700	0756	0812	0868	0924	56
778	0980	1035	1091	1147	1203	1259	1314	1370	1426	1482	56
779	1537	1593	1649	1705	1760	1816	1872	1928	1983	2039	56
780	2095	2150	2206	2262	2317	2373	2429	2484	2540	2595	56
781	2651	2707	2762	2818	2873	2929	2985	3040	3096	3151	56
782	3207	3262	3318	3373	3429	3484	3540	3595	3651	3706	56
783	3762	3817	3873	3928	3984	4039	4094	4150	4205	4261	55
784	4316	4371	4427	4482	4538	4593	4648	4704	4759	4814	55
785	4870	4925	4980	5036	5091	5146	5201	5257	5312	5367	55
786	5423	5478	5533	5588	5644	5699	5754	5809	5864	5920	55
787	5975	6030	6085	6140	6195	6251	6306	6361	6416	6471	55
788	6526	6581	6636	6692	6747	6802	6857	6913	6967	7022	55
789	7077	7132	7187	7242	7297	7352	7407	7462	7517	7572	55
790	7627	7682	7737	7792	7847	7902	7957	8012	8067	8122	55
791	8176	8231	8286	8341	8396	8451	8506	8561	8615	8670	55
792	8725	8780	8835	8890	8944	8999	9054	9109	9164	9218	55
793	9273	9328	9383	9437	9492	9547	9602	9656	9711	9766	55
794	9821	9875	9930	9985							55
90					0039	0094	0149	0203	0258	0312	55
795	0357	0412	0476	0531	0586	0640	0695	0749	0804	0859	55
796	0913	0968	1022	1077	1131	1186	1240	1295	1349	1404	55
797	1458	1513	1567	1622	1676	1731	1785	1840	1894	1948	54
798	2003	2057	2112	2166	2221	2275	2329	2384	2438	2492	54
799	2547	2601	2655	2710	2764	2818	2873	2927	2981	3036	54
800	3090	3144	3198	3253	3307	3361	3416	3470	3524	3578	54
801	3632	3687	3741	3795	3849	3903	3958	4012	4066	4120	54
802	4174	4228	4283	4337	4391	4445	4499	4553	4607	4661	54
803	4715	4770	4824	4878	4932	4986	5040	5094	5148	5202	54
804	5256	5310	5364	5418	5472	5526	5580	5634	5688	5742	54
805	5796	5850	5904	5958	6012	6065	6119	6173	6227	6281	54
806	6335	6389	6443	6497	6550	6604	6658	6712	6766	6820	54
807	6873	6927	6981	7035	7089	7142	7196	7250	7304	7358	54
808	7411	7465	7519	7573	7626	7680	7734	7787	7841	7895	54
809	7948	8002	8056	8109	8163	8217	8270	8324	8378	8431	54
810	8485	8539	8592	8646	8699	8753	8807	8860	8914	8967	54

N.	0	1	2	3	4	5	6	7	8	9	D.
811	909021	9074	9128	9181	9235	9288	9342	9395	9449	9502	54
812	9556	9609	9663	9716	9770	9823	9877	9930	9984		53
91										0037	53
813	0090	0144	0197	0251	0304	0358	0411	0464	0518	0571	53
814	0624	0678	0731	0784	0838	0891	0944	0998	1051	1104	53
815	1158	1211	1264	1317	1371	1424	1477	1530	1584	1637	53
816	1690	1743	1797	1850	1903	1956	2009	2063	2116	2169	53
817	2222	2275	2328	2381	2435	2488	2541	2594	2647	2700	53
818	2753	2806	2859	2913	2966	3019	3072	3125	3178	3231	53
819	3284	3337	3390	3443	3496	3549	3602	3655	3708	3761	53
820	3814	3867	3920	3973	4026	4079	4131	4184	4237	4290	53
821	4343	4396	4449	4502	4555	4608	4660	4713	4766	4819	53
822	4872	4925	4977	5030	5083	5136	5189	5241	5294	5347	53
823	5400	5453	5505	5558	5611	5664	5716	5769	5822	5874	53
824	5927	5980	6033	6085	6138	6191	6243	6296	6349	6401	53
825	6454	6507	6559	6612	6664	6717	6770	6822	6875	6927	53
826	6980	7033	7085	7138	7190	7243	7295	7348	7400	7453	53
827	7505	7558	7610	7663	7715	7768	7820	7873	7925	7978	52
828	8030	8083	8135	8188	8240	8292	8345	8397	8450	8502	52
829	8555	8607	8659	8712	8764	8816	8869	8921	8973	9026	52
830	9078	9130	9183	9235	9287	9340	9392	9444	9496	9549	52
831	9601	9653	9705	9758	9810	9862	9914	9967			52
92									0019	0071	52
832	0123	0175	0228	0280	0332	0384	0436	0489	0541	0593	52
833	0645	0697	0749	0801	0853	0906	0958	1010	1062	1114	52
834	1166	1218	1270	1322	1374	1426	1478	1530	1582	1634	52
835	1686	1738	1790	1842	1894	1946	1998	2050	2102	2154	52
836	2206	2258	2310	2362	2414	2466	2518	2570	2622	2674	52
837	2725	2777	2829	2881	2933	2985	3037	3088	3140	3192	52
838	3244	3296	3348	3399	3451	3503	3555	3607	3658	3710	52
839	3762	3814	3865	3917	3969	4021	4072	4124	4176	4228	52
840	4279	4331	4383	4434	4486	4538	4589	4641	4693	4744	52
841	4796	4848	4899	4951	5002	5054	5106	5157	5209	5260	52
842	5312	5364	5415	5467	5518	5570	5621	5673	5724	5776	52
843	5828	5879	5931	5982	6034	6085	6137	6188	6239	6291	52
844	6342	6394	6445	6497	6548	6600	6651	6702	6754	6805	51
845	6857	6908	6959	7011	7062	7114	7165	7216	7268	7319	51
846	7370	7422	7473	7524	7576	7627	7678	7730	7781	7832	51
847	7883	7935	7986	8037	8088	8140	8191	8242	8293	8345	51
848	8396	8447	8498	8549	8601	8652	8703	8754	8805	8856	51
849	8908	8959	9010	9061	9112	9163	9214	9266	9317	9368	51
850	9419	9470	9521	9572	9623	9674	9725	9776	9827	9878	51
851	9930	9981									51
93			0032	0083	0134	0185	0236	0287	0338	0389	51
852	0440	0491	0541	0592	0643	0694	0745	0796	0847	0898	51
853	0949	1000	1051	1102	1153	1203	1254	1305	1356	1407	51
854	1458	1509	1560	1610	1661	1712	1763	1814	1864	1915	51
855	1966	2017	2068	2118	2169	2220	2271	2321	2372	2423	51
856	2474	2524	2575	2626	2677	2727	2778	2829	2879	2930	51
857	2981	3031	3082	3133	3183	3234	3285	3335	3386	3437	51
858	3487	3538	3588	3639	3690	3740	3791	3841	3892	3943	51
859	3993	4044	4094	4145	4195	4246	4296	4347	4397	4448	51
860	4498	4549	4599	4650	4700	4751	4801	4852	4902	4953	50
861	5003	5054	5104	5154	5205	5255	5306	5356	5406	5457	50
862	5507	5558	5608	5658	5709	5759	5809	5860	5910	5960	50
863	6011	6061	6111	6162	6212	6262	6313	6363	6413	6463	50
864	6514	6564	6614	6664	6715	6765	6815	6865	6916	6966	50
865	7016	7066	7116	7167	7217	7267	7317	7367	7418	7468	50
866	7518	7568	7618	7668	7718	7769	7819	7869	7919	7969	50
867	8019	8069	8119	8169	8219	8269	8319	8370	8420	8470	50
868	8520	8570	8620	8670	8720	8770	8820	8870	8920	8970	50

N°	0	1	2	3	4	5	6	7	8	9	D.
869	93)020	9070	9120	9170	9220	9270	9319	9369	9419	9469	50
870	9519	9569	9619	9669	9719	9769	9819	9868	9918	9968	50
871	940018	0068	0118	0168	0218	0267	0317	0367	0417	0467	50
872	0516	0566	0616	0666	0716	0765	0815	0865	0915	0964	50
873	1014	1064	1114	1163	1213	1263	1313	1362	1412	1462	50
874	1511	1561	1611	1660	1710	1760	1809	1859	1909	1958	50
875	2008	2058	2107	2157	2205	2256	2306	2355	2405	2454	50
876	2504	2554	2603	2653	2701	2752	2801	2851	2900	2950	50
877	3000	3049	3099	3148	3198	3247	3297	3346	3396	3445	49
878	3494	3544	3593	3643	3692	3742	3791	3841	3899	3939	49
879	3989	4038	4088	4137	4186	4236	4285	4335	4384	4433	49
880	4483	4532	4581	4631	4680	4729	4779	4828	4877	4927	49
881	4976	5025	5074	5124	5173	5222	5272	5321	5370	5419	49
882	5469	5518	5567	5616	5665	5715	5764	5813	5862	5911	49
883	5961	6010	6059	6108	6157	6207	6256	6305	6354	6403	49
884	6452	6501	6550	6600	6649	6698	6747	6796	6845	6894	49
885	6943	6992	7041	7090	7139	7189	7238	7287	7336	7385	49
886	7434	7483	7532	7581	7630	7679	7728	7777	7826	7875	49
887	7924	7973	8021	8070	8119	8168	8217	8266	8315	8364	49
888	8413	8462	8511	8560	8608	8657	8706	8755	8804	8853	49
889	8902	8951	8999	9048	9097	9146	9195	9244	9292	9341	49
890	9390	9439	9488	9536	9585	9634	9683	9731	9780	9829	49
891	9878	9926	9975								49
	95			0024	0073	0121	0170	0219	0267	0316	49
892	0365	0413	0462	0511	0560	0608	0657	0705	0754	0803	49
893	0851	0900	0949	0997	1046	1095	1143	1192	1240	1289	49
894	1337	1386	1435	1483	1532	1580	1629	1677	1726	1774	49
895	1823	1872	1920	1969	2017	2066	2114	2163	2211	2259	48
896	2308	2356	2405	2453	2502	2550	2599	2647	2696	2744	48
897	2792	2841	2889	2938	2986	3034	3083	3131	3180	3228	48
898	3276	3325	3373	3421	3470	3518	3566	3615	3663	3711	48
899	3760	3808	3856	3905	3953	4001	4049	4098	4146	4194	48
900	4242	4291	4339	4387	4435	4484	4532	4580	4628	4677	48
901	4725	4773	4821	4869	4918	4966	5014	5062	5110	5158	48
902	5206	5255	5303	5352	5399	5447	5495	5543	5592	5640	48
903	5688	5736	5784	5832	5880	5928	5976	6024	6072	6120	48
904	6168	6216	6264	6312	6361	6409	6457	6505	6553	6601	48
905	6649	6697	6745	6792	6840	6888	6936	6984	7032	7080	48
906	7128	7176	7224	7272	7320	7368	7416	7464	7511	7559	48
907	7607	7655	7703	7751	7799	7847	7894	7942	7990	8038	48
908	8086	8134	8181	8229	8277	8325	8373	8420	8468	8516	48
909	8564	8612	8659	8707	8755	8803	8850	8898	8946	8994	48
910	9041	9089	9137	9184	9232	9280	9328	9375	9423	9471	48
911	9518	9566	9614	9661	9709	9757	9804	9852	9900	9947	48
912	9995										48
	96		0042	0090	0138	0185	0233	0281	0328	0376	0423	48
913	0471	0518	0566	0613	0661	0709	0756	0804	0851	0899	48
914	0946	0994	1041	1089	1136	1184	1231	1279	1326	1374	47
915	1421	1469	1516	1563	1611	1658	1706	1753	1801	1848	47
916	1895	1943	1990	2038	2085	2132	2180	2227	2275	2322	47
917	2369	2417	2464	2511	2559	2606	2653	2701	2748	2795	47
918	2843	2890	2937	2985	3032	3079	3126	3174	3221	3268	47
919	3315	3363	3410	3457	3504	3552	3599	3646	3693	3741	47
920	3788	3835	3882	3929	3977	4024	4071	4118	4165	4212	47
921	4260	4307	4354	4401	4448	4495	4542	4590	4637	4684	47
922	4731	4778	4825	4872	4919	4966	5013	5060	5108	5155	47
923	5202	5249	5296	5343	5390	5437	5484	5531	5578	5625	47
924	5672	5719	5766	5813	5860	5907	5954	6001	6048	6095	47
925	6142	6189	6236	6283	6329	6376	6423	6470	6517	6564	47
926	6611	6658	6705	6752	6798	6845	6892	6939	6986	7033	47
927	7080	7127	7173	7220	7267	7314	7361	7407	7454	7501	47

N.	0	1	2	3	4	5	6	7	8	9	D.
928	.967548	7595	7642	7688	7735	7782	7829	7875	7922	7969	47
929	8016	8062	8109	8156	8203	8249	8296	8343	8389	8436	47
930	8483	8530	8576	8623	8670	8716	8763	8810	8856	8903	47
931	8950	8996	9043	9090	9136	9183	9229	9276	9323	9369	47
932	9416	9462	9509	9556	9602	9649	9695	9742	9788	9835	47
933	9884	9928	9975								47
	97			0021	0068	0114	0161	0207	0254	0300	47
934	0347	0393	0440	0486	0533	0579	0626	0672	0719	0765	46
935	0812	0858	0904	0951	0997	1044	1090	1137	1183	1229	46
936	1276	1322	1369	1415	1461	1508	1554	1600	1647	1693	46
937	1740	1786	1832	1879	1925	1971	2018	2064	2110	2156	46
938	2203	2249	2295	2342	2388	2434	2480	2527	2573	2619	46
939	2666	2712	2758	2804	2851	2897	2943	2989	3035	3082	46
940	3128	3174	3220	3266	3313	3359	3405	3451	3497	3543	46
941	3590	3636	3682	3728	3774	3820	3866	3913	3959	4005	46
942	4051	4097	4143	4189	4235	4281	4327	4373	4420	4466	46
943	4512	4558	4604	4650	4696	4742	4788	4834	4880	4926	46
944	4972	5018	5064	5110	5156	5202	5248	5294	5340	5386	46
945	5432	5478	5524	5570	5615	5661	5707	5753	5799	5845	46
946	5891	5937	5983	6019	6075	6121	6166	6212	6258	6304	46
947	6350	6396	6442	6487	6533	6579	6625	6671	6717	6762	46
948	6808	6854	6900	6946	6991	7037	7083	7129	7175	7220	46
949	7266	7312	7358	7403	7449	7495	7541	7586	7632	7678	46
950	7724	7769	7815	7861	7906	7952	7998	8043	8089	8135	46
951	8180	8226	8272	8317	8363	8409	8454	8500	8546	8591	46
952	8637	8683	8728	8774	8819	8865	8911	8956	9002	9047	46
953	9093	9138	9184	9230	9275	9321	9366	9412	9457	9503	46
954	9548	9594	9639	9685	9730	9776	9821	9867	9912	9958	46
955	980003	0049	0094	0140	0185	0231	0276	0322	0367	0412	45
956	0458	0503	0549	0594	0640	0685	0730	0776	0821	0867	45
957	0912	0957	1003	1048	1093	1139	1184	1229	1275	1320	45
958	1365	1411	1456	1501	1547	1592	1637	1683	1728	1773	45
959	1819	1864	1909	1954	2000	2045	2090	2135	2181	2226	45
960	2271	2316	2362	2407	2452	2497	2543	2588	2633	2678	45
961	2723	2769	2814	2859	2904	2949	2994	3040	3085	3130	45
962	3175	3220	3265	3310	3356	3401	3446	3491	3536	3581	45
963	3626	3671	3716	3762	3807	3852	3897	3942	3987	4032	45
964	4077	4122	4167	4212	4257	4302	4347	4392	4437	4482	45
965	4527	4572	4617	4662	4707	4752	4797	4842	4887	4932	45
966	4977	5022	5067	5112	5157	5202	5247	5292	5337	5382	45
967	5426	5471	5516	5561	5606	5651	5696	5741	5786	5830	45
968	5875	5920	5965	6010	6055	6100	6144	6189	6234	6279	45
969	6324	6369	6413	6458	6503	6548	6593	6637	6682	6727	45
970	6772	6816	6861	6906	6951	6995	7040	7085	7130	7174	45
971	7219	7264	7309	7353	7398	7443	7487	7532	7577	7622	45
972	7666	7711	7756	7800	7845	7890	7934	7979	8024	8068	45
973	8113	8157	8202	8247	8291	8336	8381	8425	8470	8514	45
974	8559	8603	8648	8693	8737	8782	8826	8871	8915	8960	45
975	9005	9049	9094	9138	9183	9227	9272	9316	9361	9405	45
976	9450	9494	9539	9583	9628	9672	9717	9761	9806	9850	44
977	9895	9939	9983								44
	99			0028	0072	0117	0161	0206	0250	0294	44
978	0339	0383	0428	0472	0516	0561	0605	0650	0694	0738	44
979	0783	0827	0871	0916	0960	1004	1049	1093	1137	1182	44
980	1226	1270	1315	1359	1403	1448	1492	1536	1580	1625	44
981	1669	1713	1757	1802	1846	1890	1934	1979	2023	2067	44
982	2111	2156	2200	2244	2288	2333	2377	2421	2465	2509	44
983	2553	2598	2642	2686	2730	2774	2818	2863	2907	2951	44
984	2995	3039	3083	3127	3172	3216	3260	3304	3348	3392	44
985	3436	3480	3524	3568	3613	3657	3701	3745	3789	3833	44
986	3877	3921	3965	4009	4053	4097	4141	4185	4229	4273	44

C

N.	0	1	2	3	4	5	6	7	8	9	D.
987	994317	4361	4405	4449	4493	4537	4581	4625	4669	4713	44
988	4757	4801	4845	4889	4933	4777	5021	5064	5108	5152	44
989	5196	5240	5284	5328	5372	5416	5460	5504	5547	5591	44
990	5635	5679	5723	5767	5811	5855	5898	5942	5986	6030	44
991	6074	6117	6161	6205	6249	6293	6336	6380	6424	6468	44
992	6512	6555	6599	6643	6687	6730	6774	6818	6862	6905	44
993	6949	6993	7037	7080	7124	7168	7212	7255	7299	7343	44
994	7386	7430	7474	7517	7561	7605	7648	7692	7736	7779	44
995	7823	7867	7910	7954	7998	8041	8085	8128	8172	8216	44
996	8259	8303	8346	8390	8434	8477	8521	8564	8608	8652	44
997	8695	8739	8782	8826	8869	8913	8956	9000	9043	9087	44
998	9130	9174	9218	9261	9305	9348	9392	9435	9478	9522	44
999	9565	9609	9652	9696	9739	9783	9826	9870	9913	9957	43

A

TABLE

OF

Logarithmic Sines, Tangents, and Secants, to every Point, and quarter Point, of the Compass. Also to every Degree and Minute of the Quadrant.

P.	Sine	Co-secant	Tangent	Co-tang.	Secant	Co-sine	P.
0 0	0.000000	infinite	0.000000	infinite	10.000000	10.000000	8.0
0 1/4	8.690795	11.309215	8.691319	11.308681	10.000523	9.999477	7.3/4
0 1/2	8.991302	11.008698	8.993398	11.006602	10.002096	9.997904	7.1/2
0 3/4	9.166520	10.833480	9.171246	10.828754	10.004726	9.995274	7.1/4
0 1	9.290236	10.709764	9.298662	10.701338	10.008426	9.991574	7.0
1 1/4	9.385571	10.614429	9.398785	10.601215	10.013214	9.986786	6.3/4
1 1/2	9.462824	10.537176	9.481939	10.518061	10.019115	9.980885	6.1/2
1 3/4	9.527488	10.472512	9.553647	10.446353	10.026159	9.973841	6.1/4
2.0	9.582840	10.417160	9.617224	10.382776	10.034385	9.965615	6.0
2 1/4	9.630092	10.369908	9.674829	10.325171	10.043837	9.956163	5.3/4
2 1/2	9.673387	10.326613	9.727957	10.272043	10.054570	9.945430	5.1/2
2 3/4	9.711050	10.288950	9.777700	10.222300	10.066650	9.933350	5.1/4
3.0	9.744739	10.255261	9.824893	10.175107	10.080154	9.919846	5.0
3 1/4	9.775027	10.224973	9.870199	10.129801	10.095172	9.904828	4.3/4
3 1/2	9.802359	10.197641	9.914173	10.085827	10.111815	9.888185	4.1/2
3 3/4	9.827084	10.172916	9.957295	10.042705	10.130211	9.869789	4.1/4
4.0	9.849485	10.150515	10.000000	10.000000	10.150515	9.849485	4.0
	Co-sine	Secant	Co-tang.	Tangent	Co-secant	Sine	P.

M	Sine	D.	Co-secant	Tangent	D.	Co-tang.	Secant	D.	Co-sine	
0	0,000000	--	Infinite	0,000000	--	Infinite	10,000000		10,000000	60
1	6,463726	501717	13,536274	6,463726	501717	13,536274	000000	00	000000	59
2	764756	293485	235244	764756	293483	235244	000000	00	000000	58
3	940847	208231	059153	940847	208231	059153	000000	00	000000	57
4	7,065786	161517	12,934214	7,065786	161517	12,934214	000000	00	000000	56
5	162696	131968	837304	162696	131969	837304	000000	00	000000	55
6	241877	111575	758123	241878	111578	758122	000001	01	9,999999	54
7	308824	96653	691176	308825	99653	691175	000001	01	999999	53
8	366816	85254	633184	366817	85254	633183	000001	01	999999	52
9	417968	76263	582032	417970	76263	582030	000002	01	999998	51
10	463725	68988	536275	463727	68988	536273	000002	01	999998	50
11	7,505118	62981	12,494882	7,505120	62981	12,494880	10,000002	01	9,999998	49
12	542906	57936	457094	542909	57933	457091	000003	01	999997	48
13	577668	53641	422332	577672	53642	422328	000003	01	999997	47
14	609853	49938	390147	609857	49939	390143	000004	01	999996	46
15	639816	46714	360184	639820	46715	360180	000004	01	999996	45
16	667844	43881	332156	667849	43882	332151	000005	01	999995	44
17	694173	41372	305827	694179	41373	305821	000005	01	999995	43
18	718997	39135	281003	719003	39130	280997	000006	01	999994	42
19	742477	37127	257523	742484	37128	257516	000007	01	999993	41
20	764754	35315	235246	764761	35136	235239	000007	01	979993	40
21	7,785943	33672	12,214057	7,785951	33673	12,214049	10,000008	01	9,999992	39
22	806146	32175	193854	806155	32170	193845	000009	01	999991	38
23	825451	30805	174549	825460	30806	174540	000010	01	999990	37
24	843934	29547	156066	843944	29549	156056	000011	02	999989	36
25	861662	28388	138338	861074	28390	138326	000012	02	999988	35
26	878695	27317	121305	878708	27318	121292	000012	02	999988	34
27	895085	26323	104915	895099	26325	104901	000013	02	999987	33
28	910879	25399	089121	910894	25401	089106	000014	02	999986	32
29	926119	24538	073881	926134	24540	073866	000015	02	999985	31
30	940842	23733	059158	940858	23735	059142	000017	02	999983	30
31	7,955082	22980	12,044918	7,955100	22981	12,044900	10,000018	02	9,999982	29
32	968870	22273	031130	968889	22275	031111	000019	02	999981	28
33	982233	21608	017767	982253	21610	017747	000020	02	999980	27
34	995198	20981	004802	995219	20983	004781	000021	02	999979	26
35	8,007782	20390	11,992218	8,007804	20392	11,992191	000023	02	999977	25
36	020021	19831	979979	020045	19833	979955	000024	02	999976	24
37	031919	19302	968081	031945	19305	968055	000025	02	999975	23
38	043501	18801	956499	043527	18803	956473	000027	02	999973	22
39	054781	18325	945219	054809	18327	945191	000028	02	999972	21
40	065776	17872	934224	065806	17874	934194	000029	02	999971	20
41	8,076500	17441	11,923500	8,076531	17444	11,923469	10,000031	02	9,999969	19
42	086965	17031	913035	086997	17034	913003	000032	02	999968	18
43	097183	16639	902817	097217	16642	902783	000034	02	999966	17
44	107167	16265	892833	107202	16268	892797	000036	03	999964	16
45	116926	15908	883074	116963	15910	883037	000037	03	999963	15
46	126471	15566	873529	126510	15568	873490	000039	03	999961	14
47	135810	15238	864190	135851	15241	864149	000041	03	999959	13
48	144953	14924	855047	144996	14927	855004	000042	03	999958	12
49	153907	14622	846093	153952	14625	846048	000044	03	999956	11
50	162681	14333	837319	162727	14336	837273	000046	03	999954	10
51	8,171280	14054	11,828720	8,171328	14057	11,648672	10,000048	03	9,999952	9
52	179713	13786	820287	179763	13790	820237	000050	03	999950	8
53	187985	13529	812015	188036	13532	811964	000052	03	999948	7
54	196102	13280	803898	196156	13284	803844	000054	03	999946	6
55	204070	13041	795930	204126	13044	795874	000056	03	999944	5
56	211895	12810	788105	211953	12814	788047	000058	04	999942	4
57	219581	12587	780419	219641	12590	780359	000060	04	999940	3
58	227134	12372	772866	227195	12376	772805	000062	04	999938	2
59	234557	12164	765443	234621	12168	765379	000064	04	999936	1
60	241855	11963	758145	241921	11967	758079	000066	04	999934	0
	Co-fine		Secant	Co-tang.		Tangent	Co-fecant		Sine	M

89 Degrees

M	Sine	D.	Co-fecant	Tangent	D.	Co-tang.	Secant	D.	Co-fine	
0	8,241855	11963	11,758145	8,241921	11967	11,758079	10,000066	04	9,999934	60
1	249033	11768	750967	249102	11772	750898	000068	04	999932	59
2	256094	11580	743906	256165	11584	743835	000071	04	999929	58
3	263042	11398	736958	263115	11402	736885	000073	04	999927	57
4	269881	11221	730119	269956	11225	730044	000075	04	999925	56
5	276614	11050	723386	276691	11054	723309	000078	04	999922	55
6	283243	10883	716757	283343	10887	716677	000080	04	999920	54
7	289773	10721	710227	289856	10726	710144	000082	04	999918	53
8	296207	10565	703793	296292	10570	703708	000085	04	999915	52
9	302549	10413	697454	302634	10418	697366	000087	04	999913	51
10	308794	10266	691206	308884	10270	691116	000090	04	999910	50
11	8,314954	10122	11,685046	8,315046	10126	11,684954	10,000093	04	9,999907	49
12	321027	9982	678973	321122	9987	678878	000093	04	999905	48
13	327016	9847	672984	327114	9851	672886	000098	04	999902	47
14	332924	9714	667076	333025	9719	666975	000101	05	999899	46
15	338753	9586	661247	338856	9590	661144	000103	05	999897	45
16	344504	9460	655496	344610	9465	655390	000106	05	999894	44
17	350181	9338	649819	350289	9343	649711	000109	05	999891	43
18	355783	9219	644217	355895	9224	644105	000112	05	999888	42
19	361315	9103	638685	361430	9108	638570	000115	05	999885	41
20	366777	8990	633223	366895	8995	633105	000118	05	999882	40
21	8,372171	8880	11,627829	8,372292	8885	11,627708	10,000121	05	9,999879	39
22	377499	8772	622501	377622	8777	622378	000124	05	999876	38
23	382762	8667	617238	382889	8672	617111	000127	05	999873	37
24	387962	8564	612038	388092	8570	611908	000130	05	999870	36
25	393101	8464	606899	393234	8470	606766	000133	05	999867	35
26	398179	8366	601821	398315	8371	601685	000136	05	999864	34
27	403199	8271	596801	403338	8276	596662	000139	05	999861	33
28	408161	8177	591839	408304	8182	591696	000142	05	999858	32
29	413068	8086	586932	413213	8091	586787	000146	05	999854	31
30	417919	7996	582081	418068	8002	581932	000149	06	999851	30
31	8,422717	7909	11,577283	8,422869	7914	11,577131	10,000152	06	9,999848	29
32	427462	7823	572538	427618	7830	572382	000156	06	999844	28
33	432156	7740	567844	432315	7745	567685	000159	06	999841	27
34	436800	7657	563200	436962	7663	563038	000162	06	999838	26
35	441394	7577	558606	441560	7583	558440	000166	06	999834	25
36	445941	7499	554059	446110	7505	553890	000169	06	999831	24
37	450440	7422	549560	450613	7428	549387	000173	06	999827	23
38	454893	7346	545107	455070	7352	544930	000177	06	999823	22
39	459301	7273	540699	459481	7279	540519	000180	06	999820	21
40	463665	7200	536335	463849	7206	536151	000184	06	999816	20
41	8,467985	7129	11,532015	8,468172	7135	11,531828	10,000188	06	9,999812	19
42	472263	7060	527737	472454	7066	527546	000191	06	999809	18
43	476498	6991	523502	476693	6998	523307	000195	06	999805	17
44	480693	6924	519307	480892	6931	519108	000199	06	999801	16
45	484848	6859	515152	485050	6865	514950	000203	07	999797	15
46	488963	6794	511037	489170	6801	510830	000207	07	999793	14
47	493040	6731	506960	493250	6738	506750	000210	07	999790	13
48	497078	6669	502922	497293	6676	502707	000214	07	999786	12
49	501080	6608	498920	501298	6615	498702	000218	07	999782	11
50	505045	6548	494955	505267	6555	494733	000222	07	999778	10
51	8,508974	6489	11,491026	8,509200	6496	11,490800	10,000226	07	9,999774	9
52	512867	6431	487133	513098	6439	486902	000231	07	999769	8
53	516726	6375	483274	516961	6382	483039	000235	07	999765	7
54	520551	6319	479449	520790	6326	479210	000239	07	999761	6
55	524343	6264	475657	524586	6272	475414	000243	07	999757	5
56	528102	6211	471898	528349	6218	471651	000247	07	999753	4
57	531828	6158	468172	532080	6165	467920	000252	07	999748	3
58	535523	6106	464477	535779	6113	464221	000256	07	999744	2
59	539186	6055	460814	539447	6062	460553	000260	07	999740	1
60	542819	6004	457181	543084	6012	456916	000265	07	999735	0
	Co-fine		Secant	Co-tang.		Tangent	Co-fecant		Sine	M

M	Sine	D.	Co-secant	Tangent	D.	Co-tang.	Secant	D.	Co-sine	M
0	8.542819	6004	11,457181	8,543084	6012	11,456916	10,000265	07	9.999735	60
1	546422	5955	453578	546691	5962	453309	000269	07	999731	59
2	549995	5906	450005	550268	5914	449732	000274	07	999726	58
3	553539	5858	446461	553817	5866	446183	000278	08	999722	57
4	557054	5811	442946	557336	5819	442664	000283	08	999717	56
5	560540	5765	439460	560828	5773	439172	000287	08	999713	55
6	563999	5719	436001	564291	5727	435709	000292	08	999708	54
7	567431	5674	432569	567727	5682	432273	000296	08	999704	53
8	570836	5630	429164	571137	5638	428863	000301	08	999699	52
9	574214	5587	425786	574520	5595	425480	000306	08	999694	51
10	577566	5544	422434	577877	5552	422123	000311	08	999689	50
11	8.580892	5502	11,419108	8,581208	5510	11,418792	10.000315	08	9.999685	49
12	584193	5460	415807	584514	5468	415486	000320	08	999680	48
13	587469	5419	412531	587795	5427	412205	000325	08	999675	47
14	590721	5379	409279	591051	5387	408949	000330	08	999670	46
15	593948	5339	406052	594283	5347	405717	000335	08	999665	45
16	597152	5300	402848	597492	5308	402508	000340	08	999660	44
17	600332	5261	399668	600677	5270	399323	000345	08	999655	43
18	603489	5223	396511	603839	5232	396161	000350	08	999650	42
19	606623	5186	393377	606978	5194	393022	000355	09	999645	41
20	609734	5149	390266	610094	5158	389906	000360	09	999640	40
21	8.612823	5112	11,387177	8,613189	5121	11,386811	10,000365	09	9.999635	39
22	615891	5076	384109	616262	5085	383738	000371	09	999629	38
23	618937	5041	381063	619313	5050	380687	000376	09	999624	37
24	621962	5006	378038	622343	5015	377657	000381	09	999619	36
25	624965	4972	375035	625352	4981	374648	000386	09	999614	35
26	627948	4938	372052	628340	4947	371660	000392	09	999608	34
27	630911	4904	369089	631308	4913	368692	000397	09	999603	33
28	633854	4871	366146	634256	4880	365744	000403	09	999597	32
29	636776	4839	363224	637184	4848	362816	000408	09	999592	31
30	639680	4806	360320	640093	4816	359907	000414	09	999586	30
31	8,642563	4775	11,357437	8,642982	4784	11,357018	10,000420	09	9.999580	29
32	645428	4743	354572	645853	4753	354147	000425	09	999575	28
33	648274	4712	351726	648704	4722	351296	000430	09	999570	27
34	651102	4682	348898	651537	4691	348463	000436	09	999564	26
35	653911	4652	346089	654352	4661	345648	000442	10	999558	25
36	656702	4622	343298	657149	4631	342851	000447	10	999553	24
37	659475	4592	340525	659928	4602	340072	000453	10	999547	23
38	662230	4563	337770	662689	4573	337311	000459	10	999541	22
39	664968	4535	335032	665433	4544	334567	000465	10	999535	21
40	667689	4506	332311	668160	4516	331840	000471	10	999529	20
41	8,670393	4479	11,329607	8,670870	4488	11,329130	10,000476	10	9.999524	19
42	673080	4451	326920	673563	4461	326437	000482	10	999518	18
43	675751	4424	324249	676239	4434	323701	000488	10	999512	17
44	678405	4397	321595	678900	4417	321100	000494	10	999506	16
45	681043	4370	318957	681544	4380	318456	000500	10	999500	15
46	683665	4344	316335	684172	4354	315828	000507	10	999493	14
47	686272	4318	313728	686784	4328	313216	000518	10	999483	13
48	688863	4292	311137	689381	4303	310619	000519	10	999481	12
49	691438	4267	308563	691963	4277	308037	000525	10	999475	11
50	693998	4242	306002	694529	4252	305471	000531	10	999469	10
51	8,696543	4217	11,303457	8,697081	4228	11,302919	10,000537	11	9.999463	9
52	699073	4192	300927	699617	4203	300383	000544	11	999456	8
53	701588	4168	298411	702139	4179	297861	000550	11	999450	7
54	704090	4144	295910	704646	4155	295354	000557	11	999443	6
55	706577	4121	293423	707140	4132	292860	000563	11	999437	5
56	709049	4097	290951	709618	4108	290382	000569	11	999431	4
57	711507	4074	288493	712083	4085	287917	000576	11	999424	3
58	713952	4051	286048	714534	4062	285465	000582	11	999418	2
59	716383	4029	283617	716972	4040	283028	000589	11	999411	1
60	718800	4006	281200	719396	4017	280604	000596	11	999404	0
	Co-sine		Secant	Co-tang		Tangent	Co-secant		Sine	M

M	Sine	D.	Co-secant	Tangent	D.	Co-tang.	Secant	D.	Co-fine	
0	8,718800	4006	11,281200	8,719396	4017	11,280604	10,000596	11	9,999404	60
1	721204	3984	278796	721806	3995	278194	000602	11	999398	59
2	723595	3962	276405	724204	3974	275796	000609	11	999391	58
3	725972	3941	274028	726588	3952	273412	000616	11	999384	57
4	728337	3919	271663	728959	3930	271041	000622	11	999378	56
5	730688	3898	269312	731317	3909	268683	000629	11	999371	55
6	733027	3877	266973	733663	3889	266337	000636	12	999364	54
7	735354	3857	264646	735996	3868	264004	000643	12	999357	53
8	737667	3836	262333	738317	3848	261683	000650	12	999350	52
9	739969	3816	260031	740626	3827	259374	000657	12	999343	51
10	742259	3796	257741	742922	3807	257078	000664	12	999336	50
11	8,744536	3776	11,255464	8,745207	3787	11,254793	10,000671	12	9,999329	49
12	746802	3756	253198	747479	3768	252521	000678	12	999322	48
13	749055	3737	250945	749740	3749	250260	000685	12	999315	47
14	751297	3717	248703	751989	3729	248011	000692	12	999308	46
15	753528	3698	246472	754227	3710	245773	000699	12	999301	45
16	755747	3679	244253	756453	3692	243547	000706	12	999294	44
17	757955	3661	242045	758668	3673	241332	000714	13	999286	43
18	760151	3642	239849	760872	3655	239128	000721	12	999279	42
19	762337	3624	237663	763065	3636	236935	000728	12	999272	41
20	764511	3606	235489	765246	3618	234754	000735	13	999265	40
21	8,766675	3588	11,233325	8,767417	3600	11,232583	10,000743	12	9,999257	39
22	768828	3570	231172	769578	3583	230422	000750	13	999250	38
23	770970	3553	229030	771727	3565	228273	000758	13	999242	37
24	773101	3535	226899	773866	3548	226134	000765	13	999235	36
25	775223	3518	224777	775995	3531	224005	000773	13	999227	35
26	777333	3501	222667	778114	3514	221886	000780	13	999220	34
27	779434	3484	220566	780222	3497	219778	000788	13	999212	33
28	781524	3467	218476	782320	3480	217680	000795	13	999205	32
29	783605	3451	216395	784408	3464	215592	000803	13	999197	31
30	785675	3431	214325	786486	3447	213514	000811	13	999189	30
31	8,787736	3418	11,212264	8,788554	3431	11,211446	10,000819	13	9,999181	29
32	789787	3402	210213	790613	3415	209387	000826	13	999174	28
33	791828	3386	208172	792662	3399	207338	000834	13	999166	27
34	793859	3370	206141	794701	3383	205299	000842	13	999158	26
35	795881	3354	204119	796731	3368	203269	000850	13	999150	25
36	797894	3339	202106	798752	3352	201248	000858	13	999142	24
37	799897	3323	200103	800763	3337	199237	000866	13	999134	23
38	801892	3308	198108	802765	3322	197235	000874	13	999126	22
39	803876	3293	196124	804758	3307	195242	000882	13	999118	21
40	805852	3278	194148	806742	3297	193258	000890	13	999110	20
41	8,807819	3263	11,192181	8,808717	3278	11,191283	10,000898	13	9,999102	19
42	809777	3249	190223	810683	3262	189317	000906	14	999094	18
43	811726	3234	188274	812641	3248	187359	000914	14	999086	17
44	813667	3219	186333	814589	3233	185411	000923	14	999077	16
45	815599	3205	184401	816529	3219	183471	000931	14	999069	15
46	817522	3191	182478	818461	3205	181539	000939	14	999061	14
47	819436	3177	180564	820384	3191	179616	000947	14	999053	13
48	821343	3163	178657	822298	3177	177702	000956	14	999044	12
49	823240	3149	176760	824205	3163	175795	000964	14	999036	11
50	825130	3135	174870	826103	3150	173897	000973	14	999027	10
51	8,827011	3122	11,172989	8,827992	3136	11,172008	10,000981	14	9,999019	9
52	828884	3108	171116	829874	3123	170126	000990	14	999010	8
53	830749	3095	169251	831748	3110	168252	000998	14	999002	7
54	832607	3082	167393	833613	3096	166387	001002	14	998993	6
55	834456	3069	165544	835471	3083	164529	001016	14	998984	5
56	836297	3056	163703	837321	3070	162679	001024	14	998976	4
57	838130	3043	161870	839163	3057	160837	001033	15	998967	3
58	839956	3030	160044	840998	3045	159002	001042	15	998958	2
59	841774	3017	158226	842825	3032	157175	001050	15	998950	1
60	843585	3005	156415	844644	3019	155356	001059	15	998941	0
	Co-fine		Secant	Co-tang.		Tangent	Co-fecant		Sine	M

M	Sine	D.	Co-secant	Tangent	D.	Co-tang.	Secant	D.	Co-sine	
0	8,843585	3005	11,156415	8,844644	3019	11,155356	10,001059	15	9,998941	60
1	845387	2992	154613	846455	3007	153545	001068	15	998932	59
2	847183	2980	152817	848260	2995	151740	001077	15	998923	58
3	848971	2967	151029	850057	2982	149943	001086	15	998914	57
4	850751	2955	149249	851846	2970	148154	001095	15	998905	56
5	852525	2943	147475	853628	2958	146372	001104	15	998896	55
6	854291	2931	145709	855403	2946	144597	001113	15	998887	54
7	856049	2919	143951	857171	2935	142829	001122	15	998878	53
8	857801	2907	142199	858932	2923	141068	001131	15	998869	52
9	859546	2896	140454	860686	2911	139314	001140	15	998860	51
10	861283	2884	138717	862433	2900	137567	001149	15	998851	50
11	8,863014	2873	11,136986	8,864173	2888	11,135827	10,001159	15	9,998841	49
12	864738	2861	135262	865906	2877	134094	001168	15	998832	48
13	866455	2850	133545	867632	2866	132368	001177	16	998823	47
14	868165	2839	131835	869351	2854	130649	001187	16	998813	46
15	869868	2828	130132	871064	2843	128936	001196	16	998804	45
16	871565	2818	128435	872770	2832	127230	001205	16	998795	44
17	873255	2806	126745	874469	2821	125531	001215	16	998785	43
18	874938	2795	125062	876162	2811	123838	001224	16	998776	42
19	876615	2786	123385	877849	2800	122151	001234	16	998766	41
20	878285	2773	121715	879529	2789	120471	001243	16	998757	40
21	8,879949	2763	11,120051	8,881202	2779	11,118798	10,001253	16	9,998747	39
22	881607	2782	118393	882869	2768	117131	001262	16	998738	38
23	883258	2752	116742	884530	2758	115470	001272	16	998728	37
24	884903	2731	115097	886185	2747	113815	001282	16	998718	36
25	886542	2721	113458	887833	2737	112167	001291	16	998709	35
26	888174	2711	111826	889476	2727	110524	001301	16	998699	34
27	889801	2700	110199	891112	2717	108888	001311	16	998689	33
28	891421	2690	108579	892742	2707	107258	001321	16	998679	32
29	893035	2680	106965	894366	2697	105634	001331	17	998669	31
30	894643	2670	105357	895984	2687	104016	001341	17	998659	30
31	8,896246	2660	11,103754	8,897596	2677	11,102404	10,001351	17	9,998649	29
32	897842	2651	102158	899203	2667	100797	001361	17	998639	28
33	899432	2641	100568	900803	2658	099197	001371	17	998629	27
34	901017	2631	098983	902398	2648	097602	001381	17	998619	26
35	902596	2622	097404	903987	2638	096013	001391	17	998609	25
36	904169	2612	095831	905570	2629	094430	001401	17	998599	24
37	905736	2603	094264	907147	2620	092853	001411	17	998589	23
38	907297	2593	092703	908719	2610	091281	001422	17	998578	22
39	908853	2584	091147	910285	2601	089715	001432	17	998568	21
40	910404	2575	089596	911846	2592	088154	001442	17	998558	20
41	8,911949	2566	11,088051	8,913401	2583	11,086599	10,001452	17	9,998548	19
42	913488	2556	086512	914951	2574	085049	001463	17	998537	18
43	915022	2547	084978	916495	2565	083505	001473	17	998527	17
44	916550	2538	083450	918034	2556	081966	001484	18	998516	16
45	918073	2529	081927	919568	2547	080432	001494	18	998506	15
46	919591	2520	080409	921096	2538	078904	001505	18	998495	14
47	921103	2512	078897	922619	2530	077381	001515	18	998485	13
48	922610	2503	077390	924136	2521	075864	001526	18	998474	12
49	924112	2494	075888	925649	2512	074351	001536	18	998464	11
50	925609	2486	074391	927156	2503	072844	001547	18	998453	10
51	8,927100	2477	11,072900	8,928658	2495	11,071342	10,001558	18	9,998442	9
52	928587	2469	071413	930155	2486	069845	001569	18	998431	8
53	930068	2460	069932	931647	2478	068353	001579	18	998421	7
54	931544	2452	068456	933134	2470	066866	001590	18	998410	6
55	933015	2443	066985	934616	2461	065384	001601	18	998399	5
56	934481	2435	065519	936093	2453	063907	001612	18	998388	4
57	935942	2427	064058	937565	2445	062435	001623	18	998377	3
58	937398	2419	062602	939032	2437	060968	001634	18	998366	2
59	938850	2411	061150	940494	2430	059506	001645	18	998355	1
60	940296	2463	059704	941952	2421	058048	001656	18	998344	0
	Co-sine		Secant	Co-tang.		Tangent	Co-secant		Sine	M

Sine	D.	Co-secant	Tangent	D.	Co-tang.	Secant	D	Co-sine	
8.940296	2403	11,059704	8.941952	2421	11,058048	10,001656	19	9.998344	60
941738	2394	058262	943404	2413	056596	001667	19	999333	59
943174	2387	056826	944852	2405	055148	001678	19	998322	58
944606	2379	055394	946295	2397	053705	001689	19	998311	57
946034	2371	053966	947734	2390	052266	001700	19	998300	56
947456	2363	052544	949168	2382	050832	001711	19	998289	55
948874	2355	051126	950597	2374	049403	001723	19	998277	54
950287	2348	049713	952021	2366	047979	001734	19	998266	53
951696	2340	048304	953441	2360	046559	001745	19	998255	52
953100	2332	046900	954856	2351	045144	001757	19	998243	51
954499	2325	045601	956262	2344	043733	001768	19	998232	50
8.955894	2317	11.044106	8.957674	2337	11.042326	10.001780	19	9.998220	49
957284	2310	042716	959075	2329	040925	001791	19	998209	48
958670	2302	041330	960473	2322	039527	001803	19	998197	47
960052	2295	039948	961866	2314	038134	001814	19	998186	46
961429	2288	038571	963255	2307	036745	001826	19	998174	45
962801	2280	037199	964639	2300	035361	001837	19	998163	44
964170	2273	035830	966019	2293	033981	001849	19	998151	43
965534	2266	034466	967394	2286	032606	001861	20	998139	42
966893	2259	033107	968766	2279	031234	001872	20	998128	41
968249	2253	031751	970133	2271	029867	001884	20	998116	40
8.969600	2244	11.030400	8.971496	2265	11.028504	10.001896	20	9.998104	39
970947	2238	029053	972855	2257	027145	001908	20	998092	38
972289	2231	027711	974209	2251	025791	001920	20	998080	37
973628	2224	026372	975560	2244	024440	001932	20	998068	36
974962	2217	025038	976906	2237	023094	001944	20	998056	35
976293	2210	023707	978248	2230	021752	001956	20	998044	34
977619	2203	022381	979586	2223	020414	001968	20	998032	33
978941	2197	021059	980921	2217	019079	001980	20	998020	32
980259	2190	019741	982251	2210	017749	001992	20	998008	31
981573	2183	018427	983577	2204	016423	002004	20	997996	30
8.982883	2177	11.017117	8.984899	2197	11.015101	10.002016	20	9.997985	29
984189	2170	015811	986217	2191	013783	002028	20	997972	28
984491	2163	014509	987532	2184	012468	002041	20	997959	27
986789	2157	013211	988842	2178	011158	002053	20	997947	26
988083	2150	011917	990149	2171	009851	002065	21	997935	25
989374	2144	010626	991451	2165	008549	002078	21	997922	24
990660	2138	009340	992750	2158	007250	002090	21	997910	23
991943	2131	008057	994045	2152	005955	002103	21	997897	22
993222	2125	006778	995337	2146	004663	002115	21	997885	21
994497	2119	005503	996624	2140	003376	002128	21	997872	20
8.995768	2112	11.004232	8.997908	2134	11.002092	10.002140	21	9.997360	19
997036	2106	002964	999188	2127	000812	002153	21	997847	18
998299	2100	001701	9,000465	2121	10.999535	002165	21	997835	17
999560	2094	000441	001738	2115	998262	002178	21	997822	16
9.000816	2087	10.999184	003007	2109	996993	002191	21	997809	15
002069	2081	997931	004272	2103	995728	002203	21	997797	14
003318	2076	996682	005534	2097	994466	002216	21	997784	13
004563	2070	995437	006792	2091	993208	002229	21	997771	12
005805	2064	994195	008047	2085	991953	002242	21	997758	11
007044	2058	992956	009298	2080	990702	002255	21	997745	10
9.008278	2052	10.991722	9.010546	2074	10.989454	10.002268	21	9.997732	9
009510	2046	990490	011790	2068	988210	002281	21	997719	8
010737	2040	989263	013031	2062	986969	002294	22	997706	7
011962	2034	988038	014268	2056	985732	002307	22	997693	6
013182	2029	986818	015502	2051	984498	002320	22	997680	5
014400	2023	985600	016732	2045	983268	002333	22	997667	4
015613	2017	984387	017959	2040	982041	002346	22	997654	3
016824	2012	983176	019183	2033	980817	002359	22	997641	2
018031	2006	981969	020403	2028	979597	002372	22	997628	1
019235	2000	980765	021620	2023	978380	002386	23	997614	0
Co-fine		Secant	Co-tang.		Tangent	Co-fecant		Sine	M

Degrees

M	Sine	D.	Co-fecant	Tangent	D.	Co-tang.	Secant	D.	Co-fine	
0	9,019235	2000	10 980765	9,021620	2023	10 978380	10,002386	22	9,997614	60
1	020435	1995	979565	022834	2017	977166	002399	22	997601	59
2	021632	1989	978368	024045	2011	975956	002412	22	997588	58
3	022825	1984	977175	025251	2006	974749	002426	22	997574	57
4	024016	1978	975984	026455	2000	973545	002437	22	997561	56
5	025203	1973	974797	027655	1995	972345	002453	22	997547	55
6	026386	1967	973614	028852	1990	971148	002466	23	997534	54
7	027567	1962	972433	030046	1985	969954	002480	23	997520	53
8	028744	1957	971256	031237	1979	968763	002493	23	997507	52
9	029918	1951	970082	032425	1974	967575	002507	23	997493	51
10	031089	1947	968911	033609	1969	966391	002520	23	997480	50
11	9 032257	1941	10.967743	9,034791	1964	10,965209	10,002534	23	9,997466	49
12	033421	1936	966579	035969	1958	964031	002548	23	997452	48
13	034582	1930	965418	037144	1953	962856	002561	23	997439	47
14	035741	1925	964259	038316	1948	961684	002575	23	997425	46
15	036896	1920	963104	039485	1943	960515	002589	23	997411	45
16	038048	1915	961952	040651	1938	959349	002603	23	997397	44
17	039197	1910	960803	041813	1933	958187	002617	23	997383	43
18	040342	1905	959658	042973	1928	957027	002631	23	997369	42
19	041485	1899	958515	044130	1923	955870	002645	23	997355	41
20	042625	1894	957375	045284	1918	954716	002659	24	997341	40
21	9,043762	1889	10,956238	9,046434	1913	10,953566	10,002673	24	9,997327	39
22	044895	1884	955105	047582	1908	952418	002687	24	997313	38
23	046026	1879	953974	048727	1903	951273	002701	24	997299	37
24	047154	1875	952846	049869	1898	950131	002715	24	997285	36
25	048279	1870	951721	051008	1893	948992	002729	24	997271	35
26	049400	1865	950600	052144	1889	947856	002743	24	997257	34
27	050519	1860	949481	053277	1884	946723	002758	24	997242	33
28	051635	1855	948365	054407	1879	945593	•002772	24	997228	32
29	052749	1850	947251	055535	1874	944465	002786	24	997214	31
30	053859	1845	946141	056659	1870	943341	002801	24	997199	30
31	9,054966	1841	10.945034	9,057781	1865	10,942219	10,002815	24	9,997185	29
32	056071	1836	943929	058900	1860	941100	002830	24	997170	28
33	057172	1831	942828	060016	1855	939984	002844	24	997156	27
34	058271	1827	941729	061130	1851	938870	002859	24	997141	26
35	059367	1822	940633	062240	1846	937760	002873	24	997127	25
36	060460	1817	939540	063348	1842	936652	002888	24	997112	24
37	061551	1813	938449	064453	1837	935547	002902	24	997098	23
38	062639	1808	937361	065556	1833	934444	002917	25	997083	22
39	063724	1804	936276	066655	1828	933345	002932	25	997068	21
40	064806	1799	935194	067752	1824	932248	002947	25	997053	20
41	9,065885	1794	10,934115	9,068846	1819	10,931154	10,002961	25	9,997039	19
42	066962	1790	933038	069938	1815	930062	002976	25	997024	18
43	068036	1786	931964	071027	1810	928973	002991	25	997009	17
44	069107	1781	930893	072113	1806	927887	003006	25	996994	16
45	070176	1777	929824	073197	1802	926803	003021	25	996979	15
46	071242	1772	928758	074278	1797	925722	003036	25	996964	14
47	072306	1768	927694	075356	1793	924644	003051	25	996949	13
48	073366	1763	926634	076432	1789	923568	003066	25	996934	12
49	074424	1759	925576	077505	1784	922495	003081	25	996919	11
50	075480	1755	924520	078576	1780	921424	003096	25	996904	10
51	9,076533	1750	10,923467	9 079644	1776	10,920356	10,003111	25	9,996889	
52	077583	1746	922417	080710	1772	919290	003126	25	996874	8
53	078631	1742	921369	081773	1767	918227	003142	25	996858	7
54	079676	1738	920324	082833	1763	917167	003157	25	996843	6
55	080719	1733	919281	083891	1759	916109	003172	25	996828	5
56	081759	1729	918241	084947	1755	915053	003188	26	996812	4
57	082797	1725	917203	086000	1751	914000	003203	26	996797	3
58	083832	1721	916168	087050	1747	912950	003218	26	996628	
59	084864	1717	915136	088098	1743	911902	003234	26	996766	1
60	085894	1713	914106	089144	1738	910856	003249	26	996751	0
	Co-fine		Secant	Co-tang.		Tangent	Co-fecant		Sine	M

M	Sine	D.	Co-fecant	Tangent	D.	Co-tang.	Secant	D.	Co-fine	
0	9,085894	1713	10,914106	9,089744	1738	10,910856	10,003249	26	9,996751	60
1	086922	1709	913078	090187	1734	909813	003265	26	996735	59
2	087947	1704	912053	091228	1730	908772	003280	26	996720	58
3	088970	1700	911030	092266	1727	907734	003296	26	996704	57
4	089990	1696	910010	093302	1722	906698	003312	26	996688	56
5	091008	1692	908992	094336	1719	905664	003327	26	996673	55
6	092024	1688	907976	095367	1715	904633	003343	26	996657	54
7	093037	1684	906963	096395	1711	903605	003359	26	996641	53
8	094047	1680	905953	097422	1707	902578	003375	26	996625	52
9	095056	1676	904944	098446	1703	901554	003390	26	996610	51
10	096062	1673	903938	099468	1699	900532	003406	26	996594	50
11	9,097065	1668	10,902935	9,100487	1695	10,899513	10,003422	27	9,996578	49
12	098066	1665	901934	101504	1691	898496	003418	27	996562	48
13	099065	1661	900935	102519	1687	897481	003454	27	996546	47
14	100062	1657	899938	103532	1684	896468	003470	27	996530	46
15	101056	1653	898944	104542	1680	895458	003486	27	996514	45
16	102048	1649	897952	105550	1676	894450	003502	27	996498	44
17	103037	1645	896963	106556	1672	893444	003518	27	996482	43
18	104025	1641	895975	107559	1669	892441	003535	27	996465	42
19	105010	1638	894990	108560	1665	891440	003551	27	996449	41
20	105992	1634	894008	109559	1661	890441	003567	27	996433	40
21	9,106973	1630	10,893027	9,110556	1658	10,889444	10,003583	27	9,996417	39
22	107951	1627	892049	111551	1654	888449	003600	27	996400	38
23	108927	1623	891073	112543	1650	887457	003616	27	996384	37
24	109901	1619	890099	113533	1646	886467	003632	27	996368	36
25	110873	1616	889127	114521	1643	885479	003649	27	996351	35
26	111842	1612	888158	115507	1639	884493	003665	27	996335	34
27	112809	1608	887191	116491	1636	883509	003682	27	996318	33
28	113774	1605	886226	117472	1632	882528	003698	28	996302	32
29	114737	1601	885263	118452	1629	881548	003715	28	996285	31
30	115698	1597	884302	119429	1625	880571	003731	28	996269	30
31	9,116656	1594	10,883344	9,120404	1622	10,879596	10,003748	28	9,996252	29
32	117613	1590	882387	121377	1618	878623	003765	28	996235	28
33	118567	1587	881433	122348	1615	877652	003781	28	996219	27
34	119519	1583	880481	123317	1611	876683	003798	28	996202	26
35	120469	1580	879531	124284	1607	875716	003815	28	996185	25
36	121417	1576	878583	125249	1604	874751	003832	28	996168	24
37	122362	1573	877638	126211	1601	873789	003849	28	996151	23
38	123306	1569	876694	127172	1597	872828	003866	28	996134	22
39	124248	1566	875752	128130	1594	871870	003883	28	996117	21
40	125187	1562	874813	129087	1591	870913	003900	28	996100	20
41	9,126125	1559	10,873875	9,130041	1587	10,869959	10,003917	29	9,996083	19
42	127060	1556	872940	130994	1584	869006	003934	29	996066	18
43	127993	1552	872007	131944	1581	868056	003951	29	996049	17
44	128925	1549	871075	132893	1577	867107	003968	29	996032	16
45	129854	1545	870146	133839	1574	866161	003985	29	996015	15
46	130781	1542	869219	134784	1571	865216	004002	29	995998	14
47	131706	1538	868294	135726	1567	864274	004020	29	995980	13
48	132630	1535	867370	136667	1564	863333	004037	29	995963	12
49	133551	1532	866449	137605	1561	862395	004054	29	995946	11
50	134470	1529	865530	138542	1558	861458	004073	29	995928	10
51	9,135387	1525	10,864613	9,139476	1555	10,860524	10,004089	29	9,995911	9
52	136303	1522	863697	140409	1551	859591	004106	29	995894	8
53	137216	1519	862784	141340	1548	858660	004124	29	995876	7
54	138128	1516	861872	142269	1545	857731	004141	29	995859	6
55	139037	1512	860963	143196	1542	856804	004159	29	995841	5
56	139944	1509	860056	144121	1539	855879	004177	29	995823	4
57	140850	1506	859150	145044	1535	854956	004194	29	995806	3
58	141754	1503	858246	145966	1532	854034	004212	29	995788	2
59	142655	1500	857345	146885	1529	853115	004229	29	995771	1
60	143555	1496	856445	147803	1526	852197	004247	29	995753	0
	Cofine		Secant	Co-tang		Tangent	Co-fecant		Sine	M

M	Sine	D.	Co-secant	Tangent	D.	Co-tang.	Secant	D.	Co-sine	
0	9,143555	1496	10,856445	9,147803	1526	10,852197	10 004247	30	9 995753	6
1	144453	1493	855547	148718	1523	851282	004265	30	995735	5
2	145349	1490	854651	149632	1520	850368	004283	30	995717	5
3	146243	1487	853757	150544	1517	849456	004301	30	995699	5
4	147136	1484	852864	151454	1514	848546	004319	30	995681	5
5	148026	1481	851974	152363	1511	847637	004336	30	995664	5
6	148915	1478	851085	153269	1508	846731	004354	30	995646	5
7	149802	1475	850198	154174	1505	845826	004372	30	995628	5
8	150686	1472	849314	155077	1502	844923	004390	30	995610	5
9	151569	1469	848431	155978	1499	844022	004409	30	995591	5
10	152451	1466	847549	156877	1496	843123	004427	30	995573	5
11	9,153330	1463	10,846670	9,157775	1493	10,842225	10,004445	30	9 995555	4
12	154208	1460	845792	158671	1490	841329	004463	30	995537	4
13	155083	1457	844917	159565	1487	840435	004481	31	995519	4
14	155957	1454	844043	160457	1484	839543	004499	31	995501	4
15	156830	1451	843170	161347	1481	838653	004518	31	995482	4
16	157700	1448	842300	162236	1479	837764	004536	31	995464	4
17	158569	1445	841431	163123	1476	836877	004554	31	995446	4
18	159435	1442	840565	164008	1473	835992	004573	31	995427	4
19	160301	1439	839699	164892	1470	835108	004591	31	995409	4
20	161164	1436	838836	165774	1467	834226	004610	31	995390	4
21	9,162025	1433	10,837975	9,166654	1464	10,833346	10,004628	31	9 995372	3
22	162885	1430	837115	167532	1461	832468	004647	31	995353	3
23	163743	1427	836257	168409	1458	831591	004666	31	995334	3
24	164600	1424	835400	169284	1455	830716	004684	31	995316	3
25	165454	1421	834546	170157	1453	829843	004703	31	995297	3
26	166307	1419	833693	171029	1450	828971	004722	31	995278	3
27	167159	1416	832841	171899	1447	828101	004740	31	995260	3
28	168008	1413	831992	172767	1444	827233	004759	32	995241	3
29	168856	1410	831144	173634	1442	826366	004778	32	995222	3
30	169702	1407	830298	174499	1439	825501	004797	32	995203	3
31	9,170547	1405	10,829453	9,175562	1436	10,824638	10,004816	32	9,995184	2
32	171389	1402	828611	176224	1433	823776	004835	32	995165	2
33	172230	1399	827770	177084	1431	822916	004854	32	995146	2
34	173070	1396	826930	177942	1428	822058	004873	32	995127	2
35	173908	1394	826092	178799	1425	821201	004892	32	995108	2
36	174744	1391	825256	179655	1423	820345	004911	32	995089	2
37	175578	1388	824422	180508	1420	819492	004930	32	995070	2
38	176411	1386	823589	181360	1417	818640	004949	32	995051	2
39	177242	1383	822758	182211	1415	817789	004968	32	995032	2
40	178072	1380	821928	183059	1412	816941	004987	32	995013	2
41	9,178900	1377	10,821100	9,183907	1409	10,816093	10 005007	32	9,994993	1
42	179726	1374	820274	184752	1407	815248	005026	32	994974	1
43	180551	1372	819449	185597	1404	814403	005045	32	994955	1
44	181374	1369	818626	186439	1402	813561	005065	32	994935	1
45	182196	1366	817804	187280	1399	812720	005084	33	994916	1
46	183016	1364	816984	188120	1396	811880	005104	33	994896	1
47	183834	1361	816166	188958	1393	811042	005123	33	994877	1
48	184651	1359	815349	189794	1391	810206	005143	33	994857	1
49	185466	1356	814534	190620	1389	809371	005162	33	994838	1
50	186280	1353	813720	191462	1386	808538	005182	33	994818	1
51	9,187092	1351	10,812908	9,192294	1384	10 807706	10,005202	33	9,994798	
52	187903	1348	812097	193124	1381	806876	005221	33	994779	
53	188712	1346	811288	193953	1379	806047	005241	33	994759	
54	189519	1343	810481	194780	1376	805220	005261	33	994739	
55	190325	1341	809675	195606	1374	804394	005281	33	994719	
56	191130	1338	808870	196430	1371	803570	005300	33	994700	
57	191933	1336	808067	197253	1369	802747	005320	33	994680	
58	192734	1333	807266	198074	1366	801926	005340	33	994660	
59	193534	1330	806466	198894	1364	801106	005360	33	994640	
60	194332	1328	805668	199713	1361	800287	005380	33	994620	
M	Co-fine		Secant	Co-tang.		Tangent	Co-secant		Sine	M

M	Sine	D.	Co-fecant	Tangent	D.	Co-tang.	Secant	D.	Co-fine	
0	9.194332	1328	10.805668	9.199713	1361	10,800287	10,005380	33	9.994620	60
1	195129	1326	804871	200529	1359	799171	005400	33	994600	59
2	195925	1323	804075	201345	1356	798655	005420	33	994580	58
3	196719	1321	803281	202159	1354	797841	005440	34	994560	57
4	197511	1318	802489	202971	1352	797029	005460	34	994540	56
5	198302	1316	801698	203782	1349	796218	005481	34	994519	55
6	199091	1313	800909	204592	1347	795408	005501	34	994499	54
7	199879	1311	800121	205400	1345	794600	005521	34	994479	53
8	200666	1308	799334	206207	1342	793793	005541	34	994459	52
9	201451	1306	798549	207013	1340	792987	005562	34	994438	51
10	202234	1304	797766	207817	1338	792183	005582	34	994418	50
11	9.203017	1301	10,796983	9,208619	1335	10,791381	10,005603	34	9.994397	49
12	203797	1299	796203	209420	1333	790580	005623	34	994377	48
13	204577	1296	795423	210220	1331	789780	005643	34	994357	47
14	205354	1294	794646	211018	1328	788982	005664	34	994336	46
15	206131	1292	793869	211815	1326	788185	005684	34	994316	45
16	206906	1289	793094	212611	1324	787389	005705	34	994295	44
17	207679	1287	792321	213405	1321	786595	005726	35	994274	43
18	208452	1285	791548	214198	1319	785802	005746	35	994254	42
19	209222	1282	790778	214989	1317	785011	005767	35	994233	41
20	209992	1280	790008	215780	1315	784220	005788	35	994212	40
21	9.210760	1278	10,789240	9,216568	1312	10,783432	10,005809	35	9.994191	39
22	211526	1275	788474	217356	1310	782644	005829	35	994171	38
23	212291	1273	787709	218142	1308	781858	005850	35	994150	37
24	213055	1271	786945	218926	1305	781074	005871	35	994129	36
25	213818	1268	786182	219710	1303	780290	005892	35	994108	35
26	214579	1266	785421	220492	1301	779508	005913	35	994087	34
27	215338	1264	784662	221272	1299	778728	005934	35	994066	33
28	216097	1261	783903	222052	1297	777948	005955	35	994045	32
29	216854	1259	783146	222830	1294	777170	005976	35	994024	31
30	217609	1257	782391	223606	1292	776394	005997	35	994003	30
31	9.218363	1255	10,781637	9,224382	1290	10,775618	10,006019	35	9.993981	29
32	219116	1253	780884	225156	1288	774844	006040	35	993960	28
33	219868	1250	780132	225929	1286	774071	006061	35	993939	27
34	220618	1248	779382	226700	1284	773300	006082	35	993918	26
35	221367	1246	778633	227471	1281	772529	006104	36	993896	25
36	222115	1244	777885	228239	1279	771761	006125	36	993875	24
37	222861	1242	777139	229007	1277	770993	006146	36	993854	23
38	223606	1239	776394	229773	1275	770227	006168	36	993832	22
39	224349	1237	775651	230539	1273	769461	006189	36	993811	21
40	225092	1235	774908	231302	1271	768698	006211	36	993789	20
41	9.225833	1233	10,774167	9,232065	1269	10,767935	10,006232	36	9.993768	19
42	226573	1231	773427	232826	1267	767174	006254	36	993746	18
43	227311	1228	772689	233586	1265	766414	006275	36	993725	17
44	228048	1226	771952	234345	1262	765655	006297	36	993703	16
45	228784	1224	771216	235103	1260	764897	006319	36	993681	15
46	229518	1222	770482	235859	1258	764141	006340	36	993660	14
47	230252	1220	769748	236614	1256	763386	006362	36	993638	13
48	230984	1218	769016	237368	1254	762632	006384	36	993616	12
49	231714	1216	768286	238110	1252	761880	006406	37	993594	11
50	232444	1214	767556	238872	1250	761128	006428	37	993572	10
51	9.233172	1212	10,766828	9,239622	1248	10,760378	10,006450	37	9.993550	9
52	233899	1209	766101	240371	1246	759629	006472	37	993528	8
53	234625	1207	765375	241118	1244	758882	006494	37	993506	7
54	235349	1205	764651	241865	1242	758135	006516	37	993484	6
55	236073	1203	763927	242610	1240	757390	006538	37	993462	5
56	236795	1201	763205	243354	1238	756646	006560	37	993440	4
57	237515	1199	762485	244097	1236	755903	006582	37	993418	3
58	238235	1197	761765	244839	1234	755161	006604	37	993396	2
59	238953	1195	761047	245579	1232	754421	006626	37	993374	1
60	239670	1193	760330	246319	1230	753681	006649	37	993351	0
	Co-fine		Secant	Co-tang		Tangent	Co-fecant		Sine	M

M	Sine	D.	Co-secant	Tangent	D.	Co-tang.	Secant	D.	Co-sine	
0	9,239560	1193	10,760330	9,246319	1230	10,753681	10,006669	37	9,993351	60
1	240386	1191	759614	247057	1228	752943	006671	37	993329	59
2	241101	1189	758899	247794	1226	752206	006693	37	993307	58
3	241814	1187	758186	248530	1224	751470	006715	37	993285	57
4	242526	1185	757474	249264	1222	750736	006738	37	993262	56
5	243237	1183	756763	249998	1220	750002	006760	37	993240	55
6	243947	1181	756053	250730	1218	749270	006783	38	993217	54
7	244656	1179	755344	251461	1217	748539	006805	38	993195	53
8	245363	1177	754637	252191	1215	747809	006828	38	993172	52
9	246069	1175	753931	252920	1213	747080	006851	38	993149	51
10	246775	1173	753225	253648	1211	746352	006873	38	993127	50
11	9,247478	1171	10,752522	9,254374	1209	10,745626	10,006896	38	9,993104	49
12	248181	1169	751819	255100	1207	744900	006919	38	993081	48
13	248883	1167	751117	255824	1205	744176	006941	38	993059	47
14	249583	1165	750417	256547	1203	743453	006964	38	993036	46
15	250282	1163	749718	257269	1201	742731	006987	38	993013	45
16	250980	1161	749020	257990	1200	742010	007010	38	992990	44
17	251677	1159	748323	258710	1198	741290	007033	38	992967	43
18	252373	1158	747627	259429	1196	740571	007056	38	992944	42
19	253067	1156	746933	260146	1194	739854	007079	38	992921	41
20	253761	1154	746239	260863	1192	739137	007102	38	992898	40
21	9,254453	1152	10,745547	9,261578	1191	10,738422	10,007125	38	9,992875	39
22	255144	1150	744856	262292	1189	737708	007148	38	992852	38
23	255834	1148	744166	263005	1187	736995	007171	39	992829	37
24	256523	1146	743477	263717	1185	736283	007194	39	992806	36
25	257211	1144	742789	264428	1183	735572	007217	39	992783	35
26	257898	1142	742102	265138	1181	734862	007241	39	992759	34
27	258583	1141	741417	265847	1179	734153	007264	39	992736	33
28	259268	1139	740732	266555	1178	733445	007287	39	992713	32
29	259951	1137	740049	267261	1176	732739	007310	39	992690	31
30	260633	1135	739367	267967	1174	732033	007334	39	992666	30
31	9,261314	1133	10,738686	9,268671	1172	10,731329	10,007357	39	9,992643	29
32	261994	1131	738006	269375	1170	730625	007381	39	992619	28
33	262673	1130	737327	270077	1169	729923	007404	39	992596	27
34	263351	1128	736649	270779	1167	729221	007428	39	992572	26
35	264027	1126	735973	271479	1165	728521	007451	39	992549	25
36	264703	1124	735297	272178	1164	727822	007475	39	992525	24
37	265377	1122	734623	272876	1162	727124	007499	39	992501	23
38	266051	1120	733949	273573	1160	726427	007522	40	992478	22
39	266723	1119	733277	274269	1158	725731	007546	40	992454	21
40	267395	1117	732605	274964	1157	725036	007570	40	992430	20
41	9,268065	1115	10,731935	9,275658	1155	10,724342	10,007594	40	9,992406	19
42	268734	1113	731266	276351	1153	723649	007618	40	992382	18
43	269402	1111	730598	277043	1151	722957	007641	40	992359	17
44	270069	1110	729931	277734	1150	722266	007665	40	992335	16
45	270735	1108	729265	278424	1148	721576	007689	40	992311	15
46	271400	1106	728600	279113	1147	720887	007713	40	992287	14
47	272064	1105	727936	279801	1145	720199	007737	40	992263	13
48	272726	1103	727274	280488	1143	719512	007761	40	992239	12
49	273388	1101	726612	281174	1141	718826	007786	40	992214	11
50	274049	1099	725951	281858	1140	718142	007810	40	992190	10
51	9,274708	1098	10,725292	9,282542	1138	10,717458	10,007834	40	9,992166	9
52	275367	1096	724633	283225	1136	716775	007858	40	992142	8
53	276024	1094	723976	283907	1135	716093	007883	41	992117	7
54	276681	1092	723319	284588	1133	715412	007907	41	992093	6
55	277337	1091	722663	285268	1131	714732	007931	41	992069	5
56	277991	1089	722009	285947	1130	714053	007956	41	992044	4
57	278644	1087	721356	286624	1128	713376	007980	41	992020	3
58	279297	1086	720703	287301	1126	712699	008004	41	991996	2
59	279948	1084	720052	287977	1125	712023	008029	41	991971	1
60	280599	1082	719401	288652	1123	711348	008053	41	991947	0
	Co-fine		S ceant	Co-tang.		Tangent	Secant		Sine	M

M	Sine	D.	Co-fecant	Tangent	D.	Co-tang.	Secant	D.	Co-fine	
0	9,280599	1082	10,719401	9,288652	1123	10,711348	10,008053	41	9,991947	60
1	281248	1081	718752	289326	1122	710674	008078	41	991922	59
2	281897	1079	718103	289999	1120	710001	008103	41	991897	58
3	282544	1077	717456	290671	1118	709329	008127	41	991873	57
4	283190	1076	716810	291342	1117	708658	008152	41	991848	56
5	283836	1074	716164	292013	1115	707987	008177	41	991823	55
6	284480	1072	715520	292682	1114	707318	008201	41	991799	54
7	285124	1071	714876	293350	1112	706650	008226	42	991774	53
8	285766	1069	714234	294017	1111	705983	008251	42	991749	52
9	286408	1067	713592	294684	1109	705316	008276	42	991724	51
0	287048	1066	712952	295349	1107	704651	008301	42	991699	50
11	9,287687	1064	10,712313	9,296013	1106	10,703987	10,008326	42	9,991674	49
12	288326	1063	711674	296677	1104	703323	008351	42	991649	48
13	288964	1061	711036	297339	1103	702661	008376	42	991624	47
14	289600	1059	710400	298001	1101	701999	008401	42	991599	46
15	290236	1058	709764	298662	1100	701338	008426	42	991574	45
16	290870	1056	709130	299322	1098	700678	008451	42	991549	44
17	291504	1054	708496	299980	1096	700020	008476	42	991524	43
18	292137	1053	707863	300638	1095	699362	008502	42	991498	42
19	292768	1051	707232	301295	1093	698705	008527	42	991473	41
20	293399	1050	706601	301951	1092	698049	008552	42	991448	40
21	9,294029	1048	10,705971	9,302607	1090	10,697393	10,008578	42	9,991422	39
22	294658	1046	705342	303261	1089	696739	008603	42	991397	38
23	295286	1045	704714	303914	1087	696086	008628	42	991372	37
24	295913	1043	704087	304567	1086	695433	008654	43	991346	36
25	296539	1042	703461	305218	1084	694782	008679	43	991321	35
26	297164	1040	702836	305869	1083	694131	008705	43	991295	34
27	297788	1039	702212	306519	1081	693481	008730	43	991270	33
28	298412	1037	701588	307168	1080	692832	008756	43	991244	32
29	299034	1036	700966	307815	1078	692185	008782	43	991218	31
30	299655	1034	700345	308463	1077	691537	008807	43	991193	30
31	9,300276	1032	10,699724	9,309109	1075	10,690891	10,008833	43	9,991167	29
32	300895	1031	699105	309754	1074	690246	008859	43	991141	28
33	301514	1029	698486	310398	1073	689602	008885	43	991115	27
34	302132	1028	697868	311042	1071	688958	008910	43	991090	26
35	302748	1026	697252	311685	1070	688315	008936	43	991064	25
36	303364	1025	696636	312327	1068	687673	008962	43	991038	24
37	303979	1023	696021	312967	1067	687033	008988	43	991012	23
38	304593	1022	695407	313608	1065	686392	009014	43	990986	22
39	305207	1020	694793	314247	1064	685753	009040	43	990960	21
40	305819	1019	694181	314885	1062	685115	009066	44	990934	20
41	9,306430	1017	10,693570	9,315523	1061	10,684477	10,009092	44	9,990908	19
42	307041	1016	692959	316159	1060	683841	009118	44	990882	18
43	307650	1014	692350	316795	1058	683205	009145	44	990855	17
44	308259	1013	691741	317430	1057	682570	009171	44	990829	16
45	308867	1011	691133	318064	1055	681936	009197	44	990803	15
46	309474	1010	690526	318697	1054	681303	009223	44	990777	14
47	310080	1008	689920	319329	1053	680671	009250	44	990750	13
48	310685	1007	689315	319961	1051	680039	009276	44	990724	12
49	311289	1005	688711	320592	1050	679408	009303	44	990697	11
50	311893	1004	688107	321222	1048	678778	009329	44	990671	10
51	9,312495	1003	10,687505	9,321851	1047	10,678149	10,009356	44	9,990644	9
52	313097	1001	686903	322479	1045	677521	009382	44	990618	8
53	313698	1000	686302	323106	1044	676894	009409	44	990591	7
54	314297	998	685703	323733	1043	676267	009435	44	990565	6
55	314896	997	685104	324358	1041	675642	009462	44	990538	5
56	315495	996	684505	324983	1040	675017	009489	45	990511	4
57	316092	994	683908	325607	1039	674393	009515	45	990485	3
58	316689	993	683311	326231	1037	673769	009542	45	990458	2
59	317284	991	682716	326853	1036	673147	009569	45	990431	1
60	317879	990	682121	327475	1035	672525	009596	45	990404	0
	Co-fine		Secant	Co-tang.		Tangent	Co-fecant		Sine	M

M	Sine	D.	Co-secant	Tangent	D.	Co-tang.	Secant	D.	Co-sine	
0	9.317879	990	10,682121	9,327474	1035	10,672526	10,009590	45	9,990404	60
1	318473	988	681527	328095	1033	671905	009622	45	990378	59
2	319066	987	680934	328715	1032	671285	009649	45	990351	58
3	319658	986	680342	329334	1030	670666	009676	45	990324	57
4	320249	984	679751	329953	1029	670047	009703	45	990297	56
5	320840	983	679160	330570	1028	669430	009730	45	990270	55
6	321430	982	678570	331187	1026	668813	009757	45	990243	54
7	322019	980	677981	331803	1025	668197	009785	45	990215	53
8	322607	979	677393	332418	1024	667582	009812	45	990188	52
9	323194	977	676806	333033	1023	666967	009839	45	990161	51
10	323780	976	676220	333646	1021	666354	009866	45	990134	50
11	9,324306	975	10,675634	9,334259	1020	10,665741	10,009893	46	9,990107	49
12	324950	973	675050	334871	1019	665129	009921	46	990079	48
13	325534	972	674466	335482	1017	664518	009948	46	990052	47
14	326117	970	673883	336093	1016	663907	009975	46	990025	46
15	326700	969	673300	336702	1015	663298	010003	46	989997	45
16	327281	968	672719	337311	1013	662689	010030	46	989970	44
17	327862	966	672138	337919	1012	662081	010058	46	989942	43
18	328442	965	671558	338527	1011	661473	010085	46	989915	42
19	329021	964	670979	339133	1010	660867	010113	46	989887	41
20	329599	962	670401	339739	1008	660261	010140	46	989860	40
21	9,330176	961	10,669824	9,340344	1007	10,659656	10,010168	46	9,989832	39
22	330753	960	669247	340948	1006	659052	010196	46	989804	38
23	331329	958	668671	341552	1004	658448	010223	46	989777	37
24	331903	957	668097	342155	1003	657845	010251	47	989749	36
25	332478	956	667522	342757	1002	657243	010279	47	989721	35
26	333051	954	666949	343358	1000	656642	010307	47	989693	34
27	333624	953	666376	343958	999	656042	010335	47	989665	33
28	334195	952	665805	344558	998	655442	010363	47	989637	32
29	334766	950	665234	345157	997	654843	010391	47	989609	31
30	335337	949	664663	345755	996	654245	010418	47	989582	30
31	9,335906	948	10,664094	9,346353	994	10,653647	10,010447	47	9,989553	29
32	336475	945	663525	346949	993	653051	010475	47	989525	28
33	337043	945	662957	347545	992	652455	010503	47	989497	27
34	337610	944	662390	348141	991	651859	010531	47	989469	26
35	338176	943	661824	348735	990	651265	010559	47	989441	25
36	338742	941	661258	349329	988	650671	010587	47	989413	24
37	339306	940	660694	349922	987	650078	010616	47	989384	23
38	339871	939	660129	350514	986	649486	010644	47	989356	22
39	340434	937	659566	351106	985	648894	010672	47	989328	21
40	340996	936	659004	351697	983	648303	010700	47	989300	20
41	9,341558	935	10,658442	9,352287	982	10,647713	10,010729	47	9,989271	19
42	342119	934	657881	352876	981	647124	010757	47	989243	18
43	342679	932	657321	353465	980	646535	010786	47	989214	17
44	343239	931	656761	354053	979	645947	010814	47	989186	16
45	343797	930	656203	354640	977	645360	010843	47	989157	15
46	344355	929	655645	355227	976	644773	010872	48	989128	14
47	344912	927	655088	355813	975	644187	010900	48	989100	13
48	345469	926	654531	356398	974	643602	010929	48	989071	12
49	346024	925	653976	356982	973	643018	010958	48	989042	11
50	346579	924	653421	357566	971	642434	010986	48	989014	10
51	9,347134	922	10,652866	9,358149	970	10,641851	10,011015	48	9,988985	9
52	347687	921	652313	358731	969	641269	011044	48	988956	8
53	348240	920	651760	359313	968	640687	011073	48	988927	7
54	348792	919	651208	359893	967	640107	011102	48	988898	6
55	349343	917	650657	360474	966	639526	011131	48	988869	5
56	349893	916	650107	361053	965	638947	011160	48	988840	4
57	350443	915	649557	361632	963	638368	011189	48	988811	3
58	350992	914	649008	362210	962	637790	011218	49	988782	2
59	351540	913	648460	362787	961	637213	011247	49	988753	1
60	352088	911	647912	363363	960	636636	011276	49	988724	0
	Cosine		Secant	Co-tang.		Tangent	Co-secant		Sine	M

M	Sine	D.	Co-fecant	Tangent	D.	Co-tang.	Secant	D.	Co-fine	
0	9,352088	911	10,647912	9,363364	960	10,636636	10,011276	49	9,988724	60
1	352635	910	647365	363940	959	636060	011305	49	988695	59
2	353181	909	646819	364515	958	635485	011334	49	988666	58
3	353726	908	646274	365090	957	634910	011364	49	988636	57
4	354271	907	645729	365664	955	634336	011393	49	988607	56
5	354815	905	645185	366237	954	633763	011422	49	988578	55
6	355358	904	644642	366810	953	633190	011452	49	988548	54
7	355901	903	644099	367382	952	632618	011481	49	988519	53
8	356443	902	643557	367953	951	632047	011511	49	988489	52
9	356984	901	643016	368524	950	631476	011540	49	988460	51
10	357524	899	642476	369094	949	630906	011570	49	988430	50
11	9,358064	898	10,641936	9,363663	948	10,630337	10,011599	49	9,988401	49
12	358603	897	641397	370232	946	629768	011629	49	988371	48
13	359141	896	640859	370799	945	629201	011658	49	988342	47
14	359678	895	640322	371367	944	628633	011688	50	988312	46
15	360215	893	639785	371933	943	628067	011718	50	988282	45
16	360752	892	639249	372499	942	627501	011748	50	988252	44
17	361287	891	638713	373064	941	626936	011777	50	988223	43
18	361822	890	638178	373629	940	626371	011807	50	988193	42
19	362356	889	637644	374193	939	625807	011837	50	988163	41
20	362889	888	637111	374756	938	625244	011867	50	988133	40
21	9,363422	887	10,636578	9,375319	937	10,624681	10,011897	50	9,988103	39
22	363954	885	636046	375881	935	624119	011927	50	988073	38
23	364485	884	635515	376442	934	623558	011957	50	988043	37
24	365016	883	634984	377003	933	622997	011987	50	988013	36
25	365546	882	634454	377563	932	622437	012017	50	987983	35
26	366075	881	633925	378122	931	621878	012048	50	987952	34
27	366604	880	633396	378681	930	621319	012078	50	987922	33
28	367131	879	632869	379239	929	620761	012108	50	987892	32
29	367659	877	632341	379797	928	620203	012138	50	987862	31
30	368185	876	631815	380354	927	619646	012168	51	987832	30
31	9,368711	875	10,631289	9,380910	926	10,619090	10,012199	51	9,987801	29
32	369236	874	630764	381466	925	618534	012229	51	987771	28
33	369761	873	630239	382020	924	617980	012260	51	987740	27
34	370285	872	629715	382575	923	617425	012290	51	987710	26
35	370808	871	629192	383129	922	616871	012321	51	987679	25
36	371330	870	628670	383682	921	616318	012351	51	987649	24
37	371852	869	628148	384234	920	615766	012382	51	987618	23
38	372373	867	627627	384786	919	615214	012412	51	987588	22
39	372894	866	627106	385337	918	614663	012443	51	987557	21
40	373414	865	626586	385888	917	614112	012474	51	987526	20
41	9,373933	864	10,626067	9,386438	915	10,613562	10,012505	51	9,987495	19
42	374452	863	625548	386987	914	613013	012535	51	987465	18
43	374970	862	625030	387536	913	612464	012566	51	987434	17
44	375487	861	624513	388084	912	611916	012597	52	987403	16
45	376003	860	623997	388631	911	611369	012628	52	987372	15
46	376519	859	623481	389178	910	610822	012659	52	987341	14
47	377035	858	622965	389724	909	610276	012690	52	987310	13
48	377549	857	622451	390270	908	609730	012721	52	987279	12
49	378063	856	621937	390815	907	609185	012752	52	987248	11
50	378577	854	621423	391360	906	608640	012783	52	987217	10
51	9,379089	853	10,620911	9,391903	905	10,608097	10,012814	52	9,987186	9
52	379601	852	620399	392447	904	607553	012845	52	987155	8
53	380113	851	619887	392989	903	607011	012876	52	987124	7
54	380624	850	619376	393531	902	606469	012908	52	987092	6
55	381134	849	618866	394073	900	605927	012939	52	987061	5
56	381643	848	618357	394614	900	605386	012970	52	987030	4
57	382152	847	617848	395154	899	604846	013002	52	986998	3
58	382661	846	617339	395694	898	604306	013033	52	986967	2
59	383168	845	616832	396233	897	603767	013064	52	986936	1
60	383675	844	616325	396771	896	603229	013096	52	986904	0
	Co-fine		Secant	Co-tang.		Tangent	Co-fecant		Sine	M

M	Sine	D.	Co-secant	Tangent	D.	Co-tang.	Secant	D.	Co-sine	
0	9.383675	844	10.616325	9.396771	896	10.603229	10.013096	52	9.986904	60
1	384182	843	615818	397309	896	602691	013127	53	986873	59
2	384687	842	615313	397846	895	602154	013159	53	986841	58
3	385192	841	614808	398383	894	601617	013191	53	986809	57
4	385697	840	614303	398919	893	601081	013222	53	986778	56
5	386201	839	613799	399455	892	600545	013254	53	986746	55
6	386704	838	613296	399990	891	600010	013286	53	986714	54
7	387207	837	612793	400524	890	599476	013317	53	986683	53
8	387709	836	612291	401058	889	598942	013349	53	986651	52
9	388210	835	611790	401591	888	598409	013381	55	986619	51
10	388711	834	611289	402124	887	597876	013413	53	986587	50
11	9.389211	833	10.610789	9.402656	886	10.597344	10.013445	53	9.986555	49
12	389711	832	610289	403187	885	596813	013477	53	986523	48
13	390210	831	609790	403718	884	596282	013509	53	986491	47
14	390708	830	609292	404249	883	595751	013541	53	986459	46
15	391206	828	608794	404778	882	595222	013573	53	986427	45
16	391703	827	608297	405308	881	594692	013605	53	986395	44
17	392199	826	607801	405836	880	594164	013637	54	986363	43
18	392695	825	607305	406364	879	593636	013669	54	986331	42
19	393191	824	606809	406892	878	593108	013701	54	986299	41
20	393685	823	606315	407419	877	592581	013734	54	986266	40
21	9.394179	822	10.605821	9.407945	876	10.592055	10.013766	54	9.986234	39
22	394673	821	605327	408471	875	591529	013798	54	986202	38
23	395166	820	604834	408997	874	591003	013831	54	986169	37
24	395658	819	604342	409521	874	590479	013863	54	986137	36
25	396150	818	603850	410045	873	589955	013896	54	986104	35
26	396641	817	603359	410569	872	589431	013928	54	986072	34
27	397132	817	602868	411092	871	588908	013961	54	986039	33
28	397622	816	602379	411615	870	588385	013993	54	986007	32
29	398111	815	601889	412137	869	587863	014026	54	985974	31
30	398600	814	601400	412658	868	587342	014058	54	985942	30
31	9.399088	813	10.600912	9.413179	867	10.586821	10.014091	55	9.985909	29
32	399575	812	600425	413699	866	586301	014124	55	985876	28
33	400062	811	599938	414219	865	585781	014157	55	985843	27
34	400549	810	599451	414738	864	585262	014189	55	985811	26
35	401035	809	598965	415257	864	584743	014222	55	985778	25
36	401520	808	598480	415775	863	584225	014255	55	985745	24
37	402005	807	597995	416293	862	583707	014288	55	985712	23
38	402489	806	597511	416810	861	583190	014321	55	985679	22
39	402972	805	597028	417326	860	582674	014354	55	985646	21
40	403455	804	596545	417842	859	582158	014387	55	985613	20
41	9.403938	803	10.596062	9.418358	858	10.581642	10.014420	55	9.985580	19
42	404420	802	595580	418873	857	581127	014453	55	985547	18
43	404901	801	595099	419387	856	580613	014486	55	985514	17
44	405382	800	594618	419901	855	580099	014520	55	985480	16
45	405862	799	594138	420415	855	579585	014553	55	985447	15
46	406341	798	593659	420927	854	579073	014586	56	985414	14
47	406820	797	593180	421440	853	578560	014620	56	985380	13
48	407299	796	592701	421952	852	578048	014653	56	985347	12
49	407777	795	592223	422463	851	577537	014686	56	985314	11
50	408254	794	591746	422974	850	577026	014720	56	985280	10
51	9.408731	794	10.591269	9.423484	849	10.576516	10.014753	56	9.985247	9
52	409207	793	590793	423993	848	576007	014787	56	985213	8
53	409682	792	590318	424503	848	575497	014820	56	985180	7
54	410157	791	589843	425011	847	574989	014854	56	985146	6
55	410632	790	589368	425519	846	574481	014887	56	985113	5
56	411106	789	588894	426027	845	573973	014921	56	985079	4
57	411579	788	588421	426534	844	573466	014955	56	985045	3
58	412052	787	587948	427041	843	572959	014989	56	985011	2
59	412524	786	587476	427547	843	572453	015022	56	984978	1
60	412996	785	587004	428052	842	571948	015056	56	984944	0
	Co-sine		Secant	Co-tang.		Tangent	Co-secant		sine	M

E.

	Sine.	D.	Co-secant	Tangent	D.	Co-tang.	Secant	D.	Co-sine	
	9.412996	785	10.587004	9.428052	843	10.571948	10.015056	57	9.984944	60
	413467	784	586533	428557	841	571443	015090	57	984910	59
	413938	783	586061	429062	840	570938	015124	57	984876	58
	414408	783	585592	429566	839	570434	015158	57	984842	57
	414878	782	585122	430070	838	569930	015192	57	984808	56
	415347	781	584653	430573	838	569427	015226	57	984774	55
	415815	780	584185	431075	837	568925	015260	57	984740	54
7	416283	779	583717	431577	836	568423	015294	57	984706	53
	416751	778	583249	432079	835	567921	015328	57	984672	52
9	417217	777	582783	432580	834	567420	015363	57	984637	51
	417684	776	582316	433080	833	566920	015397	57	984603	50
1	9.418149	775	10.581851	9.433580	832	10.566420	10.015431	57	9.984569	49
2	418615	774	581385	434080	832	565920	015465	57	984535	48
3	419079	773	580921	434579	831	565421	015500	57	984500	47
4	419544	773	580456	435078	830	564922	015534	57	984466	46
5	420007	772	579993	435576	829	564424	015568	58	984432	45
6	420470	771	579530	436073	828	563927	015603	58	984397	44
7	420933	770	579067	436570	828	563430	015637	58	984363	43
8	421395	769	578605	437067	827	562933	015672	58	984328	42
9	421857	768	578143	437563	826	562437	015706	58	984294	41
0	422318	767	577682	438059	825	561941	015741	58	984259	40
11	9.422778	767	10.577222	9.438554	824	10.561446	10.015776	58	9.984224	39
12	423238	766	576762	439048	823	560952	015810	58	984190	38
13	423697	765	576303	439543	823	560457	015845	58	984155	37
14	424156	764	575844	440036	822	559964	015880	58	984120	36
15	424615	763	575385	440529	821	559471	015915	58	984085	35
16	425073	762	574927	441022	820	558978	015950	58	984050	34
17	425530	761	574470	441514	819	558486	015985	58	984015	33
18	425987	760	574013	442006	819	557994	016019	58	983981	32
19	426443	760	573557	442497	818	557503	016054	58	983946	31
20	426899	759	573101	442988	817	557012	016089	58	983911	30
31	9.427354	758	10.572646	9.443479	816	10.556521	10.016125	58	9.983875	29
32	427809	757	572191	443968	816	556032	016160	59	983840	28
33	428263	756	571737	444458	815	555542	016195	59	983805	27
34	428717	755	571283	444947	814	555053	016230	59	983770	26
35	429170	754	570830	445435	813	554565	016265	59	983735	25
36	429623	753	570377	445923	812	554077	016300	59	983700	24
37	430075	752	569925	446411	812	553589	016336	59	983664	23
38	430527	752	569473	446898	811	553102	016371	59	983629	22
39	430978	751	569022	447384	810	552616	016406	59	983594	21
40	431429	750	568571	447870	809	552130	016442	59	983558	20
41	9.431879	749	10.568121	9.448356	809	10.551644	10.016477	59	9.983523	19
42	432329	749	567671	448841	808	551159	016513	59	983487	18
43	432778	748	567222	449326	807	550674	016548	59	983452	17
44	433226	747	566774	449810	806	550190	016584	59	983416	16
45	433675	746	566325	450294	806	549706	016619	59	983381	15
46	434122	745	565878	450777	805	549223	016655	59	983345	14
47	434569	744	565431	451260	804	548740	016691	59	983309	13
48	435016	744	564984	451743	803	548257	016727	60	983273	12
49	435462	743	564538	452225	802	547775	016762	60	983238	11
50	435908	742	564092	452706	802	547294	016798	60	983202	10
1	9.436353	741	10.563647	9.453187	801	10.546813	10.016834	60	9.983166	9
2	436798	740	563202	453668	800	546332	016870	60	983130	8
3	437242	740	562758	454148	799	545852	016906	60	983094	7
4	437686	739	562314	454628	799	545372	016942	60	983058	6
5	438129	738	561871	455107	798	544893	016978	60	983022	5
6	438572	737	561428	455586	797	544414	017014	60	982986	4
7	439014	736	560986	456064	796	543936	017050	60	982950	3
8	439456	736	560544	456542	796	543458	017086	60	982914	2
9	439897	735	560103	457019	795	542981	017122	60	982878	1
0	440338	734	559662	457496	794	542504	017158	60	982842	0
	Co-sine		Secant	Co-tang.		Tangent	Co-secant		Sine	M

74 Degrees.

M	Sine	D.	Co-secant	Tangent	D.	Co-tang.	Secant	D.	Co-sine	
0	9,440338	734	10,559662	9,457496	794	10,542504	10,017158	60	9,982842	60
1	440778	733	559222	457973	793	542027	017195	60	982805	59
2	441218	732	558782	458449	793	541551	017231	61	982769	58
3	441658	731	558342	458925	792	541075	017267	61	982733	57
4	442096	731	557904	459400	791	540600	017304	61	982696	56
5	442535	730	557465	459875	790	540125	017340	61	982660	55
6	442973	729	557027	460349	790	539651	017376	61	982624	54
7	443410	728	556590	460823	789	539177	017413	61	982587	53
8	443847	727	556153	461297	788	538703	017449	61	982551	52
9	444284	727	555716	461770	788	538230	017486	61	982514	51
10	444720	726	555280	462242	787	537758	017523	61	982477	50
11	9,445155	725	10,554845	9,462714	786	10,537286	10,017559	61	9,982441	49
12	445590	724	554410	463186	785	536814	017596	61	982404	48
13	446025	723	553975	463658	785	536342	017633	61	982367	47
14	446459	723	553541	464130	784	535872	017669	61	982331	46
15	446893	722	553107	464599	783	535401	017706	61	982294	45
16	447326	721	552674	465069	783	534931	017743	61	982257	44
17	447759	720	552241	465539	782	534461	017780	62	982220	43
18	448191	720	551809	466008	781	533992	017817	62	982183	42
19	448623	719	551377	466476	780	533524	017854	62	982146	41
20	449054	718	550946	466945	780	533055	017891	62	982109	40
21	9,449485	717	10,550515	9,467413	779	10,532587	10,017928	62	9,982072	39
22	449915	716	550085	467880	778	532120	017965	62	982035	38
23	450345	716	549655	468347	778	531653	018002	62	981998	37
24	450775	715	549225	468814	777	531186	018039	62	981961	36
25	451204	714	548796	469280	776	530720	018076	62	981924	35
26	451632	713	548368	469746	775	530254	018114	62	981886	34
27	452060	713	547940	470211	775	529789	018151	62	981849	33
28	452488	712	547512	470676	774	529324	018188	62	981812	32
29	452915	712	547085	471141	773	528859	018226	62	981774	31
30	453342	710	546658	471605	773	528395	018263	62	981737	30
31	9,453768	710	10,546232	9,472068	772	10,527932	10,018301	63	9,981699	29
32	454194	709	545806	472532	771	527468	018338	63	981662	28
33	454619	708	545381	472995	771	527005	018375	63	981625	27
34	455044	707	544956	473457	770	526543	018413	63	981587	26
35	455469	707	544531	473919	799	526081	018451	63	981549	25
36	455893	706	544107	474381	769	525619	018488	63	981512	24
37	456316	705	543684	474842	768	525158	018526	63	981474	23
38	456739	704	543261	475303	767	524697	018564	63	981436	22
39	457162	704	542838	475763	767	524237	018601	63	981399	21
40	457584	703	542416	476223	766	523777	018639	63	981361	20
41	9,458006	702	10,541994	9,476683	765	10,523317	10,018677	63	9,981323	19
42	458427	702	541573	477142	765	522858	018715	63	981285	18
43	458848	701	541152	477601	764	522399	018753	63	981247	17
44	459268	700	540732	478059	763	521941	018791	63	981209	16
45	459688	699	540312	478517	763	521483	018829	63	981171	15
46	460108	698	539892	478975	762	521025	018867	64	981133	14
47	460527	698	539473	479432	761	520568	018905	64	981095	13
48	460946	697	539054	479889	761	520111	018943	64	981057	12
49	461364	696	538636	480345	760	519655	018981	64	981019	11
50	461782	695	538218	480801	759	519199	019019	64	980981	10
51	9,462199	695	10,537801	9,481257	759	10,518743	10,019058	64	9,980942	9
52	462616	694	537384	481712	758	518288	019096	64	980904	8
53	463032	693	536968	482167	757	517833	019134	64	980866	7
54	463448	693	536552	482621	757	517379	019173	64	980827	6
55	463864	692	536136	483075	756	516925	019211	64	980789	5
56	464279	691	535721	483529	755	516471	019250	64	980750	4
57	464694	690	535306	483982	755	516018	019288	64	980712	3
58	465108	690	534892	484435	754	515565	019327	64	980673	2
59	465522	689	534478	484887	753	515113	019365	64	980635	1
60	465935	688	534065	485339	753	514661	019404	64	980596	0
	Co-fine		Secant	Co-tang.		Tangent	Co-fecant		Sine	M

M	Sine	D.	Co-secant	Tangent	D.	Co-tang.	Secant	D.	Co-fine	
0	9,465935	688	10,534065	9,485339	753	10,514661	10,019404	64	9,980596	60
1	466348	688	533652	485791	752	514209	019442	64	980558	59
2	466761	687	533239	486242	751	513758	019481	65	980519	58
3	467173	687	532827	486693	751	513307	019520	65	980480	57
4	467585	685	532415	487143	750	512857	019558	65	980442	56
5	467996	685	532004	487593	749	512407	019597	65	980403	55
6	468407	684	531593	488043	749	511957	019636	65	980364	54
7	468817	683	531183	488492	748	511508	019675	65	980325	53
8	469227	683	530773	488941	747	511059	019714	65	980286	52
9	469637	682	530363	489390	747	510610	019753	65	980247	51
10	470046	681	529954	489838	746	510162	019792	65	980208	50
11	9,470455	680	10,529545	9,490286	746	10,509714	10,019831	65	9,980169	49
12	470863	680	529137	490733	745	509267	019870	65	980130	48
13	471271	679	528729	491180	744	508820	019909	65	980091	47
14	471679	678	528321	491627	744	508373	019948	65	980052	46
15	472086	678	527914	492073	743	507927	019988	65	980012	45
16	472492	677	527508	492519	743	507481	020027	65	979973	44
17	472898	676	527102	492965	742	507035	020066	66	979934	43
18	473304	676	526696	493410	741	506590	020105	66	979895	42
19	473710	675	526290	493854	740	506146	020143	66	979855	41
20	474115	674	525885	494299	740	505701	020184	66	979816	40
21	9,474519	674	10,525481	9,494743	740	10,505257	10,020224	66	9,979776	39
22	474923	673	525027	495186	739	504814	020263	66	979737	38
23	475327	672	524673	495630	738	504370	020303	66	979697	37
24	475730	672	524270	496073	737	503927	020342	66	979658	36
25	476133	671	523867	496515	737	503485	020382	66	979618	35
26	476536	670	523464	496957	736	503043	020421	66	979579	34
27	476938	669	523062	497399	736	502601	020461	66	979539	33
28	477340	669	522660	497841	735	502159	020501	66	979499	32
29	477741	668	522259	498282	734	501718	020541	66	979459	31
30	478142	667	521858	498722	734	501278	020580	66	979420	30
31	9,478543	667	10,521457	9,499163	733	10,500837	10,020620	66	9,979380	29
32	478942	666	521058	499603	733	500397	020660	66	979340	28
33	479342	665	520658	500042	732	499958	020700	67	979300	27
34	479741	665	520259	500481	731	499519	020740	67	979260	26
35	480140	664	519860	500920	731	499080	020780	67	979220	25
36	480539	663	519461	501359	730	498641	020820	67	979180	24
37	480937	663	519063	501797	730	498203	020860	67	979140	23
38	481324	662	518666	502235	729	497765	020900	67	979100	22
39	481731	661	518269	502672	728	497328	020941	67	979059	21
40	482128	661	517874	503109	728	496891	020981	67	979019	20
41	9,482525	660	10,517475	9,503546	727	10,496454	10,021021	67	9,978979	19
42	482921	659	517079	503982	727	496018	021061	67	978939	18
43	483316	659	516684	504418	726	495582	021102	67	978898	17
44	483712	658	516288	504854	725	495146	021142	67	978858	16
45	484107	657	515893	505289	725	494711	021183	67	978817	15
46	484501	657	515499	505724	724	494276	021223	67	978777	14
47	484895	656	515105	506159	724	493841	021264	67	978736	13
48	485289	655	514711	506593	723	493407	021304	68	978696	12
49	485682	655	514318	507027	722	492973	021345	68	978655	11
50	486075	654	513925	507460	722	492540	021385	68	978615	10
51	9,486467	653	10,513533	9,507893	721	10,492107	10,021426	68	9,978574	9
52	486860	653	513140	508326	721	491674	021467	68	978533	8
53	487251	652	512749	508759	720	491241	021507	68	978493	7
54	487643	651	512357	509191	719	490809	021548	68	978452	6
55	488033	651	511967	509622	719	490378	021589	68	978411	5
56	488424	650	511576	510054	718	489946	021630	68	978370	4
57	488814	650	511186	510485	718	489515	021671	68	978329	3
58	489204	649	510796	510916	717	489084	021712	68	978288	2
59	489593	648	510407	511346	716	488654	021753	68	978247	1
60	489982	648	510018	511776	716	488224	021794	68	978206	0
	Co-fine		Secant	Co-tang.		Tangent	Co-secant			M

M	Sine	D.	Co-secant	Tangent	D.	Co-tang.	Secant		Co-sine	
0	9,489982	648	10,510018	9,511776	716	10,488224	10,021794	68	9,978206	60
1	490371	648	509629	512206	716	487794	021835	68	978165	59
2	490759	647	509241	512635	715	487365	021876	68	978124	58
3	491147	646	508853	513064	714	486936	021917	69	978083	57
4	491535	646	508465	513493	714	486507	021958	69	978042	56
5	491922	645	508078	513921	713	486079	021999	69	978001	55
6	492308	644	507692	514349	713	485651	022041	69	977959	54
7	492695	644	507305	514777	713	485223	022082	69	977918	53
8	493081	643	506919	515204	712	484796	022123	69	977877	52
9	493466	642	506534	515631	711	484369	022165	69	977835	51
10	493851	642	506149	516057	710	483943	022206	69	977794	50
11	9,494236	641	10,505764	9,516484	710	10,483516	10,022248	69	9,977752	49
12	494621	641	505379	516910	709	483090	022289	69	977711	48
13	495005	640	504995	517335	709	482665	022331	69	977669	47
14	495388	639	504612	517761	708	482239	022372	69	977628	46
15	495772	639	504228	518185	708	481815	022414	69	977586	45
16	496154	638	503846	518610	707	481390	022456	70	977544	44
17	496537	637	503463	519034	706	480966	022497	70	977503	43
18	496919	637	503081	519458	706	480542	022539	70	977461	42
19	497301	636	502699	519882	705	480118	022581	70	977419	41
20	497682	636	502318	520305	705	479695	022623	70	977377	40
21	9,498063	635	10,501937	9,520728	704	10,479272	10,022665	70	9,977335	39
22	498444	634	501556	521151	703	478849	022707	70	977293	38
23	498824	634	501176	521573	703	478427	022749	70	977251	37
24	499204	633	500796	521995	703	478005	022791	70	977209	36
25	499584	632	500416	522417	702	477583	022833	70	977167	35
26	499963	632	500037	522838	702	477162	022875	70	977125	34
27	500342	631	499658	523259	701	476741	022917	70	977083	33
28	500721	631	499279	523680	701	476320	022959	70	977041	32
29	501099	630	498901	524100	700	475900	023001	70	976999	31
30	501470	629	498524	524520	699	475480	023043	70	976957	30
31	9,501854	629	10,498146	9,524939	699	10,475061	10,023086	70	9,976914	29
32	502231	628	497769	525358	698	474642	023128	71	976872	28
33	502607	628	497393	525778	698	474222	023170	71	976830	27
34	502984	627	497016	526197	697	473803	023213	71	976787	26
35	503360	626	496640	526615	697	473385	023255	71	976745	25
36	503735	626	496265	527033	696	472967	023298	71	976702	24
37	504110	625	495890	527451	696	472549	023340	71	976660	23
38	504485	625	495515	527868	695	472132	023383	71	976617	22
39	504860	624	495140	528285	695	471715	023420	71	976574	21
40	505234	623	494766	528702	694	471298	023468	71	976532	20
41	9,505608	623	10,494392	9,529119	693	10,470881	10,023511	71	9,976489	19
42	505981	622	494019	529535	693	470465	023554	71	976446	18
43	506354	622	493646	529950	693	470050	023596	71	976404	17
44	506727	621	493273	530366	692	469634	023639	71	976361	16
45	507099	620	492901	530781	691	469219	023682	71	976318	15
46	507471	620	492529	531196	691	468804	023725	71	976275	14
47	507843	619	492157	531611	690	468389	023768	72	976232	13
48	508214	619	491786	532025	690	467975	023811	72	976189	12
49	508585	618	491415	532439	689	467561	023854	72	976146	11
50	508956	618	491044	532853	689	467147	023897	72	976103	10
51	9,509326	617	10,490674	9,533266	688	10,466734	10,023940	72	9,976060	9
52	509696	616	490304	533679	688	466321	023983	72	976017	8
53	510065	616	489935	534092	687	465908	024026	72	975974	7
54	510434	615	489566	534504	687	465496	024070	72	975930	6
55	510803	615	489197	534916	686	465084	024113	72	975887	5
56	511172	614	488828	535328	686	464672	024156	72	975844	4
57	511540	613	488460	535739	685	464261	024200	72	975800	3
58	511907	613	488093	536150	685	463850	024243	72	975757	2
59	512275	612	487725	536561	684	463439	024286	72	975714	1
60	512642	612	487358	536972	684	463028	024330	72	975670	0
	Co-sine		Secant	Co-tang.		Tangent	Co-secant		Sine	M

M	Sine	D.	Co-secant	Tangent	D.	Co-tang.	Secant	D	Co-sine	
0	9.512642	612	10,487358	9.536972	684	10.463028	10,024330	72	9.975670	60
1	513009	611	486991	537382	683	462618	024373	73	975627	59
2	513375	611	486625	537792	683	462208	024417	73	975583	58
3	513741	610	486259	538202	682	461798	024461	73	975539	57
4	514107	609	485893	538611	682	461389	024504	73	975496	56
5	514472	609	485528	539020	681	460980	024548	73	975452	55
6	514837	608	485163	539429	681	460571	024592	73	975408	54
7	515202	608	484798	539837	680	460163	024635	73	975365	53
8	515566	607	484434	540245	680	459755	024679	73	975321	52
9	515930	607	484070	540653	679	459347	024723	73	975277	51
10	516294	606	483706	541061	679	458939	024767	73	975233	50
11	9.516657	605	10,483343	9.541468	678	10.458532	10,024811	73	9.975189	49
12	517020	605	482980	541875	678	458125	024855	73	975145	48
13	517382	604	482618	542281	677	457719	024899	73	975101	47
14	517745	604	482255	542688	677	457312	024943	73	975057	46
15	518107	603	481893	543094	676	456906	024987	73	975013	45
16	518468	603	481532	543499	676	456501	025031	74	974969	44
17	518829	602	481171	543905	675	456095	025075	74	974925	43
18	519190	601	480810	544310	675	455690	025120	74	974880	42
19	519551	601	480449	544715	674	455285	025164	74	974836	41
20	519911	600	480089	545119	674	454881	025208	74	974792	40
21	9.520271	600	10,479729	9.545524	673	10,454476	10,025253	74	9.974747	39
22	520631	599	479369	545928	673	454072	025297	74	974703	38
23	520990	599	479010	546331	672	453669	025341	74	974659	37
24	521349	598	478651	546735	672	453265	025386	74	974614	36
25	521707	598	478293	547138	671	452862	025430	74	974570	35
26	522066	597	477934	547540	671	452460	025475	74	974525	34
27	522424	596	477576	547943	670	452057	025519	74	974481	33
28	522781	596	477219	548345	670	451655	025564	74	974436	32
29	523138	595	476862	548747	669	451253	025609	74	974391	31
30	523495	595	476505	549149	669	450851	025653	75	974347	30
31	9.523852	594	10,476148	9.549550	668	10,450450	10,025698	75	9.974302	29
32	524208	594	475792	549951	668	450049	025743	75	974257	28
33	524564	593	475436	550352	667	449648	025788	75	974212	27
34	524920	593	475080	550752	667	449248	025833	75	974167	26
35	525275	592	474725	551152	666	448848	025878	75	974122	25
36	525630	591	474370	551552	666	448448	025923	75	974077	24
37	525984	591	474016	551952	665	448048	025968	75	974032	23
38	526339	590	473661	552351	665	447649	026013	75	973987	22
39	526693	590	473307	552750	665	447250	026058	75	973942	21
40	527046	589	472954	553149	664	446851	026103	75	973897	20
41	9.527400	589	10,472600	9.553548	664	10,446452	10,026148	75	9.973852	19
42	527753	588	472247	553946	663	446054	026193	75	973807	18
43	528105	588	471895	554344	663	445656	026239	75	973761	17
44	528458	587	471542	554741	662	445259	026284	76	973716	16
45	528810	587	471190	555139	662	444861	026329	76	973671	15
46	529161	586	470839	555536	661	444464	026375	76	973625	14
47	529513	586	470487	555933	661	444067	026420	76	973580	13
48	529864	585	470136	556329	660	443671	026465	76	973535	12
49	530215	585	469785	556725	660	443275	026511	76	973489	11
50	530565	584	469435	557121	659	442879	026556	76	973444	10
51	9.530915	584	10,469085	9.557517	659	10,442483	10,026602	76	9.973398	9
52	531265	583	468735	557913	659	442087	026648	76	973352	8
53	531614	582	468386	558308	658	441692	026693	76	973307	7
54	531963	582	468037	558702	658	441298	026739	76	973261	6
55	532312	581	467688	559097	657	440903	026785	76	973215	5
56	532661	581	467339	559491	657	440509	026831	76	973169	4
57	533009	580	466991	559885	656	440115	027876	76	973124	3
58	533357	580	466643	560279	656	439721	026922	76	973078	2
59	533704	579	466296	560673	655	439327	026968	77	973032	1
60	534052	578	465948	561066	655	438934	027014	77	972986	0
	Co-sine		Secant	Co-tang.		Tangent	Co-secant		Sine	M

6876

M	Sine	D.	Co-secant	Tangent	D.	Co-tang.	Secant	D.	Co-sine	
0	9.534052	578	10.465948	9.561066	655	10.438934	10.027014	77	9.972986	60
1	534399	577	465601	561459	654	438541	027060	77	972940	59
2	534745	577	465255	561851	654	438149	027106	77	972894	58
3	535092	577	464908	562244	653	437756	027152	77	972848	57
4	535438	576	464562	562636	653	437364	027198	77	972802	56
5	535783	576	464217	563028	653	436972	027245	77	972755	55
6	536129	575	463871	563419	652	436581	027291	77	972709	54
7	536474	574	463526	563811	652	436189	027337	77	972663	53
8	536818	574	463182	564202	651	435798	027383	77	972617	52
9	537163	573	462837	564592	651	435408	027430	77	972570	51
10	537507	573	462493	564983	650	435017	027476	77	972524	50
11	9.537851	572	10.462149	9.565373	650	10.434627	10.027522	77	9.972478	49
12	538194	572	461806	565763	649	434237	027569	78	972431	48
13	538538	571	461462	566153	649	433847	027615	78	972385	47
14	538880	571	461120	566542	649	433458	027662	78	972338	46
15	539223	570	460777	566932	648	433068	027709	78	972291	45
16	539565	570	460435	567320	648	432680	027755	78	972245	44
17	539907	569	460093	567709	647	432291	027802	78	972198	43
18	540249	569	459751	568098	647	431902	027849	78	972151	42
19	540590	568	459410	568486	646	431514	027896	78	972105	41
20	540931	568	459069	568873	646	431127	027942	78	972058	40
21	9.541272	567	10.458728	9.569261	645	10.430739	10.027989	78	9.972011	39
22	541613	567	458387	569648	645	430352	028036	78	971964	38
23	541953	566	458047	570035	645	429965	028083	78	971917	37
24	542293	566	457707	570422	644	429578	028130	78	971870	36
25	542632	565	457368	570809	644	429191	028177	78	971823	35
26	542971	565	457029	571195	643	428805	028224	78	971776	34
27	543310	564	456690	571581	643	428419	028271	79	971729	33
28	543649	564	456351	571967	642	428033	028318	79	971682	32
29	543987	563	456013	572352	642	427648	028365	79	971635	31
30	544325	563	455675	572738	642	427262	028412	79	971588	30
31	9.544663	562	10.455337	9.573123	641	10.426877	10.028460	79	9.971540	29
32	545000	562	455000	573507	641	426493	028507	79	971493	28
33	545338	561	454662	573892	640	426108	028554	79	971446	27
34	545674	561	454326	574276	640	425724	028602	79	971398	26
35	546011	560	453989	574660	639	425340	028649	79	971351	25
36	546347	560	453653	575044	639	424956	028697	79	971303	24
37	546683	559	453317	575427	639	424573	028744	79	971256	23
38	547019	559	452981	575810	638	424190	028792	79	971208	22
39	547354	558	452646	576193	638	423807	028839	79	971161	21
40	547689	558	452311	576576	637	423424	028887	79	971113	20
41	9.548024	557	10.451976	9.576958	637	10.423042	10.028934	80	9.971066	19
42	548359	557	451641	577341	636	422659	028982	80	971018	18
43	548693	556	451307	577723	636	422277	029030	80	970970	17
44	549027	556	450973	578104	636	421896	029078	80	970922	16
45	549360	555	450640	578486	635	421514	029126	80	970874	15
46	549693	555	450307	578867	635	421133	029173	80	970827	14
47	550026	554	449974	579248	634	420752	029221	80	970779	13
48	550359	554	449641	579629	634	420371	029269	80	970731	12
49	550692	553	449308	580009	634	419991	029317	80	970683	11
50	551024	553	448976	580389	633	419611	029365	80	970635	10
51	9.551356	552	10.448644	9.580769	633	10.419231	10.029414	80	9.970586	9
52	551687	552	448313	581149	632	418851	029462	80	970538	8
53	552018	552	447982	581528	632	418472	029510	80	970490	7
54	552349	551	447651	581907	632	418093	029558	80	970442	6
55	552680	551	447320	582286	631	417714	029606	80	970394	5
56	553010	550	446990	582665	631	417335	029655	81	970345	4
57	553341	550	446659	583043	630	416957	029703	81	970297	3
58	553670	549	446330	583422	630	416578	029751	81	970249	2
59	554000	549	446000	583800	629	416200	029800	81	970200	1
60	554329	548	445671	584177	629	415823	029848	81	970152	0
	Co-sine		Secant	Co-tang.		Tangent	Co-secant		Sine	M

Sine	D.	Co-secant	Tangent	D.	Co-tang.	Secant	D.	Co-sine	
554329	548	10,445671	9,584177	629	10,,15823	10,029848	81	9,970152	60
554658	548	445342	584555	629	415445	029897	81	970103	59
554987	547	445013	584932	628	415068	029945	81	970055	58
555315	547	444685	585309	628	414691	029994	81	970006	57
555643	546	444357	585686	627	414314	030043	81	969957	56
555971	546	444029	586062	627	413938	030091	81	969909	55
556299	546	443701	586439	627	413561	030140	81	969860	54
556626	545	443374	586815	626	413185	030189	81	969811	53
556953	544	443047	587190	626	412810	030238	81	969762	52
557280	544	442720	587566	625	412434	030286	81	969714	51
557606	543	442394	587941	625	412059	030335	81	969665	50
557932	543	10,442068	9,588316	625	10,411684	10,030384	82	9,969616	49
558256	543	441742	588691	624	411309	030433	82	969567	48
558583	542	441417	589066	624	410934	030482	82	969518	47
558909	542	441091	589440	623	410560	030531	82	969469	46
559234	542	440766	589814	623	410186	030580	82	969420	45
559558	541	440442	590188	623	409812	030630	82	969370	44
559883	540	440117	590562	622	409438	030679	82	969321	43
560207	540	439793	590935	622	409065	030728	82	969272	42
560531	539	439469	591308	622	408692	030777	82	969223	41
560855	539	439145	591681	621	408319	030827	82	969173	40
561176	538	10,438822	9,592054	621	10,407946	10,030876	82	9,969124	39
561501	538	438499	592426	620	407574	030925	82	969075	38
561824	537	438176	592798	620	407202	030975	82	969025	37
562146	537	437854	593171	619	406829	031024	82	968976	36
562468	536	437532	593542	619	406458	031074	83	968926	35
562790	536	437210	593914	618	406086	031123	83	968877	34
563112	536	436888	594285	618	405715	031173	83	968827	33
563433	535	436567	594656	618	405344	031223	83	968777	32
563755	535	436245	595027	617	404973	031272	83	968728	31
564075	534	435925	595398	617	404602	031322	83	968678	30
564396	534	10,435604	9,595768	617	10,404232	10,031372	83	9,968628	29
564716	533	435284	596138	616	403862	031422	83	968578	28
565030	533	434964	596508	616	403492	031472	83	968528	27
565355	532	434644	596878	616	403122	031522	83	968479	26
565675	532	434324	597247	615	402753	031571	83	968429	25
565995	531	434005	597616	615	402384	031621	83	968379	24
566314	531	433686	597985	615	402015	031671	83	968329	23
566634	531	433368	598354	614	401646	031722	83	968278	22
566953	530	433049	598722	614	401278	031772	84	968228	21
567269	530	432731	599091	613	400909	031822	84	968178	20
567567	529	10,432413	9,599459	613	10,400541	10,031872	84	9,968128	19
567904	529	432096	599827	613	400173	031922	84	968078	18
568222	528	431778	600194	612	399806	031973	84	968027	17
568539	528	431461	600562	612	399438	032023	84	967977	16
568855	528	431145	600929	611	399071	032073	84	967927	15
569172	527	430828	601296	611	398704	032124	84	967876	14
569486	527	430512	601662	611	398338	032174	84	967826	13
569804	526	430196	602029	610	397971	032225	84	967775	12
570120	526	429880	602395	610	397605	032275	84	967725	11
570435	525	429565	602761	610	397239	032326	84	967674	10
570751	525	10,429249	9,603127	609	10,396873	10,032376	84	9,967624	9
571066	524	428934	603493	609	396507	032427	84	967573	8
571380	524	428620	603858	609	396142	032478	85	967522	7
571695	523	428305	604223	608	395777	032529	85	967471	6
572009	523	427991	604588	608	395412	032579	85	967421	5
572323	523	427677	604953	607	395047	032630	85	967370	4
572636	522	427364	605317	607	394683	032681	85	967319	3
572950	522	427050	605682	607	394318	032732	85	967268	2
573263	522	426737	606046	606	393954	032783	85	967217	1
573575	521	426425	606410	606	393590	032834	85	967166	0
Co-fine		Secant	Co-tang		Tangent	Co-fecant		Sine	M

M	Sine	D.	Co-secant	Tangent	D.	Co-tang.	Secant	D.	Co-sine	
0	9.573575	521	10.426425	9.606410	606	10.393590	10.032834	85	9.967166	60
1	573888	520	426112	606773	606	393227	032885	85	967115	59
2	574200	520	425800	607137	605	392863	032936	85	967064	58
3	574512	519	425488	607500	605	392500	032987	85	967013	57
4	574824	519	425176	607863	604	392137	033031	85	966961	56
5	575136	519	424864	608225	604	391775	033090	85	966910	55
6	575447	518	424553	608588	604	391412	033141	85	966859	54
7	575758	518	424242	608950	603	391050	033192	85	966808	53
8	576069	517	423931	609312	603	390688	033244	86	966756	52
9	576379	517	423621	609674	603	390326	033295	86	966705	51
10	576689	516	423311	610036	602	389964	033347	86	966653	50
11	9.576999	516	10.423001	9.610397	602	10.389603	10.033398	86	9.966602	49
12	577309	516	422691	610759	602	389241	033450	86	966550	48
13	577618	515	422382	611120	601	388880	033501	86	966499	47
14	577927	515	422073	611480	601	388520	033553	86	966447	46
15	578236	514	421764	611841	601	388159	033605	86	966395	45
16	578545	514	421455	612201	600	387799	033656	86	966344	44
17	578853	513	421147	612561	600	387439	033708	86	966292	43
18	579162	513	420838	612921	600	387079	033760	86	966240	42
19	579469	513	420531	613281	599	386719	033812	86	966188	41
20	579777	512	420223	613641	599	386359	033864	86	966136	40
21	9.580085	512	10.419915	9.614000	598	10.386000	10.033915	87	9.966085	39
22	580392	511	419608	614359	598	385641	033967	87	966033	38
23	580699	511	419301	614718	598	385282	034019	87	965981	37
24	581005	511	418995	615077	597	384923	034072	87	965928	36
25	581312	510	418688	615435	597	384565	034124	87	965876	35
26	581618	510	418382	615793	597	384207	034176	87	965824	34
27	581924	509	418076	616151	596	383849	034228	87	965772	33
28	582229	509	417771	616509	596	383491	034280	87	965720	32
29	582535	509	417465	616867	596	383133	034332	87	965668	31
30	582840	508	417160	617224	595	382776	034385	87	965615	30
31	9.583145	508	10.416855	9.617581	595	10.382418	10.034437	87	9.965563	29
32	583449	507	416551	617939	595	382061	034489	87	965511	28
33	583754	507	416246	618295	594	381705	034542	87	965458	27
34	584058	506	415942	618652	594	381348	034594	87	965406	26
35	584361	506	415639	619008	594	380992	034647	88	965353	25
36	584665	506	415335	619364	593	380636	034699	88	965301	24
37	584968	505	415032	619721	593	380279	034752	88	965248	23
38	585272	505	414728	620076	593	379924	034805	88	965195	22
39	585574	504	414426	620432	592	379568	034857	88	965143	21
40	585877	504	414123	620787	592	379213	034910	88	965090	20
41	9.586179	503	10.413821	9.621142	592	10.378858	10.034963	88	9.965037	19
42	586482	503	413518	621497	591	378503	035016	88	964984	18
43	586783	503	413217	621852	591	378148	035069	88	964931	17
44	587085	502	412915	622207	590	377793	035121	88	964879	16
45	587386	502	412614	622561	590	377439	035174	88	964826	15
46	587688	501	412312	622915	590	377085	035227	88	964773	14
47	587988	501	412012	623269	589	376731	035281	88	964719	13
48	588289	501	411711	623623	589	376377	035334	89	964666	12
49	588590	500	411410	623976	589	376024	035386	89	964613	11
50	588890	500	411110	624330	588	375670	035440	89	964560	10
51	9.589190	499	10.410810	9.624683	588	10.375317	10.035493	89	9.964507	9
52	589489	499	410511	625036	588	374964	035546	89	964454	8
53	589789	499	410211	625388	587	374612	035600	89	964400	7
54	590088	498	409912	625741	587	374259	035653	89	964347	6
55	590387	498	409613	626093	587	373907	035706	89	964294	5
56	590686	497	409314	626445	586	373555	035760	89	964240	4
57	590984	497	409016	626797	586	373203	035813	89	964187	3
58	591282	497	408718	627149	586	372851	035867	89	964133	2
59	591580	496	408420	627501	585	372499	035920	89	964080	1
60	591878	496	408122	627852	585	372148	035974	89	964026	0
	Co-sine		Secant	Co-tang.		Tangent	Co-secant		Sine	M

026

M	Sine	D.	Co-secant	Tangent	D.	Co-tang.	Secant	D.	Co-fine	
0	9.591878	496	10.408122	9.627852	585	10.372148	10.035974	89	9.963226	60
1	59 17?	495	407825	628203	585	371797	036028	89	963972	59
2	592473	495	407527	628554	585	371446	036081	89	963919	58
3	592770	495	407230	628905	584	371095	036135	90	963865	57
4	593067	494	406933	629255	584	270745	036189	90	963811	56
5	593363	494	406637	629606	583	370394	036243	90	963757	55
6	593659	493	406341	629956	583	370044	036296	90	963704	54
7	593955	493	406045	630306	583	369694	036350	90	963650	53
8	594251	493	405749	630656	583	369344	036404	90	963596	52
9	594547	492	405453	631005	582	368995	036458	90	963542	51
10	594842	492	405158	631355	582	368645	036512	90	963488	50
11	9.595137	491	10.404863	9.631704	582	10.368296	10.036566	90	9.963434	49
12	595432	491	404568	632053	581	367947	036621	90	963379	48
13	595727	491	404273	632401	581	367599	036675	90	963325	47
14	596021	490	403979	632750	581	367250	036729	90	963271	46
15	596315	490	403685	633098	580	366902	036783	90	963217	45
16	596609	489	403391	633447	580	366553	036837	90	963163	44
17	596903	489	403097	633795	580	366205	036892	91	963108	43
18	597196	48?	402804	634143	579	365857	036946	91	963054	42
19	597490	488	402510	634490	579	365510	037001	91	962999	41
20	597783	488	402217	634838	579	365162	037055	91	962945	40
21	9.598075	487	10.401925	9.635185	578	10.364815	10.037110	91	9.962890	39
22	598368	487	401632	635532	578	364468	037164	91	962836	38
23	598660	487	401340	635879	578	364121	037219	91	962781	37
24	598952	486	401048	636226	577	363774	037273	91	962727	36
25	599244	486	400756	636572	577	363428	037328	91	962672	35
26	599536	485	400464	636919	577	363081	037383	91	962617	34
27	599827	485	400173	637265	577	362735	037438	91	962562	33
28	600118	484	399882	637611	576	362389	037493	91	962508	32
29	600409	484	399591	637956	576	362044	037547	91	962453	31
30	600700	484	399300	638302	576	361698	037602	92	962398	30
31	9.600990	48?	10.399010	9.638647	575	10.361353	10.037657	92	9.962343	29
32	601180	483	398720	638992	575	361008	037712	92	962288	28
33	601570	483	398430	639337	575	360663	037767	92	962233	27
34	601860	482	398140	639682	574	360318	037822	92	962178	26
35	602150	482	397850	640027	574	359973	037877	92	962123	25
36	602439	482	397561	640371	574	359629	037933	92	962067	24
37	602728	481	397272	640716	573	359284	037988	92	962012	23
38	603017	481	396983	641060	573	358940	038043	92	961957	22
39	603305	481	396695	641404	573	358596	038098	92	961902	21
40	603594	480	396406	641747	572	358253	038154	92	961846	20
41	9.603882	480	10.396118	9.642091	572	10.357909	10.038209	92	9.961791	19
42	604170	479	395830	642434	572	357566	038265	92	961735	18
43	604457	479	395543	642777	572	357223	038320	92	961680	17
44	604745	479	395255	643120	571	356880	038376	93	961624	16
45	605032	478	394968	643463	571	356537	038431	93	961569	15
46	605319	478	394681	643806	571	356194	038487	93	961513	14
47	605606	478	394394	644148	570	355852	038542	93	961458	13
48	605892	477	394108	644490	570	355510	038598	93	961402	12
49	606179	477	393821	644832	570	355168	038654	93	961346	11
50	606465	476	393535	645174	569	354826	038710	93	961290	10
51	9.606751	476	10.393249	9.645516	569	10.354484	10.038765	93	9.961235	9
52	607036	476	392964	645857	569	354143	038821	93	961179	8
53	607322	475	392678	646199	569	353801	038877	93	961123	7
54	607607	475	392393	646540	568	353460	038933	93	961067	6
55	607892	474	392108	646881	568	353119	038989	93	961011	5
56	608177	474	391823	647222	568	352778	039045	93	960955	4
57	608461	474	391539	647562	567	352438	039101	93	960899	3
58	608745	473	391255	647903	567	352097	039157	94	960843	2
59	609029	473	390971	648243	567	351757	039214	94	960786	1
60	609313	473	390687	648583	566	351417	039270	94	960730	0
	Co-fine		Secant	Co-tang.		Tangent	Co-fecant		Sine	M

66 Degrees

M	Sine	D.	Co-secant	Tangent	D.	Co-tang	Secant	D.	Co-sine	
0	9,609313	473	10,390687	9,648583	566	10,351417	10,039270	94	9,960730	60
1	609597	472	390403	648923	566	351077	039326	94	960674	59
2	609880	472	390120	649263	566	350737	039382	94	960618	58
3	610163	472	389837	649602	566	350398	039439	94	960561	57
4	610447	471	389553	649942	565	350058	039495	94	960505	56
5	610729	471	389271	650281	565	349719	039552	94	960448	55
6	611012	470	388988	650620	565	349380	039608	94	960392	54
7	611294	470	388706	650959	564	349041	039665	94	960335	53
8	611576	470	388424	651297	564	348703	039721	94	960279	52
9	611858	469	388142	651636	564	348364	039778	94	960222	51
10	612140	469	387860	651974	563	348026	039835	94	960165	50
11	9,612421	469	10,387579	9,652312	563	10,347688	10,039891	95	9,960109	49
12	612702	468	387298	652650	563	347350	039948	95	960052	48
13	612983	468	387017	652988	563	347012	040005	95	959995	47
14	613264	467	386736	653326	562	346674	040061	95	959938	46
15	613545	467	386455	653663	562	346337	040118	95	959882	45
16	613825	467	386175	654000	562	346000	040175	95	959825	44
17	614105	466	385895	654337	561	345663	040234	95	959768	43
18	614385	466	385615	654674	561	345326	040289	95	959711	42
19	614665	466	385335	655011	561	344989	040346	95	959654	41
20	614944	465	385056	655348	561	344652	040404	95	959596	40
21	9,615223	465	10,384777	9,655684	560	10,344316	10,040461	95	9,959539	39
22	615502	465	384498	656020	560	343980	040518	95	959482	38
23	615781	464	384219	656356	560	343644	040575	95	959425	37
24	616060	464	383940	656692	559	343308	040632	95	959368	36
25	616338	464	383662	657028	559	342972	040690	96	959310	35
26	616616	463	383384	657364	559	342636	040747	96	959253	34
27	616894	463	383106	657699	559	342301	040805	96	959195	33
28	617172	462	382828	658034	558	341966	040862	96	959138	32
29	617450	462	382550	658369	558	341631	040919	96	959081	31
30	617727	462	382273	658704	558	341296	040977	96	959023	30
31	9,618004	461	10,381996	9,659039	558	10,340961	10,041035	96	9,958965	29
32	618281	461	381719	659373	557	340627	041092	96	958908	28
33	618558	461	381442	659708	557	340292	041150	96	958850	27
34	618834	460	381166	660042	556	339958	041208	96	958792	26
35	619110	460	380890	660376	556	339624	041266	96	958734	25
36	619386	460	380614	660710	556	339290	041323	96	958677	24
37	619662	459	380338	661043	556	338957	041381	96	958619	23
38	619938	459	380062	661377	556	338623	041439	96	958561	22
39	620213	459	379787	661710	555	338290	041497	97	958503	21
40	620488	458	379512	662043	555	337957	041555	97	958445	20
41	9,620763	458	10,379237	9,662376	555	10,337624	10,041613	97	9,958387	19
42	621038	457	378962	662709	554	337291	041671	97	958329	18
43	621313	457	378687	663042	554	336958	041729	97	958271	17
44	621587	457	378413	663375	554	336625	041788	97	958212	16
45	621861	456	378139	663707	554	336293	041846	97	958154	15
46	622135	456	377865	664039	553	335961	041904	97	958096	14
47	622409	456	377591	664371	553	335629	041962	97	958038	13
48	622682	455	377318	664703	553	335297	042021	97	957979	12
49	622956	455	377044	665035	553	334965	042079	97	957921	11
50	623229	455	376771	665366	552	334634	042137	97	957863	10
51	9,623502	454	10,376498	9,665697	552	10,334303	10,042196	98	9,957804	9
52	623774	454	376226	666029	552	333971	042254	98	957746	8
53	624047	454	375953	666360	551	333640	042313	98	957687	7
54	624319	453	375681	666691	551	333309	042372	68	957628	6
55	624591	453	375409	667021	551	332979	042430	98	957570	5
56	624863	453	375137	667352	551	332648	042489	98	957511	4
57	625135	452	374865	667682	550	332318	042548	98	957452	3
58	625406	452	374594	668013	550	331987	042607	98	957393	2
59	625677	452	374323	668343	550	331657	042665	98	957335	1
60	625948	451	374052	668672	550	331328	042724	98	957276	0
	Co-sine		Secant	Co-tang.		Tangent	Co-secant		Sine	M

M	Sine	D.	Co-fecant	Tangent	D.	Co-tang.	Secant	D.	Co-fine	
0	9,625946	451	10,374054	9,668673	550	10,331327	10,042724	98	9,957276	60
1	626219	451	373781	669002	549	330998	042783	98	957217	59
2	626490	451	373510	669332	549	330668	042842	98	957158	58
3	626760	450	373240	669661	549	330339	042901	98	957099	57
4	627030	450	372970	669991	548	330009	042960	98	957040	56
5	627300	450	372700	670320	548	329680	043019	98	956981	55
6	627570	449	372430	670649	548	329351	043079	99	956921	54
7	627840	449	372160	670977	548	329023	043138	99	956862	53
8	628109	449	371892	671306	547	328694	043197	99	956803	52
9	628378	448	371622	671634	547	328366	043256	99	956744	51
10	628647	448	371353	671963	547	328037	043316	99	956684	50
11	9,628916	447	10,371084	9,672291	547	10,327709	10,043375	99	9,956625	49
12	629185	447	370815	672619	546	327381	043434	99	956566	48
13	629453	447	370547	672947	546	327053	043494	99	956506	47
14	629721	446	370279	673274	546	326726	043553	99	956447	46
15	629989	446	370011	673602	546	326398	043613	99	956387	45
16	630257	446	369743	673929	545	326071	043673	99	956327	44
17	630524	446	369476	674257	545	325743	043732	99	956268	43
18	630792	445	369208	674584	545	325416	043792	100	956208	42
19	631059	445	368941	674910	544	325090	043852	100	956148	41
20	631326	445	368674	675237	544	324763	043911	100	956089	40
21	9,631593	444	10,368407	9,675564	544	10,324436	10,043971	100	9,956029	39
22	631859	444	368141	675890	544	324110	044031	100	955969	38
23	632125	444	367875	676216	543	323784	044091	100	955909	37
24	632392	443	367608	676543	543	323457	044151	100	955849	36
25	632658	443	367342	676869	543	323131	044211	100	955789	35
26	632923	443	367077	677194	543	322806	044271	100	955729	34
27	633189	442	366811	677520	542	322480	044331	100	955669	33
28	633454	442	366546	677846	542	322154	044391	100	955609	32
29	633719	442	366281	678171	542	321829	044452	100	955548	31
30	633984	441	366016	678496	542	321504	044512	100	955488	30
31	9,634249	441	10,365751	9,678821	541	10,321179	10,044572	101	9,955428	29
32	634514	440	365486	679146	541	320854	044632	101	955368	28
33	634778	440	365222	679471	541	320529	044693	101	955307	27
34	635042	440	364958	679795	541	320205	044753	101	955247	26
35	635306	439	364694	680120	540	319880	044814	101	955186	25
36	635570	439	364430	680444	540	319556	044874	101	955126	24
37	635833	439	364167	680768	540	319232	044935	101	955065	23
38	636097	438	363903	681092	540	318908	044995	101	955005	22
39	636360	438	363640	681416	539	318584	045056	101	954944	21
40	636623	438	363377	681743	539	318260	045117	101	954883	20
41	9,636886	437	10,363114	9,682063	539	10,317937	10,045177	101	9,954823	19
42	637148	437	362852	682387	539	317613	045238	101	954762	18
43	637411	437	362589	682710	538	317290	045299	101	954701	17
44	637673	437	362327	683033	538	316967	045360	101	954640	16
45	637935	436	362065	683356	538	316644	045421	101	954579	15
46	638197	436	361803	683679	538	316321	045482	102	954518	14
47	638458	436	361542	684001	537	315999	045543	102	954457	13
48	638720	435	361280	684324	537	315676	045604	102	954396	12
49	638981	435	361019	684646	537	315354	045665	102	954335	11
50	639242	435	360758	684968	537	315032	045726	102	954274	10
51	9,639503	434	10,360497	9,685290	536	10,314710	10,045787	102	9,954213	9
52	639764	434	360236	685612	536	314388	045848	102	954152	8
53	640024	434	359976	685934	536	314066	045910	102	954090	7
54	640284	433	359716	686255	536	313745	045971	102	954029	6
55	640544	433	359456	686577	535	313423	046032	102	953968	5
56	640804	433	359196	686898	535	313102	046094	102	953906	4
57	641064	432	358936	687219	535	312781	046155	102	953845	3
58	641323	432	358677	687540	535	312460	046217	102	953783	2
59	641583	432	358417	687861	534	312139	046278	103	953722	1
60	641842	431	358158	688182	534	311818	046340	103	953660	0
	Co-fine		Secant	Co-tang.		Tangent	Co-fecant		Sine	M

M	Sine	D	Co-secant	Tangent	D	Co-tang	Secant	D	Co-sine	
0	9.641842	432	10.358158	9.688182	534	10.311818	10.046340	103	9.953660	60
1	642101	432	357899	688502	534	311498	046401	103	953599	59
2	642360	431	357640	688823	534	311177	046463	103	953537	58
3	642618	430	357382	689143	533	310857	046525	103	953475	57
4	642876	430	357124	689463	533	310537	046587	103	953413	56
5	643135	430	356865	689783	533	310217	046648	103	953352	55
6	643393	430	356607	690103	533	309897	046710	103	953290	54
7	643650	429	356350	690423	533	309577	046772	103	953228	53
8	643908	429	356092	690742	532	309258	046834	103	953166	52
9	644165	429	355835	691062	532	308938	046896	103	953104	51
10	644423	428	355577	691381	532	308619	046958	103	953042	50
11	9,644680	428	10,355320	9,691700	531	10,308300	10,047020	104	9,952980	49
12	644936	428	355064	692019	531	307981	047082	104	952918	48
13	645193	427	354807	692338	531	307662	047145	104	952855	47
14	645450	427	354550	692656	531	307344	047207	104	952793	46
15	645706	427	354294	692975	531	307025	047269	104	952731	45
16	645962	426	354038	693293	530	306707	047331	104	952669	44
17	646218	426	353782	693611	530	306388	047394	104	952606	43
18	646474	426	353526	693930	530	306070	047456	104	952544	42
19	646729	425	353271	694248	530	305752	047519	104	952481	41
20	646984	425	353016	694566	529	305434	047581	104	952419	40
21	9,647239	425	10,352761	9,694883	529	10,305117	10,047644	104	9,952356	39
22	647494	424	352506	695201	529	304799	047706	104	952294	38
23	647749	424	352251	695518	529	304482	047769	104	952231	37
24	648004	424	351996	695836	529	304164	047831	105	952168	36
25	648258	424	351742	696153	528	303847	047895	105	952105	35
26	648512	423	351488	696470	528	303530	047957	105	952043	34
27	648766	423	351234	696787	528	303213	048020	105	951980	33
28	649020	423	350980	697103	528	302897	048083	105	951917	32
29	649274	422	350726	697420	527	302580	048146	105	951854	31
30	649527	422	350473	697736	527	302264	048209	105	951791	30
31	9,649781	422	10,350219	9,698053	527	10,301947	10,048272	105	9,951728	29
32	650034	422	349966	698369	527	301631	048335	105	951665	28
33	650287	421	349713	698685	526	301315	048398	105	951602	27
34	650539	421	349461	699001	526	300999	048461	105	951539	26
35	650792	421	349208	699316	526	300684	048524	105	951476	25
36	651044	420	348956	699632	526	300368	048588	105	951412	24
37	651297	420	348703	699947	526	300053	048651	106	951349	23
38	651549	420	348451	700263	525	299737	048714	106	951286	22
39	651800	419	348200	700578	525	299422	048778	106	951222	21
40	652052	419	347948	700893	525	299107	048841	106	951159	20
41	9,652304	419	10,347696	9,701208	524	10,298792	10,048904	106	9,951096	19
42	652555	418	347445	701523	524	298477	048968	106	951032	18
43	652806	418	347194	701837	524	298163	049032	106	950968	17
44	653057	418	346943	702152	524	297848	049095	106	950905	16
45	653307	418	346693	702466	524	297534	049159	106	950841	15
46	653558	417	346442	702780	523	297220	049222	106	950778	14
47	653808	417	346192	703095	523	296905	049286	106	950714	13
48	654059	417	345941	703409	523	296591	049350	106	950650	12
49	654309	416	345691	703723	523	296277	049414	106	950586	11
50	654558	416	345442	704036	522	295964	049478	107	950522	10
51	9,654808	416	10,345192	9,704350	522	10,295650	10,049542	107	9,950458	9
52	655058	415	344942	704663	522	295337	049606	107	950394	8
53	655307	415	344693	704977	522	295023	049670	107	950330	7
54	655556	415	344444	705290	522	294710	049734	107	950266	6
55	655805	415	344195	705603	521	294397	049798	107	950202	5
56	656054	414	343946	705916	521	294084	049862	107	950138	4
57	656302	414	343698	706228	521	293772	049926	107	950074	3
58	656551	414	343449	706541	521	293459	049990	107	950009	2
59	656799	413	343201	706854	521	293146	050055	107	949945	1
60	657047	413	342953	707166	520	292834	050119	107	949881	0
	Co-fine		Secant	Co-tang.		Tangent	Co-fecant		Sine	M

049862

M	Sine	D.	Co-secant	Tangent	D.	Co-tang.	Secant	D.	Co-fine	
0	9,657047	413	10,342953	9,707166	520	10,292834	10,050119	107	9,949881	60
1	657295	413	342705	707478	520	292522	050184	107	949816	59
2	657542	412	342458	707790	520	292210	050248	107	949752	58
3	657790	412	342210	708102	520	291898	050312	108	949688	57
4	658037	412	341963	708414	519	291586	050377	108	949623	56
5	658484	412	341716	708726	519	291274	050442	108	949558	55
6	658531	411	341469	709037	519	290963	050506	108	949494	54
7	658778	411	341222	709349	519	290651	050571	108	949429	53
8	659025	411	340975	709660	519	290340	050636	108	949364	52
9	659271	410	340729	709971	518	290029	050700	108	949300	51
10	659517	410	340483	710282	518	289718	050765	108	949235	50
11	9,659762	410	10,340237	9,710593	518	10,289407	10,050830	108	9,949170	49
12	660009	409	339991	710904	518	289096	050895	108	949105	48
13	660255	409	339745	711215	518	288785	050960	108	949040	47
14	660500	409	339500	711525	517	288475	051025	108	948975	46
15	660746	409	339254	711836	517	288164	051090	108	948910	45
16	660991	408	339009	712146	517	287854	051155	108	948845	44
17	661236	408	338764	712456	517	287544	051220	109	948780	43
18	661481	408	338519	712766	516	287234	051285	109	948715	42
19	661726	407	338274	713076	516	286924	051350	109	948650	41
20	661970	407	338030	713386	516	286614	051416	109	948584	40
21	9,662214	407	10,337786	9,713696	516	10,286304	10,051481	109	9,948519	39
22	662459	407	337541	714005	516	285995	051546	109	948454	38
23	662703	406	337297	714314	515	285686	051612	109	948388	37
24	662946	406	337054	714624	515	285376	051677	109	948323	36
25	663190	406	336810	714933	515	285067	051743	109	948257	35
26	663433	405	336567	715242	515	284758	051808	109	948192	34
27	663677	405	336323	715551	514	284449	051874	109	948126	33
28	663920	405	336080	715860	514	284140	051940	109	948060	32
29	664163	405	335837	716168	514	283832	052005	110	947995	31
30	664406	404	335594	716477	514	283523	052071	110	947929	30
31	9,664648	404	10,335352	9,716785	514	10,283215	10,052137	110	9,947863	29
32	664891	404	335109	717093	513	282907	052203	110	947797	28
33	665133	403	334867	717401	513	282599	052269	110	947731	27
34	665375	403	334625	717709	513	282291	052335	110	947665	26
35	665617	403	334383	718017	513	281983	052400	110	947600	25
36	665859	402	334141	718325	513	281675	052467	110	947533	24
37	666100	402	333900	718633	512	281367	052533	110	947467	23
38	666342	402	333658	718940	512	281060	052599	110	947401	22
39	666583	402	333417	719248	512	280752	052665	110	947335	21
40	666824	401	333176	719555	512	280445	052731	110	947269	20
41	9,667065	401	10,332935	9,719862	512	10,280138	10,052797	110	9,947203	19
42	667305	401	332695	720169	511	279831	052864	111	947136	18
43	667546	401	332454	720476	511	279524	052930	111	947070	17
44	667786	400	332214	720783	511	279217	052936	111	947004	16
45	668026	400	331974	721089	511	278911	053063	111	946937	15
46	668267	400	331733	721396	511	278604	053129	111	946871	14
47	668506	499	331494	721702	510	278298	053196	111	946804	13
48	668746	399	331254	722009	510	277991	053262	111	946738	12
49	668986	399	331014	722315	510	277685	053329	111	946671	11
50	669225	399	330775	722621	510	277379	053396	111	946604	10
51	9,669464	398	10,330536	9,722927	510	10,277073	10,053462	111	9,946538	9
52	669703	398	330297	723232	509	276768	053529	111	946471	8
53	669942	398	330058	723538	509	276462	053596	111	946404	7
54	670181	397	329819	723844	509	276156	053663	111	946337	6
55	670419	397	329581	724149	509	275851	053730	112	946270	5
56	670658	397	329342	724454	509	275546	053797	112	946203	4
57	670896	397	329104	724759	508	275241	053864	112	946136	3
58	671134	396	328866	725065	508	274935	053931	112	946069	2
59	671372	396	328628	725369	508	274631	053998	112	946002	1
60	671609	396	328391	725674	508	274326	054065	112	945935	0
	Co-fine		Secant	Co-tang.		Tangent	Co-secant		Sine	M

M	Sine	D	Co-fecant	Tangent	D.	Co-tang	Secant	D	Co-fine	
0	9.671609	396	10.328391	9.725674	508	10.274320	10.054065	112	9.945935	60
1	671847	395	328153	725979	508	274021	054132	112	945868	59
2	672084	395	327916	726284	507	273716	054200	112	945800	58
3	672321	395	327679	726588	507	273412	054267	112	945733	57
4	672558	395	327442	726892	507	273108	054334	112	945666	56
5	672795	394	327205	727197	507	272803	054402	112	945598	55
6	673032	394	326968	727501	507	272499	054469	112	945531	54
7	673268	394	326732	727805	506	272195	054536	113	945464	53
8	673505	394	326495	728109	506	271891	054604	113	945396	52
9	673741	393	326259	728412	506	271588	054672	113	945328	51
10	673977	393	326023	728716	506	271284	054739	113	945261	50
11	9.674213	393	10.325787	9.729020	506	10.270980	10.054807	113	9.945193	49
12	674448	392	325552	729323	505	270677	054875	113	945125	48
13	674684	392	325316	729626	505	270374	054942	113	945058	47
14	674919	392	325081	729929	505	270071	055010	113	944990	46
15	675155	392	324845	730233	505	269767	055078	113	944922	45
16	675390	391	324610	730535	505	269465	055146	113	944854	44
17	675624	391	324376	730838	504	269162	055214	113	944786	43
18	675859	391	324141	731141	504	268859	055282	113	944718	42
19	676094	391	323906	731444	504	268556	055350	113	944650	41
20	676328	390	323672	731746	504	268254	055418	114	944582	40
21	9.676562	390	10.323438	9.732048	504	10.267952	10.055486	114	9.944513	39
22	676796	390	323204	732351	503	267649	055554	114	944446	38
23	677030	390	322970	732653	503	267347	055623	114	944377	37
24	677264	389	322736	732955	503	267045	055691	114	944309	36
25	677498	389	322502	733257	503	266743	055759	114	944241	35
26	677731	389	322269	733558	503	266442	055828	114	944172	34
27	677964	388	322036	733860	502	266140	055896	114	944104	33
28	678197	388	321803	734162	502	265838	055964	114	944036	32
29	678430	388	321570	734463	502	265537	056033	114	943967	31
30	678663	388	321337	734764	502	265236	056101	114	943899	30
31	9.678895	387	10.321105	9.735066	502	10.264934	10.056170	114	9.943830	29
32	679128	387	320872	735367	502	264633	056239	114	943761	28
33	679360	387	320640	735668	501	264332	056307	115	943693	27
34	679592	387	320408	735969	501	264031	056376	115	943624	26
35	679824	386	320176	736269	501	263731	056445	115	943555	25
36	680056	386	319944	736570	501	263430	056514	115	943486	24
37	680288	386	319712	736871	501	263129	056583	115	943417	23
38	680519	385	319481	737171	500	262829	056652	115	943348	22
39	680750	385	319250	737471	500	262529	056721	115	943279	21
40	680982	385	319018	737771	500	262229	056790	115	943210	20
41	9.681213	385	10.318787	9.738071	500	10.261929	10.056859	115	9.943141	19
42	681443	384	318557	738371	500	261629	056928	115	943072	18
43	681674	384	318326	738671	499	261329	056997	115	943003	17
44	681905	384	318095	738971	499	261029	057066	115	942934	16
45	682135	384	317865	739271	499	260729	057136	115	942854	15
46	682365	383	317635	739570	499	260430	057205	116	942795	14
47	682595	383	317405	739870	499	260130	057275	116	942725	13
48	682825	383	317175	740169	499	259831	057344	116	942656	12
49	683055	383	316945	740468	498	259532	057413	116	942587	11
50	683284	382	316716	740767	498	259233	057483	116	942517	10
51	9.683514	382	10.316486	9.741066	498	10.258934	10.057552	116	9.942448	9
52	683743	382	316257	741365	498	258635	057622	116	942378	8
53	683972	381	316028	741664	498	258336	057692	116	942308	7
54	684201	381	315799	741962	497	258038	057761	116	942239	6
55	684430	381	315570	742261	497	257739	057831	116	942169	5
56	684658	381	315342	742559	497	257441	057901	116	942099	4
57	684887	380	315113	742858	497	257142	057971	116	942029	3
58	685115	380	314885	743156	497	256844	058041	116	941959	2
59	685343	380	314657	743454	497	256546	058111	117	941889	1
60	685571	380	314429	743752	496	256248	058181	117	941819	0
	Co-fine		Secant	Co-tang		Tangent	Co-fecant		Sine	M

M	Sine	D.	Co-secant	Tangent	D.	Co-tang	Secant	D.	Co-fine	
0	9,685571	380	10,314429	9,743754	496	10,256248	10,058181	117	9,941819	60
1	685799	379	314201	744050	496	255950	058251	117	941749	59
2	686027	379	313973	744348	496	255652	058321	117	941679	58
3	686254	379	313746	744645	425	255355	058391	117	941609	57
4	686482	379	313518	744943	496	255057	058461	117	941539	56
5	686709	378	313291	745240	495	254760	058531	117	941469	55
6	686936	378	313064	745538	495	254462	058602	117	941398	54
7	687163	378	312837	745835	495	254165	058672	117	941328	53
8	687389	378	312611	746132	495	253868	058742	117	941258	52
9	687616	377	312384	746429	495	253571	058813	117	941187	51
10	687843	377	312157	746726	495	253274	058883	117	941117	50
11	9,688069	377	10,311931	9,747023	494	10,252977	10,058954	118	9,941046	49
12	688295	377	311705	747319	494	252681	059025	118	940975	48
13	688521	376	311479	747616	494	252384	059095	118	940905	47
14	688747	376	311253	747913	494	252087	059166	118	940834	46
15	688972	376	311028	748209	494	251791	059237	118	940763	45
16	689198	376	310802	748505	493	251495	059307	118	940693	44
17	689423	375	310577	748801	493	251199	059378	118	940622	43
18	689648	375	310352	749097	493	250903	059449	118	940551	42
19	689873	375	310127	749393	493	250607	059520	118	940480	41
20	690098	375	309902	749689	493	250311	059591	118	940409	40
21	9,690323	374	10,309677	9,749985	493	10,250015	10,059661	118	9,940338	39
22	690548	374	309452	750281	492	249719	059733	118	940267	38
23	690772	374	309228	750576	492	249424	059804	118	940196	37
24	690996	374	309004	750872	492	249128	059875	119	940125	36
25	691220	373	308780	751167	492	248833	059947	119	940053	35
26	691444	373	308556	751462	492	248538	060018	119	939982	34
27	691668	373	308332	751757	492	248243	060089	119	939911	33
28	691892	373	308108	752052	491	247948	060160	119	939840	32
29	692115	372	307885	752347	491	247653	060232	119	939768	31
30	692339	372	307661	752642	491	247358	060303	119	939697	30
31	9,692562	372	10,307438	9,752937	491	10,247063	10,060375	119	9,939625	29
32	692785	371	307215	753231	491	246769	060446	119	939554	28
33	693008	371	306992	753526	491	246474	060518	119	939482	27
34	693231	371	306769	753820	490	246180	060590	119	939410	26
35	693453	371	306547	754115	490	245885	060661	119	939339	25
36	693676	370	306324	754409	490	245591	060733	120	939267	24
37	693898	370	306102	754703	490	245297	060805	120	939195	23
38	694120	370	305880	754997	490	245003	060877	120	939123	22
39	694342	370	305658	755291	489	244709	060949	120	939051	21
40	694564	369	305436	755585	489	244415	061020	120	938980	20
41	9,694786	369	10,305214	9,755878	489	10,244122	10,061092	120	9,938908	19
42	695007	369	304993	756172	489	243828	061164	120	938836	18
43	695229	369	304771	756465	489	243535	061237	120	938763	17
44	695450	368	304550	756759	489	243241	061309	120	938691	16
45	695671	368	304329	757052	489	242948	061381	120	938619	15
46	695892	368	304108	757345	488	242655	061453	120	938547	14
47	696113	368	303887	757638	488	242362	061525	120	938475	13
48	696334	367	303666	757931	488	242069	061598	121	938402	12
49	696554	367	303446	758224	488	241776	061670	121	938330	11
50	696775	367	303225	758517	488	241483	061742	121	938258	10
51	9,696995	367	10,303005	9,758810	488	10,241190	10,061815	121	9,938185	9
52	697215	366	302785	759102	487	240898	061887	121	938113	8
53	697435	366	302565	759395	487	240605	061960	121	938040	7
54	697654	366	302346	759687	487	240313	062033	121	937967	6
55	697874	366	302126	759979	487	240021	062105	121	937895	5
56	698094	365	301906	760272	487	239728	062178	121	937822	4
57	698313	365	301687	760564	487	239436	062251	121	937749	3
58	698532	365	301468	760856	486	239144	062324	121	937676	2
59	698751	365	301249	761148	486	238852	062397	121	937603	1
60	698970	364	301030	761439	486	238561	062469	121	937531	0
	Co-fine		Secant	Co-tang.		Tangent	Co-fecant		Sine	M

M	Sine	D.	Co-secant	Tangent	D.	Co-tang.	Secant	D.	Co-sine	
0	9,698970	364	10,301030	9,761439	486	10,238561	10,062469	121	9,937531	60
1	699183	364	300811	761731	486	238269	062542	122	937458	59
2	699407	364	300593	762023	486	237977	062615	122	937385	58
3	699626	364	300374	762314	486	237686	062688	122	937312	57
4	699844	363	300156	762606	485	237394	062762	122	937238	56
5	700062	363	299938	762897	485	237103	062835	122	937165	55
6	700280	363	299720	763188	485	236812	062908	122	937092	54
7	700498	363	299502	763479	485	236521	062981	122	937019	53
8	700716	363	299284	763770	485	236230	063054	122	936946	52
9	700933	362	299067	764061	485	235939	063128	122	936872	51
10	701151	362	298849	764352	484	235648	063201	122	936799	50
11	9,701368	362	10,298632	9,764643	484	10,235357	10,063275	122	9,936725	49
12	701585	362	298415	764933	484	235067	063348	123	936652	48
13	701802	361	298198	765224	484	234776	063422	123	936578	47
14	702019	361	297981	765514	484	234486	063495	123	936505	46
15	702236	361	297764	765805	484	234195	063569	123	936431	45
16	702452	361	297548	766095	484	233905	063643	123	936357	44
17	702669	360	297331	766385	483	233615	063716	123	936284	43
18	702885	360	297115	766675	483	233325	063790	123	936210	42
19	703101	360	296899	766965	483	233035	063864	123	936136	41
20	703317	360	296683	767255	483	232745	063938	123	936062	40
21	9,703533	359	10,296467	9,767545	483	10,232455	10,064012	123	9,935988	39
22	703749	359	296251	767834	483	232166	064086	123	935914	38
23	703964	359	296036	768124	482	231876	064160	123	935840	37
24	704179	359	295821	768414	482	231586	064234	124	935766	36
25	704395	359	295605	768703	482	231297	064308	124	935692	35
26	704610	358	295390	768992	482	231008	064382	124	935618	34
27	704825	358	295175	769281	482	230719	064457	124	935543	33
28	705040	358	294960	769570	482	230430	064531	124	935469	32
29	705254	358	294746	769860	481	230140	064605	124	935395	31
30	705469	357	294531	770148	481	229852	064680	124	935320	30
31	9,705683	357	10,294317	9,770437	481	10,229563	10,064754	124	9,935246	29
32	705897	357	294103	770726	481	229274	064829	124	935171	28
33	706112	357	293888	771015	481	228985	064903	124	035097	27
34	706326	356	293674	771303	481	228697	064978	124	935022	26
35	706539	356	293461	771592	481	228408	065052	124	934948	25
36	706753	356	293247	771880	480	228120	065127	124	934873	24
37	706967	356	293033	772168	480	227832	065202	125	934798	23
38	707180	355	292820	772457	480	227543	065277	125	934723	22
39	707393	355	292607	772745	480	227255	065351	125	934647	21
40	707606	355	292394	773033	480	226967	065426	125	934574	20
41	9,707819	355	10,292181	9,773321	480	10,226679	10,065501	125	9,934499	19
42	708032	354	291968	773608	479	226392	065576	125	934424	18
43	708245	354	291755	773896	479	226104	065651	125	934349	17
44	708458	354	291542	774184	479	225816	065726	125	934274	16
45	708670	354	291330	774471	479	225529	065801	125	934199	15
46	708882	353	291118	774759	479	225241	065877	125	934123	14
47	709094	353	290906	775046	479	224954	065952	125	934048	13
48	709306	353	290694	775333	479	224667	066027	125	933973	12
49	709518	353	290482	775621	478	224379	066102	126	933898	11
50	709730	353	290270	775908	478	224092	066178	126	933822	10
51	9,709941	352	10,290059	9,776195	478	10,223805	10,066253	126	9,933747	9
52	710153	352	289847	776482	478	223518	066329	126	933671	8
53	710364	352	289636	776769	478	223231	066404	126	933596	7
54	710575	352	289425	777056	478	222944	066480	126	933520	6
55	710786	351	289214	777342	478	222658	066556	126	933444	5
56	710997	351	289003	777628	477	222372	066631	126	933369	4
57	711208	351	288792	777915	477	222085	066707	126	933293	3
58	711419	351	288581	778201	477	221799	066783	126	933217	2
59	711629	350	288371	778487	477	221513	066859	126	933141	1
60	711839	350	288161	778774	477	221226	066934	126	933066	0
	Co-sine		Secant	Co-tang.		Tangent	Co-secant		Sine	

M	Sine	D.	Co-secant	Tangent	D.	Co-tang'	Secant	D.	Co-sine	
0	9,711859	350	10,288161	9,778774	477	10,221226	10,066936	126	9,933000	60
1	712049	350	287951	779060	477	220940	067010	127	932990	59
2	712260	350	287740	779346	476	220654	067086	127	932914	58
3	712469	349	287531	779632	476	220368	067162	127	932838	57
4	712679	349	287321	779918	476	220082	067238	127	932762	56
5	712889	349	287111	780203	476	219797	067315	127	932685	55
6	713098	349	286902	780489	476	219511	067391	127	932609	54
7	713308	349	286692	780775	475	219225	067467	127	932533	53
8	713517	348	286483	781060	476	218940	067543	127	932457	52
9	713726	348	286274	781346	475	218654	067620	127	932380	51
10	713935	348	286065	781631	475	218369	067696	127	932304	50
11	9,714144	348	10,285856	9,781916	475	10,218084	10,067772	127	9,932228	49
12	714352	347	285648	782201	475	217799	067849	127	932151	48
13	714561	347	285439	782486	475	217514	067925	128	932075	47
14	714769	347	285231	782771	475	217229	068002	128	931998	46
15	714978	347	285022	783056	475	216944	068079	128	931921	45
16	715186	347	284814	783341	475	216659	068155	128	931845	44
17	715394	346	284606	783626	474	216374	068232	128	931768	43
18	715601	346	284399	783910	474	216090	068309	128	931691	42
19	715809	346	284191	784195	474	215805	068386	128	931614	41
20	716017	346	283983	784479	474	215521	068463	128	931537	40
21	9,716224	345	10,283776	9,784764	474	10,215236	10,068540	128	9,931460	39
22	716432	345	283568	785048	474	214952	068617	128	931383	38
23	716639	345	283361	785332	473	214668	068694	128	931306	37
24	716846	345	283154	785616	473	214384	068771	129	931229	36
25	717053	345	282947	785900	473	214100	068848	129	931152	35
26	717259	344	282741	786184	473	213816	068925	129	931075	34
27	717466	344	282534	786468	473	213532	069002	129	930998	33
28	717673	344	282327	786752	473	213248	069079	129	930921	32
29	717879	344	282121	787036	473	212964	069157	129	930843	31
30	718085	343	281915	787319	473	212681	069234	129	930766	30
31	9,718291	343	10,281709	9,787603	472	10,212397	10,069311	129	9,930688	29
32	718497	343	281503	787886	472	212114	069389	129	930611	28
33	718703	343	281297	788170	472	211830	069467	129	930533	27
34	718909	343	281091	788453	472	211547	069544	129	930456	26
35	719114	342	280886	788736	472	211264	069622	129	930378	25
36	719320	342	280680	789019	472	210981	069700	130	930300	24
37	719525	342	280475	789302	471	210698	069777	130	930223	23
38	719730	342	280270	789585	471	210415	069855	130	930145	22
39	719935	341	280065	789868	471	210132	069933	130	930067	21
40	720140	341	279860	790151	471	209849	070011	130	929989	20
41	9,720345	341	10,279655	9,790433	471	10,209567	10,070089	130	9,929911	19
42	720549	341	279451	790716	471	209284	070167	130	929833	18
43	720754	340	279246	790999	471	209001	070245	130	929755	17
44	720958	340	279042	791281	471	208719	070323	130	929677	16
45	721162	340	278838	791563	470	208437	070401	130	929599	15
46	721366	340	278634	791846	470	208154	070479	130	929521	14
47	721570	339	278430	792128	470	207872	070558	130	929442	13
48	721774	339	278226	792410	470	207590	070636	131	929364	12
49	721978	339	278022	792692	470	207308	070714	131	929286	11
50	722181	339	277819	792974	470	207026	070793	131	929207	10
51	9,722385	339	10,277615	9,793256	470	10,206744	10,070871	131	9,929129	9
52	722588	339	277412	793538	469	206462	070950	131	929050	8
53	722791	338	277209	793819	469	206181	071028	131	928972	7
54	722994	338	277006	794101	469	205899	071107	131	928893	6
55	723197	338	276803	794383	469	205617	071186	131	928814	5
56	723400	338	276600	794664	469	205336	071264	131	928736	4
57	723603	337	276397	794945	469	205055	071343	131	928657	3
58	723805	337	276195	795227	469	204773	071422	131	928578	2
59	724007	337	275993	795508	468	204492	071501	131	928499	1
60	724210	337	275790	795789	468	204211	071580	131	928420	0
	Co-sine		Secant	Co-tang.		Tangent	Co-secant		Sine	M

M	Sine	D.	Co-fec nt	Tangent	D.	Co-tang.	Secant	D.	Co fine	
0	9,724210	337	10,275790	9,795769	468	10,204211	10 075580	132	9,928420	60
1	724412	337	275588	796070	468	203930	071658	132	928342	59
2	724614	336	275386	796351	468	203649	071737	132	928263	58
3	724816	336	275184	796632	468	203368	071817	132	928183	57
4	725017	336	274983	796913	468	203087	071896	132	928104	56
5	725219	336	274781	797194	468	202806	071975	132	928025	55
6	725420	335	274580	797475	468	202525	072055	132	927946	54
7	725622	335	274378	797755	467	202245	072133	132	927867	53
8	725823	335	274177	798036	467	201964	072213	132	927787	52
9	726024	335	273976	798316	467	201684	072292	132	927708	51
10	726225	335	273775	798596	467	201404	072371	132	927629	50
11	9,726420	334	10,273574	9,798877	467	10 201123	10,072451	132	9,927549	49
12	726626	334	273374	799157	467	200843	072531	133	927469	48
13	726827	334	273173	799437	467	200563	072610	133	927390	47
14	727027	334	272973	799717	467	200283	072690	133	927310	46
15	727228	334	272772	799997	466	200003	072769	133	927231	45
16	727428	333	272572	800277	466	199723	072849	133	927151	44
17	727628	333	272372	800557	466	199443	072929	133	927071	43
18	727828	333	272172	800836	466	199164	073009	133	926991	42
19	728027	333	271973	801116	466	198884	073089	133	926911	41
20	728227	333	271773	801395	466	198604	073169	133	926831	40
21	9,728427	332	10,271573	9,801675	465	10,198325	10,073249	133	9,926751	39
22	728626	332	271374	801955	465	198045	073329	133	926671	38
23	728825	332	271175	802234	465	197766	073409	133	926591	37
24	729024	332	270976	802513	465	197487	073489	134	926511	36
25	729223	331	270777	802792	465	197208	073569	134	926431	35
26	729422	331	270578	803072	465	196928	073649	134	926351	34
27	729621	331	270379	803351	465	196649	073730	134	926270	33
28	729820	331	270180	803630	465	196370	073810	134	926190	32
29	730018	330	269982	803908	465	196092	073890	134	926110	31
30	730216	330	269784	804187	465	195813	073971	134	926029	30
31	9,730415	330	10,269585	9,804466	464	10,195534	10,074051	134	9,925949	29
32	730613	330	269387	804745	464	195255	074132	134	925868	28
33	730811	330	269189	805023	464	194977	074212	134	925788	27
34	731009	329	268991	805302	464	194698	074293	134	925707	26
35	731206	329	268794	805580	464	194420	074374	134	925626	25
36	731404	329	268596	805859	464	194141	074455	135	925545	24
37	731602	329	268398	806137	464	193863	074535	135	925465	23
38	731799	329	268201	806415	463	193585	074616	135	925384	22
39	731996	328	268004	806693	463	193307	074697	135	925303	21
40	732193	328	267807	806971	463	193029	074778	135	925222	20
41	9,732390	328	10,267610	9,807249	463	10,192751	10,074859	135	9,925141	19
42	732587	328	267413	807527	463	192473	074940	135	925060	18
43	732784	328	267216	807805	463	192195	075021	135	924979	17
44	732980	327	267020	808083	463	191917	075103	135	924897	16
45	733177	327	266823	808361	463	191639	075184	135	924816	15
46	733373	327	266627	808638	462	191362	075265	136	924735	14
47	733569	327	266431	808916	462	191084	075347	136	924653	13
48	733765	326	266235	809193	462	190807	075428	136	924572	12
49	733961	326	266039	809471	462	190529	075509	136	924491	11
50	734157	326	265843	809748	462	190252	075591	136	924409	10
51	9,734353	326	10,265647	9,810025	462	10,189975	10 075672	136	9 924328	9
52	734548	326	265452	810302	462	189698	075754	136	924246	8
53	734744	325	265256	810580	462	189420	075836	136	924164	7
54	734939	325	265061	810857	462	189143	075917	136	924083	6
55	735135	325	264865	811134	461	188866	075999	136	924001	5
56	735330	325	264670	811410	461	188590	076081	136	923919	4
57	735525	325	264475	811687	461	188313	076163	136	923837	3
58	735719	324	264281	811964	461	188036	076245	137	923755	2
59	735914	324	264086	812241	461	187759	076327	137	923673	1
60	736109	324	263891	812517	461	187483	076409	137	923591	0
	Co-fine		Secant	Co-tang.		Tangent	Co-fecan		Sine	M

M	Sine	D.	Co-fecant	Tangent	D.	Co-tang	Secant	D.	Co-fine	
0	9,736109	324	10,263891	9,812517	461	10,187483	10,076409	137	9,923%,1	60
1	736303	324	263697	812794	461	187206	076491	137	923509	59
2	736498	324	263502	813070	461	186930	076573	137	923427	58
3	736692	323	263308	813347	460	186653	076655	137	923345	57
4	736886	323	263114	813623	460	186377	076737	137	923263	56
5	737080	323	262920	813899	460	186101	076819	137	923181	55
6	737274	323	262726	814175	460	185825	076902	137	923098	54
7	737467	323	262533	814452	460	185548	076984	137	923016	53
8	737681	322	262339	814728	460	185272	077067	137	922933	52
9	737855	322	262145	815004	460	184996	077149	137	922851	51
10	738048	322	261952	815279	460	184721	077232	138	922768	50
11	9,738241	322	10,261759	9,815555	459	10,184445	10,077314	138	9,922686	49
12	738434	322	261566	815831	459	184169	077397	138	922603	48
13	738627	321	261373	816107	459	183893	077480	138	922520	47
14	738820	321	261180	816382	459	183618	077562	138	922438	46
15	739013	321	260987	816658	459	183342	077645	138	922355	45
16	739205	321	260795	816933	459	183067	077728	138	922272	44
17	739398	321	260602	817209	459	182791	077811	138	922189	43
18	739590	320	260410	817484	459	182516	077894	138	922106	42
19	739783	320	260217	817759	459	182241	077977	138	922023	41
20	739975	320	260025	818035	458	181965	078060	138	921940	40
21	9,740167	320	10,259833	9,818310	458	10,181690	10,078143	139	9,921857	39
22	740359	320	259641	818585	458	181415	078226	139	921774	38
23	740550	319	259450	818860	458	181140	078309	139	921691	37
24	740742	319	259258	819135	458	180865	078393	139	921607	36
25	740934	319	259066	819410	458	180590	078476	139	921524	35
26	741125	319	258875	819684	458	180316	078559	139	921441	34
27	741316	319	258684	819959	458	180041	078643	139	921357	33
28	741508	318	258492	820234	458	179766	078726	139	921274	32
29	741699	318	258301	820508	457	179492	078810	139	921190	31
30	741889	318	258111	820783	457	179217	078893	139	921107	30
31	9,742080	318	10,257920	9,821057	457	10,178943	10,078977	139	9,921023	29
32	742271	318	257729	821332	457	178668	079061	140	920939	28
33	742462	317	257538	821606	457	178394	079144	140	920856	27
34	742652	317	257348	821880	457	178120	079228	140	920772	26
35	742842	317	257158	822154	457	177846	079312	140	920688	25
36	743033	317	256967	822429	457	177571	079396	140	920604	24
37	743223	317	256777	822703	457	177297	079480	140	920520	23
38	743413	316	256587	822977	456	177023	079564	140	920436	22
39	743602	316	256398	823250	456	176750	079648	140	920352	21
40	743792	316	256208	823524	456	176476	079732	140	920268	20
41	9,743982	316	10,256018	9,823798	456	10,176202	10,079816	140	9,920184	19
42	744171	316	255829	824072	456	175928	079901	140	920099	18
43	744361	315	255639	824345	456	175655	079985	140	920015	17
44	744550	315	255450	824619	456	175381	080069	141	919931	16
45	744739	315	255261	824893	456	175107	080154	141	919846	15
46	744928	315	255072	825166	456	174834	080238	141	919762	14
47	745117	315	254883	825439	455	174561	080323	141	919677	13
48	745306	314	254694	825713	455	174287	080407	141	919593	12
49	745494	314	254506	825986	455	174014	080492	141	919508	11
50	745683	314	254317	826259	455	173741	080576	141	919424	10
51	9,745871	314	10,254129	9,826532	455	10,173468	10,080661	141	9,919339	9
52	746059	314	253941	826805	455	173195	080746	141	919254	8
53	746248	313	253752	827078	455	172922	080831	141	919169	7
54	746436	313	253564	827351	455	172649	080915	141	919085	6
55	746624	313	253376	827624	455	172376	081000	142	919000	5
56	746812	313	253188	827897	454	172103	081085	142	918915	4
57	746999	313	253001	828170	454	171830	081170	142	918830	3
58	747187	312	252813	828442	454	171558	081255	142	918745	2
59	747374	312	252626	828715	454	171285	081341	142	918659	1
60	747562	312	252438	828987	454	171013	081426	142	918574	0
	Co-fine		Secant	Co-tang.		Tangent	Co-fecant		Sine	M

M	Sine	D.	Co-fecant	Tangent	D.	Co-tang.	Secant	D.	Co-fine	
0	9.747562	312	10,252438	9,818987	454	10,171013	10,081426	142	9,918574	60
1	747749	312	252251	829260	454	170740	081511	142	918189	59
2	747936	312	252064	829532	454	170468	081596	142	918404	58
3	748123	311	251877	829805	454	170195	081682	142	918318	57
4	748310	311	251690	830077	454	169923	081767	142	918233	56
5	748497	311	251503	830349	453	169651	081853	142	918147	55
6	748683	311	251317	830622	453	169379	081938	143	918062	54
7	748870	311	251130	830893	453	169107	082024	143	917976	53
8	749056	310	250944	831165	453	168835	082109	143	917891	52
9	749242	310	250758	831437	453	168563	082195	143	917805	51
10	749429	310	250571	831709	453	168291	082281	143	917719	50
11	9,749615	310	10,250385	9,831981	453	10,168019	10,082366	143	9,917634	49
12	749801	310	250199	832253	453	167747	082452	143	917548	48
13	749987	309	250013	832525	453	167475	082538	143	917462	47
14	750172	309	249828	832796	453	167204	082624	143	917376	46
15	750358	309	249642	833068	452	166932	082710	143	917290	45
16	750543	309	249457	833339	452	166661	082796	143	917204	44
17	750729	309	249271	833611	452	166389	082881	144	917118	43
18	750914	308	249086	833882	452	166118	082968	144	917032	42
19	751099	308	248901	834154	452	165846	083055	144	916945	41
20	751284	308	248716	834425	452	165575	083141	144	916859	40
21	9,751469	308	10,248531	9,834696	452	10,165304	10,083227	144	9,916773	39
22	751654	308	248346	834967	452	165033	083313	144	916687	38
23	751839	308	248161	835238	452	164762	083400	144	916600	37
24	752023	307	247977	835509	452	164491	083486	144	916514	36
25	752208	307	247792	835780	451	164220	083573	144	916427	35
26	752392	307	247608	836051	451	163949	083659	144	916341	34
27	752576	307	247424	836322	451	163678	083746	144	916254	33
28	752760	307	247240	836593	451	163407	083833	145	916167	32
29	752944	306	247056	836864	451	163136	083920	145	916080	31
30	753128	306	246872	837134	451	162866	084006	145	915994	30
31	9,753312	306	10,246688	9,837405	451	10,162595	10,084093	145	9,915907	29
32	753495	306	246505	837675	451	162325	084180	145	915820	28
33	753679	306	246321	837946	451	162054	084267	145	915733	27
34	753862	305	246138	838216	451	161784	084354	145	915646	26
35	754046	305	245954	838487	450	161513	084441	145	915559	25
36	754229	305	245771	838757	450	161243	084528	145	915472	24
37	754412	305	245588	839027	450	160973	084615	145	915385	23
38	754595	305	245405	839297	450	160703	084703	145	915297	22
39	754778	304	245222	839568	450	160432	084790	145	915210	21
40	754960	304	245040	839838	450	160162	084877	146	915123	20
41	9,755143	304	10,244857	9,840108	450	10,159892	10,084965	146	9,915035	19
42	755326	304	244674	840378	450	159622	085052	146	914948	18
43	755508	304	244492	840647	450	159353	085140	146	914860	17
44	755690	304	244310	840917	449	159083	085227	146	914773	16
45	755872	303	244128	841187	449	158813	085315	146	914685	15
46	756054	303	243946	841457	449	158543	085402	146	914598	14
47	756236	303	243764	841726	449	158274	085490	146	914510	13
48	756418	303	243582	841996	449	158004	085578	146	914422	12
49	756600	303	243400	842266	449	157734	085666	146	914334	11
50	756782	302	243218	842535	449	157465	085754	147	914246	10
51	9,756963	302	10,243037	9,842805	449	10,157195	10,085842	147	9,914158	9
52	757144	302	242856	843074	449	156926	085930	147	914070	8
53	757326	302	242674	843343	449	156657	086018	147	913982	7
54	757507	302	242493	843612	449	156388	086106	147	913894	6
55	757688	301	242312	843882	448	156118	086194	147	913806	5
56	757869	301	242131	844151	448	155849	086282	147	913718	4
57	758050	301	241950	844420	448	155580	086370	147	913630	3
58	758230	301	241770	844689	448	155311	086459	147	913541	2
59	758411	301	241589	844958	448	155042	086547	147	913453	1
60	758591	301	241409	845227	448	154773	086636	147	913364	0
	Co-fine		Secant	Co-tang.		Tangent	Co-fecant		Sine	M

M	Sine	D.	Co-secant	Tangent	D.	Co-tang.	Secant	D.	Co-sine	M
0	9,755591	301	10,244409	9,845227	448	10,154773	10,086635	147	9,913365	60
1	758772	300	241228	845496	448	154504	086724	147	913276	59
2	758952	300	241048	845764	448	154236	086813	148	913187	58
3	757132	300	240868	846033	448	153967	086901	148	913099	57
4	759312	300	240688	846302	448	153698	086990	148	913010	56
5	759492	300	240508	846570	447	153430	087078	148	912922	55
6	759672	299	240328	846839	447	153161	087167	148	912833	54
7	759851	299	240149	847107	447	152893	087256	148	912744	53
8	760031	299	239969	847376	447	152624	087344	148	912655	52
9	760211	299	239789	847644	447	152356	087434	148	912566	51
10	760390	299	239610	847913	447	152087	087523	148	912477	50
11	9,760569	298	10,239431	9,848161	447	10,151819	10,087611	148	9,912388	49
12	760748	298	239252	848449	447	151551	087701	149	912299	48
13	760927	298	239073	848717	447	151283	087790	149	912210	47
14	761106	298	238894	848986	447	151014	087879	149	912121	46
15	761285	298	238715	849254	447	150745	087969	149	912031	45
16	761464	298	238536	849522	447	150478	088058	149	911942	44
17	761542	297	238358	849790	446	150210	088147	149	911853	43
18	761821	297	238179	850058	446	149942	088237	149	911763	42
19	761999	297	238001	850325	446	149675	088326	149	911674	41
20	762177	297	237823	850593	446	149407	088416	149	911584	40
21	9,762356	297	10,237544	9,850861	446	10,149139	10,088505	149	9,911495	39
22	762534	296	237466	851129	446	148871	088595	149	911405	38
23	762712	296	237288	851396	446	148604	088685	150	911315	37
24	762889	296	237111	851664	446	148336	088774	150	911226	36
25	763067	296	236933	851931	446	148069	088864	150	911136	35
26	763245	296	236755	852199	446	147801	088954	150	911046	34
27	763422	296	236578	852466	446	147534	089044	150	910956	33
28	763600	295	236400	852733	445	147267	089134	150	910866	32
29	763777	295	236223	853001	445	146999	089224	150	910776	31
30	763954	295	236046	853268	445	146732	089314	150	910686	30
31	9,764131	295	10,235869	9,853535	445	10,146465	10,089404	150	9,910596	29
32	764308	295	235692	853802	445	146198	089494	150	910506	28
33	764485	294	235515	854069	445	145931	089585	150	910415	27
34	764662	294	235338	854336	445	145664	089675	151	910325	26
35	764838	294	235162	854603	445	145397	089765	151	910235	25
36	765015	294	234985	854870	445	145130	089856	151	910144	24
37	765191	294	234809	855137	445	144863	089946	151	910054	23
38	765367	294	234633	855404	445	144596	090037	151	909963	22
39	765544	293	234456	855671	444	144329	090127	151	909873	21
40	765720	293	234280	855938	444	144062	090218	151	909782	20
41	9,765896	293	10,234104	9,856204	444	10,143796	10,090309	151	9,909691	19
42	766072	293	233928	856471	444	143529	090399	151	909601	18
43	766247	293	233753	856737	444	143263	090490	151	909510	17
44	766423	293	233577	857004	444	142996	090581	151	909419	16
45	766598	292	233402	857270	444	142730	090672	152	909328	15
46	766774	292	233226	857537	444	142463	090763	152	909237	14
47	766949	292	233051	857803	444	142197	090854	152	909146	13
48	767124	292	232876	858069	444	141931	090945	152	909055	12
49	767300	292	232700	858336	443	141664	091036	152	908964	11
50	767475	291	232525	858602	443	141398	091127	152	908873	10
51	9,767649	291	10,232351	9,858868	443	10,141132	10,091219	152	9,908781	9
52	767824	291	232176	859134	443	140866	091310	152	908690	8
53	767999	291	232001	859400	443	140600	091401	152	908599	7
54	768173	291	231827	859666	443	140334	091493	152	908507	6
55	768348	290	231652	859932	443	140068	091584	153	908416	5
56	768522	290	231478	860198	443	139802	091676	153	908324	4
57	768697	290	231303	860464	443	139536	091767	153	908233	3
58	768871	290	231129	860730	443	139270	091859	153	908141	2
59	769045	290	230955	860995	443	139005	091951	153	908049	1
60	769219	290	230781	861261	443	138739	092042	153	907958	0
	Co-sine		Secant	Co-tang.		Tangent	Co-secant		Sine	M

M	Sine	D.	Co-fecant	Tangent	D.	Co-tang	Secant	D.	Co-fine	
0	9,769119	290	10,230781	9 861261	443	10,138739	10,092042	153	9.907958	60
1	769393	289	230607	861527	443	138473	092134	153	907866	59
2	769566	289	230434	861792	442	138208	092226	153	907774	58
3	769740	289	230260	862058	442	137942	092318	153	907682	57
4	769913	289	230087	862323	442	137677	092410	153	907590	56
5	770087	287	229913	862589	442	137411	092502	153	907498	55
6	770260	288	229740	862854	442	137146	092594	153	907406	54
7	770433	288	229567	863119	442	136881	092686	154	907314	53
8	770606	288	229394	863385	442	136615	092778	154	907222	52
9	770779	288	229221	863650	442	136350	092871	154	907129	51
10	770952	283	229048	863915	442	136085	092963	154	907037	50
11	9,771125	288	10 228875	9 864180	442	10,135820	10,093055	154	9 906945	49
12	771298	287	228702	864445	442	135555	093148	154	906852	48
13	771470	287	228530	864710	442	135290	093240	154	906760	47
14	771643	287	228357	864975	431	135025	093333	154	906667	46
15	771815	287	228185	865240	441	134760	093425	154	906575	45
16	771987	287	228013	865505	441	134495	093518	154	906482	44
17	772159	287	227841	865770	441	134230	093611	155	906389	43
18	772331	286	227669	866035	441	133965	093704	155	906296	42
19	772503	286	227497	866300	441	133700	093796	155	906204	41
20	772675	286	227325	866564	441	133436	093889	155	906111	40
21	9,772847	286	10,227153	9,866829	441	10,133171	10,093981	155	9.906018	39
22	773018	286	226982	867094	441	132906	094075	155	905925	38
23	773190	286	226810	867358	441	132642	094168	155	905832	37
24	773361	285	226639	867623	441	132377	094261	155	905739	36
25	773533	285	226467	867887	441	132113	094355	155	905645	35
26	773704	285	226296	868152	440	131848	094448	155	905552	34
27	773875	285	226125	868416	440	131584	094541	155	905459	33
28	774046	285	225954	868680	440	131320	094634	156	905366	32
29	774217	285	225783	868945	440	131055	094728	156	905272	31
30	774388	284	225612	869209	440	130791	094821	156	905179	30
31	9,774558	284	10,225442	9,869473	440	10,130527	10,094915	156	9,905085	29
32	774729	284	225271	869737	440	130263	095008	156	904992	28
33	774899	284	225101	870001	440	129999	095102	156	904898	27
34	775070	284	224930	870265	440	129735	095196	156	904804	26
35	775240	284	224760	870529	440	129471	095289	156	904711	25
36	775410	283	224590	870793	440	129207	095383	156	904617	24
37	775580	283	224420	871057	440	128943	095477	156	904523	23
38	775750	283	224250	871321	440	128679	095571	157	904429	22
39	775920	283	224080	871585	440	128415	095665	157	904335	21
40	776090	283	223910	871849	439	128151	095759	157	904241	20
41	9,776259	283	10,223741	9,872112	439	10,127888	10,095853	157	9 904147	19
42	776429	282	223571	872376	439	127624	095947	157	904053	18
43	776598	282	223402	872640	439	127360	096041	157	903959	17
44	776768	282	223232	872903	439	127097	096136	157	903864	16
45	776937	282	223063	873167	439	126833	096230	157	903770	15
46	777106	282	222894	873430	439	126570	096324	157	903676	14
47	777275	281	222725	873694	439	126306	096419	157	903581	13
48	777444	281	222556	873957	439	126043	096513	157	903487	12
49	777613	281	222387	874220	439	125780	096608	158	903392	11
50	777781	281	222219	874484	439	125516	096702	158	903298	10
51	9,777950	281	10,222050	9,874747	439	10,125253	10,096797	158	9,903203	9
52	778119	281	221881	875010	439	124990	096892	158	903108	8
53	778287	280	221713	875273	438	124727	096986	158	903014	7
54	778455	280	221545	875536	438	124464	097081	158	902919	6
55	778624	280	221376	875800	438	124200	097176	158	902824	5
56	778792	280	221208	876063	438	123937	097271	158	902729	4
57	778960	280	221040	876326	438	123674	097366	158	902634	3
58	779128	280	220872	876589	438	123411	097461	159	902539	2
59	779295	279	220705	876851	438	123149	097556	159	902444	1
60	779463	279	220537	877114	438	122886	097651	159	902349	0
	Co-fine		Secant	Co-tang		Tangent	Co-fecant		Sine	M

M	Sine	D	Co-secant	Tangent	D.	Co-tang	Secant	D.	Co-sine	
0	9,779463	279	10,220537	9,877114	438	10,122886	10,097651	159	9,902349	60
1	779631	279	220369	877377	438	122623	097747	159	902253	59
2	779798	279	220202	877640	438	122360	097842	159	902158	58
3	779966	279	220034	877903	438	122097	097937	159	902063	57
4	780133	279	219867	878165	438	121835	098033	159	901967	56
5	780300	278	219700	878428	438	121572	098128	159	901872	55
6	780467	278	219533	878691	438	121309	098224	159	901776	54
7	780634	278	219366	878953	437	121047	098319	159	901681	53
8	780801	278	219199	879216	437	120784	098415	159	901585	52
9	780968	278	219032	879478	437	120522	098510	159	901490	51
10	781134	278	218866	879741	437	120259	098606	160	901394	50
11	9,781301	277	10,218699	9,880003	437	10,119997	10,098702	160	9,901298	49
12	781468	277	218532	880266	437	119734	098798	160	901202	48
13	781634	277	218366	880528	437	119472	098894	160	901106	47
14	781800	277	218200	880790	437	119210	098990	160	901010	46
15	781966	277	218034	881052	437	118948	099086	160	900914	45
16	782132	277	217868	881314	437	118686	099182	160	900818	44
17	782298	276	217702	881576	437	118424	099278	160	900722	43
18	782464	276	217536	881839	437	118161	099374	160	900626	42
19	782630	276	217370	882101	437	117899	099471	160	900529	41
20	782796	276	217204	882363	436	117637	099567	161	900433	40
21	9,782961	276	10,217039	9,882625	436	10,117375	10,099663	161	9,900337	39
22	783127	276	216873	882887	436	117113	099760	161	900240	38
23	783292	275	216708	883148	436	116852	099856	161	900144	37
24	783457	275	216543	883410	436	116590	099953	161	900047	36
25	783623	275	216377	883672	436	116328	100049	161	899951	35
26	783788	275	216212	883934	436	116066	100146	161	899854	34
27	783953	275	216047	884196	436	115804	100243	161	899757	33
28	784118	275	215882	884457	436	115543	100340	161	899660	32
29	784282	274	215718	884719	436	115281	100436	161	899564	31
30	784447	274	215553	884980	436	115020	100533	162	899467	30
31	9,784612	274	10,215388	9,885242	436	10,114758	10,100630	162	9,899370	29
32	784776	274	215224	885503	436	114497	100727	162	899273	28
33	784941	274	215059	885765	436	114285	100824	162	899176	27
34	785105	274	214895	886026	436	113974	100922	162	899078	26
35	785269	273	214731	886288	436	113712	101019	162	898981	25
36	785433	273	214567	886549	435	113451	101116	162	898884	24
37	785597	273	214403	886810	435	113190	101213	162	898787	23
38	785761	273	214239	887072	435	112928	101311	162	898689	22
39	785925	273	214075	887333	435	112667	101408	162	898592	21
40	786089	273	213911	887594	435	112406	101506	163	898494	20
41	9,786252	272	10,213748	9,887855	435	10,112145	10,101603	163	9,898397	19
42	786416	272	213584	888116	435	111884	101701	163	898299	18
43	786579	272	213421	888377	435	111623	101798	163	898202	17
44	786742	272	213258	888639	435	111361	101896	163	898104	16
45	786906	272	213094	888900	435	111100	101994	163	898006	15
46	787069	272	212931	889160	435	110840	102092	163	897908	14
47	787232	271	212768	889421	435	110579	102190	163	897810	13
48	787395	271	212605	889682	435	110318	102288	163	897712	12
49	787557	271	212443	889943	435	110057	102386	163	897614	11
50	787720	271	212280	890204	434	109796	102484	163	897516	10
51	9,787883	271	10,212117	9,890465	434	10,109535	10,102582	164	9,897418	9
52	788045	271	211955	890725	434	109275	102680	164	897320	8
53	788208	271	211792	890986	434	109014	102778	164	897222	7
54	788370	270	211630	891246	434	108753	102877	164	897123	6
55	788532	270	211408	891507	434	108493	102975	164	897025	5
56	788694	270	211305	891768	434	108232	103074	164	896926	4
57	788856	270	211144	892028	434	107972	103172	164	896828	3
58	789018	270	210982	892289	434	107711	103271	164	896729	2
59	789180	270	210820	892549	434	107451	103369	164	896631	1
60	789342	269	210658	892810	434	107190	103468	164	896532	0
	Co-sine		Secant	Co-tang		Tangent	Co-secant		Sine	M

M	Sine	D.	Co-secant	Tangent	D.	C o-tang	Secant	D.	Co-fine	
0	9,789342	269	10,210658	9,892810	434	10,107190	10,103468	164	9,896532	60
1	789504	269	210496	893070	434	106930	103567	165	896433	59
2	789665	269	210335	893331	434	106669	103665	165	896335	58
3	789827	269	210173	893591	434	106409	103764	165	896236	57
4	789988	269	210012	893851	434	106149	103863	165	896137	56
5	790149	269	209851	894111	434	105889	103961	165	896039	55
6	790310	268	209690	894371	434	105629	104061	163	895939	
7	790471	268	209529	894632	433	105368	104160	165	89	
8	790632	268	209368	894892	433	105108	104259	165	89	
9	790793	268	209207	895152	433	104848	104359	165	89	51
10	790954	268	209046	895412	433	104588	104458	165	895542	50
11	9,791115	268	10,208885	9,895672	433	10,104328	10,104557	166	9,895443	49
12	791275	267	208725	895932	433	104068	104657	166	895343	48
13	791436	267	208564	896192	433	103808	104756	166	895244	47
14	791596	267	208404	896452	433	103548	104855	166	895145	46
15	791757	267	208243	896712	433	103288	104955	166	895045	45
16	791917	267	208083	896971	433	103029	105055	166	894945	44
17	792077	267	207923	897231	433	102769	105154	166	894846	43
18	792237	266	207763	897491	433	102509	105254	166	894746	42
19	792397	266	207603	897751	433	102249	105354	166	894646	41
20	792557	266	207443	898010	433	101990	105454	166	894546	40
21	9,792716	266	10,207284	9,898270	433	10,101730	10,105554	167	9,894446	39
22	792876	266	207124	898530	433	101470	105654	167	894346	38
23	793035	266	206965	898789	433	101211	105754	167	894246	37
24	793195	265	206805	899049	432	100951	105854	167	894146	36
25	793354	265	206646	899308	432	100692	105954	167	894046	35
26	793514	265	206486	899568	432	100432	106054	167	893946	34
27	793673	265	206327	899827	432	100173	106154	167	893846	33
28	793832	265	206168	900086	432	099914	106255	167	893745	32
29	793991	265	206009	900346	432	099654	106355	167	893645	31
30	794150	264	205850	900605	432	099395	106456	167	893544	30
31	9,794308	264	10,205692	9,900864	432	10,099136	10,106556	168	9,893444	29
32	794467	264	205533	901124	432	098876	106657	168	893343	28
33	794626	264	205374	901383	432	098617	106757	168	893243	27
34	794784	264	205216	901642	432	098358	106858	168	893142	26
35	794942	264	205058	901901	432	098099	106959	168	893041	25
36	795101	264	204899	902160	432	097840	107060	168	892940	24
37	795259	263	204741	902419	432	097581	107161	168	892839	23
38	795417	263	204583	902679	432	097321	107262	168	892738	22
39	795575	263	204425	902938	432	097062	107362	168	892636	21
40	795733	263	204267	903197	431	096803	107464	168	892536	20
41	9,795891	263	10,204109	9,903455	431	10,096545	10,107565	169	9,892435	19
42	796049	263	203951	903714	431	096286	107666	169	892334	18
43	796206	263	203794	903973	431	096027	107767	169	892233	17
44	796364	262	203636	904232	431	095768	107868	169	892132	16
45	796521	262	203479	904491	431	095509	107970	169	892030	15
46	796679	262	203321	904750	431	095250	108071	169	891929	14
47	796836	262	203164	905008	431	094992	108173	169	891827	13
48	796993	262	203007	905267	431	094733	108274	169	891726	12
49	797150	262	202850	905526	431	094474	108376	169	891624	11
50	797307	261	202693	905784	431	094216	108477	170	891523	10
51	9,797464	261	10,202536	9,906043	431	10,093957	10,108579	170	9,891421	9
52	797621	261	202379	906302	431	093698	108681	170	891319	8
53	797777	261	202223	906560	431	093440	108783	170	891217	7
54	797934	261	202066	906819	431	093181	108885	170	891115	6
55	798091	261	201909	907077	431	092923	108987	170	891013	5
56	798247	261	201753	907336	431	092664	109089	170	890911	4
57	798403	260	201597	907594	431	092406	109191	170	890809	3
58	798560	260	201440	907852	431	092148	109293	170	890707	2
59	798716	260	201284	908111	430	091889	109395	170	890605	1
60	798872	260	201118	908369	430	091631	109497	170	890503	0
	Co-fine			Secant	Co-tang.		Tangent	Co-secant		Sine	M

M	Sine	D.	Co-secant	Tangent	D.	Co-tang	Secant	D.	Co-sine	
0	9,798872	260	10,201128	9,908369	430	10,091631	10,109497	170	9,890503	60
1	799028	260	200972	908628	430	091372	109600	171	890400	59
2	799184	260	200816	908886	430	091114	109702	171	890298	58
3	799339	259	200661	909144	430	090856	109805	171	890195	57
4	799495	259	200505	909402	430	090598	109907	171	890093	56
5	799651	259	200349	909660	430	090340	110010	171	889990	55
6	799806	259	200194	909918	430	090082	110112	171	889888	54
7	799962	259	200038	910177	430	089823	110215	171	889785	53
8	800117	259	199883	910435	430	089565	110318	171	889682	52
9	800272	258	199728	910693	430	089307	110421	171	889579	51
10	800427	258	199573	910951	430	089049	110523	171	889477	50
11	9,800582	258	10,199418	9,911209	430	10,088791	10,110626	172	9,889374	49
12	800737	258	199263	911467	430	088533	110729	172	889271	48
13	800892	258	199108	911724	430	088276	110832	172	889168	47
14	801047	258	198953	911982	430	088018	110936	172	889064	46
15	801201	258	198799	912240	430	087760	111039	172	888961	45
16	801356	257	198644	912498	430	087502	111142	172	888858	44
17	801511	257	198489	912756	430	087244	111245	172	888755	43
18	801665	257	198335	913014	429	086986	111349	172	888651	42
19	801819	257	198181	913271	429	086729	111452	172	888548	41
20	801973	257	198027	913529	429	086471	111556	173	888444	40
21	9,802118	257	10,197872	9,913787	429	10,086213	10,111659	173	9,888341	39
22	802282	256	197718	914044	429	085956	111763	173	888237	38
23	802436	256	197564	914302	429	085698	111866	173	888134	37
24	802589	256	197411	914560	429	085440	111970	173	888030	36
25	802743	256	197257	914817	429	085183	112074	173	887926	35
26	802897	256	197103	915075	429	084925	112178	173	887822	34
27	803050	256	196950	915332	429	084668	112282	173	887718	33
28	803204	256	196796	915590	429	084410	112386	173	887614	32
29	803357	255	196643	915847	429	084153	112490	173	887510	31
30	803510	255	196489	916104	429	083896	112594	174	887406	30
31	9,803664	255	10,196336	9,916362	429	10,083638	10,112698	174	9,887302	29
32	803817	255	196183	916619	429	083381	112802	174	887198	28
33	803970	255	196030	916877	429	083123	112907	174	887093	27
34	804123	255	195877	917134	429	082866	113011	174	886989	26
35	804276	254	195724	917391	429	082609	113115	174	886885	25
36	804428	254	195572	917648	429	082352	113220	174	886780	24
37	804581	254	195419	917905	429	082095	113324	174	886676	23
38	804734	254	195266	918163	428	081837	113429	174	886571	22
39	804886	254	195114	918420	428	081580	113534	174	886466	21
40	805039	254	194961	918677	428	081323	113638	175	886362	20
41	9,805191	254	10,194809	9,918934	428	10,081066	10,113743	175	9,886257	19
42	805343	253	194657	919191	428	080809	113848	175	886152	18
43	805495	253	194505	919448	428	080552	113953	175	886047	17
44	805647	253	194353	919705	428	080295	114058	175	885942	16
45	805799	253	194201	919962	428	080038	114163	175	885837	15
46	805951	253	194049	920219	428	079781	114268	175	885732	14
47	806103	253	193897	920476	428	079524	114373	175	885627	13
48	806254	253	193746	920732	428	079268	114478	175	885522	12
49	806406	252	193594	920990	428	079010	114584	175	885416	11
50	806557	252	193443	921247	428	078753	114689	176	885311	10
51	9,806709	252	10,193291	9,921503	428	10,078497	10,114795	176	9,885205	9
52	806860	252	193140	921760	428	078240	114900	176	885100	8
53	807011	252	192989	922017	428	077983	115006	176	884994	7
54	807163	252	192837	922274	428	077726	115111	176	884889	6
55	807314	252	192686	922530	428	077470	115217	179	884783	5
56	807465	251	192535	922787	428	077213	115323	176	884677	4
57	807615	251	192385	923044	428	076956	115428	176	884572	3
58	807766	251	192234	923300	428	076700	115534	176	884466	2
59	807917	251	192083	923557	427	076443	115640	176	884360	1
60	808067	251	191933	923813	427	076187	115746	177	884254	0
	Co-fine		Secant	Co-tang.		Tangent	Co-fecant		Sine	M

M	Sine	D.	Co-secant	Tangent	D.	Co-tang.	Secant	D.	Co-sine	
0	9 808067	251	10,191933	9,923813	427	10,076187	10,115746	177	9,884254	60
1	808218	251	191782	924070	427	075930	115852	177	884148	59
2	808368	251	191632	924327	427	075673	115958	177	884042	58
3	808519	250	191481	924583	427	075417	116064	177	883936	57
4	808669	250	191331	924840	427	075160	116171	177	883829	56
5	808819	250	191181	925096	427	074904	116277	177	883723	55
6	808969	250	191031	925352	427	074648	116383	177	883617	54
7	809119	250	190881	925609	427	074391	116490	177	883510	53
8	809269	250	190731	925865	427	074135	116596	177	883404	52
9	809419	249	190581	926122	427	073878	116703	178	883297	51
10	809569	249	190431	926378	427	073622	116809	178	883191	50
11	9,809718	249	10,190282	9,926634	427	10,073366	10,116916	178	9,883084	49
12	809868	249	190132	926890	427	073110	117023	178	882977	48
13	810017	249	189983	927147	427	072853	117129	178	882871	47
14	810167	249	189833	927403	427	072597	117236	178	882764	46
15	810316	248	189684	927659	427	072341	117343	178	882657	45
16	810465	248	189535	927915	427	072085	117450	178	882550	44
17	810614	248	189386	928171	427	071829	117557	178	882443	43
18	810763	248	189237	928427	427	071573	117664	179	882336	42
19	810912	248	189088	928683	427	071317	117771	179	882229	41
20	811061	248	188939	928940	427	071060	117879	179	882121	40
21	9,811210	248	10,188790	9,929196	427	10,070804	10,117986	179	9,882014	39
22	811358	247	188642	929452	427	070548	118093	179	881907	38
23	811507	247	188493	929708	427	070292	118201	179	881799	37
24	811655	247	188345	929964	426	070036	118308	179	881692	36
25	811804	247	188196	930220	426	069780	118416	179	881584	35
26	811952	247	188048	930475	426	069525	118523	179	881477	34
27	812100	247	187900	930731	426	069269	118631	179	881360	33
28	812248	247	187752	930987	426	069013	118739	180	881261	32
29	812396	246	187604	931243	426	068757	118847	180	881153	31
30	812544	246	187456	931499	426	068501	118954	180	881046	30
31	9,812692	246	10,187308	9,931755	426	10,068245	10,119062	180	9,880938	29
32	812840	246	187160	932010	426	067990	119170	180	880830	28
33	812988	246	187012	932266	426	067734	119278	180	880722	27
34	813135	246	186865	932522	426	067478	119387	180	880613	26
35	813283	246	186717	932778	426	067222	119495	180	880505	25
36	813430	245	186570	933033	426	066967	119603	180	880397	24
37	813578	245	186422	933289	426	066711	119711	181	880289	23
38	813725	245	186275	933545	426	066455	119820	181	880180	22
39	813872	245	186128	933800	426	066200	119928	181	880072	21
40	814019	245	185981	934056	426	065944	120037	181	879963	20
41	9,814166	245	10,185834	9,934311	426	10,065689	10,120145	181	9,879855	19
42	814313	245	185687	934567	426	065433	120254	181	879746	18
43	814460	244	185540	934823	426	065177	120363	181	879637	17
44	814607	244	185393	935078	426	064922	120471	181	879529	16
45	814752	244	185247	935333	426	064667	120580	181	879420	15
46	814900	244	185100	935589	426	064411	120689	181	879311	14
47	815046	244	184954	935844	426	064156	120798	182	879202	13
48	815193	244	184807	936100	426	063900	120907	182	879093	12
49	815339	244	184661	936355	426	063645	121016	182	878984	11
50	815485	243	184515	936610	426	063390	121125	182	878875	10
51	9,815632	243	10,184368	9,936866	425	10,063134	10,121234	182	9,878766	9
52	815778	243	184222	937121	425	062879	121344	182	878656	8
53	815924	243	184076	937376	425	062624	121453	182	878547	7
54	816069	243	183931	937632	425	062368	121562	182	878438	6
55	816215	243	183785	937887	425	062113	121672	182	878328	5
56	816361	243	183639	938142	425	061858	121781	183	878219	4
57	816507	232	183493	938398	425	061602	121891	183	878109	3
58	816652	242	183348	938653	425	061347	122001	183	877999	2
59	816798	242	183202	938908	425	061092	122110	183	877890	1
60	816943	242	183057	939163	425	060837	122220	183	877780	0
	Co-sine		Secant	Co-tang.		Tangent	Co-secan·		Sine	M

H 2

M	Sine	D.	Co-secant	Tangent	D.	C o-tang	Secant	D.	C o-sine	
0	9,816943	242	10,183057	9,939163	425	10,060837	10,122220	183	9,877780	60
1	817088	242	182912	939418	425	060582	122330	183	877670	59
2	817233	242	182767	939673	425	060327	122440	183	877560	58
3	817379	242	182621	939929	425	060071	122550	183	877450	57
4	817524	241	182476	940183	425	059817	122660	183	877340	56
5	817668	241	182332	940438	425	059562	122770	184	877230	55
6	817813	241	182187	940694	425	059306	122880	184	877120	54
7	817958	241	182042	940949	425	059051	122990	184	877010	53
8	818103	241	181897	941204	425	058796	123101	184	876899	52
9	818247	241	181753	941458	425	058542	123211	184	876789	51
10	818392	241	181608	941714	425	058286	123322	184	876678	50
11	9,818536	240	10,181464	9,941968	425	10,058032	10,123432	184	9,876568	49
12	818681	240	181319	942223	425	057777	123543	184	876457	48
13	818825	240	181175	942478	425	057522	123653	184	876347	47
14	818969	240	181031	942733	425	057267	123764	185	876236	46
15	819113	240	180887	942988	425	057012	123875	185	876125	45
16	819257	240	180743	943243	425	056757	123986	185	876014	44
17	819401	240	180599	943498	425	056502	124096	185	875904	43
18	819545	239	180455	943752	425	056248	124207	185	875793	42
19	819689	239	180311	944007	425	055993	124318	185	875682	41
20	819832	239	180168	944262	425	055738	124429	185	875571	40
21	9,819976	239	10,180024	9,944517	425	10,055483	10,124541	185	9,875459	39
22	820120	239	179880	944771	424	055229	124652	185	875348	38
23	820263	239	179737	945026	424	054974	124763	185	875237	37
24	820406	239	179594	945281	424	054719	124874	186	875126	36
25	820550	238	179450	945535	424	054465	124986	186	875014	35
26	820693	238	179307	945790	424	054210	125097	186	874903	34
27	820836	238	179164	946045	424	053955	125209	186	874791	33
28	820979	238	179021	946299	424	053701	125320	186	874680	32
29	821122	238	178878	946554	424	053446	125432	186	874568	31
30	821265	238	178735	946808	424	053192	125544	186	874456	30
31	9,821407	238	10,178593	9,947063	424	10,052937	10,125656	186	9,874344	29
32	821550	238	178450	947318	424	052682	125768	187	874232	28
33	821693	237	178307	947572	424	052428	125879	187	874121	27
34	821835	237	178165	947826	424	052174	125991	187	874009	26
35	821977	237	178023	948081	424	051919	126104	187	873896	25
36	822120	237	177880	948336	424	051664	126216	187	873784	24
37	822262	237	177738	948590	424	051410	126328	187	873672	23
38	822404	237	177596	948844	424	051156	126440	187	873560	22
39	822546	237	177454	949099	424	050901	126552	187	873448	21
40	822688	236	177312	949355	424	050647	126665	187	873335	20
41	9,822830	236	10,177170	9,949607	424	10,050393	10,126777	187	9,873223	19
42	822972	236	177028	949862	424	050138	126890	188	873110	18
43	823114	236	176886	950116	424	049884	127002	188	872998	17
44	823255	236	176745	950370	424	049630	127115	188	872885	16
45	823397	236	176603	950625	424	049375	127228	188	872772	15
46	823539	236	176461	950879	424	049121	127341	188	872659	14
47	823680	235	176320	951133	424	048867	127453	188	872547	13
48	823821	235	176179	951388	424	048612	127566	188	872434	12
49	823963	235	176037	951642	424	048358	127679	188	872321	11
50	824104	235	175896	951896	424	048104	127792	188	872208	10
51	9,824245	235	10,175755	9,952150	424	10,047850	10,127905	189	9,872095	9
52	824386	235	175614	952405	424	047595	128019	189	871981	8
53	824527	235	175473	952659	424	047341	128132	189	871868	7
54	824668	234	175332	952913	424	047087	128245	189	871755	6
55	824808	234	175192	953167	423	046833	128359	189	871641	5
56	824949	234	175051	953421	423	046579	128472	189	871528	4
57	825090	234	174910	953675	423	046325	128586	189	871414	3
58	825230	234	174770	953929	423	046071	128699	189	871301	2
59	825371	234	174629	954183	423	045817	128813	189	871187	1
60	825511	234	174489	954437	423	045563	128927	190	871073	0
	Co-sine		Secant	Co-tang		Tangent	Co-secant		Sine	M

M	Sine	D.	Co-fecant	Tangent	D.	Co-tang.	Secant	D.	C o-fine	
0	9,825511	234	10,174489	9,954437	423	10,045563	10,128927	190	9,871075	60
1	825651	233	174349	954691	423	045309	129040	190	870960	59
2	825791	233	174209	954945	423	045055	129154	190	870846	58
3	825931	233	174069	955200	423	044800	129268	190	870732	57
4	826071	233	173929	955454	423	044546	129382	190	870618	56
5	826211	233	173789	955707	423	044293	129496	190	870504	55
6	826351	233	173649	955961	423	044039	129610	190	870390	54
7	826491	233	173509	956215	423	043785	129724	190	870276	53
8	826631	233	173369	956469	423	043531	129839	190	870161	52
9	826770	232	173230	956723	423	043277	129953	191	870047	51
10	826910	232	173090	956977	423	043023	130067	191	869933	50
11	9,827049	232	10,172951	9,957231	423	10,042769	10,130182	191	9,869818	49
12	827189	232	172811	957485	423	042515	130296	191	869704	48
13	827328	232	172672	957739	423	042261	130411	191	869589	47
14	827467	232	172533	957993	423	042007	130526	191	869474	46
15	827606	232	172394	958246	423	041754	130649	191	869360	45
16	827745	232	172255	958500	423	041500	130755	191	869245	44
17	827884	231	172116	958754	423	041246	130870	191	869130	43
18	828023	231	171977	959008	423	040991	130985	192	869015	42
19	828162	231	171838	959262	423	040738	131100	192	868900	41
20	828301	231	171699	959516	423	040484	131215	192	868785	40
21	9,828439	231	10,171561	9,959769	423	10,040231	10,131330	192	9,868670	39
22	828578	231	171422	960023	423	039977	131445	192	868555	38
23	828716	231	171284	960277	423	039723	131560	192	868440	37
24	828855	230	171145	960531	423	039469	131676	192	868324	36
25	828993	230	171007	960784	423	039216	131791	192	868209	35
26	829131	230	170869	961038	423	038962	131907	192	868093	34
27	829269	230	170731	961291	423	038709	132022	193	867978	33
28	829407	230	170593	961545	423	038455	132138	193	867862	32
29	829545	230	170455	961799	423	038201	132253	193	867747	31
30	829683	230	170317	962052	423	037948	132369	193	867631	30
31	9,829821	229	10,170179	9,962306	423	10,037694	10,132485	193	9,867515	29
32	829959	229	170041	962560	423	037440	132601	193	867399	28
33	830097	229	169903	962813	423	037187	132717	193	867283	27
34	830234	229	169766	963067	423	036933	132833	193	867167	26
35	830372	229	169628	963320	423	036680	132949	193	867051	25
36	830509	229	169491	963574	423	036426	133065	194	866935	24
37	830646	229	169354	963827	423	036173	133181	194	866819	23
38	830784	229	169216	964081	423	035919	133297	194	866703	22
39	830921	228	169079	964335	423	035665	133414	194	866586	21
40	831058	228	168942	964588	423	035412	133530	194	866470	20
41	9,831195	228	10,168805	9,964842	422	10,035158	10,133647	194	9,866353	19
42	831332	228	168668	965095	422	034905	133763	194	866237	18
43	831469	228	168531	965349	422	034651	133880	194	866120	17
44	831606	228	168394	965602	422	034398	133996	195	866004	16
45	831742	228	168258	965855	422	034145	134113	195	865887	15
46	831879	228	168121	966109	422	033891	134230	195	865770	14
47	832015	227	167985	966362	422	033638	134347	195	865653	13
48	832152	227	167848	966616	422	033384	134464	195	865536	12
49	832288	227	167712	966869	422	033131	134581	195	865419	11
50	832425	227	167575	967123	422	032877	134698	195	865302	10
51	9,832561	227	10,167439	9,967376	422	10,032624	10,134815	195	9,865185	9
52	832697	227	167303	967629	422	032371	134932	195	865068	8
53	832833	227	167167	967883	422	032117	135050	195	864950	7
54	832969	226	167031	968136	422	031864	135167	196	864833	6
55	833105	226	166895	968389	422	031611	135284	196	864716	5
56	833241	226	166759	968643	422	031357	135402	196	864598	4
57	833377	226	166623	968896	422	031104	135519	196	864481	3
58	833512	226	166488	969149	422	030851	135637	196	864363	2
59	833648	226	166352	969403	422	030597	135755	196	864245	1
60	833783	226	166217	969656	422	030344	135873	196	864127	0
	Co-fine		Secant	Co-tang.		Tangent	Co-fecant		Sine	M

M	Sine	D.	Co-secant	Tangent	D.	Co-tang.	Secant	D.	Co-sine	
0	9,835783	226	10,166217	9,969656	422	10,030344	10,135873	196	9,864127	60
1	833919	225	166081	969909	422	030091	135990	196	864010	59
2	834054	225	165946	970162	422	029838	136108	197	863892	58
3	834189	225	165811	970416	422	029584	136226	197	863774	57
4	834325	225	165675	970669	422	029331	136344	197	863656	56
5	834460	225	165540	970922	422	029078	136462	197	863538	55
6	834595	225	165405	971175	422	028825	136581	197	863419	54
7	834730	225	165270	971429	422	028571	136699	197	863301	53
8	834865	225	165135	971682	422	028318	136817	197	863183	52
9	834999	224	165001	971935	422	028065	136936	197	863064	51
10	835134	224	164866	972188	422	027812	137054	198	862946	50
11	9,835269	224	10,164731	9,972441	422	10,027559	10,137173	198	9,862827	49
12	835403	224	164597	972694	422	027306	137291	198	862709	48
13	835538	224	164462	972948	422	027052	137410	198	862590	47
14	835672	224	164328	973201	422	026799	137529	198	862471	46
15	835807	224	164193	973454	422	026546	137647	198	862353	45
16	835941	224	164059	973707	422	026293	137766	198	862234	44
17	836075	223	163925	973960	422	026040	137885	198	862115	43
18	836209	223	163791	974213	422	025787	138004	198	861996	42
19	836343	223	163657	974466	422	025534	138123	198	861877	41
20	836477	223	163523	974719	422	025281	138242	199	861758	40
21	9,836611	223	10,163389	9,974973	422	10,025027	10,138362	199	9,861638	39
22	836745	223	163255	975226	422	024774	138481	199	861519	38
23	836878	223	163122	975479	422	024521	138600	199	861400	37
24	837012	222	162988	975732	422	024268	138720	199	861280	36
25	837146	222	162854	975985	422	024015	138839	199	861161	35
26	837279	222	162721	976238	422	023762	138959	199	861041	34
27	837412	222	162588	976491	422	023509	139078	199	860922	33
28	837546	222	162454	976744	422	023256	139198	199	860802	32
29	837679	222	162321	976997	422	023003	139318	200	860682	31
30	837812	222	162188	977250	422	022750	139438	200	860562	30
31	9,837945	222	10,162055	9,977503	422	10,022497	10,139558	200	9,860442	29
32	838078	221	161922	977756	422	022244	139678	200	860322	28
33	838211	221	161789	978009	422	021991	139798	200	860202	27
34	838344	221	161656	978262	422	021738	139918	200	860082	26
35	838477	221	161523	978515	422	021485	140038	200	859962	25
36	838610	221	161390	978768	422	021232	140158	200	859842	24
37	838742	221	161258	979021	422	020979	140279	201	859721	23
38	838875	221	161125	979274	422	020726	140399	201	859601	22
39	839007	221	160993	979527	422	020473	140520	201	859480	21
40	839140	220	160860	979780	422	020220	140640	201	859360	20
41	9,839272	220	10,160728	9,980033	422	10,019967	10,140761	201	9,859239	19
42	839404	220	160596	980286	422	019714	140881	201	859119	18
43	839536	220	160464	980538	422	019462	141002	201	858998	17
44	839668	220	160332	980791	421	019209	141123	201	858877	16
45	839800	220	160200	981044	421	018956	141244	202	858756	15
46	839932	220	160068	981297	421	018703	141365	202	858635	14
47	840064	219	159936	981550	421	018450	141486	202	858514	13
48	840196	219	159804	981803	421	018197	141607	202	858393	12
49	840328	219	159672	982056	421	017944	141728	202	858272	11
50	840459	219	159541	982309	421	017691	141849	202	858151	10
51	9,840591	219	10,159409	9,982562	421	10,017438	10,141971	202	9,858029	9
52	840722	219	159278	982814	421	017186	142092	202	857908	8
53	840854	219	159146	983067	421	016933	142214	202	857786	7
54	840985	219	159015	983320	421	016680	142335	203	857665	6
55	841116	218	158884	983573	421	016427	142457	203	857543	5
56	841247	218	158753	983826	421	016174	142578	203	857422	4
57	841378	218	158622	984079	421	015921	142700	203	857300	3
58	841509	218	158491	984331	421	015669	142822	203	857178	2
59	841640	218	158360	984584	421	015416	142944	203	857056	1
60	841771	218	158229	984837	421	015163	143066	203	856934	0
	Co-sine		Secant	Co-tang.		Tangent	Co-secant		Sine	M

M	Sine	D.	Co-secant	Tangent	D.	Co-tang.	Secant	D.	Co-sine	
0	9,841771	218	10,158229	9,984837	421	10,015163	10,143066	203	9,856934	60
1	841902	218	158098	985090	421	014910	143188	203	856812	59
2	842033	218	157967	985343	421	014657	143310	204	856690	58
3	842163	217	157837	985596	421	014404	143432	204	856568	57
4	842294	217	157706	985848	421	014152	143554	204	856446	56
5	842424	217	157576	986101	421	013899	143677	204	856323	55
6	842555	217	157445	986354	421	013646	143799	204	856201	54
7	842685	217	157315	986607	421	013393	143922	204	856078	53
8	842815	217	157185	986860	421	013140	144044	204	855956	52
9	842946	217	157054	987112	421	012888	144167	204	855833	51
10	843076	217	156924	987365	421	012635	144289	205	855711	50
11	9,843206	216	10,156794	9,987618	421	10,012382	10,144412	205	9,855588	49
12	843336	216	156664	987871	421	012129	144535	205	855465	48
13	843466	216	156534	988123	421	011877	144658	205	855342	47
14	843595	216	156405	988376	421	011624	144781	205	855219	46
15	843725	216	156275	988629	421	011371	144904	205	855096	45
16	843855	216	156145	988882	421	011118	145027	205	854973	44
17	843984	216	156016	989134	421	010866	145150	205	854850	43
18	844114	216	155886	989387	421	010613	145273	206	854727	42
19	844243	215	155757	989640	421	010360	145397	206	854603	41
20	844372	215	155628	989893	421	010107	145520	206	854480	40
21	9,844502	215	10,155498	9,990145	421	10,009855	10,145644	206	9,854356	39
22	844631	215	155369	990398	421	009602	145767	206	854233	38
23	844760	215	155240	990651	421	009349	145891	206	854109	37
24	844889	215	155111	990903	421	009097	146014	206	853986	36
25	845018	215	154982	991156	421	008844	146138	206	853862	35
26	845147	215	154853	991409	421	008591	146262	206	853738	34
27	845276	214	154724	991662	421	008338	146386	207	853614	33
28	845405	214	154595	991914	421	008086	146510	207	853490	32
29	845533	214	154467	992167	421	007833	146634	207	853366	31
30	845662	214	154338	992420	421	007580	146758	207	853242	30
31	9,845790	214	10,154210	9,992672	421	10,007328	10,146882	207	9,853118	29
32	845919	214	154081	992925	421	007075	147006	207	852994	28
33	846047	214	153953	993178	421	006822	147131	207	852869	27
34	846175	214	153825	993430	421	006570	147255	207	852745	26
35	846304	214	153696	993683	421	006317	147380	207	852620	25
36	846432	213	153568	993936	421	006064	147504	208	852496	24
37	846560	213	153440	994189	421	005811	147629	208	852371	23
38	846688	213	153312	994441	421	005559	147753	208	852247	22
39	846816	213	153184	994694	421	005306	147878	208	852122	21
40	846944	213	153056	994947	421	005053	148003	208	851997	20
41	9,847071	213	10,152929	9,995199	421	10,004801	10,148128	208	9,851872	19
42	847199	213	152801	995452	421	004548	148253	208	851747	18
43	847327	213	152673	995705	421	004295	148378	208	851622	17
44	847454	212	152546	995957	421	004043	148503	209	851497	16
45	847582	212	152418	996210	421	003790	148628	209	851372	15
46	847709	212	152291	996463	421	003537	148754	209	851246	14
47	847836	212	152164	996715	421	003285	148879	209	851121	13
48	847964	212	152036	996968	421	003032	149004	209	850996	12
49	848091	212	151909	997221	421	002779	149130	209	850870	11
50	848218	212	151782	997473	421	002527	149255	209	850745	10
51	9,848345	212	10,151655	9,997726	421	10,002274	10,149381	209	9,850619	9
52	848472	211	151528	997979	421	002021	149507	210	850493	8
53	848599	211	151401	998231	421	001769	149632	210	850368	7
54	848726	211	151274	998484	421	001516	149758	210	850242	6
55	848852	211	151148	998737	421	001263	149884	210	850116	5
56	848979	211	151021	998989	421	001011	150010	210	849990	4
57	849106	211	150894	999242	421	000758	150136	210	849864	3
58	849232	211	150768	999495	421	000505	150263	210	849737	2
59	849359	211	150641	999747	421	000253	150389	210	849611	1
60	849485	211	150515	10,00000	421	000000	150515	210	849485	0
	Co-sine		Secant	Co-tang.		Tangent	Co-secant		Sine	M

207

Ms	1 Degree		2 Degrees		3 Degrees		4 Degrees		5 Degrees		6 Degree		Ms
Dif.	Lat.	Dep.	Lat.	Dep.	Lat.	Dep.	Lat.	Dep.	Lat.	Dep.	Lat.	Dep.	Dif.
1	01.0	00.0	01.0	00.0	01.0	00.1	01.0	00.1	01.0	00.1	01.0	00.1	1
2	02.0	00.0	02.0	00.1	02.0	00.1	02.0	00.1	02.0	00.2	02.0	00.2	2
3	03.0	00.1	03.0	00.1	03.0	00.2	03.0	00.2	03.0	00.3	03.0	00.3	3
4	04.0	00.1	04.0	00.1	04.0	00.2	04.0	00.3	04.0	00.3	04.0	00.4	4
5	05.0	00.1	05.0	00.2	05.0	00.3	05.0	00.3	05.0	00.4	05.0	00.5	5
6	06.0	00.1	06.0	00.2	06.0	00.3	06.0	00.4	06.0	00.5	06.0	00.6	6
7	07.0	00.1	07.0	00.2	07.0	00.4	07.0	00.5	07.0	00.6	07.0	00.7	7
8	08.0	00.1	08.0	00.3	08.0	00.4	08.0	00.6	08.0	00.7	08.0	00.8	8
9	09.0	00.2	09.0	00.3	09.0	00.5	09.0	00.6	09.0	00.8	08.9	00.9	9
10	10.0	00.2	10.0	00.3	10.0	00.5	10.0	00.7	10.0	00.9	09.9	01.0	10
11	11.0	00.2	11.0	00.4	11.0	00.6	11.0	00.8	11.0	01.0	10.9	01.1	11
12	12.0	00.2	12.0	00.4	12.0	00.6	12.0	00.8	12.0	01.0	11.9	01.3	12
13	13.0	00.2	13.0	00.5	13.0	00.7	13.0	00.9	12.9	01.1	12.9	01.4	13
14	14.0	00.2	14.0	00.5	14.0	00.7	14.0	01.0	13.9	01.2	13.9	01.5	14
15	15.0	00.3	15.0	00.5	15.0	00.8	15.0	01.0	14.9	01.3	14.9	01.6	15
16	16.0	00.3	16.0	00.6	16.0	00.8	16.0	01.1	15.9	01.4	15.9	01.7	16
17	17.0	00.3	17.0	00.6	17.0	00.9	17.0	01.2	16.9	01.5	16.9	01.8	17
18	18.0	00.3	18.0	00.6	18.0	00.9	18.0	01.3	17.9	01.6	17.9	01.9	18
19	19.0	00.3	19.0	00.7	19.0	01.0	19.0	01.3	18.9	01.7	18.9	02.0	19
20	20.0	00.4	20.0	00.7	20.0	01.0	20.0	01.4	19.9	01.7	19.9	02.1	20
21	21.0	00.4	21.0	00.7	21.0	01.1	20.9	01.5	20.9	01.8	20.9	02.2	21
22	22.0	00.4	22.0	00.8	22.0	01.1	21.9	01.5	21.9	01.9	21.9	02.3	22
23	23.0	00.4	23.0	00.8	23.0	01.2	22.9	01.6	22.9	02.0	22.9	02.4	23
24	24.0	00.4	24.0	00.8	24.0	01.3	23.9	01.7	23.9	02.1	23.9	02.5	24
25	25.0	00.4	25.0	00.9	25.0	01.3	24.9	01.7	24.9	02.2	24.9	02.6	25
26	26.0	00.5	26.0	00.9	26.0	01.4	25.9	01.8	25.9	02.3	25.9	02.7	26
27	27.0	00.5	27.0	00.9	27.0	01.4	26.9	01.9	26.9	02.4	26.9	02.8	27
28	28.0	00.5	28.0	01.0	28.0	01.5	27.9	02.0	27.9	02.4	27.8	02.9	28
29	29.0	00.5	29.0	01.0	29.0	01.5	28.9	02.0	28.9	02.5	28.8	03.0	29
30	30.0	00.5	30.0	01.1	30.0	01.6	29.9	02.1	29.9	02.6	29.8	03.1	30
31	31.0	00.5	31.0	01.1	31.0	01.6	30.9	02.2	30.9	02.7	30.8	03.2	31
32	32.0	00.6	32.0	01.1	32.0	01.7	31.9	02.2	31.9	02.8	31.8	03.3	32
33	33.0	00.6	33.0	01.2	33.0	01.7	32.9	02.3	32.9	02.9	32.8	03.4	33
34	34.0	00.6	35.0	01.2	34.0	01.8	33.9	02.4	33.9	03.0	33.8	03.6	34
35	35.0	00.6	35.0	01.2	35.0	01.8	34.9	02.4	34.9	03.1	34.8	03.7	35
36	36.0	00.6	36.0	01.3	35.9	01.9	35.9	02.5	35.9	03.1	35.8	03.8	36
37	37.0	00.6	37.0	01.3	36.9	01.9	36.9	02.6	36.9	03.2	36.8	03.9	37
38	38.0	00.7	38.0	01.3	37.9	02.0	37.9	02.7	37.9	03.3	37.8	04.0	38
39	39.0	00.7	39.0	01.4	38.9	02.0	38.9	02.7	38.9	03.4	38.8	04.1	39
40	40.0	00.7	40.0	01.4	39.9	02.1	39.9	02.8	39.8	03.5	39.8	04.2	40
41	41.0	00.7	41.0	01.4	40.9	02.1	40.9	02.9	40.8	03.6	40.8	04.3	41
42	42.0	00.7	42.0	01.5	41.9	02.2	41.9	02.9	41.8	03.7	41.8	04.4	42
43	43.0	00.8	43.0	01.5	42.9	02.2	42.9	03.0	42.8	03.8	42.8	04.5	43
44	44.0	00.8	44.0	01.5	43.9	02.3	43.9	03.1	43.8	03.8	43.8	04.6	44
45	45.0	00.8	45.0	01.6	44.9	02.4	44.9	03.1	44.8	03.9	44.8	04.7	45
46	46.0	00.8	46.0	01.6	45.9	02.4	45.9	03.2	45.8	04.0	45.7	04.8	46
47	47.0	00.8	47.0	01.6	46.9	02.5	46.9	03.3	46.8	04.1	46.7	04.9	47
48	48.0	00.8	48.0	01.7	47.9	02.5	47.9	03.4	47.8	04.2	47.7	05.0	48
49	49.0	00.8	49.0	01.7	48.9	02.6	48.9	03.4	48.8	04.3	48.7	05.1	49
50	50.0	00.9	50.0	01.7	50.0	02.6	49.9	03.5	49.8	04.4	49.7	05.2	50
51	51.0	00.9	51.0	01.8	51.3	02.7	50.9	03.6	50.8	04.4	50.7	05.3	51
52	52.0	00.9	52.0	01.8	52.9	02.7	51.9	03.6	51.8	04.5	51.7	05.4	52
53	53.0	00.9	53.0	01.8	53.9	02.8	52.9	03.7	52.8	04.6	52.7	05.5	53
54	54.0	00.9	54.0	01.9	54.9	02.8	53.9	03.8	53.8	04.7	53.7	05.6	54
55	55.0	01.0	55.0	01.9	55.9	02.9	54.9	03.8	54.8	04.8	54.7	05.7	55
56	56.0	01.0	56.0	02.0	56.9	02.9	55.9	03.9	55.8	04.9	55.7	05.9	56
57	57.0	01.0	57.0	02.0	56.9	03.0	56.8	04.0	56.8	05.0	56.7	06.0	57
58	58.0	01.0	58.0	02.0	57.9	03.0	57.9	04.0	57.8	05.1	57.7	06.1	58
59	59.0	01.0	59.0	02.1	58.9	03.1	58.9	04.1	58.8	05.1	58.7	06.2	59
Dif.	Dep.	Lat.	Dep.	Lat.	Dep.	Lat.	Dep.	Lat.	Dep.	Lat.	Dep.	Lat.	Dif.
Ms	89 Degrees		88 Degrees		87 Degree		86 Degrees		85 Degrees		84 Degrees		Ms.

M. diff	1 Degree lat.	dep.	2 Degrees lat.	dep.	3 Degrees lat.	dep.	4 Degrees lat.	dep.	5 Degrees lat.	dep.	6 Degrees lat.	dep.	M. dist
60	60.0	01.1	60.0	02.1	59.9	03.1	59.9	04.2	59.8	05.2	59.7	06.3	60
61	61.0	01.1	61.0	02.1	60.9	03.2	60.9	04.3	60.8	05.3	60.7	06.4	61
62	62.0	01.1	62.0	02.2	61.9	03.2	61.9	04.3	61.8	05.4	61.7	06.5	62
63	63.0	01.1	63.0	02.2	62.9	03.3	62.8	04.4	62.8	05.5	62.7	06.6	63
64	64.0	01.1	64.0	02.2	63.9	03.3	63.8	04.5	63.8	05.6	63.6	06.7	64
65	65.0	01.1	65.0	02.3	64.9	03.4	64.8	04.5	64.8	05.7	64.6	06.8	65
66	66.0	01.2	66.0	02.3	65.9	03.5	65.8	04.6	65.7	05.8	65.6	06.9	66
67	67.0	01.2	67.0	02.3	66.9	03.5	66.8	04.7	66.7	05.8	66.6	07.0	67
68	68.0	01.2	68.0	02.4	67.9	03.6	67.8	04.7	67.7	05.9	67.6	07.1	68
69	69.0	01.2	69.0	02.4	68.9	03.6	68.8	04.8	68.7	06.0	68.6	07.2	69
70	70.0	01.2	70.0	02.4	69.9	03.7	69.8	04.9	69.7	06.1	69.0	07.3	70
71	71.0	01.2	71.0	02.5	70.9	03.7	70.8	05.0	70.7	06.2	70.6	07.4	71
72	72.0	01.3	72.0	02.5	71.9	03.8	71.8	05.0	71.7	06.3	71.6	07.5	72
73	73.0	01.3	73.0	02.5	72.9	03.8	72.8	05.1	72.7	06.4	72.6	07.6	73
74	74.0	01.3	74.0	02.6	73.9	03.9	73.8	05.2	73.7	06.5	73.6	07.7	74
75	75.0	01.3	75.0	02.6	74.9	03.9	74.8	05.2	74.7	06.5	74.6	07.8	75
76	76.0	01.3	76.0	02.7	75.9	04.0	75.8	05.3	75.7	06.6	75.6	07.9	76
77	77.0	01.3	77.0	02.7	76.9	04.0	76.8	05.4	76.7	06.7	76.6	08.0	77
78	78.0	01.4	78.0	02.7	77.9	04.1	77.8	05.4	77.7	06.8	77.5	08.1	78
79	79.0	01.4	79.0	02.8	78.9	04.1	78.8	05.5	78.7	06.9	78.6	08.3	79
80	80.0	01.4	80.0	02.8	79.9	04.2	79.8	05.6	79.7	07.0	79.6	08.4	80
81	81.0	01.4	81.0	02.8	80.9	04.2	80.8	05.7	80.7	07.1	80.6	08.5	81
82	82.0	01.4	81.9	02.9	81.9	04.3	81.8	05.7	81.7	07.2	81.5	08.6	82
83	83.0	01.5	82.9	02.9	82.9	04.3	82.8	05.8	82.7	07.2	82.5	08.7	83
84	84.0	01.5	83.9	02.9	83.9	04.4	83.8	05.9	83.7	07.3	83.5	08.8	84
85	85.0	01.5	84.9	03.0	84.9	04.4	84.8	05.9	84.7	07.4	84.5	08.9	85
86	86.0	01.5	85.9	03.0	85.9	04.5	85.8	06.0	85.7	07.5	85.5	09.0	86
87	87.0	01.5	86.9	03.0	86.9	04.6	86.8	06.1	86.7	07.6	86.5	09.1	87
88	88.0	01.5	87.9	03.1	87.9	04.6	87.8	06.1	87.7	07.7	87.5	09.2	88
89	89.0	01.6	88.9	03.1	88.9	04.7	88.8	06.2	88.7	07.8	88.5	09.3	89
90	90.0	01.6	89.9	03.1	89.9	04.7	89.8	06.3	89.7	07.8	89.5	09.4	90
91	91.0	01.6	90.9	03.2	90.9	04.8	90.8	06.4	90.7	07.9	90.5	09.5	91
92	92.0	01.6	91.9	03.2	91.9	04.8	91.8	06.4	91.6	08.0	91.5	09.6	92
93	93.0	01.6	92.9	03.2	92.9	04.9	92.8	06.5	92.6	08.1	92.5	09.7	93
94	94.0	01.6	93.9	03.3	93.9	04.9	93.8	06.6	93.6	08.2	93.5	09.8	94
95	95.0	01.7	94.9	03.3	94.9	05.0	94.8	06.6	94.6	08.3	94.5	09.9	95
96	96.0	01.7	95.9	03.4	95.9	05.0	95.8	06.7	95.6	08.4	95.5	10.0	96
97	97.0	01.7	96.9	03.4	96.9	05.1	96.8	06.8	96.6	08.5	96.5	10.1	97
98	98.0	01.7	97.9	03.4	97.9	05.1	97.8	06.8	97.6	08.5	97.5	10.2	98
99	99.0	01.7	98.9	03.5	98.9	05.2	98.8	06.9	98.6	08.6	98.5	10.3	99
100	100.0	01.7	99.9	03.5	99.9	05.2	99.8	07.0	99.6	08.7	99.5	10.5	100
200	200.0	03.5	199.9	07.0	199.7	10.5	199.5	13.9	199.2	17.4	198.9	20.9	200
300	299.9	05.2	299.8	10.5	299.6	15.7	299.3	20.9	298.9	26.1	298.4	31.4	300
400	399.9	07.0	399.8	14.0	399.5	20.9	399.0	27.9	398.5	34.9	397.8	41.8	400
500	499.9	08.7	499.7	17.5	499.3	26.2	498.8	34.9	498.1	43.0	497.3	52.3	500
600	599.9	10.5	599.6	20.9	599.2	31.4	598.5	41.8	597.7	52.3	596.7	62.7	600
700	699.9	12.2	699.6	24.4	699.0	36.6	698.3	48.8	697.3	61.0	696.2	73.2	700
800	799.9	14.0	799.5	27.9	798.9	41.9	798.1	55.8	797.0	69.7	795.6	83.6	800
900	899.8	15.7	899.5	31.4	898.8	47.1	897.8	62.8	896.6	78.4	895.1	94.1	900
1	0.1	0.0	0.1	0.0	0.1	0.0	0.1	0.0	0.1	0.0	0.1	0.0	1
2	0.2	0.0	0.2	0.0	0.2	0.0	0.2	0.0	0.2	0.0	0.2	0.0	2
3	0.3	0.0	0.3	0.0	0.3	0.0	0.3	0.0	0.3	0.0	0.3	0.0	3
4	0.4	0.0	0.4	0.0	0.4	0.0	0.4	0.0	0.4	0.0	0.4	0.0	4
5	0.5	0.0	0.5	0.0	0.5	0.0	0.5	0.0	0.5	0.0	0.5	0.1	5
6	0.6	0.0	0.6	0.0	0.6	0.0	0.6	0.0	0.6	0.1	0.6	0.1	6
7	0.7	0.0	0.7	0.0	0.7	0.0	0.7	0.0	0.7	0.1	0.7	0.1	7
8	0.8	0.0	0.8	0.0	0.8	0.0	0.8	0.1	0.8	0.1	0.8	0.1	8
9	0.9	0.0	0.9	0.0	0.9	0.0	0.9	0.1	0.9	0.1	0.9	0.1	9
diff	dep.	lat.	dep.	lat.	dep.	lat.	dep.	lat.	dep.	lat.	dep.	lat.	diff
Ts.	89 Degrees		88 Degrees		87 Degrees		86 Degrees		85 Degrees		84 Degrees		Ta.

Ms dift	7 Degrees lat.	dep.	8 Degrees lat.	dep.	9 Degrees lat.	dep.	10 Degrees lat.	dep	11 Degrees lat.	dep.	12 Degrees lat.	dep.	dift
1	01.0	00.1	01.0	00.1	01.0	00.2	01.0	00.2	01.0	00.2	01.0	00.2	1
2	02.0	00.2	02.0	00.3	02.0	00.3	02.0	00.3	02.0	00.4	02.0	00.4	2
3	03.0	00.4	03.0	00.4	03.0	00.5	03.0	00.5	02.9	00.6	02.9	00.6	3
4	04.0	00.5	04.0	00.6	04.0	00.6	03.9	00.7	03.9	00.8	03.9	00.8	4
5	05.0	00.6	05.0	00.7	04.9	00.8	04.9	00.9	04.9	01.0	04.9	01.0	5
6	06.0	00.7	05.9	00.8	05.9	00.9	05.9	01.0	05.9	01.1	05.9	01.2	6
7	06.9	00.9	06.9	01.0	06.9	01.1	06.9	01.2	06.9	01.3	06.8	01.5	7
8	07.9	01.0	07.9	01.1	07.9	01.3	07.9	01.4	07.9	01.5	07.8	01.7	8
9	08.9	01.1	08.9	01.3	08.9	01.4	08.9	01.6	08.8	01.7	08.8	01.9	9
10	09.9	01.2	09.9	01.4	09.9	01.6	09.8	01.7	09.8	01.9	09.8	02.1	10
11	10.9	01.3	10.9	01.5	10.9	01.7	10.8	01.9	10.8	02.1	10.8	02.3	11
12	11.9	01.5	11.9	01.7	11.9	01.9	11.8	02.1	11.8	02.3	11.7	02.5	12
13	12.9	01.6	12.9	01.8	12.8	02.0	12.8	02.3	12.8	02.5	12.7	02.7	13
14	13.9	01.7	13.9	01.9	13.8	02.2	13.8	02.4	13.7	02.7	13.7	02.9	14
15	14.9	01.8	14.9	02.1	14.8	02.3	14.8	02.6	14.7	02.9	14.7	03.1	15
16	15.9	01.9	15.8	02.2	15.8	02.5	15.8	02.8	15.7	03.1	15.6	03.3	16
17	16.9	02.1	16.8	02.4	16.8	02.7	16.7	02.9	16.7	03.2	16.6	03.5	17
18	17.9	02.2	17.8	02.5	17.8	02.8	17.7	03.1	17.7	03.4	17.6	03.7	18
19	18.9	02.3	18.8	02.6	18.8	03.0	18.7	03.3	18.7	03.6	18.6	04.0	19
20	19.9	02.4	19.8	02.8	19.8	03.1	19.7	03.5	19.6	03.8	19.6	04.2	20
21	20.8	02.6	20.8	02.9	20.7	03.3	20.7	03.6	20.6	04.0	20.5	04.4	21
22	21.8	02.7	21.8	03.1	21.7	03.4	21.7	03.8	21.6	04.2	21.5	04.6	22
23	22.8	02.8	22.8	03.2	22.7	03.6	22.7	04.0	22.6	04.4	22.5	04.8	23
24	23.8	02.9	23.8	03.3	23.7	03.8	23.6	04.2	23.6	04.6	23.5	05.0	24
25	24.8	03.0	24.8	03.5	24.7	03.9	24.6	04.3	24.5	04.8	24.5	05.2	25
26	25.8	03.2	25.7	03.6	25.7	04.1	25.6	04.5	25.5	05.0	25.4	05.4	26
27	26.8	03.3	26.7	03.8	26.7	04.2	26.6	04.7	26.5	05.2	26.4	05.6	27
28	27.8	03.4	27.7	03.9	27.7	04.4	27.6	04.9	27.5	05.3	27.4	05.8	28
29	28.8	03.5	28.7	04.0	28.6	04.5	28.6	05.0	28.5	05.5	28.4	06.0	29
30	29.8	03.7	29.7	04.2	29.6	04.7	29.5	05.2	29.4	05.7	29.3	06.2	30
31	30.8	03.8	30.7	04.3	30.6	04.8	30.5	05.4	30.4	05.9	30.3	06.4	31
32	31.8	03.9	31.7	04.5	31.6	05.0	31.5	05.5	31.4	06.1	31.3	06.7	32
33	32.8	04.0	32.7	04.6	32.6	05.2	32.5	05.7	32.4	06.3	32.3	06.9	33
34	33.7	04.1	33.7	04.7	33.6	05.3	33.5	05.9	33.3	06.5	33.3	07.1	34
35	34.7	04.3	34.7	04.9	34.6	05.5	34.5	06.1	34.4	06.7	34.2	07.3	35
36	35.7	04.4	35.7	05.0	35.6	05.6	35.5	06.2	35.3	06.9	35.2	07.5	36
37	36.7	04.5	36.6	05.2	36.5	05.8	36.4	06.4	36.3	07.1	36.2	07.7	37
38	37.7	04.6	37.6	05.3	37.5	05.9	37.4	06.6	37.3	07.3	37.2	07.9	38
39	38.7	04.8	38.6	05.4	38.5	06.1	38.4	06.8	38.3	07.4	38.1	08.1	39
40	39.7	04.9	39.6	05.6	39.5	06.3	39.4	06.9	39.3	07.6	39.1	08.3	40
41	40.7	05.0	40.6	05.7	40.5	06.4	40.4	07.1	40.2	07.8	40.1	08.5	41
42	41.7	05.1	41.6	05.8	41.5	06.6	41.4	07.3	41.2	08.0	41.1	08.7	42
43	42.7	05.2	42.6	06.0	42.5	06.7	42.3	07.5	42.2	08.2	42.1	08.9	43
44	43.7	05.4	43.6	06.1	43.5	06.9	43.3	07.6	43.2	08.4	43.0	09.2	44
45	44.7	05.5	44.6	06.3	44.4	07.0	44.3	07.8	44.3	08.6	44.0	09.4	45
46	45.7	05.6	45.6	06.4	45.4	07.2	45.3	08.0	45.2	08.8	45.0	09.6	46
47	46.6	05.7	46.5	06.5	46.4	07.4	46.3	08.1	46.1	09.0	46.0	09.8	47
48	47.6	05.8	47.5	06.7	47.4	07.5	47.3	08.3	47.1	09.2	46.9	10.0	48
49	48.6	06.0	48.5	06.8	48.4	07.7	48.3	08.5	47.9	09.3	47.9	10.2	49
50	49.6	06.1	49.5	07.0	49.4	07.8	49.2	08.7	49.1	09.5	48.9	10.4	50
51	50.6	06.2	50.5	07.1	50.4	08.0	50.2	08.8	50.1	09.7	49.9	10.6	51
52	51.6	06.3	51.5	07.2	51.4	08.1	51.2	09.0	51.0	09.9	50.9	10.8	52
53	52.6	06.5	52.5	07.4	52.3	08.3	52.2	09.2	52.0	10.1	51.8	11.0	53
54	53.6	06.6	53.5	07.5	53.3	08.4	53.2	09.4	53.0	10.3	52.8	11.2	54
55	54.6	06.7	54.5	07.7	54.3	08.6	54.2	09.5	54.0	10.5	53.8	11.4	55
56	55.6	06.8	55.5	07.8	55.3	08.8	55.1	09.7	55.0	10.7	54.8	11.6	56
57	56.6	06.9	56.4	07.9	56.3	08.9	56.1	09.9	56.0	10.9	55.8	11.9	57
58	57.6	07.1	57.4	08.1	57.3	09.1	57.1	10.1	56.9	11.1	56.7	12.1	58
59	58.6	07.2	58.4	08.2	58.3	09.2	58.1	10.2	57.9	11.3	57.7	12.3	59
dift	dep.	lat.	dep.	lat.	dep.	lat.	dep.	lat.	dep.	lat.	dep.	lat.	dift
Ms	83 Degrees		82 Degrees		81 Degrees		80 Degrees		79 Degrees		78 Degrees		Ms

Ms	7 Degrees		8 Degrees		9 Degrees		10 Degrees		11 Degrees		12 Degrees		Ms
diſt	lat.	dep.	lat.	dep.	lat.	dep.	lat.	dep.	lat.	dep.	lat.	dep.	diſt
60	59.6	07.3	59.4	08.4	59.3	09.4	59.1	10.4	58.9	11.4	58.7	12.5	60
61	60.5	07.4	60.4	08.5	60.2	09.5	60.1	10.6	59.9	11.6	59.7	12.7	61
62	61.5	07.6	61.4	08.6	61.2	09.7	61.1	10.8	60.9	11.8	60.6	12.9	62
63	62.5	07.7	62.4	08.8	62.2	09.9	62.0	10.9	61.8	12.0	61.6	13.1	63
64	63.5	07.8	63.4	08.9	63.2	10.0	63.0	11.1	62.8	12.2	62.6	13.3	64
65	64.5	07.9	64.4	09.0	64.2	10.2	64.0	11.3	63.8	12.4	63.6	13.5	65
66	65.5	08.0	65.4	09.2	65.2	10.3	65.0	11.5	64.8	12.6	64.6	13.7	66
67	66.5	08.2	66.4	09.3	66.2	10.5	66.0	11.6	65.8	12.8	65.5	13.9	67
68	67.5	08.3	67.3	09.5	67.2	10.6	67.0	11.8	66.7	13.0	66.5	14.1	68
69	68.5	08.4	68.3	09.6	68.2	10.8	68.0	12.0	67.7	13.2	67.5	14.4	69
70	69.5	08.5	69.3	09.7	69.1	10.9	68.9	12.2	68.7	13.4	68.5	14.6	70
71	70.5	08.6	70.3	09.9	70.1	11.1	69.9	12.4	69.7	13.5	69.4	14.8	71
72	71.5	08.8	71.3	10.0	71.1	11.3	70.9	12.5	70.7	13.7	70.4	15.0	72
73	72.5	08.9	72.3	10.2	72.1	11.4	71.9	12.7	71.7	14.9	71.4	15.2	73
74	73.4	09.0	73.3	10.3	73.1	11.6	72.9	12.8	72.6	14.1	72.4	15.4	74
75	74.4	09.1	74.3	10.4	74.1	11.7	73.9	13.0	73.6	14.3	73.4	15.6	75
76	75.4	09.3	75.3	10.6	75.1	11.9	74.8	13.2	74.6	14.5	74.3	15.8	76
77	76.4	09.4	76.3	10.7	76.1	12.0	75.8	13.4	75.6	14.7	75.3	16.0	77
78	77.4	09.5	77.2	10.9	77.0	12.2	76.8	13.5	76.6	14.9	76.3	16.2	78
79	78.4	09.6	78.2	11.0	78.0	12.4	77.8	13.7	77.5	15.1	77.3	16.4	79
80	79.4	09.7	79.2	11.1	79.0	12.5	78.8	13.9	78.5	15.3	78.2	16.6	80
81	80.4	09.9	80.2	11.3	80.0	12.7	79.8	14.1	79.5	15.5	79.2	16.8	81
82	81.4	10.0	81.2	11.4	81.0	12.8	80.8	14.2	80.5	15.6	80.2	17.1	82
83	82.4	10.1	82.2	11.6	82.0	13.0	81.7	14.4	81.5	15.8	81.2	17.3	83
84	83.4	10.2	83.2	11.7	83.0	13.1	82.7	14.6	82.5	16.0	82.2	17.5	84
85	84.4	10.4	84.2	11.8	84.0	13.3	83.7	14.8	83.4	16.2	83.1	17.7	85
86	85.4	10.5	85.2	12.0	84.9	13.4	84.7	14.9	84.4	16.4	84.1	17.9	86
87	86.3	10.6	86.2	12.1	85.9	13.6	85.7	15.1	85.4	16.6	85.1	18.1	87
88	87.3	10.7	87.1	12.2	86.9	13.8	86.7	15.3	86.4	16.8	86.1	18.3	88
89	88.3	10.8	88.1	12.4	87.9	13.9	87.6	15.4	87.4	17.0	87.1	18.5	89
90	89.3	11.0	89.1	12.5	88.9	14.1	88.6	15.6	88.3	17.2	88.0	18.7	90
91	90.3	11.1	90.1	12.7	89.9	14.2	89.6	15.8	89.3	17.4	89.0	18.9	91
92	91.3	11.2	91.1	12.8	90.9	14.4	90.6	16.0	90.3	17.6	90.0	19.1	92
93	92.3	11.3	92.1	12.9	91.9	14.5	91.6	16.1	91.3	17.7	91.0	19.3	93
94	93.3	11.5	93.1	13.1	92.8	14.7	92.6	16.3	92.3	17.9	91.9	19.6	94
95	94.3	11.6	94.1	13.2	93.8	14.9	93.6	16.5	93.3	18.1	92.9	19.8	95
96	95.3	11.7	95.1	13.4	94.8	15.0	94.5	16.7	94.2	18.3	93.9	20.0	96
97	96.3	11.8	96.1	13.5	95.8	15.2	95.5	16.8	95.2	18.5	94.9	20.2	97
98	97.3	11.9	97.0	13.6	96.8	15.3	96.5	17.0	96.2	18.7	95.9	20.4	98
99	98.3	12.1	98.0	13.8	97.8	15.5	97.5	17.2	97.2	18.9	96.8	20.6	99
100	99.3	12.2	99.0	13.9	98.8	15.6	98.5	17.4	98.2	19.1	97.8	20.8	100
200	198.5	24.4	198.1	27.8	197.5	31.3	197.0	34.7	196.3	38.2	195.6	41.6	200
300	297.8	36.6	297.1	41.8	296.3	46.9	295.4	52.1	294.5	57.2	293.4	62.4	300
400	397.0	48.8	396.1	55.7	395.1	62.6	393.9	69.5	392.6	76.3	391.3	83.2	400
500	496.5	60.9	495.1	69.6	493.8	78.2	492.4	86.8	490.8	95.4	489.1	104.0	500
600	595.5	73.1	594.2	83.5	592.6	93.9	590.9	104.2	589.0	114.5	586.9	124.7	600
700	694.8	85.3	693.2	97.4	691.4	109.5	689.4	121.6	687.1	133.6	684.7	145.5	700
800	794.0	97.5	792.2	111.3	790.2	125.1	787.8	139.0	785.3	152.6	782.5	166.3	800
900	893.3	109.7	891.2	125.3	888.9	140.8	876.3	156.3	883.5	171.7	880.3	187.1	900

ʄs.													ʅ s.
1	0.1	0.0	0.1	0.0	0.1	0.0	0.1	0.0	0.1	0.0	0.1	0.0	1
2	0.2	0.0	0.2	0.0	0.2	0.0	0.2	0.0	0.2	0.0	0.2	0.0	2
3	0.3	0.0	0.3	0.0	0.3	0.0	0.3	0.1	0.3	0.1	0.3	0.1	3
4	0.4	0.0	0.4	0.1	0.4	0.1	0.4	0.1	0.4	0.1	0.4	0.1	4
5	0.5	0.1	0.5	0.1	0.5	0.1	0.5	0.1	0.5	0.1	0.5	0.1	5
6	0.6	0.1	0.6	0.1	0.6	0.1	0.6	0.1	0.6	0.1	0.6	0.1	6
7	0.7	0.1	0.7	0.1	0.7	0.1	0.7	0.1	0.7	0.1	0.7	0.1	7
8	0.8	0.1	0.8	0.1	0.8	0.1	0.8	0.1	0.8	0.2	0.8	0.2	8
9	0.9	0.1	0.9	0.1	0.9	0.1	0.9	0.2	0.9	0.2	0.9	0.2	9

diſt	dep.	lat.	dep.	lat.	dep.	lat.	dep.	lat.	dep	lat.	dep.	lat	diſt
Ts.	83 Degrees		82 Degrees		81 Degrees		80 Degrees		79 Degrees		78 Degrees		ʅ s

M. dist	13 Degrees lat.	dep.	14 Degrees lat.	dep.	15 Degrees lat.	dep.	16 Degrees lat.	dep.	17 Degrees lat.	dep.	18 Degrees lat.	dep.	M. dist
1	01.0	00.2	01.0	00.2	01.0	00.3	01.0	00.3	01.0	00.3	01.0	00.3	1
2	01.9	00.4	01.9	00.5	01.9	00.5	01.9	00.6	01.9	00.6	01.9	00.6	2
3	02.9	00.7	02.9	00.7	02.9	00.8	02.9	00.8	02.9	00.9	02.9	00.9	3
4	03.9	00.9	03.9	01.0	03.8	01.0	03.8	01.1	03.8	01.2	03.8	01.2	4
5	04.9	01.1	04.9	01.2	04.8	01.3	04.8	01.4	04.8	01.5	04.8	01.5	5
6	05.8	01.3	05.8	01.5	05.8	01.6	05.8	01.7	05.7	01.8	05.7	01.9	6
7	06.8	01.6	06.8	01.7	06.8	01.8	06.8	02.0	06.7	02.0	06.7	02.2	7
8	07.8	01.8	07.8	01.9	07.7	02.1	07.7	02.2	07.6	02.3	07.6	02.5	8
9	08.8	02.0	08.7	02.2	08.7	02.3	08.7	02.5	08.6	02.6	08.6	02.8	9
10	09.7	02.2	09.7	02.4	09.7	02.6	09.6	02.8	09.6	02.9	09.5	03.1	10
11	10.7	02.5	10.7	02.7	10.6	02.8	10.6	03.0	10.5	03.2	10.5	03.4	11
12	11.7	02.7	11.6	02.9	11.6	03.1	11.5	03.3	11.5	03.5	11.4	03.7	12
13	12.7	02.9	12.6	03.1	12.6	03.4	12.5	03.6	12.4	03.8	12.4	04.0	13
14	13.6	03.1	13.6	03.4	13.5	03.6	13.5	03.9	13.4	04.1	13.3	04.3	14
15	14.6	03.4	14.6	03.6	14.5	03.9	14.4	04.1	14.3	04.4	14.3	04.6	15
16	15.6	03.6	15.5	03.9	15.5	04.1	15.4	04.4	15.3	04.7	15.2	04.9	16
17	16.6	03.8	16.5	04.1	16.4	04.4	16.3	04.7	16.3	05.0	16.2	05.3	17
18	17.5	04.0	17.5	04.4	17.4	04.7	17.3	05.0	17.2	05.3	17.1	05.6	18
19	18.5	04.3	18.4	04.6	18.4	04.9	18.3	05.3	18.2	05.6	18.1	05.9	19
20	19.5	04.5	19.4	04.8	19.3	05.2	19.2	05.5	19.1	05.8	19.0	06.2	20
21	20.5	04.7	20.4	05.1	20.3	05.4	20.2	05.8	20.1	06.1	20.0	06.5	21
22	21.4	04.9	21.3	05.3	21.2	05.7	21.1	06.1	21.0	06.4	20.9	06.8	22
23	22.4	05.2	22.3	05.6	22.2	06.0	22.1	06.3	22.0	06.7	21.9	07.1	23
24	23.4	05.4	23.3	05.8	23.2	06.2	23.1	06.6	22.9	07.0	22.8	07.4	24
25	24.4	05.6	24.3	06.0	24.1	06.5	24.0	06.9	23.9	07.3	23.8	07.7	25
26	25.3	05.8	25.2	06.3	25.1	06.7	25.0	07.2	24.9	07.6	24.7	08.0	26
27	26.3	06.1	26.2	06.5	26.1	07.0	26.0	07.4	25.8	07.9	25.7	08.3	27
28	27.3	06.3	27.2	06.8	27.0	07.2	26.9	07.7	26.8	08.2	26.6	08.7	28
29	28.3	06.5	28.1	07.0	28.0	07.5	27.9	08.0	27.7	08.5	27.6	09.0	29
30	29.2	06.7	29.1	07.3	29.0	07.8	28.8	08.3	28.7	08.8	28.5	09.3	30
31	30.2	07.0	30.1	07.5	29.9	08.0	29.8	08.5	29.6	09.1	29.5	09.6	31
32	31.2	07.2	31.0	07.7	30.9	08.3	30.8	08.8	30.6	09.4	30.4	09.9	32
33	32.2	07.4	32.0	08.0	31.9	08.5	31.7	09.1	31.6	09.6	31.4	10.2	33
34	33.1	07.6	33.0	08.2	32.8	08.8	32.7	09.4	32.5	09.9	32.3	10.5	34
35	34.1	07.9	34.0	08.5	33.8	09.1	33.6	09.6	33.5	10.2	33.3	10.8	35
36	35.1	08.1	34.9	08.7	34.8	09.3	34.6	09.9	34.4	10.5	34.2	11.1	36
37	36.1	08.3	35.9	09.0	35.7	09.6	35.6	10.2	35.4	10.8	35.2	11.4	37
38	37.0	08.5	36.9	09.2	36.7	09.8	36.5	10.5	36.4	11.1	36.1	11.7	38
39	38.0	08.8	37.8	09.4	37.7	10.1	37.5	10.7	37.3	11.4	37.1	12.1	39
40	39.0	09.0	38.8	09.7	38.6	10.4	38.4	11.1	38.3	11.7	38.0	12.4	40
41	39.9	09.2	39.8	09.9	39.6	10.6	39.4	11.3	39.2	12.0	39.0	12.7	41
42	40.9	09.4	40.8	10.2	40.6	10.9	40.4	11.6	40.2	12.3	39.9	13.0	42
43	41.9	09.7	41.7	10.4	41.5	11.1	41.3	11.9	41.1	12.6	40.9	13.3	43
44	42.9	09.9	42.7	10.6	42.5	11.4	42.3	12.1	42.1	12.9	41.8	13.6	44
45	43.8	10.1	43.7	10.9	43.5	11.6	43.3	12.4	43.0	13.2	42.8	13.9	45
46	44.8	10.3	44.6	11.1	44.4	11.9	44.2	12.7	44.0	13.4	43.7	14.2	46
47	45.8	10.6	45.6	11.4	45.4	12.2	45.2	13.0	44.9	13.7	44.7	14.5	47
48	46.8	10.8	46.6	11.6	46.4	12.4	46.1	13.2	45.9	14.0	45.6	14.8	48
49	47.7	11.0	47.5	11.9	47.3	12.7	47.1	13.5	46.9	14.3	46.6	15.1	49
50	48.7	11.2	48.5	12.1	48.3	12.9	48.1	13.8	47.8	14.6	47.6	15.5	50
51	49.7	11.5	49.5	12.3	49.3	13.2	49.0	14.1	48.8	14.9	48.5	15.8	51
52	50.7	11.7	50.5	12.6	50.2	13.5	50.0	14.3	49.7	15.2	49.5	16.2	52
53	51.6	11.9	51.4	12.8	51.2	13.7	50.9	14.6	50.7	15.5	50.4	16.4	53
54	52.6	12.1	52.4	13.1	52.2	14.0	51.9	14.9	51.6	15.8	51.4	16.7	54
55	53.6	12.4	53.4	13.3	53.1	14.2	52.9	15.2	52.6	16.1	52.3	17.0	55
56	54.6	12.6	54.3	13.6	54.1	14.5	53.8	15.4	53.5	16.4	53.3	17.3	56
57	55.5	12.8	55.3	13.8	55.1	14.8	54.8	15.7	54.5	16.7	54.2	17.6	57
58	56.5	13.0	56.3	14.0	56.0	15.0	55.7	16.0	55.5	17.0	55.2	17.9	58
59	57.5	13.3	57.2	14.3	57.0	15.3	56.7	16.3	56.4	17.2	56.1	18.2	59
	dep.	lat.	dep.	lat.	dep.	lat.	dep.	lat.	dep.	lat.	dep.	lat.	dist

Ms	13 Degrees		14 Degrees		15 Degrees		16 Degrees		17 Degrees		18 Degrees		M
dist	lat.	dep.	lat.	dep.	lat.	dep.	lat.	dep.	lat.	dep.	lat.	dep.	dist
60	58.5	13.5	58.2	14.5	58.0	15.5	57.7	16.5	57.4	17.5	57.1	18.5	60
61	59.4	13.7	59.2	14.8	58.9	15.8	58.6	16.8	58.4	17.8	58.0	18.8	61
62	60.4	13.9	60.2	15.0	59.9	16.0	59.6	17.1	59.3	18.1	59.0	19.2	62
63	61.4	14.0	61.1	15.2	60.9	16.3	60.6	17.4	60.3	18.4	59.9	19.5	63
64	62.4	14.2	62.1	15.5	61.8	16.6	61.5	17.6	61.2	18.7	60.9	19.8	64
65	63.3	14.6	63.1	15.7	62.8	16.8	62.5	17.9	62.2	19.0	61.8	20.1	65
66	64.3	14.8	64.0	16.0	63.7	17.1	63.4	18.2	63.1	19.3	62.8	20.4	66
67	65.3	15.1	65.0	16.2	64.7	17.3	64.4	18.5	64.1	19.6	63.7	20.7	67
68	66.3	15.3	66.0	16.5	65.7	17.6	65.4	18.7	65.0	19.3	64.7	21.0	68
69	67.2	15.5	66.9	16.7	66.6	17.9	66.3	19.0	66.0	20.2	65.6	21.3	69
70	68.2	15.7	67.9	16.9	67.6	18.1	67.3	19.3	66.9	20.5	66.6	21.6	70
71	69.2	16.0	68.9	17.2	68.6	18.4	68.2	19.6	67.9	20.8	67.5	21.9	71
72	70.2	16.2	69.9	17.4	69.5	18.6	69.2	19.8	68.9	21.0	68.5	22.2	72
73	71.1	16.4	70.8	17.7	70.5	18.9	70.2	20.1	69.8	21.3	69.4	22.6	73
74	72.1	16.6	71.8	17.9	71.5	19.2	71.1	20.4	70.8	21.6	70.4	22.9	74
75	73.1	16.9	72.8	18.1	72.4	19.4	72.1	20.7	71.8	21.9	71.3	23.2	75
76	74.1	17.1	73.7	18.4	73.4	19.7	73.0	20.9	72.7	22.2	72.3	23.5	76
77	75.0	17.3	74.7	18.6	74.4	19.9	74.0	21.2	73.7	22.5	73.2	23.8	77
78	76.0	17.5	75.7	18.9	75.3	20.2	75.0	21.5	74.6	22.8	74.2	24.1	78
79	77.0	17.8	76.7	19.1	76.3	20.4	75.9	21.8	75.6	23.1	75.1	24.4	79
80	77.9	18.0	77.6	19.4	77.2	20.7	76.9	22.0	76.6	23.4	76.1	24.7	80
81	78.9	18.2	78.6	19.6	78.2	21.0	77.9	22.3	77.5	23.7	77.0	25.0	81
82	79.9	18.4	79.6	19.8	79.2	21.2	78.8	22.6	78.5	24.0	78.0	25.3	82
83	80.9	18.7	80.5	20.1	80.2	21.5	79.8	22.9	79.4	24.3	78.9	25.6	83
84	81.8	18.9	81.5	20.3	81.1	21.7	80.7	23.1	80.4	24.6	79.9	26.0	84
85	82.8	19.1	82.5	20.6	82.1	22.0	81.7	23.4	81.3	24.8	80.8	26.3	85
86	83.8	19.3	83.4	20.8	83.1	22.3	82.7	23.7	82.2	25.1	81.8	26.6	86
87	85.8	19.6	84.4	21.1	84.0	22.5	83.6	24.0	83.2	25.4	82.7	26.9	87
88	85.7	19.8	85.4	21.3	85.0	22.8	84.6	24.3	84.1	25.7	83.7	27.2	88
89	86.7	20.0	86.4	21.5	86.0	23.0	85.6	24.5	85.1	26.0	84.6	27.5	89
90	87.7	20.2	87.3	21.8	86.9	23.3	86.5	24.8	86.1	26.3	85.6	27.8	90
91	88.7	20.5	88.3	22.0	87.9	23.6	87.5	25.1	87.0	26.6	86.5	28.1	91
92	89.6	20.7	89.3	22.3	88.9	23.8	88.4	25.4	88.0	26.9	87.5	28.4	92
93	90.6	20.9	90.2	22.5	89.8	24.1	89.4	25.6	88.9	27.2	88.4	28.7	93
94	91.6	21.1	91.2	22.7	90.8	24.3	90.4	25.9	89.9	27.5	89.4	29.0	94
95	92.6	21.4	92.2	23.0	91.3	24.6	91.3	26.2	90.8	27.8	90.3	29.4	95
96	93.5	21.6	93.1	23.2	92.7	24.8	92.3	26.5	91.8	28.1	91.3	29.7	96
97	94.5	21.8	94.1	23.5	93.7	25.1	93.2	26.7	92.8	28.4	92.2	30.0	97
98	95.5	22.0	95.1	23.7	94.7	25.4	94.2	27.0	93.7	28.6	93.2	30.3	98
99	96.5	22.3	96.1	23.9	95.6	25.6	95.2	27.3	94.7	28.9	94.1	30.6	99
100	97.4	22.5	97.0	24.2	96.6	25.9	96.1	27.6	95.6	29.2	95.1	30.9	100
200	194.9	45.0	194.1	48.4	193.2	51.8	192.3	55.1	191.3	58.5	190.2	61.8	200
300	292.3	67.5	291.1	72.6	289.8	77.6	288.4	82.7	286.9	87.7	285.3	92.7	300
400	389.7	90.0	388.1	96.8	386.4	103.5	384.5	110.2	382.5	116.9	380.4	123.6	400
500	487.2	112.5	485.1	121.0	483.0	129.4	480.6	137.8	478.1	146.2	475.5	154.5	500
600	584.6	135.0	582.2	145.1	579.6	155.3	576.8	165.4	573.8	175.4	570.6	185.4	600
700	682.1	157.5	679.2	169.3	676.1	181.2	672.9	192.9	669.4	204.7	665.7	216.3	700
800	779.5	180.0	776.2	193.5	772.7	207.1	769.0	220.5	765.0	233.9	760.8	247.2	800
900	877.0	202.5	873.3	217.7	869.3	232.9	865.1	248.0	860.7	263.1	856.0	278.1	900
T's.													T's.
1	0.1	0.0	0.1	0.0	0.1	0.0	0.1	0.0	0.1	0.0	0.1	0.0	1
2	0.2	0.0	0.2	0.0	0.2	0.1	0.2	0.1	0.2	0.1	0.2	0.1	2
3	0.3	0.1	0.3	0.1	0.3	0.1	0.3	0.1	0.3	0.1	0.3	0.1	3
4	0.4	0.1	0.4	0.1	0.4	0.1	0.4	0.1	0.4	0.1	0.4	0.1	4
5	0.5	0.1	0.5	0.1	0.5	0.1	0.5	0.1	0.5	0.1	0.5	0.1	5
6	0.6	0.1	0.6	0.1	0.6	0.1	0.6	0.2	0.6	0.2	0.6	0.2	6
7	0.7	0.2	0.7	0.2	0.7	0.2	0.7	0.2	0.7	0.2	0.7	0.2	7
8	0.8	0.2	0.8	0.2	0.8	0.2	0.8	0.2	0.8	0.2	0.8	0.2	8
9	0.9	0.2	0.8	0.2	0.9	0.2	0.9	0.2	0.9	0.2	0.9	0.3	9
dist	dep.	lat.	dep.	lat.	dep.	lat.	dep.	lat.	dep.	lat.	dep.	lat	dist
T's.	77 Degrees		76 Degrees		75 Degrees		74 Degrees		73 Degrees		72 Degrees		T's.

Ms	19 Degrees		20 Degrees		21 Degrees		22 Degrees		23 Degrees		24 Degrees		Ms
dist	lat.	dep.	lat.	dep.	lat.	dep.	lat.	dep.	lat.	dep.	lat.	dep.	dist
1	00.9	00.3	00.9	00.3	00.9	00.4	00.9	00.4	00.9	00.4	00.9	00.4	1
2	01.9	00.7	01.9	00.7	01.9	00.7	01.9	00.7	01.8	00.8	01.8	00.8	2
3	02.8	01.0	02.8	01.0	02.8	01.1	02.8	01.1	02.8	01.2	02.7	01.2	3
4	03.8	01.3	03.8	01.4	03.7	01.4	03.7	01.5	03.7	01.6	03.7	01.6	4
5	04.7	01.6	04.7	01.7	04.7	01.8	04.6	01.9	04.6	01.9	04.6	02.0	5
6	05.7	02.0	05.6	02.1	05.6	02.2	05.6	02.2	05.5	02.3	05.5	02.4	6
7	06.6	02.3	06.6	02.4	06.5	02.5	06.5	02.6	06.4	02.7	06.4	02.8	7
8	07.6	02.6	07.5	02.7	07.5	02.9	07.4	03.0	07.4	03.1	07.3	03.3	8
9	08.5	02.9	08.5	03.1	08.4	03.2	08.3	03.4	08.3	03.5	08.2	03.7	9
10	09.5	03.3	09.4	03.4	09.3	03.6	09.3	03.7	09.2	03.9	09.1	04.1	10
11	10.4	03.6	10.3	03.8	10.3	03.9	10.2	04.1	10.1	04.3	10.0	04.5	11
12	11.3	03.9	11.3	04.1	11.2	04.3	11.1	04.5	11.0	04.7	11.0	04.9	12
13	12.3	04.2	12.2	04.4	12.1	04.7	12.1	04.9	12.0	05.1	11.9	05.3	13
14	13.2	04.6	13.2	04.8	13.1	05.0	13.0	05.2	12.9	05.5	12.8	05.7	14
15	14.2	04.9	14.1	05.1	14.0	05.4	13.9	05.6	13.8	05.9	13.7	06.1	15
16	15.1	05.2	15.0	05.5	14.9	05.7	14.8	06.0	14.7	06.3	14.6	06.5	16
17	16.1	05.5	16.0	05.8	15.9	06.1	15.8	06.4	15.6	06.6	15.5	06.9	17
18	17.0	05.9	16.9	06.2	16.8	06.5	16.7	06.7	16.6	07.0	16.4	07.3	18
19	18.0	06.2	17.9	06.5	17.7	06.8	17.6	07.1	17.5	07.4	17.4	07.7	19
20	18.9	06.5	18.8	06.8	18.7	07.3	18.5	07.5	18.4	07.8	18.3	08.1	20
21	19.9	06.8	19.7	07.2	19.6	07.5	19.5	07.9	19.3	08.2	19.2	08.5	21
22	20.8	07.2	20.7	07.5	20.5	07.9	20.4	08.2	20.3	08.6	20.1	08.9	22
23	21.7	07.5	21.6	07.9	21.5	08.2	21.3	08.6	21.2	09.0	21.0	09.3	23
24	22.7	07.8	22.6	08.2	22.4	08.6	22.3	09.0	22.1	09.4	21.9	09.8	24
25	23.6	08.1	23.5	08.6	23.3	09.0	23.2	09.4	23.0	09.8	22.8	10.2	25
26	24.6	08.5	24.4	08.9	24.3	09.3	24.1	09.7	23.9	10.2	23.8	10.6	26
27	25.5	08.8	25.4	09.2	25.2	09.7	25.0	10.1	24.9	10.5	24.7	11.0	27
28	26.5	09.1	26.3	09.6	26.1	10.0	26.0	10.5	25.8	10.9	25.6	11.4	28
29	27.4	09.4	27.3	09.9	27.1	10.4	26.9	10.9	26.7	11.3	26.5	11.8	29
30	28.4	09.8	28.2	10.3	28.0	10.8	27.8	11.2	27.6	11.7	27.4	12.2	30
31	29.3	10.1	29.1	10.6	28.9	11.1	28.7	11.6	28.5	12.1	28.3	12.6	31
32	30.3	10.4	30.1	10.9	29.9	11.5	29.7	12.0	29.5	12.5	29.2	13.0	32
33	31.2	10.7	31.0	11.3	30.8	11.8	30.6	12.4	30.4	12.9	30.1	13.4	33
34	32.1	11.1	32.0	11.6	31.7	12.2	31.5	12.7	31.3	13.3	31.1	13.8	34
35	33.1	11.4	32.9	12.0	32.7	12.5	32.5	13.1	32.2	13.7	32.0	14.2	35
36	34.0	11.7	33.8	12.3	33.6	12.9	33.4	13.5	33.1	14.1	32.9	14.6	36
37	35.0	12.0	34.8	12.7	34.5	13.3	34.3	13.9	34.1	14.5	33.8	15.0	37
38	35.9	12.4	35.7	13.0	35.5	13.6	35.2	14.3	35.0	14.8	34.7	15.5	38
39	36.9	12.7	36.6	13.3	36.4	14.0	36.2	14.6	35.9	15.2	35.6	15.9	39
40	37.8	13.0	37.6	13.7	37.3	14.3	37.1	15.0	36.8	15.6	36.5	16.3	40
41	38.8	13.3	38.5	14.0	38.3	14.7	38.0	15.4	37.7	16.0	37.5	16.7	41
42	39.7	13.7	39.5	14.4	39.2	15.1	38.9	15.7	38.7	16.4	38.4	17.1	42
43	40.7	14.0	40.4	14.7	40.2	15.4	39.9	16.1	39.6	16.8	39.3	17.5	43
44	41.6	14.3	41.3	15.0	41.1	15.8	40.8	16.5	40.5	17.2	40.2	17.9	44
45	42.5	14.7	42.3	15.4	42.0	16.1	41.7	16.9	41.4	17.6	41.1	18.3	45
46	43.5	15.0	43.2	15.7	42.9	16.5	42.7	17.2	42.3	18.0	42.0	18.7	46
47	44.4	15.3	44.2	16.1	43.9	16.8	43.6	17.6	43.3	18.4	42.9	19.1	47
48	45.4	15.6	45.1	16.4	44.8	17.2	44.5	18.0	44.2	18.8	43.8	19.5	48
49	46.3	16.0	46.0	16.8	45.7	17.6	45.5	18.4	45.1	19.1	44.8	19.9	49
50	47.3	16.3	47.0	17.1	46.7	17.9	46.4	18.7	46.0	19.5	45.7	20.3	50
51	48.2	16.6	47.9	17.4	47.6	18.3	47.3	19.1	46.9	19.9	46.6	20.7	51
52	49.2	16.9	48.9	17.8	48.5	18.6	48.2	19.5	47.9	20.3	47.5	21.1	52
53	50.1	17.3	49.8	18.1	49.5	19.0	49.1	19.9	48.8	20.7	48.4	21.6	53
54	51.1	17.6	50.7	18.5	50.4	19.4	50.1	20.1	49.7	21.1	49.3	22.0	54
55	52.0	17.9	51.7	18.8	51.3	19.7	51.0	20.6	50.6	21.5	50.2	22.4	55
56	52.9	18.2	52.6	19.2	52.3	20.1	51.9	21.0	51.5	21.9	51.2	22.8	56
57	53.9	18.6	53.6	19.5	53.2	20.4	52.9	21.4	52.5	22.3	52.1	23.2	57
58	54.8	18.9	54.5	19.8	54.1	20.8	53.8	21.7	53.4	22.7	53.0	23.6	58
59	55.8	19.2	55.4	20.2	55.1	21.1	54.7	22.1	54.3	23.1	53.9	24.0	59
dist	dep.	lat.	dep.	lat.	dep.	lat.	dep.	lat.	dep.	lat.	dep.	lat.	dist
Ms	71 Degrees		70 Degrees		69 Degrees		68 Degrees		67 Degrees		66 Degrees		Ms

Ms.	19 Degrees		20 Degrees		21 Degrees		22 Degrees		23 Degrees		24 Degrees		M.
dist	lat.	dep.	lat.	dep.	lat.	dep.	lat.	dep.	lat.	dep.	lat.	dep.	dist
60	56.7	19.5	56.4	20.5	56.0	21.5	55.6	22.4	55.2	23.4	54.8	24.4	60
61	57.7	19.9	57.3	20.9	56.9	21.9	56.6	22.9	56.1	23.8	55.7	24.8	61
62	58.6	20.2	58.3	21.2	57.9	22.2	57.5	23.2	57.1	24.2	56.6	25.2	62
63	59.6	20.5	59.2	21.5	58.8	22.6	58.4	23.6	58.0	24.6	57.6	25.6	63
64	60.5	20.8	60.1	21.9	59.7	22.9	59.3	24.0	58.9	25.0	58.5	26.0	64
65	61.5	21.2	61.1	22.2	60.7	23.3	60.3	24.3	59.8	25.4	59.4	26.4	65
66	62.4	21.5	62.0	22.6	61.6	23.7	61.2	24.7	60.8	25.8	60.3	26.8	66
67	63.3	21.8	63.0	22.9	62.5	24.0	62.1	25.1	61.7	26.2	61.2	27.2	67
68	64.3	22.1	63.9	23.2	63.5	24.4	63.0	25.3	62.6	26.6	62.1	27.7	68
69	65.2	22.5	64.8	23.6	64.4	24.7	64.0	25.8	63.5	27.0	63.0	28.1	69
70	66.2	22.8	65.8	23.9	65.3	25.1	64.9	26.2	64.4	27.3	63.9	28.5	70
71	67.1	23.1	66.7	24.3	66.3	25.4	65.8	26.6	65.4	27.7	64.9	28.9	71
72	68.1	23.4	67.7	24.6	67.2	25.8	66.8	27.0	66.3	28.1	65.8	29.3	72
73	69.0	23.8	68.6	25.0	68.1	26.2	67.7	27.3	67.2	28.5	66.7	29.7	73
74	70.0	24.1	69.5	25.3	69.1	26.5	68.6	27.7	68.1	28.9	67.6	30.1	74
75	70.9	24.4	70.5	25.7	70.0	26.9	69.5	28.1	69.0	29.3	68.5	30.5	75
76	71.9	24.7	71.4	26.0	70.9	27.2	70.5	28.5	70.0	29.7	69.4	30.9	76
77	72.8	25.1	72.4	26.3	71.9	27.6	71.4	28.8	70.9	30.1	70.3	31.3	77
78	73.7	25.4	73.3	26.7	72.8	28.0	72.3	29.2	71.8	30.5	71.3	31.7	78
79	74.7	25.7	74.2	27.0	73.7	28.3	73.2	29.6	72.7	30.9	72.2	32.1	79
80	75.6	26.0	75.2	27.4	74.7	28.7	74.2	30.0	73.6	31.3	73.1	32.5	80
81	76.6	26.4	76.1	27.7	75.6	29.0	75.1	30.3	74.6	31.6	74.0	32.9	81
82	77.5	26.7	77.1	28.0	76.5	29.4	76.0	30.7	75.5	32.0	74.9	33.3	82
83	78.5	27.0	78.0	28.4	77.5	29.7	77.0	31.1	76.4	32.4	75.8	33.8	83
84	79.4	27.4	78.9	28.7	78.4	30.1	77.9	31.5	77.3	32.8	76.7	34.2	84
85	80.4	27.7	79.9	29.1	79.3	30.5	78.8	31.8	78.2	33.2	77.6	34.6	85
86	81.3	28.0	80.8	29.4	80.3	30.8	79.7	32.2	79.2	33.6	78.6	35.0	86
87	82.3	28.3	81.8	29.8	81.2	31.2	80.7	32.6	80.1	34.0	79.5	35.4	87
88	83.2	28.7	82.7	30.1	82.1	31.5	81.6	33.0	81.0	34.4	80.4	35.8	88
89	84.1	29.0	83.6	30.4	83.1	31.9	82.5	33.3	81.9	34.8	81.3	36.2	89
90	85.1	29.3	84.6	30.8	84.0	32.3	83.4	33.7	82.8	35.2	82.2	36.6	90
91	86.0	29.6	85.3	31.1	84.9	32.6	84.4	34.1	83.8	35.6	83.1	37.0	91
92	87.0	30.0	86.5	31.3	85.9	33.0	85.3	34.5	84.7	35.9	84.0	37.4	92
93	87.9	30.3	87.4	31.8	86.8	33.3	86.2	34.8	85.6	36.3	85.0	37.8	93
94	88.9	30.6	88.3	32.1	87.7	33.7	87.2	35.2	86.5	36.7	85.9	38.2	94
95	89.8	30.9	89.3	32.5	88.7	34.0	88.1	35.6	87.4	37.1	86.8	38.6	95
96	90.8	31.3	90.2	32.8	89.6	34.4	89.0	36.0	88.4	37.5	87.7	39.0	96
97	91.7	31.6	91.2	33.2	90.5	34.8	89.9	36.3	89.3	37.9	88.6	39.4	97
98	92.7	31.9	92.1	33.5	91.5	35.1	90.9	36.7	90.2	38.3	89.5	39.9	98
99	93.6	32.2	93.0	33.9	92.4	35.5	91.8	37.1	91.1	38.7	90.4	40.3	99
100	94.5	32.6	94.0	34.2	93.4	35.8	92.7	37.5	92.0	39.1	91.4	40.7	100
200	189.1	65.1	187.9	68.4	186.7	71.7	185.4	74.9	184.1	78.1	182.7	81.3	200
300	283.7	97.7	281.9	102.6	280.1	107.5	278.2	112.4	276.1	117.2	274.1	122.0	300
400	378.2	130.2	375.9	136.8	373.4	143.3	370.9	149.8	368.2	156.3	365.4	162.7	400
500	472.8	162.8	469.8	171.0	466.8	179.2	463.6	187.3	460.2	195.4	456.8	203.4	500
600	567.3	195.3	563.8	205.2	560.1	215.0	556.3	224.6	552.3	234.4	548.1	244.0	600
700	661.9	227.9	657.8	239.4	653.5	250.9	649.0	262.2	644.3	273.5	639.5	284.7	700
800	756.4	260.5	751.7	273.6	746.9	286.7	741.7	299.7	736.4	312.6	730.8	325.4	800
900	850.9	293.0	845.7	307.8	840.2	322.5	834.5	337.1	828.4	351.7	822.2	366.1	900
1 s.													1 s.
1	0.1	0.0	0.1	0.0	0.1	0.0	0.1	0.0	0.1	0.0	0.1	0.0	1
2	0.2	0.1	0.2	0.1	0.2	0.1	0.2	0.1	0.2	0.1	0.2	0.1	2
3	0.3	0.1	0.3	0.1	0.3	0.1	0.3	0.1	0.3	0.1	0.3	0.1	3
4	0.4	0.1	0.4	0.1	0.4	0.1	0.4	0.1	0.4	0.2	0.4	0.2	4
5	0.5	0.2	0.5	0.2	0.5	0.2	0.5	0.2	0.5	0.2	0.5	0.2	5
6	0.6	0.2	0.6	0.2	0.6	0.2	0.6	0.2	0.6	0.2	0.5	0.2	6
7	0.7	0.2	0.7	0.2	0.7	0.3	0.6	0.3	0.6	0.3	0.6	0.3	7
8	0.8	0.3	0.8	0.3	0.7	0.3	0.7	0.3	0.7	0.3	0.7	0.3	8
9	0.9	0.3	0.8	0.3	0.8	0.3	0.8	0.3	0.8	0.4	0.8	0.4	9
dist	dep	lat.	dep	lat.	dep	lat.	dep	lat.	dep	lat.	dep	lat.	dist
1 s.	71 Degrees		70 Degrees		69 Degrees		68 Degrees		67 Degrees		66 Degrees		T s.

Di	25 Degrees		26 Degrees		27 Degrees		28 Degrees		29 Degrees		30 Degrees		Di
dist	lat.	dep.	lat.	dep.	lat.	dep.	lat.	dep.	lat.	dep.	lat.	dep.	dist
1	00.9	00.4	00.9	00.4	00.9	00.5	00.9	00.5	00.9	00.5	00.9	00.5	1
2	01.8	00.8	01.8	00.9	01.8	00.9	01.8	00.9	01.7	01.0	01.7	01.0	2
3	02.7	01.3	02.7	01.3	02.7	01.4	02.6	01.4	02.6	01.5	02.6	01.5	3
4	03.6	01.7	03.6	01.8	03.6	01.8	03.5	01.9	03.5	01.9	03.5	02.0	4
5	04.5	02.1	04.5	02.2	04.5	02.3	04.4	02.3	04.4	02.4	04.3	02.5	5
6	05.4	02.5	05.4	02.6	05.3	02.7	05.3	02.8	05.2	02.9	05.2	03.0	6
7	06.3	03.0	06.3	03.1	06.2	03.2	06.2	03.3	06.1	03.4	06.1	03.5	7
8	07.2	03.4	07.2	03.5	07.1	03.6	07.1	03.8	07.0	03.9	06.9	04.0	8
9	08.2	03.8	08.1	03.9	08.0	04.1	08.0	04.2	07.9	04.4	07.8	04.5	9
10	09.1	04.2	09.0	04.4	08.9	04.5	08.8	04.7	08.7	04.8	08.7	05.0	10
11	10.0	04.6	09.9	04.8	09.8	05.0	09.7	05.2	09.6	05.3	09.5	05.5	11
12	10.9	05.1	10.8	05.3	10.7	05.4	10.6	05.6	10.5	05.8	10.4	06.0	12
13	11.8	05.5	11.7	05.7	11.6	05.9	11.5	06.1	11.4	06.3	11.3	06.5	13
14	12.7	05.9	12.6	06.1	12.5	06.4	12.4	06.6	12.2	06.8	12.1	07.0	14
15	13.6	06.3	13.5	06.6	13.4	06.8	13.2	07.0	13.1	07.3	13.0	07.5	15
16	14.5	06.8	14.4	07.0	14.3	07.3	14.1	07.5	14.0	07.8	13.9	08.0	16
17	15.4	07.2	15.3	07.5	15.1	07.7	15.0	08.0	14.9	08.2	14.7	08.5	17
18	16.3	07.6	16.2	07.9	16.0	08.2	15.9	08.5	15.7	08.7	15.6	09.0	18
19	17.2	08.0	17.1	08.3	16.9	08.6	16.8	08.9	16.6	09.2	16.5	09.5	19
20	18.1	08.5	18.0	08.8	17.8	09.1	17.7	09.4	17.5	09.7	17.3	10.0	20
21	19.0	08.9	18.9	09.2	18.7	09.5	18.5	09.9	18.4	10.2	18.2	10.5	21
22	19.9	09.3	19.8	09.6	19.6	10.0	19.4	10.3	19.2	10.7	19.1	11.0	22
23	20.8	09.7	20.7	10.1	20.5	10.4	20.3	10.8	20.1	11.2	19.9	11.5	23
24	21.8	10.1	21.6	10.5	21.4	10.9	21.2	11.3	21.0	11.6	20.8	12.0	24
25	22.7	10.6	22.5	11.0	22.3	11.4	22.1	11.7	21.9	12.1	21.7	12.5	25
26	23.6	11.0	23.4	11.4	23.2	11.8	23.0	12.2	22.7	12.6	22.5	13.0	26
27	24.5	11.4	24.3	11.8	24.1	12.3	23.8	12.7	23.6	13.1	23.4	13.5	27
28	25.4	11.8	25.2	12.3	24.9	12.7	24.7	13.1	24.5	13.6	24.2	14.0	28
29	26.3	12.3	26.1	12.7	25.8	13.2	25.6	13.6	25.4	14.1	25.1	14.5	29
30	27.2	12.7	27.0	13.2	26.7	13.6	26.5	14.1	26.2	14.5	26.0	15.0	30
31	28.1	13.1	27.9	13.6	27.6	14.1	27.4	14.6	27.1	15.0	26.8	15.5	31
32	29.0	13.5	28.8	14.0	28.5	14.5	28.3	15.0	28.0	15.5	27.7	16.0	32
33	29.9	13.9	29.7	14.5	29.4	15.0	29.1	15.5	28.9	16.0	28.6	16.5	33
34	30.8	14.4	30.6	14.9	30.3	15.4	30.0	16.0	29.7	16.5	29.4	17.0	34
35	31.7	14.8	31.5	15.3	31.2	15.9	30.9	16.4	30.6	17.0	30.3	17.5	35
36	32.6	15.2	32.4	15.8	32.1	16.3	31.8	16.9	31.5	17.5	31.2	18.0	36
37	33.5	15.6	33.3	16.2	33.0	16.8	32.7	17.4	32.4	17.9	32.0	18.5	37
38	34.4	16.1	34.2	16.7	33.9	17.3	33.6	17.8	33.2	18.4	32.9	19.0	38
39	35.3	16.5	35.1	17.1	34.7	17.7	34.4	18.3	34.1	18.9	33.8	19.5	39
40	36.3	16.9	36.0	17.5	35.6	18.2	35.3	18.8	35.0	19.4	34.6	20.0	40
41	37.2	17.3	36.9	18.0	36.5	18.6	36.2	19.2	35.9	19.9	35.5	20.5	41
42	38.1	17.7	37.7	18.4	37.4	19.1	37.1	19.7	36.7	20.4	36.4	21.0	42
43	39.0	18.2	38.6	18.9	38.3	19.5	38.0	20.2	37.6	20.8	37.2	21.5	43
44	39.9	18.6	39.5	19.3	39.2	20.0	38.9	20.7	38.5	21.3	38.1	22.0	44
45	40.8	19.0	40.4	19.7	40.1	20.4	39.7	21.1	39.4	21.8	39.0	22.5	45
46	41.7	19.4	41.3	20.2	41.0	20.9	40.6	21.6	40.2	22.3	39.8	23.0	46
47	42.6	19.9	42.2	20.6	41.9	21.3	41.5	22.1	41.1	22.8	40.7	23.5	47
48	43.5	20.3	43.1	21.0	42.8	21.8	42.4	22.5	42.0	23.3	41.6	24.0	48
49	44.4	20.7	44.0	21.5	43.7	22.2	43.3	23.0	42.9	23.8	42.4	24.5	49
50	45.3	21.1	44.9	21.9	44.6	22.7	44.2	23.5	43.7	24.2	43.3	25.0	50
51	46.2	21.6	45.8	22.4	45.4	23.2	45.0	23.9	44.6	24.7	44.2	25.5	51
52	47.1	22.0	46.7	22.8	46.3	23.6	45.9	24.4	45.5	25.2	45.0	26.0	52
53	48.0	22.4	47.6	23.2	47.2	24.1	46.8	24.9	46.4	25.7	45.9	26.5	53
54	48.9	22.8	48.5	23.7	48.1	24.5	47.7	25.4	47.2	26.2	46.8	27.0	54
55	49.8	23.2	49.4	24.1	49.0	25.0	48.6	25.8	48.1	26.7	47.6	27.5	55
56	50.8	23.7	50.3	24.6	49.9	25.4	49.4	26.3	49.0	27.1	48.5	28.0	56
57	51.7	24.1	51.2	25.0	50.8	25.9	50.3	26.8	49.9	27.6	49.4	28.5	57
58	52.6	24.5	52.1	25.4	51.7	26.3	51.2	27.2	50.7	28.1	50.2	29.0	58
59	53.5	24.9	53.0	25.9	52.6	26.8	52.1	27.7	51.6	28.6	51.1	29.5	59
dist	dep.	lat.	dep.	lat.	dep.	lat.	dep.	lat.	dep.	lat.	dep.	lat.	dist
Mi	65 Degrees		64 Degrees		63 Degrees		62 Degrees		61 Degrees		60 Degrees		Mi

Ms.	25 Degrees		26 Degrees		27 Degrees		28 Degrees		29 Degrees		30 Degrees		Ms.
dist	lat.	dep.	lat.	dep.	lat.	dep.	lat.	dep.	lat.	dep.	lat.	dep.	dist
60	54.4	25.4	53.9	26.3	53.5	27.2	53.0	28.2	52.5	29.1	52.0	30.0	60
61	55.3	25.8	54.8	26.7	54.4	27.7	53.9	28.6	53.4	29.6	52.8	30.5	61
62	56.2	26.2	55.7	27.2	55.2	28.1	54.7	29.1	54.2	30.1	53.7	31.0	62
63	57.1	26.6	56.6	27.6	56.1	28.6	55.6	29.6	55.1	30.5	54.6	31.5	63
64	58.0	27.0	57.5	28.1	57.0	29.1	56.5	30.0	56.0	31.0	55.4	32.0	64
65	58.9	27.5	58.4	28.5	57.9	29.5	57.4	30.5	56.8	31.5	56.3	32.5	65
66	59.8	27.9	59.3	28.9	58.8	30.0	58.3	31.0	57.7	32.0	57.2	33.0	66
67	60.7	28.3	60.2	29.4	59.7	30.4	59.2	31.5	58.6	32.5	58.0	33.5	67
68	61.6	28.7	61.1	29.8	60.6	30.9	60.0	31.9	59.5	33.0	58.9	34.0	68
69	62.5	29.2	62.0	30.2	61.5	31.3	60.9	32.4	60.3	33.5	59.8	34.5	69
70	63.4	29.6	62.9	30.7	62.4	31.8	61.8	32.9	61.2	33.9	60.6	35.0	70
71	64.3	30.0	63.8	31.1	63.3	32.2	62.7	33.3	62.1	34.4	61.5	35.5	71
72	65.3	30.4	64.7	31.6	64.2	32.7	63.6	33.8	63.0	34.9	62.4	36.0	72
73	66.2	30.8	65.6	32.0	65.0	33.1	64.5	34.3	63.8	35.4	63.2	36.5	73
74	67.1	31.3	66.5	32.4	65.9	33.6	65.3	34.7	64.7	35.9	64.1	37.0	74
75	68.0	31.7	67.4	32.9	66.8	34.1	66.2	35.2	65.6	36.4	65.0	37.5	75
76	68.9	32.1	68.3	33.3	67.7	34.5	67.1	35.7	66.5	36.8	65.8	38.0	76
77	69.8	32.5	69.2	33.8	68.6	35.0	68.0	36.2	67.3	37.3	66.7	38.5	77
78	70.7	33.0	70.1	34.4	69.5	35.4	68.9	36.6	68.2	37.8	67.5	39.0	78
79	71.6	33.4	71.0	34.6	70.4	35.9	69.8	37.1	69.1	38.3	68.4	39.5	79
80	72.5	33.8	71.9	35.1	71.3	36.3	70.6	37.6	70.0	38.8	69.3	40.0	80
81	73.4	34.2	72.8	35.5	72.2	36.8	71.5	38.0	70.8	39.3	70.1	40.5	81
82	74.3	34.7	73.7	35.9	73.1	37.2	72.4	38.5	71.7	39.8	71.0	41.0	82
83	75.2	35.1	74.6	36.4	74.0	37.7	73.3	39.0	72.6	40.2	71.9	41.5	83
84	76.1	35.5	75.5	36.8	74.8	38.1	74.2	39.4	73.5	40.7	72.7	42.0	84
85	77.0	35.9	76.4	37.3	75.7	38.6	75.1	39.9	74.3	41.2	73.6	42.5	85
86	77.9	36.3	77.3	37.7	76.6	39.0	75.9	40.4	75.2	41.7	74.5	43.0	86
87	78.8	36.8	78.2	38.1	77.5	39.5	76.8	40.8	76.1	42.2	75.3	43.5	87
88	79.8	37.2	79.1	38.6	78.4	40.0	77.7	41.3	77.0	42.7	76.2	44.0	88
89	80.7	37.6	80.0	39.0	79.3	40.4	78.6	41.8	77.8	43.1	77.1	44.5	89
90	81.6	38.0	80.9	39.5	80.2	40.9	79.5	42.3	78.7	43.6	77.9	45.0	90
91	82.5	38.5	81.8	39.8	81.1	41.3	80.4	42.7	79.6	44.1	78.8	45.5	91
92	83.4	38.9	82.7	40.3	82.0	41.8	81.2	43.2	80.5	44.6	79.7	46.0	92
93	84.3	39.3	83.6	40.8	82.9	42.2	82.1	43.7	81.3	45.1	80.5	46.5	93
94	85.2	39.7	84.5	41.2	83.8	42.7	83.0	44.1	82.2	45.6	81.4	47.0	94
95	86.1	40.1	85.4	41.6	84.6	43.1	83.9	44.6	83.1	46.1	82.3	47.5	95
96	87.0	40.6	86.3	42.1	85.5	43.6	84.8	45.1	84.0	46.5	83.1	48.0	96
97	87.9	41.0	87.2	42.5	86.4	44.0	85.7	45.5	84.8	47.0	84.0	48.5	97
98	88.8	41.4	88.1	43.0	87.3	44.5	86.5	46.0	85.7	47.5	84.9	49.0	98
99	89.7	41.8	89.0	43.4	88.2	44.9	87.4	46.5	86.6	48.0	85.7	49.5	99
100	90.6	42.3	89.9	43.8	89.1	45.4	88.3	47.0	87.5	48.5	86.6	50.0	100
200	181.3	84.5	179.8	87.7	178.2	90.8	176.6	93.9	174.9	96.9	173.2	100.0	200
300	271.9	126.8	289.6	131.5	267.3	136.2	264.9	140.8	262.4	145.4	259.8	150.0	300
400	362.5	169.0	359.5	175.3	356.4	181.6	353.2	187.8	349.8	193.9	346.4	200.0	400
500	453.1	211.3	449.4	219.2	445.5	227.0	441.5	234.7	437.3	242.4	433.0	250.0	500
600	543.8	253.6	539.3	263.0	534.6	272.4	529.8	281.7	524.8	290.9	519.6	300.0	600
700	634.4	295.8	629.2	306.9	623.7	317.8	618.1	328.6	612.2	339.4	606.2	350.0	700
800	725.0	338.1	719.0	350.7	712.9	363.2	706.4	375.6	699.7	387.8	692.8	400.0	800
900	815.7	380.4	808.9	394.5	802.0	408.6	794.6	422.5	787.2	436.3	779.4	450.0	900
Ts.													Ts.
1	0.1	0.0	0.1	0.0	0.1	0.0	0.1	0.0	0.1	0.0	0.1	0.0	1
2	0.2	0.1	0.2	0.1	0.2	0.1	0.2	0.1	0.2	0.1	0.2	0.1	2
3	0.3	0.1	0.3	0.1	0.3	0.1	0.3	0.1	0.3	0.1	0.3	0.1	3
4	0.4	0.2	0.4	0.2	0.4	0.2	0.4	0.2	0.4	0.2	0.3	0.2	4
5	0.5	0.2	0.4	0.2	0.4	0.2	0.4	0.2	0.4	0.2	0.4	0.2	5
6	0.5	0.3	0.5	0.3	0.5	0.3	0.5	0.3	0.5	0.3	0.5	0.3	6
7	0.6	0.3	0.6	0.3	0.6	0.3	0.6	0.3	0.6	0.3	0.6	0.3	7
8	0.7	0.3	0.7	0.4	0.7	0.4	0.7	0.4	0.7	0.4	0.7	0.4	8
9	0.8	0.4	0.8	0.4	0.8	0.4	0.8	0.4	0.8	0.4	0.8	0.4	9
dist	dep.	lat.	dep.	lat.	dep.	lat.	dep.	lat.	dep.	lat.	dep.	lat.	dist
Ts.	65 Degrees		64 Degrees		63 Degrees		62 Degrees		61 Degrees		60 Degrees		Ts.

K

Ms	31 Degrees		32 Degrees		33 Degrees		34 Degrees		35 Degrees		36 Degrees		Ms
dift	lat.	dep.	lat.	dep.	lat.	dep.	lat.	dep.	lat.	dep.	lat.	dep.	dift
1	00.9	00.5	00.8	00.5	00.8	00.5	00.8	00.6	00.8	00.6	00.8	00.6	1
2	01.7	01.0	01.7	01.1	01.7	01.1	01.7	01.1	01.6	01.1	01.6	01.2	2
3	02.6	01.5	02.5	01.6	02.5	01.6	02.5	01.7	02.5	01.7	02.4	01.8	3
4	03.4	02.1	03.4	02.1	03.4	02.2	03.3	02.2	03.3	02.3	03.2	02.4	4
5	04.3	02.6	04.2	02.6	04.2	02.7	04.1	02.8	04.1	02.9	04.0	02.9	5
6	05.1	03.1	05.1	03.2	05.0	03.3	05.0	03.4	04.9	03.4	04.9	03.5	6
7	06.0	03.6	05.9	03.7	05.9	03.8	05.8	03.9	05.7	04.0	05.7	04.1	7
8	06.9	04.1	06.8	04.2	06.7	04.4	06.6	04.5	06.6	04.6	06.5	04.7	8
9	07.8	04.6	07.6	04.8	07.5	04.9	07.5	05.0	07.4	05.2	07.3	05.3	9
10	08.6	05.2	08.5	05.3	08.4	05.4	08.3	05.6	08.2	05.7	08.1	05.9	10
11	09.4	05.7	09.3	05.8	09.2	06.0	09.1	06.2	09.0	06.3	08.9	06.5	11
12	10.3	06.2	10.2	06.4	10.1	06.5	09.9	06.7	09.8	06.9	09.7	07.1	12
13	11.1	06.7	11.0	06.9	10.9	07.1	10.8	07.3	10.6	07.5	10.5	07.6	13
14	12.0	07.2	11.9	07.4	11.7	07.6	11.6	07.8	11.4	08.0	11.3	08.2	14
15	12.9	07.7	12.7	08.0	12.6	08.2	12.4	08.4	12.3	08.6	12.1	08.8	15
16	13.7	08.2	13.6	08.5	13.4	08.7	13.3	08.9	13.1	09.2	12.9	09.4	16
17	14.6	08.8	14.4	09.0	14.3	09.3	14.1	09.5	13.9	09.7	13.8	10.0	17
18	15.4	09.3	15.3	09.5	15.1	09.8	14.9	10.1	14.7	10.3	14.6	10.6	18
19	16.3	09.8	16.1	10.1	15.9	10.3	15.7	10.6	15.6	10.9	15.4	11.2	19
20	17.1	10.3	17.0	10.6	16.8	10.9	16.6	11.2	16.4	11.5	16.2	11.8	20
21	18.0	10.8	17.8	11.1	17.6	11.4	17.4	11.7	17.2	12.0	17.0	12.2	21
22	18.9	11.3	18.7	11.7	18.4	12.0	18.2	12.3	18.0	12.6	17.8	12.9	22
23	19.7	11.8	19.5	12.2	19.3	12.5	19.1	12.9	18.8	13.2	18.6	13.5	23
24	20.6	12.4	20.4	12.7	20.1	13.1	19.9	13.4	19.7	13.8	19.4	14.1	24
25	21.4	12.9	21.2	13.2	21.0	13.6	20.7	14.0	20.5	14.3	20.2	14.7	25
26	22.3	13.4	22.0	13.8	21.8	14.2	21.6	14.5	21.3	14.9	21.0	15.3	26
27	23.1	13.9	22.9	14.3	22.6	14.7	22.4	15.1	22.1	15.5	21.8	15.9	27
28	24.0	14.4	23.7	14.8	23.5	15.2	23.2	15.7	22.9	16.1	22.7	16.5	28
29	24.9	14.9	24.6	15.4	24.3	15.8	24.0	16.2	23.8	16.8	23.5	17.0	29
30	25.7	15.5	25.4	15.9	25.2	16.3	24.9	16.8	24.6	17.2	24.3	17.6	30
31	26.6	16.0	26.3	16.4	26.0	16.9	25.7	17.3	25.4	17.8	25.1	18.2	31
32	27.4	16.5	27.1	17.0	26.8	17.4	26.5	17.9	26.2	18.4	25.9	18.8	32
33	28.3	17.0	28.0	17.5	27.7	18.0	27.4	18.5	27.0	18.9	26.7	19.4	33
34	29.1	17.5	28.8	18.0	28.5	18.5	28.2	19.0	27.8	19.5	27.5	20.0	34
35	30.0	18.0	29.7	18.6	29.4	19.1	29.0	19.6	28.7	20.1	28.3	20.6	35
36	30.9	18.5	30.5	19.1	30.2	19.6	29.8	20.1	29.5	20.6	29.1	21.2	36
37	31.7	19.1	31.4	19.6	31.0	20.1	30.7	20.7	30.3	21.2	29.9	21.7	37
38	32.6	19.6	32.2	20.1	31.9	20.7	31.5	21.2	31.1	21.8	30.7	22.5	38
39	33.4	20.1	33.1	20.7	32.7	21.2	32.3	21.8	31.9	22.4	31.6	22.9	39
40	34.3	20.6	33.9	21.2	33.5	21.8	33.2	22.4	32.8	22.9	32.4	23.5	40
41	35.1	21.1	34.8	21.7	34.4	22.3	34.0	22.9	33.6	23.5	33.2	24.1	41
42	36.0	21.6	35.6	22.3	35.2	22.9	34.8	23.5	34.4	24.1	34.0	24.7	42
43	36.8	22.1	36.5	22.8	36.0	23.4	35.6	24.0	35.2	24.7	34.8	25.3	43
44	37.7	22.6	37.3	23.3	36.9	24.0	36.5	24.6	36.0	25.2	35.6	25.9	44
45	38.6	23.2	38.2	23.8	37.7	24.5	37.3	25.2	36.9	25.8	36.4	26.5	45
46	39.4	23.7	39.0	24.4	38.6	25.1	38.2	25.7	37.7	26.4	37.2	27.0	46
47	40.3	24.2	39.9	24.9	39.4	25.6	39.0	26.3	38.5	27.0	38.0	27.6	47
48	41.1	24.7	40.7	25.4	40.3	26.1	39.8	26.8	39.3	27.5	38.8	28.2	48
49	42.0	25.2	41.6	26.0	41.1	26.7	40.6	27.4	40.1	28.1	39.6	28.8	49
50	42.9	25.8	42.4	26.5	41.9	27.2	41.5	28.0	41.0	28.7	40.5	29.4	50
51	43.7	26.3	43.2	27.0	42.8	27.8	42.3	28.5	41.8	29.2	41.3	30.0	51
52	44.6	26.8	44.1	27.6	43.6	28.3	43.0	29.1	42.6	29.8	42.1	30.6	52
53	45.4	27.3	44.9	28.1	44.4	28.9	43.9	29.6	43.4	30.4	42.9	31.2	53
54	46.3	27.8	45.8	28.6	45.3	29.4	44.8	30.2	44.2	31.0	43.7	31.7	54
55	47.1	28.3	46.6	29.2	46.1	30.0	45.6	30.8	45.0	31.5	44.5	32.3	55
56	48.0	28.8	47.5	29.7	47.0	30.5	46.4	31.3	45.9	32.1	45.3	32.9	56
57	48.9	29.4	48.3	30.2	47.8	31.0	47.3	31.9	46.7	32.7	46.1	33.5	57
58	49.7	29.9	49.2	30.7	48.6	31.6	48.1	32.4	47.5	33.3	46.9	34.1	58
59	50.6	30.4	50.0	31.3	49.5	32.1	48.9	33.0	48.3	33.8	47.7	34.7	59
dift	dep.	lat.	dep.	lat.	dep.	lat.	dep.	lat.	dep.	lat.	dep.	lat.	dift
Ms	59 Degrees		58 Degrees		57 Degrees		56 Degrees		55 Degrees		54 Degrees		Ms

Ms	31 Degrees		32 Degrees		33 Degrees		34 Degrees		35 Degrees		36 Degrees		Ms
dist	lat.	dep.	lat.	dep.	lat.	dep.	lat.	dep.	lat.	dep.	lat.	dep.	dist
60	51.4	30.9	50.9	31.8	50.3	32.7	49.7	33.6	49.1	34.4	48.5	35.3	60
61	52.3	31.4	51.7	32.3	51.2	33.2	50.6	34.1	50.0	35.0	49.3	35.9	61
62	53.1	31.9	52.6	32.9	52.0	33.8	51.4	34.7	50.8	35.6	50.2	36.4	62
63	54.0	32.4	53.4	33.4	52.8	34.3	52.2	35.2	51.6	36.1	51.0	37.0	63
64	54.9	33.0	54.3	33.9	53.7	34.9	53.1	35.8	52.4	36.7	51.8	37.6	64
65	55.7	33.5	55.1	34.4	54.5	35.4	53.9	36.3	53.2	37.3	52.6	38.2	65
66	56.6	34.0	56.0	35.0	55.3	35.9	54.7	36.9	54.1	37.9	53.4	38.8	66
67	57.4	34.5	56.8	35.5	56.2	36.5	55.5	37.5	54.9	38.4	54.2	39.4	67
68	58.3	35.0	57.7	36.0	57.0	37.0	56.4	38.0	55.7	39.0	55.0	40.0	68
69	59.1	35.5	58.5	36.6	57.9	37.6	57.2	38.6	56.5	39.6	55.8	40.6	69
70	60.0	36.1	59.4	37.1	58.7	38.1	58.0	39.1	57.3	40.1	56.6	41.1	70
71	60.9	36.6	60.2	37.6	59.5	38.7	58.9	39.7	58.2	40.7	57.4	41.7	71
72	61.7	37.1	61.1	38.2	60.4	39.2	59.7	40.3	59.0	41.3	58.2	42.3	72
73	62.6	37.6	61.9	38.7	61.2	39.8	60.5	40.8	59.8	41.9	59.1	42.9	73
74	63.4	38.1	62.8	39.2	62.1	40.3	61.3	41.4	60.6	42.4	59.9	43.5	74
75	64.3	38.6	63.6	39.8	62.9	40.8	62.2	41.9	61.4	43.0	60.7	44.1	75
76	65.1	39.1	64.4	40.3	63.7	41.4	63.0	42.5	62.3	43.6	61.5	44.7	76
77	66.0	39.7	65.3	40.8	64.6	41.9	63.8	43.1	63.1	44.2	62.3	45.3	77
78	66.9	40.1	66.1	41.3	65.4	42.5	64.7	43.6	63.9	44.7	63.1	45.8	78
79	67.7	40.7	67.0	41.9	66.3	43.0	65.5	44.2	64.7	45.3	63.9	46.4	79
80	68.6	41.2	67.8	42.4	67.1	43.6	66.3	44.7	65.5	45.9	64.7	47.0	80
81	69.4	41.7	68.7	42.9	67.9	44.1	67.1	45.3	66.3	46.5	65.5	47.6	81
82	70.3	42.2	69.5	43.5	68.8	44.7	68.0	45.9	67.2	47.0	66.3	48.2	82
83	71.1	42.7	70.4	44.0	69.6	45.2	68.8	46.4	68.0	47.6	67.1	48.8	83
84	72.0	43.3	71.2	44.5	70.4	45.7	69.6	47.0	68.8	48.2	68.0	49.4	84
85	72.9	43.8	72.1	45.0	71.3	46.3	70.5	47.5	69.6	48.8	68.8	50.0	85
86	73.7	44.3	72.9	45.6	72.1	46.8	71.3	48.1	70.4	49.3	69.6	50.6	86
87	74.6	44.8	73.8	46.1	73.0	47.4	72.1	48.7	71.3	49.9	70.4	51.1	87
88	75.4	45.3	74.6	46.6	73.8	47.9	73.0	49.2	72.1	50.3	71.1	51.7	88
89	76.3	45.8	75.5	47.2	74.6	48.5	73.8	49.8	72.9	51.0	72.0	52.3	89
90	77.1	46.4	76.3	47.7	75.5	49.0	74.6	50.3	73.7	51.6	72.8	52.9	90
91	78.0	46.9	77.2	48.2	76.3	49.6	75.4	50.9	74.5	52.2	73.6	53.5	91
92	78.9	47.4	78.0	48.8	77.2	50.1	76.3	51.4	75.4	52.8	74.4	54.1	92
93	79.7	47.9	78.9	49.3	78.0	50.6	77.1	52.0	76.2	53.3	75.2	54.7	93
94	80.6	48.4	79.7	49.8	78.8	51.2	77.9	52.6	77.0	53.9	76.0	55.3	94
95	81.4	48.9	80.6	50.3	79.7	51.7	78.8	53.1	77.8	54.5	76.9	55.8	95
96	82.3	49.4	81.4	50.9	80.5	52.3	79.6	53.7	78.6	55.1	77.7	56.4	96
97	83.1	50.0	82.3	51.4	81.3	52.8	80.4	54.2	79.5	55.6	78.5	57.0	97
98	84.0	50.5	83.1	51.9	82.2	53.4	81.2	54.8	80.3	56.2	79.3	57.6	98
99	84.9	51.0	84.0	52.5	83.0	53.9	82.1	55.4	81.1	56.8	80.1	58.2	99
100	85.7	51.5	84.8	53.0	83.9	54.5	82.9	55.9	81.9	57.4	80.9	58.8	100
200	171.4	103.0	169.6	106.0	167.7	108.9	165.8	111.8	163.8	114.7	161.8	117.5	200
300	257.1	154.5	254.4	159.0	251.6	163.4	248.7	167.7	245.7	172.1	242.7	176.3	300
400	342.9	206.0	339.2	212.0	335.5	217.9	331.6	223.7	327.7	229.4	323.6	235.1	400
500	428.6	257.5	424.0	265.0	419.3	272.3	414.5	279.6	409.6	286.8	404.5	293.9	500
600	514.3	309.0	508.8	317.9	503.2	326.8	497.4	335.5	491.5	344.1	485.4	352.7	600
700	600.0	360.5	593.6	370.9	587.1	381.2	580.3	391.4	573.4	401.5	566.3	411.4	700
800	685.7	412.0	678.4	423.9	670.9	435.7	663.2	447.3	655.3	458.8	647.2	470.2	800
900	771.4	463.5	763.2	476.9	754.8	490.2	746.1	503.3	737.2	516.2	728.1	529.0	900
1 s.													1 s.
1	0.1	0.1	0.1	0.1	0.1	0.1	0.1	0.1	0.1	0.1	0.1	0.1	1
2	0.2	0.1	0.2	0.1	0.2	0.1	0.2	0.1	0.2	0.1	0.2	0.1	2
3	0.3	0.2	0.3	0.2	0.3	0.2	0.2	0.2	0.2	0.2	0.2	0.2	3
4	0.3	0.2	0.3	0.2	0.3	0.2	0.3	0.2	0.3	0.2	0.3	0.2	4
5	0.4	0.3	0.4	0.3	0.4	0.3	0.4	0.3	0.4	0.3	0.4	0.3	5
6	0.5	0.3	0.5	0.3	0.5	0.3	0.5	0.3	0.5	0.3	0.5	0.4	6
7	0.6	0.4	0.6	0.4	0.6	0.4	0.6	0.4	0.6	0.4	0.6	0.4	7
8	0.7	0.4	0.7	0.4	0.7	0.4	0.7	0.4	0.7	0.5	0.6	0.5	8
9	0.8	0.5	0.8	0.5	0.8	0.5	0.7	0.5	0.7	0.5	0.7	0.5	9
dist	dep.	lat.	dep.	lat.	dep.	lat.	dep.	lat.	dep.	lat.	dep.	lat.	dist
Ts.	59 Degrees		58 Degrees		57 Degrees		56 Degrees		55 Degrees		54 Degrees		Ts.

M dist	37 Degrees lat.	37 Degrees dep.	38 Degree lat.	38 Degree dep.	39 Degrees lat.	39 Degrees dep.	40 Degrees lat.	40 Degrees dep.	41 Degree lat.	41 Degree dep.	42 Degrees lat.	42 Degrees dep.	M s dist
1	00.8	00.6	00.8	00.6	00.8	00.6	00.8	00.6	00.8	00.7	00.7	00.7	1
2	01.6	01.2	01.6	01.2	01.6	01.3	01.5	01.3	01.5	01.3	01.5	01.3	2
3	02.4	01.8	02.4	01.8	02.3	01.9	02.3	01.9	02.3	02.0	02.2	02.0	3
4	03.2	02.4	03.2	02.5	03.1	02.5	03.1	02.6	03.0	02.6	03.0	02.7	4
5	04.0	03.0	03.9	03.1	03.9	03.1	03.8	03.2	03.8	03.3	03.7	03.3	5
6	04.8	03.6	04.7	03.7	04.7	03.8	04.6	03.9	04.5	03.7	04.5	04.0	6
7	05.6	04.2	05.5	04.3	05.4	04.4	05.4	04.5	05.3	04.6	05.2	04.7	7
8	06.4	04.8	06.3	04.9	06.2	05.0	06.1	05.1	06.0	05.2	05.9	05.4	8
9	07.2	05.4	07.1	05.5	07.0	05.7	06.9	05.8	06.8	05.9	06.7	06.0	9
10	08.0	06.0	07.9	06.2	07.8	06.3	07.7	06.4	07.5	06.6	07.4	06.7	10
11	08.8	06.6	08.7	06.8	08.5	06.9	08.4	07.1	08.3	07.2	08.2	07.4	11
12	09.6	07.2	09.5	07.4	09.3	07.8	09.2	07.7	09.1	07.9	08.9	08.0	12
13	10.4	07.8	10.2	08.0	10.1	08.2	10.0	08.4	09.8	08.5	09.7	08.7	13
14	11.2	08.4	11.0	08.6	10.9	08.8	10.7	09.0	10.6	09.2	10.4	09.4	14
15	12.0	09.0	11.8	09.2	11.7	09.4	11.5	09.6	11.3	09.8	11.1	10.0	15
16	12.8	09.6	12.6	09.9	12.4	10.1	12.3	10.3	12.1	10.5	11.9	10.7	16
17	13.6	10.2	13.4	10.5	13.2	10.7	13.0	10.9	12.8	11.2	12.6	11.4	17
18	14.4	10.8	14.2	11.1	14.0	11.3	13.8	11.6	13.6	11.8	13.4	12.0	18
19	15.2	11.4	15.0	11.7	14.8	12.0	14.6	12.2	14.3	12.5	14.1	12.7	19
20	16.0	12.0	15.8	12.3	15.5	12.6	15.3	12.9	15.1	13.1	14.9	13.4	20
21	16.8	12.6	16.5	12.9	16.3	13.2	16.1	13.5	15.8	13.8	15.6	14.0	21
22	17.6	13.2	17.3	13.5	17.1	13.8	16.9	14.1	16.6	14.4	16.3	14.7	22
23	18.4	13.8	18.1	14.2	17.9	14.5	17.6	14.8	17.4	15.1	17.1	15.4	23
24	19.2	14.4	18.9	14.8	18.7	15.1	18.4	15.4	18.1	15.7	17.8	16.1	24
25	20.0	15.0	19.7	15.4	19.4	15.7	19.2	16.1	18.9	16.4	18.6	16.7	25
26	20.8	15.6	20.5	16.0	20.2	16.4	19.9	16.7	19.6	17.1	19.3	17.4	26
27	21.6	16.2	21.3	16.6	21.0	17.0	20.7	17.4	20.4	17.7	20.1	18.1	27
28	22.4	16.9	22.1	17.2	21.8	17.6	21.4	18.0	21.1	18.4	20.8	18.7	28
29	23.2	17.5	22.9	17.9	22.5	18.2	22.2	18.6	21.9	19.0	21.5	19.4	29
30	24.0	18.1	23.6	18.5	23.3	18.9	23.0	19.3	22.6	19.7	22.3	20.1	30
31	24.8	18.7	24.4	19.1	24.1	19.5	23.7	19.9	23.4	20.3	23.0	20.7	31
32	25.6	19.3	25.2	19.7	24.9	20.1	24.5	20.6	24.2	21.0	23.8	21.4	32
33	26.4	19.9	26.0	20.3	25.6	20.8	25.3	21.2	24.9	21.6	24.5	22.1	33
34	27.2	20.5	26.8	20.9	26.4	21.4	26.0	21.9	25.7	22.3	25.3	22.7	34
35	28.0	21.1	27.6	21.5	27.2	22.0	26.8	22.5	26.4	23.0	26.0	23.4	35
36	28.7	21.7	28.4	22.1	28.0	22.7	27.6	23.1	27.2	23.6	26.7	24.1	36
37	29.5	22.3	29.2	22.8	28.8	23.3	28.3	23.8	27.9	24.3	27.5	24.8	37
38	30.3	22.9	29.9	23.4	29.5	23.9	29.1	24.4	28.7	24.9	28.2	25.4	38
39	31.1	23.5	30.7	24.0	30.3	24.5	29.9	25.1	29.4	25.6	29.0	26.1	39
40	31.9	24.1	31.5	24.6	31.1	25.2	30.6	25.7	30.2	26.2	29.7	26.8	40
41	32.7	24.7	32.3	25.3	31.9	25.8	31.4	26.4	30.9	26.9	30.5	27.4	41
42	33.5	25.3	33.1	25.9	32.6	26.4	32.2	27.0	31.7	27.6	31.2	28.1	42
43	34.3	25.9	33.9	26.5	33.4	27.1	32.9	27.6	32.5	28.2	31.9	28.8	43
44	35.1	26.5	34.7	27.1	34.2	27.7	33.7	28.3	33.2	28.9	32.7	29.4	44
45	35.9	27.1	35.5	27.7	35.0	28.3	34.5	28.9	34.0	29.5	33.4	30.1	45
46	36.7	27.7	36.2	28.3	35.7	28.9	35.1	29.6	34.7	30.2	34.2	30.8	46
47	37.5	28.3	37.0	28.9	36.5	29.6	36.0	30.2	35.5	30.8	34.9	31.4	47
48	38.3	28.9	37.8	29.6	37.3	30.2	36.8	30.9	36.2	31.5	35.7	32.1	48
49	39.1	29.5	38.6	30.2	38.1	30.8	37.5	31.5	37.0	32.1	36.4	32.8	49
50	39.9	30.1	39.4	30.8	38.9	31.5	38.3	32.1	37.7	32.8	37.2	33.5	50
51	40.7	30.7	40.2	31.4	39.6	32.1	39.1	32.8	38.5	33.5	37.9	34.1	51
52	41.5	31.3	41.0	32.0	40.4	32.7	39.8	33.4	39.2	34.1	38.6	34.8	52
53	42.3	31.9	41.8	32.6	41.2	33.4	40.6	34.1	40.0	34.8	39.4	35.5	53
54	43.1	32.5	42.5	33.2	42.0	34.0	41.4	34.7	40.8	35.4	40.1	36.1	54
55	43.9	33.1	43.3	33.9	42.7	34.6	42.1	35.4	41.5	36.1	40.9	36.8	55
56	44.7	33.7	44.1	34.5	43.5	35.2	42.9	36.0	42.3	36.7	41.6	37.5	56
57	45.5	34.3	44.9	35.1	44.3	35.9	43.7	36.6	43.0	37.4	42.4	38.1	57
58	46.3	34.9	45.7	35.7	45.1	36.5	44.4	37.3	43.8	38.0	43.1	38.8	58
59	47.1	35.5	46.5	36.3	45.8	37.1	45.2	37.9	44.5	38.7	43.8	39.5	59
dist	dep.	lat.	dep.	lat.	dep.	lat.	dep.	lat.	dep.	lat.	dep.	lat.	dist
Ms	53 Degrees		52 Degrees		51 Degree		50 Degrees		49 Degrees		48 Degrees		Ms

Ms	37 Degree		38 Degree		39 Degrees		40 Degrees		41 Degrees		42 Degrees		M
dist	lat.	dep.	lat.	dep.	lat.	dep.	lat.	dep.	lat.	dep.	lat.	dep.	dist
60	47.9	36.1	47.3	36.9	46.6	37.8	46.0	38.6	45.3	39.4	44.6	40.1	60
61	48.7	36.7	48.1	37.6	47.4	38.4	46.7	39.2	46.0	40.0	45.3	40.8	61
62	49.5	37.3	48.9	38.2	48.2	39.0	47.5	39.9	46.8	40.7	46.1	41.5	62
63	50.3	37.9	49.6	38.8	49.0	39.6	48.3	40.5	47.5	41.3	46.8	42.1	63
64	51.1	38.5	50.4	39.4	49.7	40.3	49.0	41.1	48.3	42.0	47.5	42.8	64
65	51.9	39.1	51.2	40.0	50.5	40.9	49.8	41.8	49.1	42.6	48.3	43.5	65
66	52.7	39.7	52.0	40.6	51.3	41.5	50.6	42.4	49.8	43.3	49.0	44.2	66
67	53.5	40.3	52.8	41.3	52.1	42.2	51.3	43.1	50.6	44.0	49.8	44.8	67
68	54.3	40.9	53.6	41.9	52.8	42.8	52.1	43.7	51.3	44.6	50.5	45.5	68
69	55.1	41.5	54.4	42.5	53.6	43.4	52.9	44.4	52.1	45.3	51.3	46.2	69
70	55.9	42.1	55.2	43.1	54.4	44.1	53.6	45.0	52.8	45.9	52.0	46.8	70
71	56.7	42.7	55.9	43.7	55.2	44.7	54.4	45.6	53.6	46.6	52.8	47.5	71
72	57.5	43.3	56.7	44.3	56.0	45.3	55.2	46.3	54.3	47.2	53.5	48.2	72
73	58.3	43.9	57.5	44.9	56.7	45.9	55.9	46.9	55.1	47.9	54.2	48.8	73
74	59.1	44.5	58.3	45.6	57.5	46.6	56.7	47.6	55.8	48.5	55.0	49.5	74
75	59.9	45.1	59.1	46.2	58.3	47.2	57.4	48.2	56.6	49.2	55.7	50.2	75
76	60.7	45.7	59.9	46.8	59.1	47.8	58.2	48.9	57.4	49.9	56.5	50.8	76
77	61.5	46.3	60.7	47.4	59.8	48.5	59.0	49.5	58.1	50.5	57.2	51.5	77
78	62.3	46.9	61.5	48.0	60.6	49.1	59.7	50.1	58.9	51.2	58.0	52.2	78
79	63.1	47.5	62.2	48.6	61.4	49.7	60.5	50.8	59.6	51.8	58.7	52.0	79
80	63.9	48.1	63.0	49.3	62.2	50.3	61.3	51.4	60.4	52.5	59.4	53.5	80
81	64.7	48.7	63.8	49.9	62.9	51.0	62.0	52.1	61.1	53.1	60.2	54.2	81
82	65.5	49.3	64.6	50.5	63.7	51.6	62.8	52.7	61.9	53.8	60.9	54.9	82
83	66.3	49.9	65.4	51.1	64.5	52.2	63.6	53.4	62.6	54.4	61.7	55.5	83
84	67.1	50.6	66.2	51.7	65.3	52.9	64.3	54.0	63.4	55.1	62.4	56.2	84
85	67.9	51.2	67.0	52.3	66.1	53.5	65.1	54.6	64.2	55.8	63.2	56.9	85
86	68.7	51.8	67.8	53.0	66.8	54.1	65.9	55.3	64.9	56.1	63.9	57.5	86
87	69.5	52.4	68.6	53.6	67.6	54.7	66.6	55.9	65.7	57.1	64.6	58.2	87
88	70.3	53.0	69.3	54.2	68.4	55.4	67.4	56.6	66.4	57.7	65.4	58.9	88
89	71.1	53.6	70.1	54.8	69.2	56.0	68.2	57.2	67.2	58.4	66.1	59.5	89
90	71.9	54.2	70.9	55.4	69.9	56.6	68.9	57.9	67.9	59.0	66.9	60.2	90
91	72.7	54.8	71.7	56.0	70.7	57.3	69.7	58.5	68.7	59.7	67.6	60.9	91
92	73.5	55.4	72.5	56.6	71.5	57.9	70.5	59.1	69.4	60.4	68.4	61.6	92
93	74.3	56.0	73.3	57.3	72.3	58.7	71.2	59.8	70.2	61.0	69.1	62.2	93
94	75.1	56.6	74.1	57.9	73.0	59.2	72.0	60.4	70.9	61.7	69.9	62.9	94
95	75.9	57.2	74.9	58.5	73.8	59.8	72.8	61.1	71.7	62.3	70.6	63.6	95
96	76.7	57.8	75.6	59.1	74.6	60.4	73.5	61.7	72.5	63.0	71.3	64.2	96
97	77.5	58.4	76.4	59.7	75.4	61.1	74.3	62.4	73.2	63.6	72.1	64.9	97
98	78.3	59.0	77.2	60.3	76.2	61.6	75.1	63.0	74.0	64.3	72.8	65.6	98
99	79.1	59.6	78.0	61.0	76.9	62.3	75.8	63.8	74.7	64.9	73.6	66.2	99
100	79.9	60.2	78.8	61.6	77.7	62.9	76.6	64.3	75.5	65.6	74.3	66.9	100
200	159.7	120.3	157.6	123.1	155.4	125.9	153.2	128.6	150.9	131.2	148.6	133.8	200
300	239.6	180.5	236.4	184.7	233.1	188.8	229.8	192.8	226.4	196.8	222.9	200.7	300
400	319.4	240.7	315.2	246.3	310.9	251.7	306.4	257.1	301.9	262.4	297.3	267.6	400
500	399.3	300.9	394.0	307.8	388.6	314.7	383.0	321.4	377.4	328.0	371.6	334.6	500
600	479.1	361.1	472.8	369.4	466.3	377.6	459.6	385.7	452.8	393.6	445.9	401.5	600
700	559.0	421.2	551.6	431.0	544.0	440.5	536.2	449.9	528.3	459.2	520.2	468.4	700
800	638.9	481.4	630.4	492.5	621.7	503.5	612.8	514.2	603.8	524.8	594.5	535.3	800
900	718.8	541.6	709.2	554.1	699.4	566.4	689.4	578.5	679.2	590.4	668.8	602.2	900
T's.													T's.
1	0.1	0.1	0.1	0.1	0.1	0.1	0.1	0.1	0.1	0.1	0.1	0.1	1
2	0.2	0.1	0.2	0.1	0.2	0.1	0.2	0.1	0.2	0.1	0.2	0.1	2
3	0.2	0.2	0.2	0.2	0.2	0.2	0.2	0.2	0.2	0.2	0.2	0.2	3
4	0.3	0.2	0.3	0.2	0.3	0.3	0.3	0.3	0.3	0.3	0.3	0.3	4
5	0.4	0.3	0.4	0.3	0.4	0.3	0.4	0.3	0.4	0.3	0.4	0.3	5
6	0.5	0.4	0.5	0.4	0.5	0.4	0.5	0.4	0.5	0.4	0.5	0.4	6
7	0.6	0.4	0.6	0.4	0.5	0.4	0.5	0.4	0.5	0.5	0.5	0.5	7
8	0.6	0.5	0.6	0.5	0.6	0.5	0.6	0.5	0.6	0.5	0.6	0.5	8
9	0.7	0.5	0.7	0.6	0.7	0.5	0.7	0.6	0.6	0.6	0.7	0.6	9
diff	dep.	lat.	dep.	lat.	dep.	lat.	dep.	lat.	dep.	lat.	dep.	lat.	diff
T's.	53 Degrees		52 Degrees		51 Degrees		50 Degrees		49 Degrees		48 Degrees		T's.

Ms	43 Degrees		44 Degrees		45 Degrees		Ms	43 Degrees		44 Degrees		45 Degrees	
dist	lat.	dep.	lat.	dep.	lat.	dep	dist	lat.	dep.	lat.	dep.	lat.	dep.
1	00.7	00.7	00.7	00.7	00.7	00.7	60	43.9	40.9	43.2	41.7	42.4	42.4
2	01.5	01.4	01.4	01.4	01.4	01.4	61	44.6	41.6	43.9	42.4	43.1	43.1
3	02.2	02.0	02.2	02.1	02.1	02.1	62	45.3	42.3	44.6	43.1	43.8	43.8
4	02.9	02.7	02.9	02.8	02.8	02.8	63	46.1	43.0	45.3	43.8	44.5	44.5
5	03.7	03.4	03.6	03.5	03.5	03.5	64	46.8	43.6	46.0	44.5	45.3	45.3
6	04.4	04.1	04.3	04.2	04.2	04.2	65	47.5	44.3	46.8	45.1	46.0	46.0
7	05.1	04.8	05.0	04.9	04.9	04.9	66	48.3	45.0	47.5	45.8	46.7	46.7
8	05.9	05.5	05.8	05.6	05.7	05.7	67	49.0	45.7	48.2	46.5	47.4	47.4
9	06.6	06.1	06.5	06.3	06.4	06.4	68	49.7	46.4	48.9	47.2	48.1	48.1
10	07.3	06.8	07.2	06.9	07.1	07.1	69	50.5	47.1	49.6	47.9	48.8	48.8
11	08.0	07.5	07.9	07.6	07.8	07.8	70	51.2	47.7	50.4	48.6	49.5	49.5
12	08.8	08.2	08.6	08.3	08.5	08.5	71	51.9	48.4	51.1	49.3	50.2	50.2
13	09.5	08.9	09.4	09.0	09.2	09.2	72	52.7	49.1	51.8	50.0	50.9	50.9
14	10.2	09.5	10.1	09.7	09.9	09.9	73	53.4	49.8	52.5	50.7	51.6	51.6
15	11.0	10.2	10.8	10.4	10.6	10.6	74	54.1	50.5	53.2	51.4	52.3	52.3
16	11.7	10.9	11.5	11.1	11.3	11.3	75	54.9	51.2	53.9	52.1	53.0	53.0
17	12.4	11.6	12.2	11.8	12.0	12.0	76	55.6	51.8	54.7	52.8	53.7	53.7
18	13.2	12.3	12.9	12.5	12.7	12.7	77	56.3	52.5	55.5	53.5	54.4	54.4
19	13.9	13.0	13.7	13.2	13.4	13.4	78	57.0	53.2	56.1	54.2	55.2	55.2
20	14.6	13.6	14.4	13.9	14.1	14.1	79	57.8	53.9	56.8	54.9	55.9	55.9
21	15.4	14.3	15.1	14.6	14.8	14.8	80	58.5	54.6	57.5	55.6	56.6	56.6
22	16.1	15.0	15.8	15.3	15.6	15.6	81	59.2	55.2	58.3	56.3	57.3	57.3
23	16.8	15.7	16.5	16.0	16.3	16.3	82	60.0	55.9	59.0	57.0	58.0	58.0
24	17.6	16.6	17.3	16.7	17.0	17.0	83	60.7	56.6	59.7	57.6	58.7	58.7
25	18.3	17.1	18.0	17.4	17.7	17.4	84	61.4	57.3	60.4	58.3	59.4	59.4
26	19.0	17.7	18.7	18.1	18.4	18.4	85	62.2	58.0	61.1	59.0	60.1	60.1
27	19.7	18.4	19.4	18.8	19.1	19.1	86	62.9	58.6	61.9	59.7	60.8	60.8
28	20.5	19.1	20.1	19.4	19.8	19.8	87	63.6	59.3	62.6	60.4	61.6	61.5
29	21.2	19.8	20.9	20.1	20.5	20.5	88	64.4	60.0	63.3	61.1	62.2	62.2
30	21.9	20.5	21.6	20.8	21.2	21.2	89	65.1	60.7	64.0	61.8	62.9	62.9
31	22.7	21.1	22.3	21.5	21.9	21.9	90	65.8	61.4	64.7	62.5	63.6	63.6
32	23.4	21.8	23.0	22.1	22.6	22.6	91	66.6	62.1	65.5	63.2	64.3	64.3
33	24.1	22.5	23.7	22.9	23.3	23.3	92	67.3	62.7	66.2	63.9	65.1	65.1
34	24.9	23.2	24.5	23.6	24.0	24.0	93	68.0	63.4	66.9	64.6	65.8	65.8
35	25.6	23.9	25.2	24.3	24.7	24.7	94	68.7	64.1	67.6	65.3	66.5	66.5
36	26.3	24.5	25.9	25.0	25.5	25.5	95	69.5	64.8	68.3	66.0	67.2	67.2
37	27.1	25.2	26.6	25.7	26.2	26.2	96	70.2	65.5	69.1	66.7	67.9	67.9
38	27.8	25.9	27.3	26.4	26.9	26.9	97	70.9	66.2	69.8	67.4	68.6	68.6
39	28.5	26.6	28.1	27.1	27.6	27.6	98	71.7	66.8	70.5	68.1	69.3	69.3
40	29.3	27.3	28.8	27.8	28.3	28.3	99	72.4	67.5	71.2	68.8	70.0	70.0
41	30.0	28.0	29.5	28.5	29.0	29.0	100	73.1	68.2	71.9	69.5	70.7	70.7
42	30.7	28.6	30.2	29.2	29.7	29.7	200	146.3	136.4	143.9	138.9	141.4	141.4
43	31.4	29.3	30.9	29.9	30.4	30.4	300	219.4	204.6	215.8	208.4	212.1	212.1
44	32.2	30.0	31.6	30.6	31.1	31.1	400	292.5	272.8	287.7	277.9	282.8	282.8
45	32.9	30.7	32.4	31.3	31.8	31.8	500	365.7	341.0	359.7	347.3	353.5	353.5
46	33.6	31.4	33.1	32.0	32.5	32.5	600	438.8	409.2	431.6	416.8	424.2	424.2
47	34.4	32.1	33.8	32.6	33.2	33.2	700	511.9	477.4	503.5	486.3	495.0	495.0
48	35.1	32.7	34.5	33.3	33.9	33.9	800	585.1	545.6	575.5	555.7	565.7	565.7
49	35.8	33.4	35.2	34.0	34.6	34.6	900	658.2	613.8	647.4	625.2	636.4	636.4
50	36.6	34.1	36.0	34.7	35.4	35.4	T's						
51	37.3	34.8	36.7	35.4	36.1	36.1	1	0.1	0.1	0.1	0.1	0.1	0.1
52	38.0	35.5	37.4	36.1	36.8	36.8	2	0.1	0.1	0.1	0.1	0.1	0.1
53	38.8	36.2	38.1	36.8	37.5	37.5	3	0.2	0.2	0.2	0.2	0.2	0.2
54	39.5	36.8	38.8	37.5	38.2	38.2	4	0.3	0.3	0.3	0.3	0.3	0.3
55	40.2	37.5	39.6	38.2	38.9	38.9	5	0.4	0.3	0.4	0.3	0.4	0.4
56	41.0	38.2	40.3	38.9	39.6	39.6	6	0.4	0.4	0.4	0.4	0.4	0.4
57	41.7	38.9	41.0	39.6	40.3	40.3	7	0.5	0.5	0.5	0.5	0.5	0.5
58	42.4	39.5	41.7	40.3	41.0	41.0	8	0.6	0.5	0.6	0.6	0.6	0.6
59	43.1	40.2	42.4	41.0	41.7	41.7	9	0.7	0.6	0.6	0.6	0.6	0.6
dist	dep.	lat.	dep.	lat.	dep.	lat.	dist	dep.	lat.	dep.	lat.	dep.	lat
Ms	47 Degrees		46 Degrees		4 Points		T's	47 Degrees		46 Degrees		4 Points	

A TABLE of the RHUMBS, or Points and Quarter Points of the COMPASS, and the Angles which they make with the MERIDIAN.

North East Quadrant	North West Quadrant	Pts.	D. M. S	South East Quadrant.	South West Quadrant.
NORTH.	NORTH.	0		SOUTH.	SOUTH.
N ¼ E	N ¼ W	0 ¼	2 48 45	S ¼ E	S ¼ W
N ½ E	N ½ W	0 ½	5 37 30	S ½ E	S ½ W
N ¾ E	N ¾ W	0 ¾	8 26 15	S ¾ E	S ¾ W
N by E	N by W	1	11 15 0	S by E	S by W
N N E ¾ N	N N W ¾ N	1 ¼	14 3 45	S S E ¾ S	S S W ¾ S
N N E ½ N	N N W ½ N	1 ½	16 52 30	S S E ½ S	S S W ½ S
N N E ¼ N	N N W ¼ N	1 ¾	19 41 15	S S E ¼ S	S S W ¼ S
N N E	N N W	2	22 30 0	S S E	S S W
N N E ¼ E	N N W ¼ W	2 ¼	25 18 45	S S E ¼ E	S S W ¼ W
N N E ½ E	N N W ½ W	2 ½	28 7 30	S S E ½ E	S S W ½ W
N N E ¾ E	N N W ¾ W	2 ¾	30 56 15	S S E ¾ E	S S W ¾ W
N E by N	N W by N	3	33 45 0	S E by S	S W by S
N E ¾ N	N W ¾ N	3 ¼	36 33 45	S E ¾ S	S W ¾ S
N E ½ N	N W ½ N	3 ½	39 22 30	S E ½ S	S W ½ S
N E ¼ N	N W ¼ N	3 ¾	42 11 15	S E ¼ S	S W ¼ S
N E	N W	4	45 0 0	S E	S W
N E ¼ E	N W ¼ W	4 ¼	47 48 45	S E ¼ E	S W ¼ W
N E ½ E	N W ½ W	4 ½	50 37 30	S E ½ E	S W ½ W
N E ¾ E	N W ¾ W	4 ¾	53 26 15	S E ¾ E	S W ¾ W
N E by E	N W by W	5	56 15 0	S E by E	S W by W
E N E ¾ N	W N W ¾ N	5 ¼	59 3 45	E S E ¾ S	W S W ¾ S
E N E ½ N	W N W ½ N	5 ½	61 52 30	E S E ½ S	W S W ½ S
E N E ¼ N	W N W ¼ N	5 ¾	64 41 15	E S E ¼ S	W S W ¼ S
E N E	W N W	6	67 30 0	E S E	W S W
E N E ¼ E	W N W ¼ W	6 ¼	70 18 45	E S E ¼ E	W S W ¼ W
E N E ½ E	W N W ½ W	6 ½	73 7 30	E S E ½ E	W S W ½ W
E N E ¾ E	W N W ¾ W	6 ¾	75 56 15	E S E ¾ E	W S W ¾ W
E by N	W by N	7	78 45 0	E by S	W by S
E ¾ N	W ¾ N	7 ¼	81 33 45	E ¾ S	W ¾ S
E ½ N	W ½ N	7 ½	84 22 30	E ½ S	W ½ S
E ¼ N	W ¼ N	7 ¾	87 11 15	E ¼ S	W ¼ S
EAST	WEST	8	90 0 0	EAST	WEST

Mls	¼ Point		½ Point		¾ Point		1 Point		1¼ Points		1½ Points		M
dist	lat.	dep.	lat.	dep.	lat.	dep.	lat.	dep.	lat.	dep.	lat.	dep.	dist
1	01.0	00.0	01.0	00.1	01.0	00.1	01.0	00.2	01.0	00.2	01.0	00.3	1
2	02.0	00.1	02.0	00.2	02.0	00.3	02.0	00.4	01.9	00.5	01.9	00.6	2
3	03.0	00.1	03.0	00.3	03.0	00.4	02.9	00.6	02.9	00.7	02.9	00.9	3
4	04.0	00.2	04.0	00.4	04.0	00.6	03.9	00.8	03.9	01.0	03.8	01.2	4
5	05.0	00.2	05.0	00.5	04.9	00.7	04.9	01.0	04.9	01.2	04.8	01.5	5
6	06.0	00.3	06.0	00.6	05.9	00.9	05.9	01.2	05.8	01.5	05.7	01.7	6
7	07.0	00.3	07.0	00.7	06.9	01.0	06.9	01.4	06.8	01.7	06.7	02.0	7
8	08.0	00.4	08.0	00.8	07.9	01.2	07.8	01.6	07.8	01.9	07.7	02.3	8
9	09.0	00.4	09.0	00.9	08.9	01.3	08.8	01.8	08.7	02.2	08.6	02.6	9
10	10.0	00.5	10.0	01.0	09.9	01.5	09.8	02.0	09.7	02.4	09.6	02.9	10
11	11.0	00.5	10.9	01.1	10.9	01.6	10.8	02.1	10.7	02.7	10.5	03.2	11
12	12.0	00.6	11.9	01.2	11.9	01.8	11.8	02.3	11.6	02.9	11.5	03.5	12
13	13.0	00.6	12.9	01.3	12.9	01.9	12.8	02.5	12.6	03.2	12.4	03.8	13
14	14.0	00.7	13.9	01.4	13.8	02.1	13.7	02.7	13.6	03.4	13.4	04.1	14
15	15.0	00.7	14.9	01.5	14.8	02.2	14.7	02.9	14.6	03.6	14.4	04.4	15
16	16.0	00.8	15.9	01.6	15.8	02.3	15.7	03.1	15.5	03.9	15.3	04.6	16
17	17.0	00.8	16.9	01.7	16.8	02.5	16.7	03.3	16.5	04.1	16.3	04.9	17
18	18.0	00.9	17.9	01.8	17.8	02.6	17.7	03.5	17.5	04.4	17.2	05.2	18
19	19.0	00.9	18.9	01.9	18.8	02.8	18.6	03.7	18.4	04.6	18.2	05.5	19
20	20.0	01.0	19.9	02.0	19.8	02.9	19.6	03.9	19.4	04.9	19.1	05.8	20
21	21.0	01.0	20.9	02.1	20.8	03.1	20.6	04.1	20.4	05.1	20.1	06.1	21
22	22.0	01.1	21.9	02.2	21.8	03.2	21.6	04.3	21.3	05.3	21.1	06.4	22
23	23.0	01.1	22.9	02.2	22.8	03.4	22.6	04.5	22.3	05.6	22.0	06.7	23
24	24.0	01.2	23.9	02.3	23.7	03.5	23.5	04.7	23.3	05.8	23.0	07.0	24
25	25.0	01.2	24.9	02.4	24.7	03.7	24.5	04.9	24.3	06.1	23.9	07.3	25
26	26.0	01.3	25.9	02.5	25.7	03.8	25.5	05.1	25.2	06.3	24.9	07.5	26
27	27.0	01.3	26.9	02.6	26.7	04.0	26.5	05.3	26.2	06.6	25.8	07.8	27
28	28.0	01.4	27.9	02.7	27.7	04.1	27.5	05.5	27.2	06.8	26.8	08.1	28
29	29.0	01.4	28.9	02.8	28.7	04.3	28.4	05.7	28.1	07.0	27.8	08.4	29
30	30.0	01.5	29.9	02.9	29.7	04.4	29.4	05.9	29.1	07.3	28.7	08.7	30
31	31.0	01.5	30.9	03.0	30.7	04.5	30.4	06.0	30.1	07.5	29.7	09.0	31
32	32.0	01.6	31.8	03.1	31.7	04.7	31.4	06.2	31.0	07.8	30.6	09.3	32
33	33.0	01.6	32.8	03.2	32.6	04.8	32.4	06.4	32.0	08.0	31.6	09.6	33
34	34.0	01.7	33.8	03.3	33.6	05.0	33.3	06.6	33.0	08.3	32.5	09.9	34
35	35.0	01.7	34.8	03.4	34.6	05.1	34.3	06.8	34.0	08.5	33.5	10.2	35
36	36.0	01.8	35.8	03.5	35.6	05.3	35.3	07.0	34.9	08.7	34.4	10.5	36
37	37.0	01.8	36.8	03.6	36.6	05.4	36.2	07.2	35.9	09.0	35.4	10.7	37
38	38.0	01.9	37.8	03.7	37.6	05.6	37.3	07.4	36.9	09.2	36.4	11.0	38
39	39.0	01.9	38.8	03.8	38.6	05.7	38.3	07.6	37.8	09.5	37.3	11.3	39
40	40.0	02.0	39.8	03.9	39.6	05.9	39.2	07.8	38.8	09.7	38.3	11.6	40
41	41.0	02.0	40.8	04.0	40.6	06.0	40.2	08.0	39.8	10.0	39.2	11.9	41
42	41.9	02.1	41.8	04.1	41.5	06.2	41.2	08.2	40.7	10.2	40.2	12.2	42
43	42.9	02.1	42.8	04.2	42.5	06.3	42.2	08.4	41.7	10.4	41.1	12.5	43
44	43.9	02.2	43.8	04.3	43.5	06.5	43.2	08.6	42.7	10.7	42.1	12.8	44
45	44.9	02.2	44.8	04.4	44.5	06.6	44.1	08.8	43.7	10.9	43.1	13.1	45
46	45.9	02.3	45.8	04.5	45.5	06.7	45.1	09.0	44.6	11.2	44.0	13.4	46
47	46.9	02.3	46.8	04.6	46.5	06.9	46.1	09.2	45.6	11.4	45.0	13.6	47
48	47.9	02.4	47.8	04.7	47.5	07.0	47.1	09.4	46.6	11.7	45.9	13.9	48
49	48.9	02.4	48.8	04.8	48.5	07.2	48.1	09.6	47.5	11.9	46.9	14.2	49
50	49.9	02.5	49.8	04.9	49.5	07.3	49.0	09.8	48.5	12.1	47.8	14.5	50
51	50.9	02.5	50.8	05.0	50.4	07.5	50.0	10.0	49.5	12.4	48.8	14.8	51
52	51.9	02.6	51.7	05.1	51.4	07.6	51.0	10.1	50.4	12.6	49.8	15.1	52
53	52.9	02.6	52.7	05.2	52.4	07.8	52.0	10.3	51.4	12.9	50.7	15.4	53
54	53.9	02.7	53.7	05.3	53.4	07.9	53.0	10.5	52.4	13.1	51.7	15.7	54
55	54.9	02.7	54.7	05.4	54.4	08.1	53.9	10.7	53.4	13.4	52.6	16.0	55
56	55.9	02.8	55.7	05.5	55.4	08.2	54.9	10.9	54.3	13.6	53.6	16.3	56
57	56.9	02.8	56.7	05.6	56.4	08.4	55.9	11.1	55.3	13.9	54.5	16.5	57
58	57.9	02.8	57.7	05.7	57.4	08.5	56.9	11.3	56.3	14.1	55.5	16.8	58
59	58.9	02.9	58.7	05.8	58.4	08.7	57.9	11.5	57.2	14.3	56.5	17.1	59
dist	dep.	lat.	dep.	lat.	dep.	lat.	dep.	lat.	dep.	lat.	dep.	lat.	dist
M	7¾ Points		7½ Points		7¼ Points		7 Points		6¾ Points		6½ Points		M

M's	¼ Point		½ Point		¾ Point		1 Point		1¼ Points		1½ Points		M's
diſt	lat.	dep.	lat.	dep.	lat.	dep.	lat.	dep.	lat.	dep.	lat.	dep.	diſt
60	59.9	02.9	59.7	05.9	59.4	08.8	58.8	11.7	58.2	14.6	57.4	17.4	60
61	60.9	03.0	60.7	06.0	60.3	09.0	59.8	11.9	59.2	14.8	58.4	17.7	61
62	61.9	03.0	61.7	06.1	61.3	09.1	60.8	12.1	60.1	15.1	59.3	18.0	62
63	62.9	03.1	62.7	06.2	62.3	09.2	61.8	12.3	61.1	15.3	60.3	18.3	63
64	63.9	03.1	63.7	06.3	63.3	09.4	62.8	12.5	62.1	15.6	61.2	18.6	64
65	64.9	03.2	64.7	06.4	64.3	09.5	63.8	12.7	63.1	15.8	62.2	18.9	65
66	65.9	03.2	65.7	06.5	65.3	09.7	64.7	12.9	64.0	16.0	63.2	19.2	66
67	66.9	03.3	66.7	06.6	66.3	09.8	65.7	13.1	65.0	16.3	64.1	19.4	67
68	67.9	03.3	67.7	06.7	67.3	10.0	66.7	13.3	66.0	16.5	65.1	19.7	68
69	68.9	03.4	68.7	06.8	68.3	10.1	67.7	13.5	66.9	16.8	66.0	20.0	69
70	69.9	03.4	69.7	06.9	69.2	10.3	68.7	13.7	67.9	17.0	67.0	20.3	70
71	70.9	03.5	70.7	07.0	70.2	10.4	69.6	13.9	68.9	17.3	67.9	20.6	71
72	71.9	03.5	71.7	07.1	71.2	10.6	70.6	14.0	69.8	17.5	68.9	20.9	72
73	72.9	03.6	72.6	07.2	72.2	10.7	71.6	14.2	70.8	17.7	69.9	21.2	73
74	73.9	03.6	73.6	07.3	73.2	10.9	72.6	14.4	71.8	18.0	70.8	21.5	74
75	74.9	03.7	74.6	07.4	74.2	11.0	73.6	14.6	72.8	18.2	71.8	21.8	75
76	75.9	03.7	75.6	07.4	75.2	11.2	74.6	14.8	73.7	18.5	72.7	22.1	76
77	76.9	03.8	76.6	07.5	76.2	11.3	75.5	15.0	74.7	18.7	73.7	22.4	77
78	77.9	03.8	77.6	07.6	77.2	11.4	76.5	15.2	75.7	19.0	74.6	22.6	78
79	78.9	03.9	78.6	07.7	78.1	11.6	77.5	15.4	76.6	19.2	75.6	22.9	79
80	79.9	03.9	79.6	07.8	79.1	11.7	78.5	15.6	77.6	19.4	76.6	23.2	80
81	80.9	04.0	80.6	07.9	80.1	11.9	79.4	15.8	78.6	19.7	77.5	23.5	81
82	81.9	04.0	81.6	08.0	81.1	12.0	80.4	16.0	79.5	19.9	78.5	23.8	82
83	82.9	04.1	82.6	08.1	82.1	12.2	81.4	16.2	80.5	20.2	79.4	24.1	83
84	83.9	04.1	83.6	08.2	83.1	12.3	82.4	16.4	81.5	20.4	80.4	24.4	84
85	84.9	04.2	84.6	08.3	84.1	12.5	83.4	16.6	82.5	20.7	81.3	24.7	85
86	85.9	04.2	85.6	08.4	85.1	12.6	84.3	16.8	83.4	20.9	82.3	25.0	86
87	86.9	04.3	86.6	08.5	86.1	12.8	85.3	17.0	84.4	21.1	83.3	25.3	87
88	87.9	04.3	87.6	08.6	87.0	12.9	86.3	17.2	85.4	21.4	84.2	25.5	88
89	88.9	04.4	88.6	08.7	88.0	13.1	87.3	17.4	86.3	21.6	85.2	25.8	89
90	89.9	04.4	89.6	08.8	89.0	13.2	88.3	17.6	87.3	21.9	86.1	26.1	90
91	90.9	04.5	90.6	08.9	90.0	13.4	89.2	17.8	88.3	22.1	87.1	26.4	91
92	91.9	04.5	91.6	09.0	91.0	13.5	90.2	17.9	89.2	22.4	88.0	26.7	92
93	92.9	04.6	92.6	09.1	92.0	13.6	91.2	18.1	90.2	22.6	89.0	27.0	93
94	93.9	04.6	93.5	09.3	93.0	13.8	92.2	18.3	91.2	22.8	90.0	27.3	94
95	94.9	04.7	94.5	09.3	94.0	13.9	93.2	18.5	92.2	23.1	90.9	27.6	95
96	95.9	04.7	95.5	09.4	95.0	14.1	94.1	18.7	93.1	23.3	91.9	27.9	96
97	96.9	04.8	96.5	09.5	96.0	14.2	95.1	18.9	94.1	23.6	92.8	28.2	97
98	97.9	04.8	97.5	09.6	96.9	14.4	96.1	19.1	95.1	23.8	93.8	28.4	98
99	98.9	04.9	98.5	09.7	97.9	14.5	97.1	19.3	96.0	24.1	94.7	28.7	99
100	99.9	04.9	99.5	09.8	98.9	14.7	98.1	19.5	97.0	24.3	95.7	29.0	100
200	199.8	09.8	199.0	19.6	197.8	29.3	196.2	39.0	194.0	48.6	191.4	58.1	200
300	299.6	14.7	298.6	29.4	296.7	44.0	294.2	58.5	291.0	72.9	287.1	87.1	300
400	399.5	19.6	398.1	39.2	395.7	58.7	392.3	78.0	388.0	97.2	382.8	116.1	400
500	499.4	24.5	497.6	49.0	494.6	73.4	490.4	97.5	485.0	121.5	478.5	145.1	500
600	599.3	29.4	597.1	58.8	593.5	88.0	588.5	117.0	582.0	145.8	574.2	174.2	600
700	699.2	34.3	596.6	68.6	692.4	102.7	686.5	136.6	679.0	170.0	669.9	203.2	700
800	799.0	39.2	796.1	78.4	791.3	117.4	784.6	156.1	776.0	194.4	765.5	232.2	800
900	898.9	44.2	895.7	83.2	890.2	132.1	882.7	175.6	873.0	218.7	861.2	261.3	900
T's													T's
1	0.1	0.0	0.1	0.0	0.1	0.0	0.1	0.0	0.1	0.0	0.1	0.0	1
2	0.2	0.0	0.2	0.0	0.2	0.0	0.2	0.0	0.2	0.0	0.2	0.1	2
3	0.3	0.0	0.3	0.0	0.3	0.1	0.3	0.1	0.3	0.1	0.3	0.1	3
4	0.4	0.0	0.4	0.0	0.4	0.1	0.4	0.1	0.4	0.1	0.4	0.1	4
5	0.5	0.0	0.5	0.0	0.5	0.1	0.5	0.1	0.5	0.1	0.5	0.1	5
6	0.6	0.0	0.6	0.1	0.6	0.1	0.6	0.1	0.6	0.1	0.6	0.2	6
7	0.7	0.0	0.7	0.1	0.7	0.1	0.7	0.1	0.7	0.2	0.7	0.2	7
8	0.8	0.0	0.8	0.1	0.8	0.1	0.8	0.2	0.8	0.2	0.8	0.2	8
9	0.9	0.0	0.9	0.1	0.9	0.1	0.9	0.2	0.9	0.2	0.9	0.3	9
diff	dep.	lat.	dep.	lat.	dep.	lat.	dep.	lat.	dep.	lat.	dep.	lat.	diff
T's	7¾ Point		7½ Points		7¼ Points		7 Points		6¾ Points		6½ Points		T's

Ms dist	1¼ Points		2 Point		2¼ Points		2½ Points		2¾ Points		3 Points		Ms dist
	lat.	dep.	lat.	dep.	lat	dep.	lat.	dep.	lat.	der.	lat.	dep.	
1	00.9	00.3	00.7	00.4	00.9	00.4	00.9	00.5	00.9	00.5	00.8	00.6	1
2	01.9	00.7	01.8	00.8	01.8	00.9	01 8	00.9	01.7	01.0	01.7	01.1	2
3	02.8	01.0	02.8	01.1	02.7	01.3	02.6	01.4	02.6	01.5	02.5	01.7	3
4	03.8	01.3	03.7	01.5	03.6	01.7	03.5	01.9	03.4	02.1	03 3	02 2	4
5	04.7	01.7	04.6	01.9	04.5	02.1	04.4	02.4	04.3	02.6	04.2	02.8	5
6	05.6	02.0	05.5	02.3	05.4	02.6	05.3	02.8	05.1	03.1	05.0	03.3	6
7	06.6	02.4	06.5	02.7	06.3	03.0	06.2	03.3	06.0	03.6	05.8	03.9	7
8	07.5	02.7	07.4	03.1	07.2	03.4	07.1	03.8	06.9	04.1	06.7	04.4	8
9	08.5	03.0	08.3	03.4	08.1	03.8	07 9	04.2	07.7	04.6	07.5	05.0	9
10	09 4	03.4	09.2	03.8	09.0	04 3	08.8	04.7	08.6	05.1	08.3	05.6	10
11	10.4	03.7	10.2	04.2	09.2	04.7	09.7	05.2	09.4	05.7	09.1	06.1	11
12	11.3	04.0	11.1	04.6	10.8	05.1	10.6	05.7	10.3	06.2	10.0	06.7	12
13	12.2	04.4	12.0	05.0	11.8	05.6	11.5	06.1	11.2	06.7	10.8	07.2	13
14	13.2	04.7	12.9	05.4	12.7	06.0	12.3	06.6	12.0	07.2	11.6	07.8	14
15	14.1	05.1	13.0	05.7	13.6	06.4	13.2	07.1	12.9	07.7	12.5	08.3	15
16	15.1	05.4	14.8	06.1	14.5	06.8	14.1	07.5	13.7	08 2	13.3	08.9	16
17	16.0	05.7	15.7	06.5	15.4	07.3	15.0	08.0	14.6	08.7	14.1	09.4	17
18	16.9	06.1	16.6	06.9	16.3	07.7	15.9	08.5	15.4	09.3	15.0	10.0	18
19	17.9	06.4	17.6	07.3	17.2	08.1	16.8	09.0	16.3	09.8	15.8	10.6	19
20	18.8	06.7	18.6	07.7	18.1	08.6	17.6	09.4	17.2	10.3	16.6	11.1	20
21	19.8	07.1	19.4	08.0	19.0	09.0	18.5	09.9	18.0	10.8	17.5	11.7	21
22	20.7	07.4	20.3	08.4	19.9	09.4	19.4	10.4	18.9	11.3	18.3	12.2	22
23	21.7	07.7	21.3	08.8	20.8	09.8	20.3	10.8	19.7	11.8	19.1	12.8	23
24	22.6	08 1	22.2	09 2	21.7	10.3	21.2	11.3	20.6	12.3	20.0	13.3	24
25	23.5	08.4	23.1	09.6	22.6	10.7	22.0	11.8	21.4	12.9	20.8	13.9	25
26	24.5	08.8	24.0	10.0	23.5	11.1	22.9	12.3	22.3	13.4	21.6	14.4	26
27	25.4	09.1	24.9	10.3	24.4	11.5	23.8	12.7	23.2	13.9	22.4	15.0	27
28	26.4	09.4	25.9	10.7	25.3	12.0	24.7	13.2	24.0	14.4	23.3	15.6	28
29	27.3	09.8	26.8	11.1	26.2	12.4	25.6	13.7	24.9	14.9	24.1	16.1	29
30	28.2	10.1	27.7	11.5	27.1	12.8	26.5	14.1	25.7	15.4	24.9	16.7	30
31	29.2	10.4	28.6	11.9	28.0	13.3	27.3	14.6	26.6	15.9	25.8	17.2	31
32	30.1	10.8	29.6	12.2	28.9	13.7	28.2	15.1	27.4	16.5	26.6	17.8	32
33	31.1	11.1	30.5	12.6	29.8	14.1	29.1	15.5	28.3	17.0	27.4	18 3	33
34	32.0	11.5	31.4	13.0	30.7	14.5	30.0	16.0	29.2	17.5	28.3	18.9	34
35	33.0	11.8	32.3	13.4	31.6	15.0	30.9	16.5	30.0	18.0	29.1	19.4	35
36	33.9	12.1	33.3	13.8	32.5	15 4	31.7	17.0	30.9	18.5	29.9	20.0	36
37	34.8	12.5	34.2	14.2	33.4	15.8	32.6	17.4	31.7	19.0	30.8	20.6	37
38	35.8	12.8	35.1	14.5	34.4	16.2	33.5	17.9	32.6	19.5	31.6	21.1	38
39	36.7	13.1	36.0	14.9	35.3	16.7	34.4	18.4	33.5	20.0	32.4	21.7	39
40	37.7	13.5	37.0	15.3	36.2	17.1	35.3	18.9	34.3	20.6	33.4	22 2	40
41	38.6	13.8	37.9	15.7	37.1	17.5	36.2	19.3	35.2	21.1	34.1	22.8	41
42	39.5	14.1	38.8	16.1	38.0	18.0	37.0	19.8	36.0	21.6	34.9	23.3	42
43	40.4	14.5	39.7	16.5	38.9	18 4	37.9	20.3	36.9	22.1	35.8	23.9	43
44	41.4	14.8	40.7	16.8	39.8	18.8	38.8	21.2	37.7	22.6	36.6	24.4	44
45	42.4	15.2	41.6	17.2	40.7	19.2	39.7	21.2	38.6	23.1	37.4	25.0	45
46	43.3	15.5	42.5	17.6	41.6	19.7	40.6	21.7	39.5	23.6	38.2	25.6	46
47	44.3	15.8	43.4	18.0	42.5	20.1	41.4	22.1	40.3	24.2	39.1	26.1	47
48	45.2	16.2	44.3	18.4	43.4	20.5	42.3	22.6	41.2	24.7	39.9	26.7	48
49	46.1	16.5	45.3	18.8	44.3	21.0	43.2	23.1	42.0	25.2	40.7	27.2	49
50	47.1	16.8	46.2	19.1	45.2	21.4	44.1	23.6	42.9	25.7	41.6	27.8	50
51	48.0	17.2	47.1	19.5	46.1	21.8	45.0	24.0	43.7	26.2	41 4	28.3	51
52	49.0	17.5	48.0	19.9	47.0	22.2	45.9	24.5	44.6	26.7	43.2	28.9	52
53	49.9	17.9	49.0	20.3	47.0	22.7	46.7	25.0	45.5	27.2	44.1	29.4	53
54	50 8	18.2	49.7	20.7	48 8	23.1	47.6	25.5	46.3	27.8	44.9	30.0	54
55	51.8	18.5	50 8	21.0	49 7	23.5	48 5	25.9	47.2	28.3	45.7	30.6	55
56	52.7	18.9	51.7	21.4	50.6	23.9	49.4	26.4	48.0	28.8	46.6	31.1	56
57	53.7	19.2	52.7	21.8	51.5	24.4	50.3	26.9	48.9	29.3	47.4	31.7	57
58	54.6	19.5	53.6	22.2	52.4	24.8	51.2	27.3	49.7	29.8	48.2	32.2	58
59	55.5	19.9	54.5	22.6	53.3	25.2	52.0	27.8	50.6	30.3	49.1	32.8	59
dist	dep	lat.	dep.	lat	dep.	lat.	dep.	lat.	dep.	lat.	dep.	lat.	dist
Ms	6¼ Points		6 Points		5¾ Points		5½ Points		5¼ Points		5 Points		Ms

1

Ms dist	1¾ Points lat.	1¾ Points dep.	2 Points lat.	2 Points dep.	2¼ Points lat.	2¼ Points dep.	2½ Points lat.	2½ Points dep.	2¾ Points lat.	2¾ Points dep.	3 Points lat.	3 Points dep.	Ms dist
60	56.5	20.2	55.4	23.0	54.2	25.7	52.9	28.3	51.5	30.8	49.9	33.3	60
61	57.4	20.6	56.4	23.3	55.1	26.1	53.8	28.8	52.3	31.4	50.7	33.9	61
62	58.4	20.9	57.3	23.7	56.0	26.[illegible]	54.7	29.2	53.2	31.9	51.6	34.4	62
63	59.3	21.2	58.2	24.1	57.0	26.9	55.6	29.7	54.0	32.4	52.4	35.0	63
64	60.3	21.6	59.1	24.5	57.9	27.4	56.4	30.2	54.9	32.9	53.2	35.6	64
65	61.2	21.9	60.1	24.9	58.8	27.8	57.3	30.6	55.8	33.4	54.0	36.1	65
66	62.1	22.2	61.0	25.3	59.7	28.2	58.2	31.1	56.6	33.9	54.9	36.7	66
67	63.1	22.6	61.9	25.6	60.6	28.6	59.1	31.6	57.5	34.4	55.7	37.2	67
68	64.0	22.9	62.8	26.0	61.5	29.1	60.1	32.1	58.3	35.0	56.5	37.8	68
69	65.0	23.2	63.7	26.4	62.4	29.5	60.9	32.5	59.2	35.5	57.4	38.3	69
70	65.9	23.6	64.7	26.8	63.3	29.9	61.7	33.0	60.0	36.0	58.2	38.9	70
71	66.8	23.9	65.6	27.2	64.2	30.4	62.6	33.5	60.9	36.5	59.0	39.4	71
72	67.8	24.3	66.5	27.6	65.1	30.8	63.5	33.9	61.8	37.0	59.9	40.0	72
73	68.7	24.6	67.4	27.9	66.0	31.2	64.4	34.4	62.6	37.5	60.7	40.6	73
74	69.7	24.9	68.4	28.3	66.9	31.6	65.3	34.9	63.5	38.0	61.5	41.1	74
75	70.6	25.3	69.3	28.7	67.8	32.1	66.1	35.4	64.3	38.6	62.4	41.7	75
76	71.6	25.6	70.2	29.1	68.7	32.5	67.0	35.8	65.2	39.1	63.2	42.2	76
77	72.5	25.9	71.1	29.5	69.6	32.9	67.9	36.3	66.0	39.6	64.0	42.8	77
78	73.4	26.3	72.1	29.9	70.5	33.4	68.8	36.8	66.9	40.1	64.9	43.3	78
79	74.4	26.6	73.0	30.2	71.4	33.8	69.7	37.2	67.8	40.6	65.7	3.9	79
80	75.3	26.9	73.9	30.6	72.3	34.2	70.6	37.7	68.6	41.1	60.5	44.4	80
81	76.3	27.3	74.8	31.0	73.2	34.6	71.4	38.2	69.5	41.6	67.3	45.0	81
82	77.2	27.6	75.8	31.4	74.1	35.1	72.3	38.7	70.3	42.2	68.2	45.6	82
83	78.1	28.0	76.7	31.8	75.0	35.5	73.2	39.1	71.2	42.7	69.0	46.1	83
84	79.1	28.3	77.6	32.1	75.9	35.9	74.1	39.6	72.0	43.2	69.8	46.7	84
85	80.0	28.6	78.5	32.5	76.8	36.3	75.0	40.1	72.9	43.7	70.7	47.2	85
86	81.0	29.0	79.5	32.9	77.7	36.8	75.8	41.5	73.8	44.2	71.5	47.8	86
87	81.9	29.3	80.4	33.3	78.6	37.2	76.7	40.0	74.6	44.7	72.3	48.3	87
88	82.9	29.6	81.3	33.7	79.6	37.6	77.6	41.5	75.5	45.2	73.2	48.9	88
89	83.8	30.0	82.2	34.1	80.5	38.1	78.5	41.9	70.3	45.7	74.0	49.4	89
90	84.7	30.3	83.2	34.4	81.4	38.5	79.4	42.4	77.2	46.3	74.8	50.0	90
91	85.7	30.7	84.1	34.8	82.3	38.9	80.3	42.9	78.1	46.8	75.7	50.6	91
92	86.6	31.0	85.0	35.2	83.2	39.3	81.1	43.4	78.9	47.3	76.5	51.1	92
93	87.6	31.3	85.9	35.6	84.1	39.8	82.0	43.8	79.8	47.8	77.3	51.7	93
94	88.5	31.7	86.8	36.0	85.0	40.2	82.9	44.3	80.6	48.3	78.2	52.2	94
95	89.4	32.0	87.8	36.4	85.9	40.6	83.8	44.8	81.5	48.8	79.0	52.8	95
96	90.4	32.3	88.7	36.7	86.8	41.0	84.7	45.2	82.3	49.3	79.8	53.3	96
97	91.3	32.7	89.6	37.1	87.7	41.5	85.5	45.7	83.2	49.9	80.7	53.9	97
98	92.3	33.0	90.5	37.5	88.6	41.9	86.4	46.2	84.1	50.4	81.5	54.4	98
99	93.2	33.4	91.5	37.9	89.5	42.3	87.3	46.7	84.9	50.9	82.3	55.0	99
100	94.2	33.7	92.4	38.3	90.4	42.8	88.2	47.1	85.8	51.4	83.1	55.6	100
200	188.3	67.4	184.8	76.5	180.8	85.5	176.4	94.3	171.5	102.8	166.3	111.1	200
300	282.5	101.1	277.2	114.8	271.2	128.3	264.6	141.4	257.3	154.2	249.4	166.7	300
400	376.6	134.7	369.5	153.1	361.6	171.0	352.8	188.6	343.1	205.6	332.6	222.2	400
500	470.8	168.4	461.9	191.3	452.0	213.8	441.0	235.7	428.9	257.[illegible]	415.7	277.8	500
600	564.9	202.1	554.3	229.6	542.4	256.5	529.1	282.8	514.6	308.5	498.8	333.3	600
700	659.1	235.8	646.7	267.9	632.8	299.3	617.3	330.0	600.4	359.9	582.0	388.9	700
800	753.2	269.5	739.1	306.1	723.2	342.0	705.5	377.1	686.2	411.3	665.2	444.5	800
900	847.4	303.2	831.5	344.4	813.6	384.8	793.7	424.3	772.0	462.7	748.3	500.0	900
Ts.													Ts.
1	0.1	0.0	0.1	0.0	0.1	0.0	0.1	0.0	0.1	0.0	0.1	0.1	1
2	0.2	0.1	0.2	0.1	0.2	0.1	0.2	0.1	0.2	0.1	0.2	0.1	2
3	0.3	0.1	0.3	0.1	0.3	0.1	0.3	0.1	0.3	0.2	0.2	0.2	3
4	0.4	0.1	0.4	0.2	0.4	0.2	0.4	0.2	0.3	0.2	0.3	0.2	4
5	0.5	0.2	0.5	0.2	0.5	0.2	0.4	0.2	0.4	0.3	0.4	0.3	5
6	0.6	0.2	0.6	0.2	0.5	0.3	0.5	0.3	0.5	0.3	0.5	0.3	6
7	0.7	0.2	0.7	0.3	0.6	0.3	0.6	0.3	0.6	0.4	0.6	0.4	7
8	0.8	0.3	0.7	0.3	0.7	0.3	0.7	0.4	0.7	0.4	0.7	0.4	8
9	0.8	0.3	0.8	0.3	0.8	0.4	0.8	0.4	0.8	0.5	0.7	0.5	9
dist	dep.	lat.	dep.	lat.	dep.	lat.	dep.	lat.	dep.	lat.	dep.	lat.	dist
Ts.	6¼ Points		6 Points		5¾ Points		5½ Points		5¼ Points		5 Points		Ts.

Min.	0 Degr.	1 Degr.	2 Degr.	3 Degr.	4 Degr.	5 Degr.	6 Degr.	7 Degr.	8 Degr.	9 Degr.
0	.0	60.0	120.0	180.1	240.2	300.4	360.7	421.1	481.6	542.2
1	1.0	61.0	121.0	181.1	241.2	301.4	361.7	422.1	482.6	543.3
2	2.0	62.0	122.0	182.1	242.2	302.4	362.7	423.1	483.6	544.3
3	3.0	63.0	123.0	183.1	243.2	303.4	363.7	424.1	484.6	545.3
4	4.0	64.0	124.0	184.1	244.2	304.4	364.7	425.1	485.6	546.3
5	5.0	65.0	125.0	185.1	245.2	305.4	365.7	426.1	486.6	547.3
6	6.0	66.0	126.0	186.1	246.2	306.4	366.7	427.1	487.6	548.3
7	7.0	67.0	127.0	187.1	247.2	307.4	367.7	428.1	488.6	549.3
8	8.0	68.0	128.0	188.1	248.2	308.4	368.7	429.1	489.6	550.3
9	9.0	69.0	129.0	189.1	249.2	309.4	369.7	430.1	490.7	551.4
10	10.0	70.0	130.0	190.1	250.2	310.4	370.7	431.1	491.7	552.4
11	11.0	71.0	131.0	191.1	251.2	311.4	371.7	432.1	492.7	553.4
12	12.0	72.0	132.0	192.1	252.2	312.4	372.7	433.1	493.7	554.4
13	13.0	73.0	133.0	193.1	253.2	313.4	373.7	434.2	494.7	555.4
14	14.0	74.0	134.0	194.1	254.2	314.4	374.7	435.2	495.7	556.4
15	15.0	75.0	135.0	195.1	255.2	315.4	375.8	436.2	496.7	557.4
16	16.0	76.0	136.0	196.1	256.2	316.4	376.8	437.2	497.7	558.4
17	17.0	77.0	137.0	197.1	257.2	317.5	377.8	438.2	498.7	559.4
18	18.0	78.0	138.0	198.1	258.2	318.5	378.8	439.2	499.8	560.5
19	19.0	79.0	139.0	199.1	259.2	319.5	379.8	440.2	500.8	561.5
20	20.0	80.0	140.0	200.1	260.2	320.5	380.8	441.2	501.8	562.5
21	21.0	81.0	141.0	201.1	261.3	321.5	381.8	442.2	502.8	563.5
22	22.0	82.0	142.0	202.1	262.3	322.5	382.8	443.2	503.8	564.5
23	23.0	83.0	143.0	203.1	263.3	323.5	383.8	444.2	504.8	565.5
24	24.0	84.0	144.0	204.1	264.3	324.5	384.8	445.2	505.8	566.6
25	25.0	85.0	145.0	205.1	265.3	325.5	385.8	446.3	506.8	567.6
26	26.0	86.0	146.0	206.1	266.3	326.5	386.8	447.3	507.8	568.6
27	27.0	87.0	147.0	207.1	267.3	327.5	387.8	448.3	508.9	569.6
28	28.0	88.0	148.0	208.1	268.3	328.5	388.8	449.3	509.9	570.6
29	29.0	89.0	149.0	209.1	269.3	329.5	389.8	450.3	510.9	571.6
30	30.0	90.0	150.0	210.1	270.3	330.5	390.8	451.3	511.9	572.6
31	31.0	91.0	151.0	211.1	271.3	331.5	391.8	452.3	512.9	573.7
32	32.0	92.0	152.1	212.1	272.3	332.5	392.9	453.3	513.9	574.7
33	33.0	93.0	153.1	213.1	273.3	333.5	393.9	454.3	514.9	575.7
34	34.0	94.0	154.1	214.1	274.3	334.5	394.9	455.3	515.9	576.7
35	35.0	95.0	155.1	215.1	275.3	335.5	395.9	456.3	516.9	577.7
36	36.0	96.0	156.1	216.1	276.3	336.5	396.9	457.3	518.0	578.7
37	37.0	97.0	157.1	217.1	277.3	337.5	397.9	458.4	519.0	579.7
38	38.0	98.0	158.1	218.1	278.3	338.5	398.9	459.4	520.0	580.8
39	39.0	99.0	159.1	219.1	279.3	339.6	399.9	460.4	521.0	581.8
40	40.0	100.0	160.1	220.2	280.3	340.6	400.9	461.4	522.0	582.8
41	41.0	101.0	161.1	221.2	281.3	341.6	401.9	462.4	523.0	583.8
42	42.0	102.0	162.1	222.2	282.3	342.6	402.9	463.4	524.0	584.8
43	43.0	103.0	163.1	223.2	283.3	343.6	403.9	464.4	525.0	585.8
44	44.0	104.0	164.1	224.2	284.3	344.6	404.9	465.4	526.0	586.8
45	45.0	105.0	165.1	225.2	285.3	345.6	405.9	466.4	527.1	587.9
46	46.0	106.0	166.1	226.2	286.3	346.6	407.0	467.4	528.1	588.9
47	47.0	107.0	167.1	227.2	287.3	347.6	408.0	468.4	529.1	589.9
48	48.0	108.0	168.1	228.2	288.3	348.6	409.0	469.5	530.1	590.9
49	49.0	109.0	169.1	229.2	289.3	349.6	410.0	470.5	531.1	591.9
50	50.0	110.0	170.1	230.2	290.3	350.6	411.0	471.3	532.1	592.9
51	51.0	111.0	171.1	231.2	291.3	351.6	412.0	472.5	533.1	593.9
52	52.0	112.0	172.1	232.2	292.4	352.6	413.0	473.5	534.1	595.0
53	53.0	113.0	173.1	233.2	293.4	353.6	414.0	474.5	535.1	596.0
54	54.0	114.0	174.1	234.2	294.4	354.6	415.0	475.5	536.2	597.0
55	55.0	115.0	175.1	235.2	295.4	355.6	416.0	476.5	537.2	598.0
56	56.0	116.0	176.1	236.2	296.4	356.6	417.0	477.5	538.2	599.0
57	57.0	117.0	177.1	237.2	297.4	357.6	418.0	478.5	539.2	600.0
58	58.0	118.0	178.1	238.2	298.4	358.6	419.0	479.5	540.2	601.0
59	59.0	119.0	179.1	239.2	299.4	359.6	420.0	480.5	541.2	602.1

Min.	10 Degr.	11 Degr.	12 Degr.	13 Degr.	14 Degr.	15 Degr.	16 Degr.	17 Degr.	18 Degr.	19 Degr.	Min.
0	603.1	664.1	725.3	786.6	848.5	910.5	972.8	1035.3	1098.2	1161.5	0
1	604.1	665.1	726.4	787.8	849.5	911.5	973.8	1036.3	1099.3	1162.5	1
2	605.1	666.1	727.4	788.8	850.5	912.6	974.8	1037.4	1100.3	1163.6	2
3	606.1	667.1	728.4	789.9	851.6	913.6	975.9	1038.4	1101.4	1164.7	3
4	607.1	668.1	729.4	790.9	852.6	914.6	976.9	1039.5	1102.4	1165.7	4
5	608.2	669.2	730.5	791.9	853.6	915.7	978.0	1040.5	1103.5	1166.8	5
6	609.2	670.2	731.5	792.9	854.7	916.7	979.0	1041.6	1104.5	1167.8	6
7	610.2	671.2	732.5	794.0	855.7	917.7	980.0	1042.6	1105.6	1168.9	7
8	611.2	672.2	733.5	795.0	856.7	918.8	981.1	1043.7	1106.6	1170.0	8
9	612.2	673.2	734.5	796.0	857.8	919.8	982.1	1044.7	1107.7	1171.0	9
10	613.2	674.3	735.6	797.1	858.8	920.8	983.2	1045.8	1108.7	1172.1	10
11	614.2	675.3	735.6	798.1	859.9	921.9	964.2	1046.8	1109.8	1173.1	11
12	615.3	676.3	737.6	799.1	860.9	922.9	985.2	1047.9	1110.8	1174.2	12
13	616.3	677.3	738.6	800.2	861.9	923.9	986.3	1048.9	1111.9	1175.2	13
14	617.3	678.4	739.6	801.2	862.9	925.0	987.3	1049.9	1112.9	1176.3	14
15	618.3	679.4	740.7	802.2	864.0	926.0	988.4	1051.0	1114.0	1177.4	15
16	619.3	680.4	741.7	803.2	865.0	927.0	989.4	1052.0	1115.0	1178.4	16
17	620.3	681.4	742.7	804.2	866.0	928.1	990.4	1053.1	1116.1	1179.5	17
18	621.3	682.4	743.7	805.3	867.1	929.1	991.5	1054.1	1117.1	1180.5	18
19	622.4	683.4	744.6	806.3	868.1	930.1	992.5	1055.2	1118.2	1181.6	19
20	623.4	684.5	745.8	807.3	869.1	931.2	993.6	1056.2	1119.2	1182.7	20
21	624.4	685.5	746.8	808.4	870.1	932.2	994.6	1057.3	1120.3	1183.7	21
22	625.4	686.5	747.8	809.4	871.2	933.2	995.6	1058.3	1121.3	1184.8	22
23	626.4	687.5	748.9	810.4	872.2	934.3	996.7	1059.4	1122.4	1185.8	23
24	627.4	688.6	749.9	811.4	873.2	935.3	997.7	1060.4	1123.4	1186.9	24
25	628.5	689.6	750.9	812.5	874.3	936.3	998.8	1061.4	1124.5	1188.0	25
26	629.5	690.6	751.9	813.5	875.3	937.4	999.9	1062.5	1125.5	1189.0	26
27	630.5	691.6	753.0	814.5	876.3	938.4	1000.8	1063.5	1126.6	1190.1	27
28	631.5	692.6	754.0	815.5	877.4	939.4	1001.9	1064.6	1127.6	1191.1	28
29	632.5	693.6	755.0	816.6	878.4	940.5	1002.9	1065.6	1128.7	1192.2	29
30	633.5	694.7	756.0	817.6	879.4	941.5	1004.0	1066.7	1119.7	1193.2	30
31	634.6	695.7	757.1	818.6	880.5	942.5	1005.0	1067.7	1130.8	1194.3	31
32	645.6	696.7	758.1	819.6	881.5	943.6	1006.0	1068.8	1131.8	1195.4	32
33	636.6	697.7	759.1	820.7	882.5	944.6	1007.1	1069.8	1132.9	1196.4	33
34	637.6	698.7	760.1	821.7	883.6	945.6	1008.1	1070.9	1134.0	1197.5	34
35	638.6	699.8	761.1	822.7	884.6	946.7	1009.2	1072.0	1135.1	1198.5	35
36	639.6	700.8	762.2	823.8	885.6	947.7	1010.2	1073.0	1136.1	1199.6	36
37	640.7	701.8	763.2	824.8	886.7	948.7	1011.3	1074.1	1137.2	1200.7	37
38	641.7	702.8	764.2	825.8	887.7	949.8	1012.3	1075.1	1138.2	1201.7	38
39	642.7	703.8	765.2	826.8	888.7	950.8	1013.4	1076.2	1139.3	1202.8	39
40	643.7	704.9	766.3	827.9	889.8	951.9	1014.4	1077.2	1140.3	1203.9	40
41	644.7	705.9	767.3	828.9	890.8	952.9	1015.4	1078.3	1141.4	1204.9	41
42	645.8	706.9	768.3	829.9	891.8	953.9	1016.5	1079.3	1142.4	1206.0	42
43	646.8	707.9	769.3	831.0	892.9	955.0	1017.5	1080.4	1143.5	1207.1	43
44	647.8	709.0	770.4	832.0	893.9	956.0	1018.6	1081.4	1144.6	1208.1	44
45	648.8	710.0	771.4	833.0	894.9	957.1	1019.6	1082.5	1145.6	1209.2	45
46	649.8	711.0	772.4	834.1	896.0	958.1	1020.6	1083.5	1146.7	1210.2	46
47	650.8	712.0	773.4	835.1	897.0	959.2	1021.7	1084.6	1147.7	1211.3	47
48	651.9	713.0	774.5	836.1	898.0	960.2	1022.7	1085.6	1148.8	1212.4	48
49	652.9	714.1	775.5	837.2	899.1	961.3	1023.8	1086.7	1149.8	1213.4	49
50	653.9	715.1	776.5	838.2	900.1	962.3	1024.8	1087.7	1150.9	1214.5	50
51	654.9	716.1	777.5	839.2	901.1	963.4	1023.9	1088.8	1152.0	1215.5	51
52	655.9	717.1	778.6	840.3	902.2	964.4	1026.9	1089.8	1153.0	1216.6	52
53	657.0	718.2	779.6	841.3	903.2	965.5	1028.0	1090.9	1154.1	1217.7	53
54	658.0	719.2	780.6	842.3	904.3	966.5	1029.0	1091.9	1155.1	1218.7	54
55	659.0	720.2	781.7	843.4	905.3	967.6	1030.1	1093.0	1156.2	1219.8	55
56	660.0	721.2	782.7	844.4	906.3	968.6	1031.1	1094.0	1157.2	1220.9	56
57	661.0	722.3	783.7	845.4	907.4	969.6	1032.2	1095.1	1158.3	1221.9	57
58	662.1	723.3	784.7	846.5	908.4	970.7	1033.2	1096.1	1159.4	1223.0	58
59	663.1	724.3	785.8	847.5	909.4	971.7	1034.3	1097.2	1160.4	1224.1	59

15.6

Min.	20 Degr.	21 Degr.	22 Degr.	23 Degr.	24 Degr.	25 Degr.	26 Degr.	27 Degr.	28 Degr.	29 Degr.	Min.
0	1225.1	1289.2	1353.7	1418.6	1484.1	1550.0	1616.5	1683.5	1751.2	1819.5	0
1	1226.2	1290.3	1354.8	1419.7	1485.2	1551.1	1617.6	1684.6	1752.3	1820.6	1
2	1227.3	1291.3	1355.8	1420.8	1486.3	1552.2	1618.7	1685.8	1753.4	1821.7	2
3	1228.3	1292.4	1356.9	1421.9	1487.3	1553.3	1619.8	1686.9	1754.6	1822.9	3
4	1229.4	1293.5	1358.0	1423.0	1488.4	1554.4	1620.9	1688.0	1755.7	1824.0	4
5	1230.4	1294.5	1359.0	1424.1	1489.5	1555.5	1622.0	1689.1	1756.8	1825.2	5
6	1231.5	1295.6	1360.1	1425.1	1490.6	1556.6	1623.2	1690.3	1758.0	1826.3	6
7	1232.6	1296.7	1361.2	1426.2	1491.7	1557.7	1624.3	1691.4	1759.1	1827.5	7
8	1233.6	1297.8	1362.3	1427.3	1492.8	1558.8	1625.4	1692.5	1760.2	1828.6	8
9	1234.7	1298.8	1363.4	1428.4	1493.9	1559.9	1626.5	1693.6	1761.4	1829.7	9
10	1235.8	1299.9	1364.5	1429.5	1495.0	1561.0	1627.6	1694.8	1762.5	1830.9	10
11	1236.8	1301.0	1365.6	1430.6	1496.1	1562.1	1628.7	1695.9	1763.6	1832.0	11
12	1237.9	1302.0	1366.6	1431.7	1497.2	1563.2	1629.8	1697.0	1764.8	1833.2	12
13	1239.0	1303.1	1367.7	1432.8	1498.3	1564.3	1631.0	1698.1	1765.9	1834.3	13
14	1240.0	1304.2	1368.8	1433.9	1499.4	1565.4	1632.1	1699.3	1767.0	1835.5	14
15	1241.1	1305.3	1369.9	1434.9	1500.5	1566.5	1633.2	1700.4	1768.2	1836.6	15
16	1242.2	1306.3	1370.9	1436.0	1501.6	1567.6	1634.3	1701.5	1769.3	1837.8	16
17	1243.2	1307.4	1372.0	1437.1	1502.7	1568.7	1635.4	1702.6	1770.5	1838.9	17
18	1244.3	1308.5	1373.1	1438.2	1503.8	1569.8	1636.5	1703.8	1771.6	1840.1	18
19	1245.4	1309.6	1374.2	1439.3	1504.9	1571.0	1637.7	1704.9	1772.7	1841.2	19
20	1246.4	1310.6	1375.3	1440.4	1506.0	1572.1	1638.8	1706.0	1773.9	1842.4	20
21	1247.5	1311.7	1376.4	1441.5	1507.1	1573.2	1639.9	1707.1	1775.0	1843.5	21
22	1248.6	1312.8	1377.4	1442.6	1508.2	1574.3	1641.0	1708.3	1776.1	1844.6	22
23	1249.6	1313.8	1378.5	1443.7	1509.3	1575.4	1642.1	1709.4	1777.2	1845.8	23
24	1250.7	1314.9	1379.6	1444.8	1510.4	1576.5	1643.2	1710.5	1778.4	1846.9	24
25	1251.8	1316.0	1380.7	1445.8	1511.5	1577.6	1644.3	1711.6	1779.5	1848.1	25
26	1252.8	1317.1	1381.8	1446.9	1512.6	1578.7	1645.5	1712.8	1780.6	1849.2	26
27	1253.9	1318.1	1382.8	1448.0	1513.7	1579.8	1646.6	1713.9	1781.8	1850.4	27
28	1255.0	1319.2	1383.9	1449.1	1514.8	1580.9	1647.7	1715.0	1783.0	1851.5	28
29	1256.0	1320.3	1385.0	1450.2	1515.9	1582.0	1648.8	1716.1	1784.1	1852.7	29
30	1257.1	1321.4	1386.1	1451.3	1517.0	1583.2	1649.9	1717.3	1785.2	1853.8	30
31	1258.2	1322.5	1387.2	1452.4	1518.1	1584.3	1651.0	1718.4	1786.4	1855.0	31
32	1259.2	1323.5	1388.3	1453.5	1519.2	1585.4	1652.2	1719.5	1787.5	1856.1	32
33	1260.3	1324.6	1389.4	1454.6	1520.3	1586.5	1653.3	1720.7	1788.6	1857.2	33
34	1261.4	1325.7	1390.4	1455.6	1521.4	1587.6	1654.4	1721.8	1789.8	1858.4	34
35	1262.4	1326.7	1391.5	1456.7	1522.5	1588.7	1655.5	1722.9	1790.9	1859.6	35
36	1263.5	1327.8	1392.6	1457.8	1523.6	1589.8	1656.6	1724.0	1792.1	1860.7	36
37	1264.6	1328.9	1393.7	1458.9	1524.7	1590.9	1657.8	1725.2	1793.2	1861.9	37
38	1265.6	1330.0	1394.8	1460.0	1525.8	1592.0	1658.9	1726.3	1794.3	1863.0	38
39	1266.7	1331.0	1395.8	1461.1	1526.9	1593.2	1660.0	1727.4	1795.5	1864.2	39
40	1267.8	1332.1	1396.9	1462.2	1528.0	1594.3	1661.1	1728.6	1796.6	1865.3	40
41	1268.8	1333.2	1398.0	1463.3	1529.1	1595.4	1662.2	1729.7	1797.8	1866.5	41
42	1269.9	1334.3	1399.1	1464.4	1530.2	1596.5	1663.4	1730.8	1798.9	1867.6	42
43	1271.0	1335.3	1400.2	1465.5	1531.3	1597.6	1664.5	1731.9	1800.0	1868.8	43
44	1272.1	1336.4	1401.3	1466.6	1532.4	1598.7	1665.6	1733.1	1801.2	1869.9	44
45	1273.1	1337.5	1402.4	1467.7	1533.5	1599.8	1666.7	1734.2	1802.3	1871.1	45
46	1274.2	1338.6	1403.4	1468.8	1534.6	1600.9	1667.8	1735.3	1803.5	1872.2	46
47	1275.3	1339.7	1404.5	1469.8	1535.7	1602.0	1669.0	1736.5	1804.6	1873.4	47
48	1276.3	1340.7	1405.6	1470.9	1536.8	1603.1	1670.1	1737.6	1805.7	1874.5	48
49	1277.4	1341.8	1406.7	1472.0	1537.9	1604.3	1671.2	1738.7	1806.9	1875.7	49
50	1278.5	1342.9	1407.8	1473.1	1539.0	1605.4	1672.3	1739.9	1808.0	1876.8	50
51	1279.5	1344.0	1408.9	1474.2	1540.1	1606.5	1673.4	1741.0	1809.2	1878.0	51
52	1280.6	1345.1	1409.9	1475.3	1541.2	1607.6	1674.5	1742.1	1810.3	1879.2	52
53	1281.7	1346.1	1411.0	1476.4	1542.3	1608.7	1675.7	1743.2	1811.4	1880.3	53
54	1282.8	1347.2	1412.1	1477.5	1543.4	1609.8	1676.8	1744.4	1812.6	1881.5	54
55	1283.8	1348.3	1413.2	1478.6	1544.5	1610.9	1677.9	1745.5	1813.7	1882.6	55
56	1284.9	1349.4	1414.3	1479.7	1545.6	1612.0	1679.1	1746.6	1814.9	1883.8	56
57	1286.0	1350.4	1415.4	1480.8	1546.7	1613.1	1680.2	1747.8	1816.0	1884.9	57
58	1287.0	1351.5	1416.5	1481.9	1547.8	1614.2	1681.3	1748.9	1817.2	1886.1	58
59	1288.1	1352.6	1417.6	1483.0	1548.9	1615.4	1682.4	1750.0	1818.3	1887.2	59

Min.	30 Degr.	31 Degr.	32 Degr.	33 Degr.	34 Degr.	35 Degr.	36 Degr.	37 Degr.	38 Degr.	39 Degr.	Min.
0	1888.4	1958.0	2028.4	2099.6	2171.5	2244.3	2318.0	2392.7	2468.3	2545.0	0
1	1889.5	1959.2	2029.6	2100.7	2172.7	2245.5	2319.3	2393.9	2469.6	2546.2	1
2	1890.7	1960.4	2030.7	2101.9	2173.9	2246.8	2320.5	2395.2	2470.8	2547.5	2
3	1891.9	1961.6	2031.9	2103.1	2175.1	2248.0	2321.7	2396.4	2472.1	2548.8	3
4	1893.0	1962.7	2033.1	2104.3	2176.3	2249.2	2323.0	2397.7	2473.4	2550.1	4
5	1894.1	1963.9	2034.3	2105.5	2177.5	2250.4	2324.2	2398.9	2474.6	2551.4	5
6	1895.3	1965.0	2035.5	2106.7	2178.7	2251.6	2325.4	2400.2	2475.9	2552.7	6
7	1896.5	1966.2	2036.7	2107.9	2180.0	2252.9	2326.7	2401.4	2477.1	2554.0	7
8	1897.6	1967.4	2037.8	2109.1	2181.2	2254.1	2327.9	2402.7	2478.5	2555.3	8
9	1898.8	1968.5	2039.0	2110.3	2182.4	2255.3	2329.2	2403.9	2479.7	2556.6	9
10	1899.9	1969.7	2040.2	2111.5	2183.6	2256.5	2330.4	2405.2	2481.0	2557.8	10
11	1901.1	1970.9	2041.4	2112.7	2184.8	2257.8	2331.6	2406.4	2482.3	2559.1	11
12	1902.3	1972.0	2042.6	2113.9	2186.0	2259.0	2332.9	2407.7	2483.5	2560.4	12
13	1903.4	1973.2	2043.8	2115.1	2187.2	2260.2	2334.1	2409.0	2484.8	2561.7	13
14	1904.4	1974.5	2044.9	2116.3	2188.4	2261.4	2335.3	2410.2	2486.1	2563.0	14
15	1905.7	1975.6	2046.1	2117.5	2189.6	2262.7	2336.6	2411.5	2487.4	2564.2	15
16	1906.9	1976.8	2047.3	2118.7	2190.8	2263.9	2337.8	2412.7	2488.6	2565.6	16
17	1908.1	1977.9	2048.5	2119.8	2192.0	2265.1	2339.0	2414.0	2489.9	2566.9	17
18	1909.2	1979.1	2049.7	2121.0	2193.3	2266.3	2340.3	2415.2	2491.2	2568.2	18
19	1910.4	1980.3	2050.8	2122.2	2194.4	2267.6	2341.5	2416.5	2492.5	2569.5	19
20	1911.5	1981.4	2052.0	2123.4	2195.7	2268.8	2342.8	2417.8	2493.7	2570.7	20
21	1912.7	1982.6	2053.2	2124.6	2196.9	2270.0	2344.0	2419.0	2495.0	2572.0	21
22	1913.8	1983.7	2054.4	2125.8	2198.1	2271.2	2345.3	2420.3	2496.3	2573.3	22
23	1915.0	1984.9	2055.6	2127.0	2199.3	2272.5	2346.5	2421.5	2497.6	2574.6	23
24	1916.2	1986.1	2056.8	2128.2	2200.5	2273.7	2347.8	2422.8	2498.8	2575.9	24
25	1917.3	1987.3	2058.0	2129.4	2201.7	2274.9	2349.0	2424.0	2500.1	2577.2	25
26	1918.5	1988.4	2059.1	2130.6	2203.0	2276.1	2350.2	2425.3	2501.4	2578.5	26
27	1919.6	1989.6	2060.3	2131.8	2204.2	2277.4	2351.5	2426.5	2502.7	2579.8	27
28	1920.8	1990.8	2061.5	2133.0	2205.4	2278.6	2352.7	2427.8	2503.9	2581.1	28
29	1921.9	1992.0	2062.7	2134.2	2206.6	2279.8	2354.0	2429.1	2505.2	2582.4	29
30	1923.1	1993.1	2063.9	2135.4	2207.8	2281.0	2355.2	2430.3	2506.5	2583.7	30
31	1924.3	1994.3	2065.1	2136.6	2209.0	2282.3	2356.5	2431.6	2507.8	2585.0	31
32	1925.4	1995.5	2066.2	2137.8	2210.2	2283.5	2357.7	2432.9	2509.0	2586.3	32
33	1926.6	1996.6	2067.4	2139.0	2211.4	2284.7	2358.9	2434.1	2510.3	2587.6	33
34	1927.8	1997.8	2068.6	2140.2	2212.7	2286.0	2360.2	2435.4	2511.6	2588.9	34
35	1928.9	1999.0	2069.8	2141.4	2213.9	2287.2	2361.4	2436.7	2512.9	2590.2	35
36	1930.1	2000.2	2071.0	2142.6	2215.1	2288.4	2362.7	2437.9	2514.2	2591.5	36
37	1931.3	2001.3	2072.2	2143.8	2216.3	2289.7	2363.9	2439.2	2515.4	2592.8	37
38	1932.4	2002.5	2073.4	2145.0	2217.5	2290.9	2365.2	2440.4	2516.7	2594.1	38
39	1933.6	2003.7	2074.6	2146.2	2218.7	2292.1	2366.4	2441.7	2518.0	2595.4	39
40	1934.7	2004.9	2075.7	2147.4	2219.9	2293.3	2367.7	2443.0	2519.3	2596.7	40
41	1935.9	2006.0	2076.9	2148.6	2221.2	2294.6	2368.9	2444.2	2520.6	2598.0	41
42	1937.1	2007.2	2078.1	2149.8	2222.4	2295.8	2370.2	2445.5	2521.8	2599.3	42
43	1938.2	2008.4	2079.3	2151.0	2223.6	2297.0	2371.4	2446.8	2523.1	2600.6	43
44	1939.4	2009.6	2080.5	2152.2	2224.8	2298.3	2372.7	2448.0	2524.4	2601.9	44
45	1940.5	2010.7	2081.7	2153.4	2226.0	2299.5	2373.9	2449.3	2525.7	2603.2	45
46	1941.7	2011.9	2082.9	2154.6	2227.2	2300.7	2375.2	2450.6	2527.0	2604.5	46
47	1942.9	2013.1	2084.1	2155.8	2228.5	2302.0	2376.4	2451.8	2528.3	2605.8	47
48	1944.0	2014.3	2085.3	2157.0	2229.7	2303.2	2377.7	2453.1	2529.5	2607.1	48
49	1945.2	2015.4	2086.5	2158.2	2230.9	2304.4	2378.9	2454.3	2530.8	2608.4	49
50	1946.4	2016.6	2087.7	2159.4	2232.1	2305.7	2380.1	2455.6	2532.1	2609.7	50
51	1947.5	2017.8	2088.9	2160.7	2233.3	2306.9	2381.4	2456.9	2533.4	2611.0	51
52	1948.7	2019.0	2090.1	2161.9	2234.6	2308.1	2382.6	2458.1	2534.7	2612.3	52
53	1949.9	2020.2	2091.3	2163.1	2235.8	2309.4	2383.9	2459.4	2536.0	2613.6	53
54	1951.0	2021.3	2092.5	2164.3	2237.0	2310.6	2385.1	2460.7	2537.2	2614.9	54
55	1952.2	2022.5	2093.7	2165.5	2238.2	2311.8	2386.4	2461.9	2538.5	2616.2	55
56	1953.4	2023.7	2094.9	2166.7	2239.4	2313.1	2387.6	2463.2	2539.8	2617.5	56
57	1954.5	2024.9	2096.1	2167.9	2240.7	2314.3	2388.9	2464.5	2541.1	2618.8	57
58	1955.7	2026.0	2097.3	2169.1	2241.9	2315.5	2390.2	2465.8	2542.4	2620.1	58
59	1956.9	2027.2	2098.5	2170.3	2243.1	2316.7	2391.4	2467.0	2543.7	2621.4	59

Min.	40 Degr.	41 Degr.	42 Degr.	43 Degr.	44 Degr.	45 Degr.	46 Degr.	47 Degr.	48 Degr.	49 Degr.	Min.
0	2622.7	2701.6	2781.7	2863.1	2945.7	3030.0	3115.6	3202.8	3291.6	3382.1	0
1	2624.0	2702.9	2783.1	2864.5	2947.2	3031.4	3117.0	3204.2	3293.1	3383.6	1
2	2625.3	2704.3	2784.4	2865.8	2948.6	3032.8	3118.5	3205.7	3294.6	3385.2	2
3	2626.6	2705.6	2785.8	2867.2	2950.0	3034.2	3119.9	3207.2	3296.1	3386.7	3
4	2627.9	2706.9	2787.1	2868.6	2951.4	3035.6	3121.4	3208.6	3297.5	3388.2	4
5	2629.2	2708.3	2788.5	2870.0	2952.8	3037.0	3122.8	3210.1	3299.0	3389.7	5
6	2630.5	2709.6	2789.8	2871.3	2954.2	3038.4	3124.2	3211.6	3300.5	3391.3	6
7	2631.9	2710.9	2791.2	2872.7	2955.6	3039.8	3125.7	3213.0	3302.0	3392.8	7
8	2633.2	2712.2	2792.5	2874.1	2957.0	3041.3	3127.1	3214.5	3303.5	3394.3	8
9	2634.5	2713.6	2793.8	2875.4	2958.4	3042.7	3128.6	3216.0	3305.0	3395.9	9
10	2635.8	2714.9	2795.1	2876.8	2959.8	3044.1	3130.0	3217.4	3306.5	3397.4	10
11	2637.1	2716.2	2796.5	2878.2	2961.1	3045.5	3131.5	3218.9	3308.0	3398.9	11
12	2638.4	2717.5	2797.9	2879.5	2962.5	3047.0	3132.9	3220.4	3309.5	3400.4	12
13	2639.7	2718.9	2799.3	2880.9	2963.9	3048.4	3134.3	3221.9	3311.0	3402.0	13
14	2641.0	2720.2	2800.6	2882.3	2965.3	3049.8	3135.8	3223.3	3312.5	3403.5	14
15	2642.3	2721.5	2802.0	2883.7	2966.7	3051.2	3137.2	3224.8	3314.0	3405.0	15
16	2643.6	2722.9	2803.3	2885.0	2968.1	3052.6	3138.7	3226.3	3315.5	3406.6	16
17	2644.9	2724.2	2804.7	2886.4	2969.5	3054.1	3140.1	3227.7	3317.0	3408.1	17
18	2646.3	2725.5	2806.0	2887.8	2970.9	3055.5	3141.6	3229.2	3318.5	3409.6	18
19	2647.6	2726.9	2807.4	2889.2	2972.3	3056.9	3143.0	3230.7	3320.0	3411.2	19
20	2648.9	2728.2	2808.8	2890.5	2973.7	3058.3	3144.5	3232.2	3321.5	3412.7	20
21	2650.2	2729.5	2810.1	2891.9	2975.1	3059.7	3145.9	3233.6	3323.1	3414.2	21
22	2651.5	2730.8	2811.4	2893.3	2976.5	3061.2	3147.4	3235.1	3324.6	3415.8	22
23	2652.8	2732.2	2812.8	2894.7	2977.9	3062.6	3148.8	3236.6	3326.1	3417.3	23
24	2654.1	2733.5	2814.1	2896.0	2979.3	3064.0	3150.3	3238.1	3327.6	3418.8	24
25	2655.5	2734.8	2815.5	2897.4	2980.7	3065.4	3151.7	3239.5	3329.1	3420.4	25
26	2656.8	2736.2	2816.8	2898.8	2982.1	3066.9	3153.2	3241.0	3330.6	3421.9	26
27	2658.1	2737.5	2818.2	2900.2	2983.5	3068.3	3154.6	3242.5	3332.1	3423.5	27
28	2659.4	2738.8	2819.5	2901.5	2984.9	3069.7	3156.1	3244.0	3333.6	3425.0	28
29	2660.7	2740.2	2820.9	2902.9	2986.3	3071.1	3157.5	3245.5	3335.1	3426.5	29
30	2662.0	2741.5	2822.3	2904.3	2987.7	3072.6	3159.0	3246.9	3336.6	3428.1	30
31	2663.3	2742.9	2823.6	2905.7	2989.1	3074.0	3160.4	3248.4	3338.1	3429.6	31
32	2664.6	2744.2	2825.0	2907.1	2990.5	3075.4	3161.9	3249.9	3339.6	3431.2	32
33	2666.0	2745.5	2826.3	2908.4	2991.9	3076.9	3163.3	3251.4	3341.1	3432.7	33
34	2667.3	2746.9	2827.7	2909.7	2993.3	3078.3	3164.8	3252.9	3342.7	3434.2	34
35	2668.6	2748.2	2829.0	2911.2	2994.7	3079.7	3166.2	3254.4	3344.2	3435.8	35
36	2669.9	2749.5	2830.4	2912.6	2996.1	3081.1	3167.7	3255.8	3345.7	3437.3	36
37	2671.2	2750.9	2831.8	2914.0	2997.5	3082.6	3169.1	3257.3	3347.2	3438.9	37
38	2672.5	2752.2	2833.1	2915.3	2998.9	3084.0	3170.6	3258.8	3348.7	3440.4	38
39	2673.9	2753.5	2834.5	2916.7	3000.3	3085.4	3172.1	3260.3	3350.1	3442.0	39
40	2675.1	2754.9	2835.8	2918.1	3001.8	3086.9	3173.5	3261.8	3351.7	3443.5	40
41	2676.5	2756.2	2837.2	2919.5	3003.2	3088.3	3175.0	3263.3	3353.2	3445.0	41
42	2677.8	2757.6	2838.6	2920.9	3004.6	3089.7	3176.4	3264.7	3354.8	3446.6	42
43	2679.1	2758.9	2839.9	2922.3	3006.0	3091.2	3177.9	3266.2	3356.3	3448.1	43
44	2680.5	2760.2	2841.3	2923.6	3007.4	3092.6	3179.3	3267.7	3357.8	3449.7	44
45	2681.8	2761.5	2842.6	2925.0	3008.8	3094.0	3180.8	3269.2	3359.3	3451.2	45
46	2683.1	2762.9	2844.0	2926.4	3010.2	3095.5	3182.3	3270.7	3360.8	3452.8	46
47	2684.4	2764.3	2845.4	2927.8	3011.6	3096.9	3183.7	3272.2	3362.3	3454.3	47
48	2685.7	2765.6	2846.7	2929.2	3013.0	3098.3	3185.2	3273.7	3363.9	3455.9	48
49	2687.1	2766.9	2848.1	2930.6	3014.4	3099.8	3186.6	3275.2	3365.4	3457.4	49
50	2688.4	2768.3	2849.5	2932.0	3015.8	3101.2	3188.1	3276.6	3366.9	3459.0	50
51	2689.7	2769.6	2850.8	2933.3	3017.2	3102.6	3189.6	3278.1	3368.4	3460.5	51
52	2691.0	2771.0	2852.2	2934.7	3018.7	3104.1	3191.0	3279.6	3369.9	3462.1	52
53	2692.3	2772.3	2853.6	2936.1	3020.1	3105.6	3192.5	3281.1	3371.5	3463.6	53
54	2693.7	2773.7	2854.9	2937.5	3021.5	3107.0	3194.0	3282.6	3373.0	3465.2	54
55	2695.0	2775.0	2856.3	2938.9	3022.9	3108.4	3195.4	3284.1	3374.5	3466.7	55
56	2696.3	2776.4	2857.7	2940.3	3024.3	3109.8	3196.9	3285.6	3376.0	3468.3	56
57	2697.6	2777.7	2859.1	2941.7	3025.7	3111.2	3198.4	3287.1	3377.6	3469.8	57
58	2699.0	2779.0	2860.5	2943.1	3027.1	3112.7	3199.8	3288.6	3379.1	3471.4	58
59	2700.3	2780.4	2861.8	2944.4	3028.5	3114.1	3201.3	3290.1	3380.6	3473.0	59

M

Min.	50 Degr.	51 Degr.	52 Degr.	53 Degr.	54 Degr.	55 Degr.	56 Degr.	57 Degr.	58 Degr.	59 Degr.	Min.
0	3474.5	3568.8	3665.2	3763.8	3864.7	3968.0	4073.9	4182.6	4294.3	4409.2	0
1	3476.1	3570.4	3666.9	3765.5	3866.4	3969.7	4075.7	4184.5	4296.2	4411.1	1
2	3477.6	3572.0	3668.5	3767.1	3868.1	3971.5	4077.5	4186.3	4298.1	4413.1	2
3	3479.2	3573.6	3670.1	3768.8	3869.8	3973.2	4079.3	4188.2	4300.0	4415.0	3
4	3480.7	3575.2	3671.7	3770.4	3871.5	3975.0	4081.1	4190.0	4301.9	4417.0	4
5	3482.3	3576.8	3673.4	3772.1	3873.2	3976.7	4082.9	4191.8	4303.8	4418.9	5
6	3483.9	3578.4	3675.0	3773.8	3874.9	3978.4	4084.7	4193.7	4305.7	4420.8	6
7	3485.4	3580.0	3676.6	3775.4	3876.6	3980.2	4086.5	4195.5	4307.6	4422.8	7
8	3487.0	3581.6	3678.2	3777.1	3878.3	3982.0	4088.3	4197.4	4309.5	4424.7	8
9	3488.5	3583.2	3679.9	3778.8	3880.0	3983.7	4090.1	4199.2	4311.4	4426.7	9
10	3490.1	3584.8	3681.5	3780.4	3881.7	3985.5	4091.9	4201.1	4313.2	4428.6	10
11	3491.7	3586.4	3683.1	3782.1	3883.4	3987.2	4093.7	4202.9	4315.1	4430.6	11
12	3493.2	3588.0	3684.8	3783.8	3885.1	3989.0	4095.5	4204.7	4317.0	4432.5	12
13	3494.8	3589.5	3686.4	3785.5	3886.8	3990.7	4097.3	4206.6	4318.9	4434.5	13
14	3496.3	3591.1	3688.0	3787.1	3888.6	3992.5	4099.1	4208.4	4320.8	4436.4	14
15	3497.9	3592.7	3689.7	3788.8	3890.3	3994.2	4100.9	4210.3	4322.7	4438.4	15
16	3499.5	3594.3	3691.3	3790.5	3892.0	3996.0	4102.7	4212.1	4324.6	4440.4	16
17	3501.0	3595.9	3692.9	3792.1	3893.7	3997.7	4104.5	4214.0	4326.5	4442.3	17
18	3502.6	3597.5	3694.6	3793.8	3895.4	3999.5	4106.3	4215.8	4328.4	4444.3	18
19	3504.2	3599.1	3696.2	3795.5	3897.1	4001.3	4108.1	4217.7	4330.3	4446.2	19
20	3505.7	3600.7	3697.8	3797.2	3898.8	4003.0	4109.9	4219.5	4332.2	4448.2	20
21	3507.3	3602.3	3699.5	3798.8	3900.5	4004.8	4111.7	4221.4	4334.2	4450.2	21
22	3508.9	3603.9	3701.1	3800.5	3902.3	4006.5	4113.5	4223.2	4336.1	4452.1	22
23	3510.5	3605.5	3702.7	3802.2	3904.0	4008.3	4115.3	4225.1	4338.0	4454.1	23
24	3512.0	3607.1	3704.4	3803.9	3905.7	4010.0	4117.1	4227.0	4339.9	4456.0	24
25	3513.6	3608.7	3706.0	3805.5	3907.4	4011.8	4118.9	4228.8	4341.8	4458.0	25
26	3515.1	3610.3	3707.7	3807.2	3909.1	4013.6	4120.7	4230.7	4343.7	4460.0	26
27	3516.7	3611.9	3709.3	3808.9	3910.9	4015.3	4122.5	4232.5	4345.6	4461.9	27
28	3518.2	3613.6	3710.9	3810.6	3912.6	4017.1	4124.3	4234.4	4347.5	4463.9	28
29	3519.8	3615.2	3712.6	3812.3	3914.3	4018.9	4126.1	4236.2	4349.4	4465.9	29
30	3521.4	3616.8	3714.2	3813.9	3916.0	4020.6	4127.9	4238.1	4351.3	4467.8	30
31	3523.0	3618.4	3715.9	3815.6	3917.7	4022.4	4129.7	4240.0	4353.3	4469.8	31
32	3524.6	3620.0	3717.5	3817.3	3919.5	4024.2	4131.6	4241.8	4355.2	4471.8	32
33	3526.1	3621.6	3719.2	3819.0	3921.2	4025.9	4133.4	4243.7	4357.1	4473.8	33
34	3527.7	3623.2	3720.8	3820.7	3922.9	4027.7	4135.2	4245.6	4359.0	4475.7	34
35	3529.3	3624.8	3722.4	3822.3	3924.6	4029.5	4137.0	4247.4	4360.9	4477.7	35
36	3530.9	3626.4	3724.1	3824.0	3926.4	4031.2	4138.8	4249.3	4362.8	4479.7	36
37	3532.4	3628.0	3725.7	3825.7	3928.1	4033.0	4140.6	4251.2	4364.8	4481.7	37
38	3534.0	3629.6	3727.4	3827.4	3929.8	4034.8	4142.5	4253.0	4366.7	4483.6	38
39	3535.6	3631.3	3729.0	3829.1	3931.5	4036.6	4144.3	4254.9	4368.6	4485.6	39
40	3537.2	3632.9	3730.7	3830.8	3933.3	4038.3	4146.1	4256.8	4370.5	4487.6	40
41	3538.8	3634.5	3732.3	3832.5	3935.0	4040.1	4147.9	4258.6	4372.5	4489.6	41
42	3540.3	3636.1	3734.0	3834.2	3936.7	4041.9	4149.7	4260.5	4374.4	4491.6	42
43	3541.9	3637.7	3735.6	3835.8	3938.5	4043.6	4151.6	4262.4	4376.3	4493.5	43
44	3543.5	3639.3	3737.3	3837.5	3940.2	4045.4	4153.4	4264.3	4378.2	4495.5	44
45	3545.1	3640.9	3738.9	3839.2	3941.9	4047.2	4155.2	4266.1	4380.2	4497.5	45
46	3546.7	3642.5	3740.6	3840.9	3943.7	4049.0	4157.0	4268.0	4382.1	4499.5	46
47	3548.2	3644.2	3742.2	3842.6	3945.4	4050.8	4158.8	4269.9	4384.0	4501.5	47
48	3549.8	3645.8	3743.9	3844.3	3947.1	4052.5	4160.7	4271.8	4385.9	4503.5	48
49	3551.4	3647.4	3745.6	3846.0	3948.9	4054.3	4162.5	4273.6	4387.9	4505.5	49
50	3553.0	3649.0	3747.2	3847.7	3950.6	4056.1	4164.3	4275.5	4389.8	4507.5	50
51	3554.6	3650.6	3748.9	3849.4	3952.3	4057.9	4166.2	4277.4	4391.7	4509.4	51
52	3556.1	3652.3	3750.5	3851.1	3954.1	4059.7	4168.0	4279.3	4393.7	4511.4	52
53	3557.7	3653.9	3752.2	3852.8	3955.8	4061.4	4169.8	4281.1	4395.6	4513.4	53
54	3559.3	3655.5	3753.8	3854.5	3957.6	4063.2	4171.7	4283.0	4397.5	4515.4	54
55	3560.9	3657.1	3755.5	3856.2	3959.3	4065.0	4173.5	4284.9	4399.5	4517.4	55
56	3562.5	3658.7	3757.2	3857.9	3961.0	4066.8	4175.3	4286.8	4401.4	4519.4	56
57	3564.1	3660.4	3758.8	3859.6	3962.8	4068.6	4177.2	4288.7	4403.4	4521.4	57
58	3565.7	3662.0	3760.5	3861.3	3964.5	4070.4	4179.0	4290.6	4405.3	4523.4	58
59	3567.3	3663.6	3762.2	3863.0	3966.3	4072.1	4180.8	4292.5	4407.2	4525.4	59

Min	60 Degr.	61 Degr.	62 Degr.	63 Degr.	64 Degr.	65 Degr.	66 Degr.	67 Degr.	68 Degr.	69 Degr.	Min
0	4527.4	4649.2	4775.0	4905.0	5039.4	5178.8	5323.6	5474.0	5630.9	5794.6	0
1	4529.4	4651.3	4777.1	4907.2	5041.7	5181.2	5326.0	5476.6	5633.5	5797.4	1
2	4531.4	4653.4	4779.3	4909.4	5044.0	5183.6	5328.5	5479.2	5636.2	5800.2	2
3	4533.4	4655.5	4781.4	4911.6	5046.3	5186.0	5330.9	5481.7	5638.9	5803.0	3
4	4535.4	4657.5	4783.5	4913.8	5048.6	5188.3	5333.4	5484.3	5641.5	5805.8	4
5	4537.4	4659.6	4785.7	4916.0	5050.8	5190.7	5335.9	5486.9	5644.2	5808.6	5
6	4539.4	4661.7	4787.8	4918.2	5053.2	5193.1	5338.3	5489.4	5646.9	5811.4	6
7	4541.4	4663.7	4790.0	4920.4	5055.5	5195.4	5340.8	5492.0	5649.6	5814.2	7
8	4543.4	4665.8	4792.1	4922.6	5057.7	5197.8	5343.3	5494.6	5652.3	5617.0	8
9	4545.4	4667.9	4794.2	4924.8	5060.0	5200.2	5345.7	5497.1	5655.0	5819.8	9
10	4547.5	4669.9	4796.4	4927.1	5062.3	5202.6	5348.2	5499.7	5657.6	5822.6	10
11	4549.5	4672.0	4798.5	4929.3	5064.6	5205.0	5350.7	5502.3	5660.3	5825.4	11
12	4551.5	4674.1	4800.7	4931.5	5066.9	5207.3	5353.2	5504.9	5663.0	5828.2	12
13	4553.5	4676.2	4802.8	4933.7	5069.2	5209.7	5355.6	5507.4	5665.7	5831.0	13
14	4555.5	4678.2	4804.9	4935.9	5071.5	5212.1	5358.1	5510.0	5668.4	5833.9	14
15	4557.5	4680.3	4807.1	4938.1	5073.8	5214.5	5360.6	5512.6	5671.1	5836.7	15
16	4559.5	4682.4	4809.2	4940.4	5076.1	5216.9	5363.1	5515.2	5673.8	5839.5	16
17	4561.5	4684.5	4811.4	4942.6	5078.4	5219.3	5365.6	5517.8	5676.5	5842.3	17
18	4563.6	4686.6	4813.5	4944.8	5080.7	5221.7	5368.1	5520.4	5679.2	5845.2	18
19	4565.6	4688.6	4815.7	4947.0	5083.0	5224.1	5370.5	5523.0	5681.9	5848.0	19
20	4567.6	4690.7	4817.8	4949.3	5085.3	5226.5	5373.0	5525.6	5684.6	5850.8	20
21	4569.6	4692.8	4820.0	4951.5	5087.7	5228.9	5375.5	5528.2	5687.3	5853.7	21
22	4571.6	4694.9	4822.2	4953.7	5090.0	5231.3	5378.0	5530.8	5690.0	5856.5	22
23	4573.7	4697.0	4824.3	4956.0	5092.3	5233.7	5380.5	5533.4	5692.8	5859.3	23
24	4575.7	4699.1	4826.5	4958.2	5094.6	5236.1	5383.0	5536.0	5695.5	5862.2	24
25	4577.7	4701.2	4828.6	4960.4	5096.9	5238.5	5385.5	5538.6	5698.2	5865.0	25
26	4579.7	4703.2	4830.8	4962.7	5099.2	5240.9	5388.0	5541.2	5700.9	5867.9	26
27	4581.8	4705.3	4832.9	4964.9	5101.5	5243.3	5390.5	5543.8	5703.6	5870.7	27
28	4583.8	4707.4	4835.1	4967.1	5103.9	5245.7	5393.0	5546.4	5706.3	5873.5	28
29	4585.8	4709.5	4837.3	4969.4	5106.2	5248.1	5395.5	5549.0	5709.1	5876.4	29
30	4587.8	4711.6	4839.4	4971.6	5108.5	5250.5	5398.0	5551.6	5711.8	5879.3	30
31	4589.9	4713.7	4841.6	4973.9	5110.8	5252.9	5400.5	5554.2	5714.5	5882.1	31
32	4591.9	4715.8	4843.8	4976.1	5113.1	5255.3	5403.0	5556.8	5717.3	5885.0	32
33	4593.9	4717.9	4845.9	4978.3	5115.5	5257.7	5405.6	5559.5	5720.0	5887.8	33
34	4596.0	4720.0	4848.1	4980.6	5117.8	5260.1	5408.1	5562.1	5722.7	5890.7	34
35	4598.0	4722.1	4850.3	4982.8	5120.1	5262.6	5410.6	5564.7	5725.5	5893.6	35
36	4600.1	4724.2	4852.5	4985.1	5122.5	5265.0	5413.1	5567.3	5728.2	5896.4	36
37	4602.1	4726.3	4854.6	4987.3	5124.8	5267.4	5415.6	5569.9	5731.0	5899.3	37
38	4604.1	4728.4	4856.8	4989.6	5127.1	5269.8	5418.1	5572.6	5733.7	5902.2	38
39	4606.2	4730.5	4859.0	4991.8	5129.5	5272.3	5420.7	5575.2	5736.4	5905.1	39
40	4608.2	4732.6	4861.2	4994.1	5131.8	5274.7	5423.2	5577.8	5739.2	5907.9	40
41	4610.3	4734.7	4863.3	4996.3	5134.1	5277.1	5425.7	5580.5	5741.9	5910.8	41
42	4612.3	4736.9	4865.5	4998.6	5136.5	5279.5	5428.2	5583.1	5744.7	5913.7	42
43	4614.3	4739.0	4867.7	5000.9	5138.8	5282.0	5430.8	5585.7	5747.5	5916.6	43
44	4616.4	4741.1	4869.9	5003.1	5141.2	5284.4	5433.3	5588.4	5750.2	5919.5	44
45	4618.4	4743.2	4872.1	5005.4	5143.5	5286.8	5435.8	5591.0	5753.0	5922.4	45
46	4620.5	4745.3	4874.3	5007.6	5145.9	5289.3	5438.4	5593.7	5755.7	5925.4	46
47	4622.5	4747.4	4876.4	5009.9	5148.2	5291.7	5440.9	5596.3	5758.5	5928.1	47
48	4624.6	4749.5	4878.6	5012.2	5150.6	5294.1	5443.5	5599.0	5761.3	5931.0	48
49	4626.6	4751.7	4880.8	5014.4	5152.9	5296.6	5446.0	5601.6	5764.0	5933.9	49
50	4628.7	4753.8	4883.0	5016.7	5155.3	5299.0	5448.5	5604.3	5766.8	5936.8	50
51	4630.7	4755.9	4885.2	5019.0	5157.6	5301.5	5451.1	5606.9	5769.6	5939.7	51
52	4632.8	4758.0	4887.4	5021.2	5160.0	5303.9	5453.6	5609.6	5772.3	5942.6	52
53	4634.8	4760.1	4889.6	5023.5	5162.3	5306.4	5456.2	5612.2	5775.1	5945.5	53
54	4636.9	4762.3	4891.8	5025.8	5164.7	5308.8	5458.7	5614.9	5777.9	5948.5	54
55	4639.0	4764.4	4894.0	5028.1	5167.0	5311.3	5461.3	5617.5	5780.7	5951.4	55
56	4641.0	4766.5	4896.2	5030.3	5169.4	5313.7	5463.8	5620.2	5783.5	5954.3	56
57	4643.1	4768.6	4898.4	5032.6	5171.8	5316.2	5466.4	5622.9	5786.2	5957.2	57
58	4645.1	4770.8	4900.6	5034.9	5174.1	5318.6	5468.9	5625.5	5789.0	5960.1	58
59	4647.2	4772.9	4902.8	5037.2	5176.5	5321.1	5471.5	5628.2	5791.8	5963.0	59

Min.	70 Degr.	71 Degr.	72 Degr.	73 Degr.	74 Degr.	75 Degr.	76 Degr.	77 Degr.	78 Degr.	79 Degr.	Min.
0	5966.0	6145.7	6334.9	6534.5	6745.7	6970.3	7210.1	7467.2	7744.6	8045.7	0
1	5968.9	6148.8	6338.1	6537.9	6749.4	6974.2	7214.2	7471.7	7749.4	8051.0	1
2	5971.8	6151.9	6341.4	6541.3	6753.0	6978.1	7218.3	7476.1	7754.2	8056.2	2
3	5974.7	6155.0	6344.6	6544.7	6756.6	6981.9	7222.5	7480.6	7759.0	8061.5	3
4	5977.7	6158.0	6347.8	6548.2	6760.3	6985.8	7226.6	7485.0	7763.9	8066.8	4
5	5980.6	6161.1	6351.1	6551.6	6763.9	6989.7	7230.8	7489.5	7768.7	8072.0	5
6	5983.5	6164.2	6354.3	6555.0	6767.6	6993.6	7234.9	7494.0	7773.5	8077.3	6
7	5986.5	6167.3	6357.6	6558.5	6771.2	6997.5	7239.1	7498.5	7778.4	8082.6	7
8	5989.4	6170.4	6360.9	6561.9	6774.9	7001.4	7243.3	7502.9	7783.2	8087.9	8
9	5992.4	6173.5	6364.1	6565.4	6778.5	7005.3	7247.5	7507.4	7788.1	8093.2	9
10	5995.3	6176.6	6367.4	6568.8	6782.2	7009.2	7251.6	7511.9	7793.0	8098.5	10
11	5998.3	6179.7	6370.6	6572.3	6785.8	7013.1	7255.8	7516.4	7797.8	8103.8	11
12	6001.2	6182.8	6373.9	6575.7	6789.5	7017.0	7260.0	7520.9	7802.7	8109.2	12
13	6004.2	6185.9	6377.2	6579.2	6793.1	7020.9	7264.2	7525.4	7807.6	8114.5	13
14	6007.1	6189.0	6380.5	6582.6	6796.9	7024.8	7268.4	7530.0	7812.5	8119.8	14
15	6010.1	6192.1	6383.7	6586.1	6800.5	7028.7	7272.6	7534.5	7817.4	8125.2	15
16	6013.0	6195.2	6387.0	6589.5	6804.2	7032.7	7276.8	7539.0	7822.3	8130.6	16
17	6016.0	6198.3	6390.3	6593.0	6807.9	7036.6	7281.0	7543.6	7827.2	8135.9	17
18	6019.0	6201.4	6393.6	6596.5	6811.6	7040.5	7285.2	7548.1	7832.2	8141.3	18
19	6021.9	6204.6	6396.9	6600.0	6815.3	7044.5	7289.4	7552.7	7837.1	8146.7	19
20	6024.9	6207.7	6400.2	6603.4	6819.0	7048.4	7293.7	7557.2	7842.0	8152.1	20
21	6027.9	6210.8	6403.5	6606.9	6822.7	7052.4	7297.9	7561.8	7847.0	8157.5	21
22	6030.8	6213.9	6406.8	6610.4	6826.4	7056.3	7302.1	7566.3	7851.9	8162.9	22
23	6033.8	6217.1	6410.1	6613.9	6830.1	7060.3	7306.4	7570.9	7856.9	8168.3	23
24	6036.8	6220.2	6413.4	6617.4	6833.8	7064.2	7310.6	7575.5	7861.9	8173.7	24
25	6039.8	6223.3	6416.7	6620.9	6837.6	7068.2	7314.9	7580.1	7866.8	8179.2	25
26	6042.7	6226.5	6420.0	6624.4	6841.3	7072.2	7319.1	7584.7	7871.8	8184.6	26
27	6045.7	6229.6	6423.3	6627.9	6845.0	7076.2	7323.4	7589.3	7876.8	8190.1	27
28	6048.7	6232.7	6426.6	6631.4	6848.7	7080.1	7327.7	7593.9	7881.8	8195.5	28
29	6051.7	6235.9	6429.9	6635.0	6852.5	7084.1	7332.0	7598.5	7886.8	8201.0	29
30	6054.7	6239.0	6433.2	6638.5	6856.2	7088.1	7336.2	7603.1	7891.8	8206.5	30
31	6057.7	6242.2	6436.6	6642.0	6860.0	7092.1	7340.4	7607.7	7896.8	8212.0	31
32	6060.7	6245.3	6439.9	6645.5	6863.7	7096.1	7344.8	7612.3	7901.9	8217.5	32
33	6063.7	6248.5	6443.2	6649.1	6867.5	7100.1	7349.1	7617.0	7906.9	8223.0	33
34	6066.7	6251.7	6446.6	6652.6	6871.2	7104.1	7353.4	7621.6	7911.9	8228.5	34
35	6069.7	6254.8	6449.9	6656.1	6875.0	7108.2	7357.7	7626.3	7917.0	8234.5	35
36	6072.7	6258.0	6453.3	6659.7	6878.7	7112.2	7362.0	7630.9	7922.1	8239.6	36
37	6075.7	6261.2	6456.6	6663.2	6882.5	7116.2	7366.4	7635.6	7927.1	8245.1	37
38	6078.8	6264.3	6460.0	6666.8	6886.3	7120.2	7370.7	7640.2	7932.2	8250.7	38
39	6081.8	6267.5	6463.3	6670.3	6890.1	7124.3	7375.0	7644.9	7937.3	8256.3	39
40	6084.8	6270.7	6466.7	6673.9	6893.8	7128.3	7379.4	7649.6	7942.4	8261.8	40
41	6087.9	6273.9	6470.0	6677.4	6897.6	7132.3	7383.7	7654.3	7947.5	8267.4	41
42	6090.8	6277.1	6473.4	6681.0	6901.4	7136.4	7388.0	7659.0	7952.6	8273.0	42
43	6093.9	6280.3	6476.8	6684.6	6905.2	7140.4	7392.3	7663.7	7957.7	8278.6	43
44	6096.9	6283.5	6480.1	6688.1	6909.0	7144.5	7396.8	7668.4	7962.8	8284.2	44
45	6099.9	6286.6	6483.5	6691.7	6912.8	7148.6	7401.1	7673.1	7968.0	8289.9	45
46	6103.0	6289.8	6486.9	6695.3	6916.6	7152.6	7405.5	7677.8	7973.1	8295.5	46
47	6106.0	6293.0	6490.3	6698.9	6920.4	7156.7	7409.9	7682.6	7978.2	8301.1	47
48	6109.1	6296.2	6493.6	6702.4	6924.2	7160.8	7414.2	7687.3	7983.4	8306.8	48
49	6112.1	6299.4	6497.0	6706.0	6928.1	7164.9	7418.6	7692.0	7988.5	8312.4	49
50	6115.1	6302.7	6500.4	6709.6	6931.9	7169.0	7423.0	7696.8	7993.7	8318.1	50
51	6118.2	6305.9	6503.8	6713.2	6935.7	7173.0	7427.4	7701.5	7998.9	8323.8	51
52	6121.2	6309.1	6507.2	6716.8	6939.5	7177.1	7431.8	7706.3	8004.0	8329.4	52
53	6124.3	6312.3	6510.6	6720.4	6943.4	7181.2	7436.2	7711.0	8009.2	8335.1	53
54	6127.4	6315.5	6514.0	6724.0	6947.2	7185.3	7440.6	7715.8	8014.4	8340.8	54
55	6130.4	6318.7	6517.4	6727.6	6951.0	7189.5	7445.0	7720.6	8019.6	8346.6	55
56	6133.5	6321.9	6520.8	6731.2	6954.9	7193.6	7449.5	7725.4	8024.8	8352.3	56
57	6136.5	6325.2	6524.2	6734.9	6958.8	7197.7	7453.9	7730.2	8030.0	8358.0	57
58	6139.6	6328.4	6527.6	6738.5	6962.6	7201.8	7458.3	7735.0	8035.3	8363.7	58
59	6142.7	6331.7	6531.0	6742.1	6966.5	7205.9	7462.8	7739.8	8040.5	8369.5	59

264.4

M.n	80 Degr.	81 Degr.	82 Degr.	83 Degr.	84 Degr.	85 Degr.	86 Degr.	87 Degr.	88 Degr.	89 Degr.	Min.
0	8375.3	8739.1	9145.5	9603.9	10137.0	10764.7	11532.6	12522	13917	16300	0
1	8381.0	8745.5	9152.7	9614.1	10146.6	10776.2	11547.0	12541	13945	16357	1
2	8386.8	8751.9	9159.9	9622.4	10156.2	10787.7	11561.4	12561	13974	16416	2
3	8392.6	8758.3	9167.2	9630.6	10165.8	10799.3	11575.9	12580	14004	16476	3
4	8398.3	8764.8	9174.4	9638.9	10175.4	10810.8	11590.5	12599	14033	16537	4
5	8404.1	8771.2	9181.6	9647.2	10185.1	10822.6	11605.0	12619	14063	16599	5
6	8409.9	8777.7	9188.9	9655.5	10194.8	10834.2	11619.7	12639	14093	16662	6
7	8415.8	8784.1	9196.2	9663.8	10204.6	10845.9	11634.5	12659	14123	16726	7
8	8421.6	8790.6	9203.5	9672.2	10214.4	10857.7	11649.3	12679	14154	16792	8
9	8427.4	8797.1	9210.6	9680.6	10224.2	10869.6	11664.1	12699	14185	16858	9
10	8433.3	8803.6	9218.1	9689.0	10234.0	10881.4	11679.1	12719	14216	16926	10
11	8439.1	8810.1	9225.4	9697.4	10243.8	10893.3	11694.0	12739	14247	16996	11
12	8445.0	8816.6	9232.7	9705.8	10253.7	10905.2	11709.1	12759	14279	17067	12
13	8450.9	8823.2	9240.2	9714.2	10263.6	10917.2	11724.2	12780	14311	17140	13
14	8456.6	8829.7	9247.6	9722.7	10273.5	10929.1	11739.4	12801	14343	17213	14
15	8462.6	8836.3	9255.0	9731.2	10283.5	10941.2	11754.7	12821	14376	17288	15
16	8468.6	8842.6	9262.4	9739.7	10293.5	10953.3	11770.0	12842	14409	17366	16
17	8474.5	8849.4	9269.9	9748.3	10303.5	10965.5	11785.4	12863	14442	17444	17
18	8480.4	8856.0	9277.3	9756.8	10313.6	10977.7	11800.9	12885	14475	17526	18
19	8486.3	8862.6	9284.8	9765.4	10323.7	10989.9	11816.4	12906	14509	17609	19
20	8492.3	8869.3	9292.3	9774.0	10333.8	11002.2	11832.0	12927	14543	17695	20
21	8498.2	8875.9	9299.8	9782.7	10344.0	11014.5	11847.6	12949	14578	17780	21
22	8504.2	8882.6	9307.3	9791.3	10354.1	11026.9	11863.4	12971	14613	17870	22
23	8510.2	8889.2	9314.8	9800.0	10364.3	11039.3	11879.2	12992	14648	17962	23
24	8516.2	8895.9	9322.4	9808.6	10374.5	11051.7	11895.1	13014	14684	18056	24
25	8522.2	8902.6	9330.0	9817.3	10384.8	11064.2	11911.0	13037	14720	18153	25
26	8528.2	8909.3	9337.6	9826.1	10395.0	11076.8	11927.1	13059	14756	18252	26
27	8534.2	8916.0	9345.2	9834.8	10405.3	11089.5	11943.1	13081	14793	18355	27
28	8540.2	8922.7	9352.8	9843.6	10415.7	11102.0	11959.3	13104	14830	18461	28
29	8546.2	8929.5	9360.4	9852.4	10426.2	11114.6	11975.6	13126	14868	18570	29
30	8552.3	8936.2	9368.1	9861.3	10436.6	11127.4	11991.9	13149	14906	18682	30
31	8558.4	8943.0	9375.8	9870.1	10447.1	11140.1	12008.4	13172	14944	18799	31
32	8564.4	8949.8	9383.5	9879.0	10457.5	11152.9	12024.9	13195	14983	18920	32
33	8570.5	8956.6	9391.2	9887.8	10468.0	11165.8	12041.5	13219	15022	19045	33
34	8576.6	8963.4	9398.9	9896.7	10478.5	11178.7	12058.2	13242	15062	19174	34
35	8582.7	8970.2	9406.6	9905.7	10489.1	11191.7	12074.9	13266	15102	19309	35
36	8588.9	8977.1	9414.4	9914.6	10499.7	11204.7	12091.7	13290	15143	19449	36
37	8595.0	8983.9	9422.1	9923.5	10510.4	11217.7	12108.6	13314	15184	19596	37
38	8601.1	8990.8	9429.9	9932.6	10521.1	11230.8	12125.6	13338	15226	19749	38
39	8607.3	8997.7	9437.8	9941.7	10531.8	11244.0	12142.7	13362	15268	19908	39
40	8613.5	9004.6	9445.6	9950.8	10542.6	11257.2	12159.9	13387	15311	20076	40
41	8619.6	9011.5	9453.4	9959.8	10553.3	11270.5	12177.1	13411	15354	20252	41
42	8625.8	9018.4	9461.3	9968.9	10564.1	11283.8	12194.4	13436	15398	20438	42
43	8632.0	9025.4	9469.1	9978.0	10574.9	11297.1	12211.8	13461	15442	20635	43
44	8638.2	9032.3	9477.0	9987.2	10585.8	11310.5	12229.3	13486	15487	20843	44
45	8644.5	9039.3	9484.9	9996.3	10596.7	11324.0	12246.9	13512	15533	21065	45
46	8650.7	9046.3	9492.9	10005.5	10607.6	11337.6	12264.6	13537	15579	21302	46
47	8656.9	9053.3	9500.8	10014.8	10618.6	11351.1	12282.4	13563	15625	21557	47
48	8663.2	9060.3	9508.8	10024.0	10629.7	11364.8	12300.2	13589	15673	21832	48
49	8669.5	9067.3	9516.8	10033.3	10640.8	11378.4	12318.1	13615	15721	22132	49
50	8675.7	9074.4	9524.8	10042.6	10651.9	11392.2	12336.3	13641	15770	22459	50
51	8682.0	9081.4	9532.9	10051.9	10663.0	11406.0	12354.4	13668	15819	22821	51
52	8688.3	9088.5	9540.9	10061.3	10674.1	11419.8	12372.7	13694	15869	23226	52
53	8694.6	9095.6	9548.9	10070.6	10685.3	11433.7	12391.0	13721	15920	23685	53
54	8701.0	9102.7	9557.0	10080.0	10696.5	11447.7	12409.5	13749	15972	24211	54
55	8707.3	9109.8	9565.1	10089.4	10707.7	11461.7	12428.0	13776	16025	24842	55
56	8713.6	9116.9	9573.2	10098.9	10719.1	11475.8	12446.5	13804	16078	25609	56
57	8720.0	9124.0	9581.4	10108.4	10730.4	11489.9	12465.3	13831	16132	26598	57
58	8726.4	9131.2	9589.5	10117.9	10741.8	11504.1	12484.2	13860	16187	27992	58
59	8732.7	9138.4	9597.7	10127.4	10753.3	11518.3	12503.1	13888	16243	30375	59

A

TABLE

OF THE

SUN'S DECLINATION,

FOR THE YEARS

MDCCXCII, AND MDCCXCVI.

Each being Leap Year.

Days	Jan.	Feb.	Mar.	Apr.	May	June	July	Aug.	Sept.	Oct.	Nov.	Dec.	Days
	South	South	South	North	North	North	North	North	North	South	South	South	
	d. m.	d. m.	d. m.	d. m.	d. m.	d. m.	d. m.	d. m.	d. m.	d. m.	d. m.	d. m.	
1	23 1	17 5	7 11	4 56	15 22	22 12	23 4	17 49	7 58	3 33	14 46	21 59	1
2	22 56	16 48	6 48	5 19	15 40	22 19	23 0	17 33	7 36	3 57	15 5	22 8	2
3	22 50	16 30	6 25	5 42	15 57	22 26	22 55	17 18	7 14	4 20	15 23	22 16	3
4	22 44	16 13	6 2	6 4	16 15	22 33	22 49	17 1	6 51	4 43	15 42	22 24	4
5	22 37	15 55	5 39	6 27	16 32	22 40	22 44	16 45	6 29	5 6	16 0	22 31	5
6	22 30	15 36	5 16	6 50	16 48	22 46	22 37	16 28	6 7	5 29	16 18	22 38	6
7	22 23	15 18	4 52	7 12	17 5	22 51	22 31	16 12	5 44	5 52	16 35	22 45	7
8	22 15	14 59	4 29	7 34	17 21	22 57	22 24	15 54	5 21	6 15	16 53	22 51	8
9	22 7	14 39	4 6	7 57	17 37	23 1	22 17	15 37	4 59	6 38	17 10	22 56	9
10	21 58	14 20	3 42	8 19	17 52	23 6	22 9	15 19	4 36	7 1	17 27	23 2	10
11	21 49	14 0	3 19	8 41	18 8	23 10	22 1	15 1	4 13	7 23	17 43	23 6	11
12	21 39	13 41	2 55	9 2	18 23	23 14	21 52	14 43	3 50	7 46	17 59	23 10	12
13	21 29	13 21	2 31	9 24	18 37	23 17	21 43	14 24	3 27	8 8	18 15	23 14	13
14	21 18	13 0	2 8	9 45	18 52	23 20	21 34	14 6	3 4	8 31	18 31	23 18	14
15	21 7	12 40	1 44	10 7	19 6	23 22	21 25	13 47	2 41	8 53	18 46	23 21	15
16	20 56	12 19	1 20	10 28	19 19	23 24	21 15	13 28	2 17	9 15	19 1	23 23	16
17	20 45	11 58	0 57	10 49	19 33	23 26	21 4	13 8	1 54	9 37	19 15	23 25	17
18	20 32	11 37	0 33	11 10	19 46	23 27	20 54	12 49	1 31	9 59	19 29	23 26	18
19	20 20	11 16	0 9	11 31	19 59	23 27	20 43	12 30	1 7	10 21	19 43	23 27	19
20	20 7	10 54	0 14 (North)	11 51	20 11	23 28	20 31	12 10	0 44	10 42	19 57	23 28	20
21	19 54	10 33	0 38	12 11	20 23	23 28	20 19	11 50	0 20 (South)	11 3	20 10	23 28	21
22	19 40	10 11	1 2	12 31	20 35	23 27	20 7	11 29	0 3	11 25	20 22	23 27	22
23	19 26	9 49	1 25	12 51	20 46	23 26	19 55	11 9	0 26	11 46	20 35	23 26	23
24	19 12	9 27	1 49	13 11	20 57	23 25	19 42	10 48	0 50	12 6	20 47	23 25	24
25	18 57	9 4	2 13	13 30	21 8	23 23	19 29	10 28	1 13	12 27	20 58	23 23	25
26	18 42	8 42	2 36	13 50	21 18	23 21	19 16	10 7	1 37	12 48	21 9	23 21	26
27	18 27	8 20	2 59	14 9	21 28	23 19	19 2	9 45	2 0	13 8	21 20	23 18	27
28	18 11	7 57	3 23	14 27	21 37	23 16	18 48	9 24	2 23	13 28	21 30	23 14	28
29	17 55	7 34	3 46	14 46	21 46	23 12	18 34	9 3	2 47	13 48	21 40	23 11	29
30	17 39		4 9	15 4	21 55	23 8	18 19	8 41	3 10	14 7	21 50	23 7	30
31	17 22		4 33		22 4		18 4	8 19		14 27		23 2	31

A TABLE

OF THE

SUN'S DECLINATION,

FOR THE YEARS

MDCCXCIII, AND MDCCXCVII.

Each being the First Year after Leap Year.

Days	Jan.	Feb.	Mar.	Apr.	May	June	July	Aug.	Sept.	Oct.	Nov.	Dec.	Days
	South	South	South	North	North	North	North	North	North	South	South	South	
	d. m.	d. m.	d. m.	d. m.	d. m.	d. m.	d. m.	d. m.	d. m.	d. m.	d. m.	d. m.	
1	22 57	16 53	7 18	4 49	15 17	22 10	23 6	17 53	8 3	3 27	14 41	21 57	1
2	22 52	16 35	6 55	5 12	15 35	22 17	23 1	17 38	7 42	3 51	15 0	22 6	2
3	22 46	16 18	6 32	5 35	15 53	22 25	22 56	17 22	7 19	4 14	15 19	22 14	3
4	22 39	15 59	6 9	5 58	16 10	22 31	22 51	17 6	6 57	4 37	15 37	22 22	4
5	22 32	15 41	5 45	6 21	16 27	22 38	22 45	16 50	6 35	5 0	15 55	22 29	5
6	22 25	15 23	5 22	6 44	16 44	22 44	22 39	16 33	6 13	5 23	16 13	22 36	6
7	22 17	15 4	4 49	7 6	17 0	22 50	22 33	16 16	5 50	5 46	16 31	22 43	7
8	22 9	14 45	4 35	7 28	17 17	22 55	22 26	15 59	5 27	6 9	16 48	22 49	8
9	22 0	14 25	4 12	7 51	17 33	23 0	22 19	15 42	5 5	6 32	17 5	22 55	9
10	21 51	14 6	3 48	8 13	17 48	23 5	22 11	15 24	4 42	6 55	17 22	23 0	10
11	21 42	13 46	3 25	8 35	18 4	23 9	22 3	15 6	4 19	7 17	17 39	23 5	11
12	21 32	13 26	3 1	8 57	18 19	23 13	21 55	14 48	3 56	7 40	17 55	23 10	12
13	21 21	13 6	2 38	9 18	18 33	23 16	21 46	14 30	3 33	8 2	18 11	23 13	13
14	21 11	12 45	2 14	9 40	18 48	23 19	21 37	14 11	3 10	8 25	18 26	23 17	14
15	20 59	12 25	1 50	10 1	19 2	23 21	21 27	13 52	2 47	8 47	18 42	23 20	15
16	20 48	12 4	1 27	10 22	19 16	23 24	21 17	13 33	2 24	9 9	18 57	23 22	16
17	20 36	11 43	1 3	10 43	19 29	23 25	21 7	13 14	2 0	9 31	19 11	23 24	17
18	20 23	11 21	0 39	11 4	19 42	23 27	20 57	12 56	1 37	9 53	19 26	23 26	18
19	20 11	11 0	0 15 North	11 25	19 55	23 27	20 46	12 35	1 14	10 15	19 39	23 27	19
20	19 58	10 38	0 8	11 46	20 8	23 28	20 34	12 15	0 50	10 36	19 53	23 28	20
21	19 44	10 17	0 32	12 6	20 20	23 28	20 22	11 55	0 27	10 58	20 6	23 28	21
22	19 30	9 55	0 55	12 26	20 32	23 27	20 11	11 35	0 3 South	11 19	20 19	23 28	22
23	19 16	9 33	1 19	12 46	20 43	23 27	19 58	11 15	0 20	11 40	20 31	23 27	23
24	19 1	9 11	1 43	13 6	20 54	23 25	19 46	10 54	0 43	12 1	20 44	23 25	24
25	18 46	8 48	2 6	13 25	21 5	23 24	19 33	10 33	1 7	12 22	20 55	23 24	25
26	18 31	8 26	2 30	13 44	21 15	23 22	19 19	10 12	1 30	12 42	21 6	23 22	26
27	18 16	8 3	2 53	14 4	21 25	23 19	19 6	9 51	1 54	13 2	21 17	23 20	27
28	18 0	7 40	3 16	14 22	21 35	23 17	18 52	9 30	2 17	13 23	21 28	23 16	28
29	17 43		3 40	14 41	21 44	23 13	18 38	9 9	2 41	13 43	21 38	23 12	29
30	17 27		4 3	14 59	21 53	23 10	18 23	8 47	3 4	14 2	21 48	23 8	30
31	17 10		4 26		22 1		18 8	8 25		14 22		23 4	31

A TABLE

OF THE

SUN'S DECLINATION,

FOR THE YEARS

MDCCXC, MDCCXCIV, AND MDCCXCVIII.

Each being the Second Year after Leap Year.

Days	Jan.	Feb.	Mar.	Apr.	May	June	July	Aug.	Sept.	Oct.	Nov.	Dec.	Days
	South	South	South	North	North	North	North	North	North	South	South	South	
	d. m.	d. m.	d. m.	d. m.	d. m.	d. m.	d. m.	d. m.	d. m.	d. m.	d. m.	d. m.	
1	22 59	16 57	7 23	4 44	15 13	22 7	23 7	17 57	8 9	3 22	14 36	21 54	1
2	22 53	16 40	7 0	5 7	15 21	22 15	23 2	17 41	7 47	3 45	14 55	22 3	2
3	22 47	16 22	6 37	5 30	15 48	22 23	22 57	17 25	7 25	4 8	15 14	22 12	3
4	22 41	16 4	6 14	5 53	16 6	22 30	22 52	17 10	7 3	4 31	15 32	22 20	4
5	22 34	15 46	5 51	6 15	16 23	23 36	22 47	16 54	6 40	4 55	15 51	22 28	5
6	22 27	15 27	5 28	6 38	16 40	22 43	22 41	16 37	6 18	5 18	16 9	22 35	6
7	22 19	15 8	5 5	7 0	16 56	22 49	22 34	16 20	5 55	5 41	16 27	22 42	7
8	22 11	14 49	4 41	7 23	17 13	22 54	22 28	16 3	5 33	6 4	16 44	22 48	8
9	22 2	14 30	4 18	7 45	17 29	22 5	22 20	15 46	5 10	6 27	17 1	22 54	9
10	21 53	14 11	3 54	8 7	17 44	23 4	22 13	15 28	4 47	6 49	17 18	22 59	10
11	21 44	13 51	3 31	8 29	18 0	23 8	22 5	15 11	4 24	7 12	17 35	23 4	11
12	21 34	13 31	3 7	8 51	18 15	23 12	21 57	14 52	4 1	7 35	17 51	23 8	12
13	21 24	13 11	2 43	9 13	18 30	23 16	21 48	14 34	3 38	7 57	18 7	23 12	13
14	21 13	12 50	2 20	9 35	18 44	23 18	21 39	14 16	3 15	8 20	18 23	23 16	14
15	21 2	12 30	1 56	9 56	18 59	23 21	21 29	13 57	2 52	8 42	18 38	23 19	15
16	20 51	12 9	1 33	10 17	19 12	23 23	21 20	13 38	2 29	9 4	18 53	23 22	16
17	20 39	11 48	1 9	10 38	19 26	23 25	21 10	13 19	2 6	9 26	19 8	23 24	17
18	20 26	11 27	0 45	10 59	19 39	23 26	20 59	12 59	1 42	9 48	19 22	23 26	18
19	20 14	11 5	0 21 North	11 20	19 52	23 27	20 48	12 40	1 19	10 10	19 36	23 27	19
20	20 1	10 44	0 2	11 40	20 5	23 28	20 37	12 20	0 56	10 31	19 50	23 28	20
21	19 47	10 22	0 26	12 1	20 17	23 28	20 25	12 0	0 32	10 53	20 3	23 28	21
22	19 34	10 0	0 50	12 21	20 29	23 28	20 14	11 40	0 9 South	11 14	20 16	23 28	22
23	19 19	9 38	1 13	12 41	20 40	23 27	20 1	11 20	0 14	11 35	20 28	23 27	23
24	19 5	9 16	1 37	13 1	20 51	23 26	19 49	10 59	0 38	11 56	20 41	23 26	24
25	18 50	8 54	2 0	13 20	21 2	23 24	19 36	10 38	1 1	12 17	20 52	23 24	25
26	18 35	8 31	2 24	13 40	21 13	23 23	19 23	10 17	1 25	12 37	21 4	23 22	26
27	18 19	8 9	2 47	13 59	21 23	23 20	19 9	9 56	1 48	12 57	21 15	23 20	27
28	18 4	7 46	3 11	14 18	21 32	23 17	18 55	9 35	2 11	13 18	21 25	23 17	28
29	17 47		3 34	14 36	21 42	23 14	18 41	9 14	2 35	13 38	21 35	23 13	29
30	17 31		3 57	14 55	21 51	23 10	18 27	8 52	2 58	13 57	21 45	23 9	30
31	17 14		4 21		21 59		18 12	8 31		14 17		23 5	31

A TABLE

OF THE

SUN'S DECLINATION,

FOR THE YEARS

MDCCXCI, MDCCXCV, AND MDCCXCIX.

Each being the Third Year after Leap Year.

Days	Jan.	Feb.	Mar.	Apr.	May	June	July	Aug.	Sept.	Oct.	Nov	Dec.	Days
	South	South	South	North	North	North	North	North	North	South	South	South	
	d. m.	d. m.	d. m.	d. m.	d. m.	d. m.	d. m.	d. m.	d. m.	d. m.	d. m.	d. m.	
1	23 0	17 1	7 29	4 38	15 8	22 6	23 7	18 0	8 14	3 16	14 31	21 52	1
2	22 54	16 44	7 6	5 1	15 26	22 13	23 3	17 45	7 52	3 39	14 51	22 1	2
3	22 49	16 26	6 43	5 24	15 44	22 21	22 59	17 29	7 30	4 3	15 9	22 10	3
4	22 42	16 8	6 20	5 47	16 2	22 28	22 53	17 14	7 8	4 26	15 28	22 18	4
5	22 36	15 50	5 57	6 10	16 19	22 35	22 48	16 57	6 46	4 49	15 46	22 26	5
6	22 29	15 32	5 34	6 32	16 36	22 41	22 42	16 41	6 23	5 12	16 4	22 33	6
7	22 21	15 13	5 10	6 55	16 52	22 47	22 36	16 24	6 1	5 35	16 22	22 40	7
8	22 13	14 54	4 47	7 17	17 9	22 53	22 29	16 7	5 38	5 58	16 40	22 46	8
9	22 4	14 35	4 23	7 40	17 25	22 58	22 22	15 50	5 16	6 21	16 57	22 52	9
10	21 56	14 15	4 0	8 2	17 41	23 3	22 15	15 33	4 53	6 44	17 14	22 58	10
11	21 46	13 56	3 36	8 24	17 56	23 7	22 7	15 15	4 30	7 6	17 31	23 3	11
12	21 36	13 36	3 13	8 46	18 11	23 11	21 59	14 57	4 7	7 29	17 47	23 7	12
13	21 26	13 16	2 49	9 8	18 26	23 14	21 50	14 39	3 44	7 52	18 3	23 12	13
14	21 16	12 55	2 26	9 29	18 41	23 18	21 41	14 20	3 21	8 14	18 19	23 15	14
15	21 5	12 35	2 2	9 51	18 55	23 20	21 32	14 2	2 58	8 37	18 34	23 18	15
16	20 53	12 14	1 38	10 12	19 9	23 23	21 22	13 43	2 35	8 58	18 49	23 21	16
17	20 42	11 53	1 15	10 33	19 23	23 24	21 12	13 24	2 12	9 20	19 4	23 23	17
18	20 29	11 32	0 51	10 54	19 36	23 26	21 2	13 5	1 48	9 42	19 19	23 25	18
19	20 17	11 10	0 27	11 15	19 49	23 27	20 51	12 45	1 25	10 4	19 33	23 27	19
20	20 4	10 49	0 4	11 36	20 2	23 28	20 40	12 25	1 2	10 26	19 46	23 27	20
			North										
21	19 51	10 27	0 20	11 56	20 14	23 28	20 28	12 5	0 38	10 47	20 0	23 28	21
22	19 37	10 6	0 44	12 16	20 26	23 28	20 17	11 45	0 15	11 8	20 13	23 28	22
									South				
23	19 23	9 44	1 7	12 36	20 37	23 27	20 4	11 25	0 9	11 30	20 25	23 27	23
24	19 8	9 21	1 31	12 56	20 49	23 26	19 52	11 4	0 32	11 51	20 38	23 26	24
25	18 54	8 59	1 55	13 16	21 0	23 24	19 39	10 43	0 55	12 11	20 49	23 25	25
26	18 39	8 37	2 18	13 35	21 10	23 23	19 26	10 23	1 19	12 32	21 1	23 23	26
27	18 23	8 14	2 42	13 54	21 20	23 21	19 12	10 2	1 42	12 53	21 12	23 20	27
28	18 7	7 52	3 5	14 13	21 30	23 18	18 59	9 40	2 6	13 13	21 23	23 17	28
29	17 51		3 28	14 32	21 39	23 15	18 45	9 19	2 29	13 33	21 33	23 14	29
30	17 35		3 52	14 50	21 49	23 11	18 30	8 57	2 53	13 53	21 43	23 10	30
31	17 18		4 15		21 57		18 15	8 36		14 12		23 6	31

A TABLE of the VARIATION of the SUN'S DECLINATION, to every 10 Degrees of Longitude.

Days	10°	20°	30°	40°	50°	60°	70°	80°	90°	100°	110°	120°	130°	140°	150°	160°	170°	180°
January / July																		
1	0	0	0	1	1	1	1	1	1	1	1	2	2	2	2	2	2	2
4	0	0	0	1	1	1	1	1	1	2	2	2	2	2	2	3	3	3
7	0	0	1	1	1	1	2	2	2	2	2	2	3	3	3	3	3	4
10	0	0	1	1	1	1	2	2	2	2	3	3	3	3	4	4	4	4
13	0	1	1	1	1	2	2	2	2	3	3	3	4	4	4	4	5	5
16	0	1	1	1	1	2	2	2	3	3	3	4	4	4	4	5	5	5
19	0	1	1	1	2	2	2	3	3	3	4	4	4	5	5	5	5	6
22	0	1	1	1	2	2	3	3	3	4	4	4	5	5	5	6	6	6
25	0	1	1	1	2	2	3	3	3	4	4	5	5	5	6	6	7	7
28	0	1	1	2	2	2	3	3	4	4	5	5	5	6	6	7	7	7
31	0	1	1	2	2	3	3	3	4	4	5	5	6	6	7	7	7	8
Febr. / Aug.																		
5	0	1	1	2	2	3	3	4	4	5	5	6	6	7	7	8	8	9
10	1	1	2	2	3	3	4	4	5	5	6	6	7	7	8	8	9	9
15	1	1	2	2	3	3	4	4	5	5	6	6	7	8	8	9	9	10
20	1	1	2	2	3	3	4	5	5	6	6	7	7	8	9	9	10	10
25	1	1	2	2	3	4	4	5	5	6	6	7	7	8	9	9	10	11
30	1	1	2	2	3	4	4	5	6	6	7	7	8	9	9	10	10	11
March / Sep.																		
5	1	1	2	2	3	4	4	5	6	6	7	8	8	9	9	10	11	11
10	1	1	2	3	3	4	4	5	6	6	7	8	8	9	10	10	11	12
15	1	1	2	3	3	4	5	5	6	7	7	8	8	9	10	10	11	12
20	1	1	2	3	3	4	5	5	6	7	7	8	8	9	10	10	11	12
25	1	1	2	3	3	4	5	5	6	7	7	8	8	9	10	10	11	12
30	1	1	2	3	3	4	5	5	6	7	7	8	9	10	11	12	12	12
April / Oct.																		
5	1	1	2	3	3	4	4	5	6	6	7	8	8	9	10	11	11	
10	1	1	2	2	3	4	4	5	6	6	7	7	8	9	9	10	11	11
15	1	1	2	2	3	4	4	5	5	6	6	7	7	8	9	9	10	11
20	1	1	2	2	3	3	4	4	5	5	6	7	7	8	8	9	9	10
25	1	1	2	2	3	3	4	4	5	5	6	6	7	7	8	8	9	10
30	1	1	2	2	3	3	4	4	5	5	6	6	7	7	8	8	9	9
May / November																		
2	1	1	2	2	3	3	4	4	5	5	6	6	7	7	8	8	9	9
5	0	1	1	2	2	3	3	4	4	5	5	6	6	7	7	8	8	8
8	0	1	1	2	2	3	3	4	4	5	5	6	6	7	7	7	8	8
11	0	1	1	2	2	2	3	3	4	4	5	5	6	6	7	7	7	8
14	0	1	1	2	2	2	3	3	4	4	5	5	6	6	7	7	7	7
17	0	1	1	2	2	2	3	3	4	4	5	5	5	6	6	7	7	7
20	0	1	1	1	2	2	3	3	4	4	4	5	5	5	6	6	7	7
23	0	1	1	1	2	2	2	3	3	3	4	4	5	5	5	6	6	6
26	0	1	1	1	1	2	2	2	3	3	4	4	4	5	5	5	5	5
29	0	1	1	1	1	2	2	2	3	3	3	3	4	4	4	4	5	5
June / December																		
2	0	0	1	1	1	1	2	2	2	2	3	3	3	3	4	4		
5	0	0	1	0	1	1	1	2	2	2	2	2	2	2	3	3	3	3
8	0	0	0	1	1	1	1	1	2	2	2	2	2	2	3	3		3
11	0	0	0	0	1	1	1	1	1	1	1	2	2	2	2	3		3
14	0	0	0	0	0	1	0	1	1	1	1	1	1	1	1	2		2
17	0	0	0	0	0	0	0	0	0	1	1	1	1	1	1	2		2
20	0	0	0	0	0	0	0	0	0	0	0	0	0	0	0	1		1
23	0	0	0	0	0	0	0	0	0	0	0	0	0	0	0	0		0
26	0	0	0	0	0	0	0	0	1	0	0	1	1	1	1	0		1
29	0	0	0	0	0	1	1	1	1	1	1	1	1	1	2	2		2

A TABLE of the SUN's RIGHT ASCENSION, in time, adapted to the Third Year after Leap Year.

Days	Jan.	Feb.	Mar.	Apr.	May	June	July	Aug.	Sept.	Oct.	Nov.	Dec.	Days
	h. m.	h. m.	h. m.	h. m.	h. m.	h. m.	h. m.	h. m.	h. m.	h. m.	h. m.	h. m.	
1	18 48	21 1	22 50	0 43	2 34	4 37	6 41	8 46	10 42	12 30	14 27	16 31	1
2	18 53	21 5	22 53	0 47	2 33	4 41	6 45	8 50	10 46	12 34	14 31	16 35	2
3	18 57	21 9	22 57	0 50	2 42	4 45	6 50	8 54	10 49	12 37	14 34	16 39	3
4	19 2	21 13	23 1	0 54	2 46	4 49	6 54	8 58	10 53	12 41	14 38	16 44	4
5	19 6	21 17	23 4	0 58	2 50	4 53	6 58	9 1	10 57	12 45	14 42	16 48	5
6	19 10	21 21	23 8	1 1	2 53	4 58	7 2	9 5	11 0	12 48	14 46	16 52	6
7	19 15	21 25	23 12	1 5	2 57	5 2	7 6	9 9	11 4	12 52	14 50	16 57	7
8	19 19	21 29	23 16	1 9	3 1	5 6	7 10	9 13	11 7	12 56	14 54	17 1	8
9	19 24	21 33	23 19	1 12	3 5	5 10	7 14	9 17	11 11	12 59	14 58	17 5	9
10	19 28	21 37	23 23	1 16	3 9	5 14	7 18	9 21	11 15	13 3	15 2	17 10	10
11	19 32	21 41	23 27	1 20	3 13	5 18	7 22	9 24	11 18	13 7	15 7	17 14	11
12	19 37	21 45	23 30	1 23	3 17	5 22	7 26	9 28	11 22	13 10	15 11	17 19	12
13	19 41	21 48	23 34	1 27	3 21	5 26	7 30	9 32	11 25	13 14	15 15	17 23	13
14	19 45	21 52	23 38	1 31	3 25	5 31	7 34	9 36	11 29	13 18	15 19	17 27	14
15	19 50	21 56	23 41	1 34	3 29	5 35	7 39	9 39	11 33	13 22	15 23	17 32	15
16	19 54	22 0	23 45	1 38	3 33	5 39	7 43	9 43	11 36	13 25	15 27	17 36	16
17	19 58	22 4	23 49	1 42	3 37	5 43	7 47	9 47	11 40	13 29		17 41	17
18	20 2	22 8	23 52	1 45	3 40	5 47	7 51	9 51	11 43	13 33		17 45	18
19	20 7	22 12	23 56	1 49	3 44	5 52	7 55	9 54	11 47	13 37	15 39	17 50	19
20	20 11	22 16	23 59	1 53	3 48	5 56	7 59	9 58	11 51	13 40	15 44	17 54	20
21	20 15	22 19	0 3	1 57	3 52	6 0	8 3	10 2	11 54	13 44	15 48	17 59	21
22	20 19	22 23	0 7	2 0	3 56	6 4	8 7	10 5	11 58	13 48	15 52	18 3	22
23	20 23	22 27	0 10	2 4	4 0	6 8	8 11	10 9	12 1	13 52	15 56	18 7	23
24	20 28	22 31	0 14	2 8	4 4	6 12	8 15	10 13	12 5	13 56	16 1	18 12	24
25	20 32	22 35	0 18	2 12	4 9	6 16	8 19	10 17	12 9	13 59	16 5	18 16	25
26	20 36	22 38	0 21	2 15	4 13	6 21	8 23	10 20	12 14	14 3	16 9	18 21	26
27	20 40	22 42	0 25	2 19	4 17	6 25	8 26	10 24	12 16	14 7	16 13	18 25	27
28	20 44	22 46	0 29	2 23	4 21	6 29	8 30	10 28	12 19	14 11	16 18	18 30	28
29	20 48		0 32	2 27	4 25	6 33	8 34	10 31	12 23	14 15	16 22	18 34	29
30	20 52		0 36	2 30	4 29	6 37	8 38	10 35	12 27	14 19	16 26	18 39	30
31	20 57		0 39		4 33		8 42	10 38		14 23		18 43	31

A TABLE of the SUN's SEMIDIAMETER for each Sixth Day in the Year.

D.	Jan.	Feb.	Mar.	Apr.	May	June	July	Aug.	Sept.	Oct.	Nov	Dec.	D.
	m. s.	m. s.	m. s.	m. s.	m. s.	m. s.	m. s.	m. s.	m. s.	m. s.	m. s.	m. s.	
1	16 19	16 16	16 11	16 2	15 54	15 49	15 47	15 49	15 55	16 3	16 11	16 17	1
7	16 19	16 15	16 9	16 1	15 53	15 48	15 47	15 50	15 56	16 4	16 13	16 18	7
13	16 19	16 14	16 7	15 59	15 52	15 47	15 47	15 51	15 58	16 6	16 14	16 18	13
19	16 18	16 13	16 6	15 57	15 51	15 47	15 48	15 52	15 59	16 8	16 15	16 19	19
25	16 17	16 12	16 4	15 56	15 50	15 47	15 48	15 53	16 1	16 9	16 16	16 19	25

A TABLE

OF THE TIME OF

TRANSIT OF THE POLAR STAR OVER THE MERIDIAN.

ADAPTED TO MEAN TIME FOR THE YEAR

MDCCLXXXVIII.

Being Leap Year.

Days	Jan.	Feb.	Mar.	Apr.	May	June	July	Aug.	Sept.	Oct.	Nov.	Dec.	Days
	Even.	Even.	Even.	Even.	Morn	Morn	Morn	Morn	Morn	Morn	Even.	Even.	
	h. m.	h. m.	h. m.	h. m.	h. m.	h. m.	h. m.	h. m.	h. m.	h. m.	h. m.	h. m.	
1	6 6	4 4	2 10	12 8	10 10	8 8	6 10	4 8	2 7	0 9	10 3	8 5	1
2	6 6	4 0	2 6	12 4	10 6	8 4	6 6	4 5	2 3	0 5	9 59	8 1	2
3	5 58	3 56	2 2	12 0 Morn.	10 2	8 0	6 2	4 1	1 59	0 1	9 55	7 57	3
										Even. 11 57			
4	5 54	3 52	1 58	11 56	9 58	7 36	5 59	3 57	1 55	11 53	9 51	7 53	4
5	5 50	3 48	1 54	11 52	9 54	7 53	5 55	3 53	1 51	11 49	9 47	7 49	5
6	5 46	3 44	1 50	11 48	9 50	7 49	5 51	3 49	1 47	11 45	9 43	7 45	6
7	5 42	3 40	1 46	11 44	9 47	7 45	5 47	3 45	1 43	11 41	9 39	7 41	7
8	5 38	3 36	1 42	11 41	9 43	7 41	5 43	3 41	1 39	11 37	9 35	7 37	8
9	5 34	3 32	1 38	11 37	9 39	7 37	5 39	3 37	1 35	11 33	9 31	7 33	9
10	5 30	3 29	1 35	11 33	9 35	7 33	5 35	3 33	1 31	11 29	9 27	7 30	10
11	5 26	3 25	1 31	11 29	9 31	7 29	5 31	3 29	1 27	11 25	9 24	7 26	11
12	5 23	3 21	1 27	11 25	9 27	7 25	5 27	3 25	1 23	11 21	9 20	7 22	12
13	5 19	3 17	1 23	11 31	9 23	7 21	5 23	3 21	1 19	11 18	9 16	7 18	13
14	5 15	3 13	1 19	11 17	9 19	7 17	5 19	3 17	1 15	11 14	9 12	7 14	14
15	5 11	3 9	1 15	11 13	9 15	7 13	5 15	3 13	1 12	11 10	9 8	7 10	15
16	5 7	3 5	1 11	11 9	9 11	7 9	5 11	3 9	1 8	11 6	9 4	7 6	16
17	5 3	3 1	1 7	11 5	9 7	7 5	5 7	3 6	1 4	11 2	9 0	7 2	17
18	4 59	2 57	1 3	11 1	9 3	7 1	5 3	3 2	1 0	10 58	8 56	6 58	18
19	4 55	2 53	12 59	10 57	8 59	6 57	5 0	2 58	0 56	10 54	8 52	6 54	19
20	4 51	2 49	12 55	10 53	8 55	6 54	4 56	2 54	0 52	10 50	8 48	6 50	20
21	4 47	2 45	12 51	10 49	8 51	6 50	4 52	2 50	0 48	10 46	8 44	6 46	21
22	4 43	2 41	12 47	10 45	8 49	6 46	4 48	2 46	0 44	10 42	8 40	6 42	22
23	4 39	2 37	12 43	10 42	8 44	6 42	4 44	2 42	0 40	10 38	8 36	6 38	23
24	4 35	2 33	12 39	10 38	8 40	6 38	4 40	2 38	0 36	10 34	8 32	6 34	24
25	4 31	2 30	12 36	10 34	8 36	6 34	4 36	2 34	0 32	10 30	8 28	6 31	25
26	4 27	2 26	12 32	10 30	8 32	6 30	4 32	2 30	0 28	10 26	8 25	6 27	26
27	4 24	2 22	12 28	10 26	8 28	6 26	4 28	2 26	0 24	10 23	8 21	6 23	27
28	4 20	2 18	12 24	10 22	8 24	6 22	4 24	2 22	0 20	10 19	8 17	6 19	28
29	4 16	2 14	12 20	10 18	8 20	6 18	4 20	2 18	0 17	10 15	8 13	6 15	29
30	4 12		12 16	10 14	8 16	6 14	4 16	2 14	0 13	10 11	8 9	6 11	30
31	4 8		12 12		8 12		4 12	2 11		10 7		6 7	31

A
TABLE
OF THE
EQUATION OF TIME,
FOR THE YEARS
MDCCXCI, MDCCXCV, AND MDCCXCIX.

Each being the Third Year after Leap Year.

Days	Jan.	Feb.	Mar.	Apr.	May	June	July	Aug.	Sept.	Oct.	Nov.	Dec.	Days
	Subtr.	Subtr.	Subtr.	Subtr.	Add	Add	Subtr.	Subtr.	Add	Add	Add	Add	
	m. s.	m. s.	m. s.	m. s.	m. s.	m. s.	m. s.	m. s.	m. s.	m. s.	m. s.	m. s.	
1	4 8	14 4	12 38	3 55	3 8	2 38	3 20	5 54	0 15	10 23	16 13	10 33	1
2	4 36	14 11	12 25	3 36	3 15	2 29	3 31	5 50	0 34	10 41	16 14	10 10	2
3	5 4	14 17	12 12	3 18	3 22	2 19	3.42	5 46	0 53	11 0	16 13	9 46	3
4	5 32	14 23	11 59	3 0	3 28	2 9	3 53	5 41	1 12	11 18	16 12	9 22	4
5	5 39	14 28	11 45	2 43	3 34	1 59	4 4	5 35	1 32	11 36	16 11	8 57	5
6	6 25	14 32	11 31	2 25	3 39	1 48	4 14	5 29	1 51	11 53	16 8	8 31	6
7	6 51	14 35	11 17	2 8	3 43	1 37	4 24	5 22	2 11	12 10	16 5	8 5	7
8	7 17	14 37	11 2	1 51	3 47	1 26	4 34	5 15	2 32	12 27	16 0	7 39	8
9	7 42	14 39	10 46	1 34	3 51	1 15	4 43	5 7	2 52	12 43	15 55	7 12	9
10	8 6	14 40	10 30	1 17	3 54	1 3	4 51	4 58	3 13	12 59	15 49	6 45	10
11	8 30	14 39	10 14	1 1	3 56	0 51	5 0	4 49	3 33	13 14	15 43	6 17	11
12	8 53	14 39	9 58	0 44	3 58	0 39	5 8	4 40	3 54	13 29	15 35	5 49	12
13	9 16	14 37	9 41	0 29	3 59	0 27	5 15	4 29	4 15	13 43	15 27	5 20	13
14	9 38	14 34	9 24	0 13 (Add)	4 0	0 15	5 22	4 18	4 36	13 57	15 17	4 52	14
15	9 59	14 31	9 7	0 2	4 0	0 2 (Subtr.)	5 28	4 7	4 57	14 10	15 7	4 23	15
16	10 20	14 27	8 49	0 17	3 59	0 10	5 34	3 55	5 18	14 23	14 56	3 53	16
17	10 39	14 23	8 32	0 32	3 58	0 23	5 39	3 43	5 40	14 35	14 44	3 24	17
18	10 58	14 17	8 14	0 46	3 56	0 36	5 44	3 30	6 1	14 46	14 31	2 54	18
19	11 16	14 11	7 55	1 0	3 54	0 49	5 48	3 16	6 22	14 57	14 18	2 24	19
20	11 34	14 5	7 37	1 13	3 52	1 1	5 52	3 3	6 43	15 7	14 3	1 54	20
21	11 51	13 57	7 19	1 26	3 48	1 14	5 55	2 48	7 3	15 17	13 48	1 24	21
22	12 7	13 49	7 0	1 38	3 45	1 27	5 58	2 34	7 24	15 25	13 32	0 54	22
23	12 22	13 41	6 42	1 50	3 40	1 40	6 0	2 19	7 45	15 33	13 15	0 24	23
24	12 36	13 32	6 23	2 2	3 35	1 53	6 2	2 3	8 5	15 41	12 57	0 6 (Subtr.)	24
25	12 50	13 21	6 4	2 13	3 30	2 6	6 3	1 47	8 25	15 47	12 39	0 36	25
26	13 3	13 12	5 46	2 23	3 24	2 18	6 3	1 31	8 46	15 53	12 20	1 6	26
27	13 15	13 1	5 27	2 33	3 17	2 31	6 3	1 14	9 6	15 59	12 0	1 36	27
28	13 26	12 50	5 8	2 43	3 10	2 43	6 2	0 57	9 25	16 3	11 39	2 6	28
29	13 37		4 50	2 52	3 3	2 56	6 1	0 39	9 45	16 7	11 18	2 35	29
30	13 47		4 31	3 0	2 55	3 8	5 59	0 22	10 4	16 10	10 56	3 5	30
31	13 56		4 13		2 47		5 57	0 3		16 12		3 34	31

A TABLE of the RIGHT ASCENSION, and DECLINATION of the principal FIXED STARS; adapted to the beginning of the year 1790, with their annual variations.

Names and Situations of Stars.	Char.	Mag.	Rt. Ascension in time.	Ann. Variation.	Declination	Annual Variation.
			h. m. f.	S +	d. m. f.	S
Algenib, Extrem. of the wing of Pegasus	γ	2	0 02 27	3.07	14 00 55 N	+ 20.05
Bright star in the tail of the Whale	β	2	0 33 02	3.01	19 06 31 S	— 19.86
POLE STAR. Tail of Ursa minor	α	2	0 50 02	11.00	88 11 07 N	+ 19.06
Mirach, Girdle of Andromeda	β	2	0 58 02	3.33	34 30 10 N	+ 19.45
Achernar. String of the lower Eridanus	ι	1	1 29 53	2.25	58 18 30 S	— 18.55
Almaak. Foot of Andromeda	γ	2	1 51 04	3.61	41 18 53 N	+ 17.82
Preceding horn of the Ram	α	2	1 55 22	3.33	22 27 45 N	+ 17.60
Menkar. Jaw of the Whale	α	2	2 51 19	3.12	03 15 34 N	+ 14.76
Algol. Head of Medusa	β	2	2 54 34	3.85	40 08 03 N	+ 14.63
Algenib. Girdle of Perseus	α	1	3 09 25	4.20	49 06 00 N	+ 13.72
Aldebaran. Eye of the Bull	α	1	4 23 53	3.42	16 04 25 N	+ 08.26
Capella. Left shoulder of Auriga	α	1	5 01 11	4.37	45 46 00 N	+ 05.21
Rigel. West foot of Orion	β	1	5 04 27	2.87	08 27 22 S	— 04.88
North horn of the Bull	β	2	5 13 02	3.77	28 24 50 N	+ 04.19
Bellatrix. West shoulder of Orion	γ	2	5 13 53	3.22	06 08 43 N	+ 04.15
West star in the belt of Orion	δ	2	5 21 18	3.07	00 28 05 S	— 03.56
Betelgeux. Last shoulder of Orion	α	1	5 43 48	3.24	07 21 14 N	+ 01.61
Canopus. Foot of the ship Argo	α	1	6 19 18	1.34	52 35 15 S	+ 01.67
Syrius. Mouth of the greater Dog	α	1	6 35 53	2.64	16 26 21 S	+ 04.35
Castor. Head of Northern Twin	α	2	7 21 10	3.85	32 19 52 N	— 06.85
Procyon. Head of the lesser Dog	α	1	7 28 17	3.14	05 45 27 N	— 07.45
Pollux. Head of the Southern Twin	β	2	7 32 26	3.68	28 31 06 N	— 07.77
Oar of the ship Argo	β	1	9 10 51	0.75	68 51 18 S	+ 14.83
Heart of the lesser Lion	α	2	9 17 16	2.95	07 45 20 S	+ 15.14
Regulus. The Lion's heart	α	1	9 57 10	3.20	12 59 13 N	— 17.19
South Pointer. Light of the Great Bear	β	2	10 49 04	3.74	57 30 15 N	— 19.05
North Pointer. The same	α	2	10 50 39	3.88	62 52 54 N	— 19.09
Denob. The Lion's tail	β	2	11 38 21	3.11	15 44 46 N	— 19.95
Foot of the Cross	α	1	12 15 05	3.24	61 56 07 S	+ 20.00
The Virgin's Spike	α	1	13 14 08	3.14	10 03 34 S	+ 19.04
Last star in tail of Great Bear	η	2	13 30 16	2.41	15 22 01 N	— 18.24
Tail of the Dragon	α	2	13 58 43	1.63	65 22 59 N	— 17.46
Arcturus. Bright star in Bootes	α	1	14 06 05	2.72	20 17 16 N	— 17.15
Southern foot of the Centaur	α	1	14 25 47	4.44	56 01 57 S	+ 16.16
Southern scale of Libra	α	2	14 39 17	3.30	15 09 27 S	+ 15.46
Northern scale of Libra	β	2	15 05 44	3.22	08 35 50 S	+ 13.93
bright star in the Crown	α	2	15 25 47	2.53	27 25 53 N	— 12.56
In the neck of the Serpent	α	2	15 33 55	2.93	07 05 49 N	— 12.00
Antares. The Scorpion's heart	α	1	16 16 35	3.65	25 56 56 S	+ 08.84
Eastern knee of Ophiuchus	γ	2	16 58 21	3.44	15 27 09 N	+ 05.52
In the heel of Hercules	α	2	17 05 06	2.74	14 38 29 N	— 04.87
In the head of Serpentarius	α	2	17 25 12	2.77	12 43 35 N	— 03.12
In the head of the Dragon	γ	2	17 51 45	1.37	51 31 13 N	— 00.78
Lyra. Bright star in the Harp	α	1	18 29 49	2.01	38 35 53 N	+ 02.54
Altair. Eye of the Eagle	α	1	19 40 32	2.93	08 19 21 N	+ 08.44
Tail of the Swan	α	1	20 34 16	2.04	44 32 13 N	+ 12.46
Fomalhaut. Mouth of Southern Fish	α	1	22 46 00	3.32	30 43 48 S	— 18.98
In the shoulder of the same	β	2	22 53 37	2.68	26 56 44 N	+ 19.18
Markab. In the Wing of Pegasus	α	2	22 54 19	2.97	14 04 44 N	+ 19.20
Head of Andromeda	α	2	23 57 34	3.06	27 55 50 N	+ 20.04

A TABLE of REFRACTION.

App. Alt. d. m.	Re-fract. m. s.	App. Alt. d. m.	Re-fract. m. s.	App. Alt. d. m.	Re-fract. m. s.
0 00	33 00	10 00	5 15	51 0	0 46
0 10	31 22	10 15	5 07	52 0	0 44
0 20	29 50	10 30	5 00	53 0	0 43
0 30	28 22	10 45	4 53	54 0	0 41
0 40	27 00	11 00	4 47	55 0	0 40
0 50	25 42	11 15	4 40	56 0	0 38
1 00	24 29	11 30	4 34	57 0	0 37
1 10	23 20	11 45	4 29	58 0	0 35
1 20	22 15	12 00	4 23	59 0	0 34
1 30	21 15	12 20	4 16	60 0	0 33
1 40	20 18	12 40	4 09	61 0	0 32
1 50	29 25	13 00	4 03	62 0	0 30
2 00	18 35	13 20	3 57	63 0	0 29
2 10	17 48	13 40	3 51	64 0	0 28
2 20	17 04	14 00	3 45	65 0	0 26
2 30	16 24	14 20	3 40	66 0	0 25
2 40	15 45	14 40	3 35	67 0	0 24
2 50	15 09	15 00	3 30	68 0	0 23
3 00	14 36	15 30	3 24	69 0	0 22
3 10	14 04	16 00	3 17	70 0	0 21
3 20	13 34	16 30	3 10	71 0	0 19
3 30	13 06	17 00	3 04	72 0	0 18
3 40	12 40	17 30	2 59	73 0	0 17
3 50	12 15	18 00	2 54	74 0	0 16
4 00	11 51	18 30	2 49	75 0	0 15
4 10	11 29	19 00	2 44	76 0	0 14
4 20	11 08	19 30	2 39	77 0	0 13
4 30	10 48	20 00	2 35	78 0	0 12
4 40	10 29	20 30	2 31	79 0	0 11
4 50	10 11	21 00	2 27	80 0	0 10
5 00	9 54	21 30	2 24	81 0	0 9
5 10	9 38	22 0	2 20	82 0	0 8
5 20	9 23	23 0	2 14	83 0	0 7
5 30	9 08	24 0	2 07	84 0	0 6
5 40	8 54	25 0	2 02	85 0	0 5
5 50	8 41	26 0	1 56	86 0	0 4
6 00	8 28	27 0	1 51	87 0	0 3
6 10	8 15	28 0	1 47	88 0	0 2
6 20	8 03	29 0	1 42	89 0	0 1
6 30	7 51	30 0	1 38	90 0	0 0
6 40	7 40	31 0	1 35		
6 50	7 30	32 0	1 31		
7 00	7 20	33 0	1 28		
7 10	7 11	34 0	1 24		
7 20	7 02	35 0	1 21		
7 30	6 53	36 0	1 18		
7 40	6 45	37 0	1 16		
7 50	6 37	38 0	1 13		
8 00	6 29	39 0	1 10		
8 10	6 22	40 0	1 08		
8 20	6 15	41 0	1 05		
8 30	6 08	42 0	1 03		
8 40	6 01	43 0	1 01		
8 50	5 55	44 0	0 59		
9 00	5 48	45 0	0 57		
9 10	5 42	46 0	0 55		
9 20	5 36	47 0	0 53		
9 30	5 31	48 0	0 51		
9 40	5 25	49 0	0 49		
9 50	5 20	50 0	0 48		

PART II.

App. Alt m. s.	Re-fract. m.
3 56	12
4 23	11
4 56	10
5 35	9
6 22	8
7 15	7
8 40	6
10 30	5
13 10	4
17 24	3
25 20	2
43 30	1
51 30	¾
62 00	½
75 00	¼

A TABLE of DIP of the HORIZON.

Height of the Eye. Feet	Dip of the Hor. m. s.	Height of the Eye Feet	Dip of the Hor. m. s.	Height of the Eye Feet	Dip of the Hor. m. s.
1	0 37	13	3 26	26	4 52
2	1 21	14	3 34	28	5 03
3	1 39	15	3 42	30	5 14
4	1 55	16	3 49	35	5 39
5	2 08	17	3 56	40	6 02
6	2 20	18	4 03	45	6 24
7	2 31	19	4 10	50	6 44
8	2 42	20	4 16	60	7 23
9	2 52	21	4 22	70	7 59
10	3 01	22	4 28	80	8 32
11	3 10	23	4 34	90	9 03
12	3 18	24	4 40	100	9 33

PART II.

Height of the Eye Feet	Dip of the Hor. M.	Dist. of the Hor. Miles	Height of the Eye Feet	Dip of the Hor. M.	Dist. of the Hor Miles
2	1	1½	28	5	6½
4	2	2½	40	6	8
10	3	3¼	57	7	9½
18	4	5¼	109	8	11

A TABLE of DIP of the SEA, at different Distances from the Observer.

Dist. of the Land	Height of the Eye above the Sea in Feet.							
	5	10	15	20	25	30	35	40
Naut. Miles	dip m.	dip m.	dip m.	dip m.	dip m.	dip m.	dip m.	dip m.
¼	11	22	34	45	56	68	79	90
½	6	11	17	22	28	34	39	45
¾	4	8	12	15	19	23	27	30
1	4	6	9	12	15	17	20	23
1¼	3	5	7	9	12	14	16	19
1½	3	4	6	8	10	12	14	15
2	2	3	5	6	8	10	11	12
2½	2	3	5	6	7	8	9	10
3	2	3	4	5	6	7	8	8
3½	2	3	4	5	6	6	7	7
4	2	3	4	4	5	6	7	7
5	2	3	4	4	5	5	6	6
6	2	3	4	4	5	5	6	6

A TABLE of the SUN's PARALLAX, and of the Augmentation of the MOON's SEMIDIAMETER.

Sun's Alt. D.	Sun's Parallax S.	Moon's Alt. D.	Aug-ment. S.
00	9	5	1
10	9	10	3
20	8	15	4
30	8	20	5
40	7	25	7
50	6	30	8
55	5	35	9
60	4	40	10
65	4	45	11
70	3	50	12
75	2	55	13
80	2	60	14
85	1	70	15
90	0	80 &c.	16

A TABLE of the HEIGHT of the APPARENT LEVEL above the TRUE.

Dist.	Deduct.	Dist.	Deduct.	Dist.	Deduct.
Gunt. Chains	Inches	Statute Miles	F. Inches	Statute Miles	F. Inches
10	0.12	1	0 7.9	9	53. 8.4
20	0.50	2	2 7.8	10	66 3.5
30	1.12	3	5 11.6	11	80 2.6
40	1.99	4	10 7.3	12	95 5.6
50	3.12	5	16 6.9	13	112 0.5
60	4.48	6	23 10.6	14	129 11.3
70	6.09	7	32 5.7	15	149 2.
80	7.95	8	42 5.2	16	169 8.7

A TABLE of LINKS to be subtracted from each CHAIN, in an Ascending or Descending Line, in order to reduce it to the Horizontal Measure.

PART I.				PART II.			
Deg.	Links	Deg.	Links	D. M.	Links	D. M.	Links
1	0.02	11	1.84	4 3	¼	13 28	2¾
2	0.06	12	2.19	5 44	½	14 04	3
3	0.14	13	2.57	7 1	¾	14 39	3¼
4	0.25	14	2.97	8 7	1	15 12	3½
5	0.38	15	3.41	9 4	1¼	15 44	3¾
6	0.55	16	3.88	9 56	1½	16 16	4
7	0.75	17	4.37	10 44	1¾	16 46	4¼
8	0.98	18	4.90	11 29	2	17 15	4½
9	1.24	19	5.45	12 11	2¼	17 44	4¾
10	1.52	20	6.03	12 50	2½	18 12	5

A TABLE of ANGLES corresponding to SUBTENSES measured in Links, the Radius being Half a Chain.

L.	D. M.	L.	D. M.	L.	D. M.	L.	D. M.	L.	D. M.	L.	D. M.
6	6.53	21	24.14	36	42.12	51	61.20	66	82.36	81	108.12
7	8.02	22	25.25	37	43.26	52	62.40	67	84.08	82	110.10
8	9.11	23	26.36	38	44.40	53	64.00	68	85.42	83	112.12
9	10.20	24	27.46	39	45.54	54	65.22	69	87.16	84	114.17
10	11.29	25	28.58	40	47.10	55	66.44	70	88.52	85	116.26
11	12.38	26	30.08	41	48.24	56	68.06	71	90.28	86	118.38
12	13.47	27	31.20	42	49.40	57	69.30	72	92.06	87	120.55
13	14.56	28	32.31	43	50.56	58	70.54	73	93.46	88	123.17
14	16.06	29	33.43	44	52.12	59	72.18	74	95.28	89	125.45
15	17.15	30	34.55	45	53.30	60	73.44	75	97.11	90	128.19
16	18.25	31	36.07	46	54.46	61	75.10	76	98.56	91	131.00
17	19.34	32	37.20	47	56.04	62	76.38	77	100.42	92	133.52
18	20.44	33	38.32	48	57.22	63	78.06	78	102.32	93	136.52
19	21.54	34	39.45	49	58.41	64	79.35	79	104.22	94	140.08
20	23.04	35	40.58	50	60.00	65	81.07	80	106.16	95	143.38

M. S.	¼ Elapf. Time.	Middle Time.	Rifing.	M. S.	¼ Elapf. Time.	Middle Time.	Rifing.
00 00				30 00	0.88430	4.41073	2.93225
00 30	2.66121	2.63782	9.37654	30 30	87717	42386	94655
01 00	2.36018	2.74085	9.77860	31 00	87015	43088	96067
01 30	2.18409	3.11694	0.33079	31 30	86314	43779	97454
02 00	2.05916	24187	58066	32 00	85644	44459	98825
02 30	1.96223	33878	77418	32 30	84976	45127	3.00164
03 00	88307	41796	93284	33 00	84317	45785	01486
03 30	81613	48490	1.06673	33 30	83669	46434	02792
04 00	75814	54281	18271	34 00	83030	47073	04077
04 30	70700	59403	28502	34 30	82400	47702	05342
05 00	1.66125	3.63976	1.37653	35 00	0.81780	4.48323	3.06595
05 30	61986	68117	45931	35 30	81169	48932	07815
06 00	58208	71895	53488	36 00	80567	49536	09032
06 30	54733	75370	60440	36 30	79973	50130	10227
07 00	51515	78588	66877	37 00	79387	50716	11406
07 30	48520	81583	72869	37 30	78809	51294	12573
08 00	45718	84385	78474	38 00	78239	51864	13716
08 30	43086	87017	83739	38 30	77677	52426	14850
09 00	40605	89498	88703	39 00	77122	52981	15969
09 30	38258	91845	93399	39 30	76574	53529	17072
10 00	1.36032	3.94071	1.97854	40 00	0.76033	4.54070	3.16161
10 30	33915	96188	2.02091	40 30	75499	54604	19238
11 00	31896	98207	06131	41 00	74972	55131	20301
11 30	29967	4.00136	09991	41 30	74451	55652	21351
12 00	28120	01983	13687	42 00	73937	56166	22389
12 30	26349	03754	17223	42 30	73429	56674	23414
13 00	24647	05456	20638	43 00	72926	57177	24427
13 30	23010	07093	23915	43 30	72430	57673	25428
14 00	21432	08671	27073	44 00	71940	58163	26418
14 30	19910	10193	30120	44 30	71455	58648	27396
15 00	1.18440	4.11663	2.33063	45 00	0.70976	4.59127	3.28363
15 30	17018	13085	35910	45 30	70503	59600	29320
16 00	15642	14461	38667	46 00	70034	60069	30266
16 30	14307	15796	41338	46 30	69571	60532	31202
17 00	13013	17090	43930	47 00	69113	60990	32128
17 30	11757	18346	46447	47 30	68660	61443	33044
18 00	10536	19567	48893	48 00	68212	61891	33950
18 30	09348	20755	51271	48 30	67769	62334	34847
19 00	08193	21910	53586	49 00	67330	62773	35734
19 30	07067	23036	55841	49 30	66896	63207	36613
20 00	1.05970	4.24133	2.58039	50 00	0.66466	4.63637	3.37482
20 30	04901	25202	60181	50 30	66041	64062	38343
21 00	03857	26246	62274	51 00	65620	64483	39195
21 30	02838	27265	64316	51 30	65204	64899	40039
22 00	01843	28260	66311	52 00	64791	65312	40875
22 30	00870	29233	68262	52 30	64383	65720	41702
23 00	0.99918	30185	70169	53 00	63978	66125	42523
23 30	98988	31115	72036	53 30	63578	66525	43334
24 00	98077	32026	73863	54 00	63181	66922	44138
24 30	97184	32919	75652	54 30	62789	67314	44935
25 00	0.96310	4.33793	2.77405	55 00	0.62400	4.67703	3.45724
25 30	95454	34649	79124	55 30	62014	68089	46507
26 00	94614	35489	80809	56 00	61632	68471	47282
26 30	93791	36313	82461	56 30	61254	68849	48050
27 00	92982	37121	84083	57 00	60879	69224	48811
27 30	92189	37914	85675	57 30	60508	69595	49566
28 00	91411	38692	87238	58 00	60140	69963	50314
28 30	90646	39457	88773	58 30	59775	70328	51056
29 00	89894	40209	90282	59 00	59414	70689	51791
29 30	89156	40947	91765	59 30	59056	71047	52520

1 HOUR.

M. S.	¼ Elapf. Time.	Middle Time.	Rifing.	M. S.	¼ Elapf. Time.	Middle Time.	Rifing.
00 00	0.58720	4.71403	3.53243	30 00	0.41716	4.88387	3.88150
00 30	58348	71755	53759	30 30	41488	88615	88625
01 00	57909	72104	54670	31 00	41261	88842	89097
01 30	57663	72450	55375	31 30	41036	89067	89567
02 00	57310	72793	56074	32 00	40812	89291	90034
02 30	56970	73133	56767	32 30	40590	89513	90498
03 00	56632	73470	57455	33 00	40368	89735	90960
03 30	56298	73805	58137	33 30	40149	89954	91420
04 00	55966	74137	58814	34 00	39930	90173	91876
04 30	55637	74466	59486	34 30	39713	90390	92331
05 00	0.55311	4.74792	3.60152	35 00	0.39497	4.90606	3.92782
05 30	54987	75116	60813	35 30	39282	90821	93232
06 00	54666	75437	61469	36 00	39069	91034	93679
06 30	54347	75756	62120	36 30	38856	91247	94123
07 00	54031	76072	62766	37 00	38646	91457	94566
07 30	53718	76385	63407	37 30	38436	91667	95005
08 00	53406	76697	64043	38 00	38227	91876	95443
08 30	53097	77005	64675	38 30	38020	92083	95878
09 00	52791	77312	65302	39 00	37813	92290	96311
09 30	52488	77615	65924	39 30	37609	92494	96742
10 00	0.52186	4.77917	3.66542	40 00	0.37405	4.92698	3.97170
10 30	51886	78217	67156	40 30	37202	92901	97597
11 00	51589	78514	67756	41 00	37001	93102	98021
11 30	51294	78809	63769	41 30	36800	93303	98443
12 00	51002	79101	68969	42 00	36602	93501	98862
12 30	50711	79392	69566	42 30	36404	93699	99280
13 00	50423	79680	70158	43 00	36206	93897	99696
13 30	50137	79966	70745	43 30	36011	94092	4.00109
14 00	49852	80251	71329	44 00	35816	94287	00521
14 30	49570	80533	71909	44 30	35622	94481	00930
15 00	0.49290	4.80813	3.72485	45 00	0.35430	4.94673	4.01337
15 30	49012	81091	73057	45 30	35238	94865	01743
16 00	48736	81367	73625	46 00	35047	95056	02146
16 30	48462	81641	74189	46 30	34858	95245	02547
17 00	48189	81914	74750	47 00	34669	95434	02947
17 30	47919	82184	75307	47 30	34482	95621	03344
18 00	47650	82453	75860	48 00	34296	95807	03740
18 30	47383	82720	76409	48 30	34110	95993	04134
19 00	47110	82984	76955	49 00	33925	96178	04526
19 30	46856	83247	77498	49 30	33742	96361	04916
20 00	0.46595	4.83508	3.78037	50 00	0.33559	4.96544	4.05304
20 30	46335	83768	78573	50 30	33378	96725	05690
21 00	46077	84026	79105	51 00	33197	96906	06074
21 30	45822	84281	79635	51 30	33018	97085	06457
22 00	45567	84536	80159	52 00	32839	97264	06838
22 30	45315	84788	80682	52 30	32661	97442	07217
23 00	45064	85039	81201	53 00	32485	97618	07595
23 30	44815	85288	81717	53 30	32309	97794	07970
24 00	44567	85536	82230	54 00	32134	97969	08344
24 30	44321	85782	82739	54 30	31960	98143	08716
25 00	0.44077	4.86026	3.83246	55 00	0.31787	4.98316	4.09087
25 30	43834	86269	83749	55 30	31614	98489	09456
26 00	43593	86510	84250	56 00	31443	98660	09823
26 30	43353	86750	84748	56 30	31272	98831	10188
27 00	43114	86989	85242	57 00	31103	99000	10552
27 30	42877	87226	85734	57 30	30934	99169	10915
28 00	42643	87460	86223	58 00	30766	99337	11275
28 30	42409	87694	86709	58 30	30599	99504	11634
29 00	42176	87927	87192	59 00	30433	99670	11992
29 30	41945	88158	87672	59 30	30268	99835	12348

11 HOURS.

M. S.	¼ Elapf. Time.	Middle Time.	Rising.	M. S.	¼ Elapf. Time.	Middle Time.	Rifing.
00 00	0.30103	5.00000	4.11702	30 00	0.21555	5.08548	4.31523
00 30	29939	00164	13055	30 30	21432	08671	31801
01 00	29776	00327	13406	31 00	21309	08794	32079
01 30	29614	00489	13756	31 30	21187	08917	32356
02 00	29453	00650	14104	32 00	21066	09037	32631
02 30	29293	00810	14451	32 30	20945	09158	32906
03 00	29133	00970	14797	33 00	20824	09279	33180
03 30	28974	01129	15140	33 30	20704	09399	33453
04 00	28816	01287	15483	34 00	20585	09518	33724
04 30	28659	01444	15824	34 30	20456	09637	33995
05 00	0.28502	5.01601	4.16163	35 00	0.20348	5.09755	4.34265
05 30	28346	01757	16501	35 30	20230	09873	34534
06 00	28191	01912	16838	36 00	20113	09990	34802
06 30	28037	02066	17173	36 30	19996	10107	35069
07 00	27884	02219	17507	37 00	19880	10223	35335
07 30	27731	02372	17839	37 30	19764	10339	35601
08 00	27579	02524	18171	38 00	19649	10454	35865
08 30	27428	02675	18500	38 30	19534	10569	36128
09 00	27277	02826	18828	39 00	19420	10683	36391
09 30	27127	02976	19156	39 30	19306	10797	36652
10 00	0.26978	5.03125	4.19482	40 00	0.19193	5.10910	4.36913
10 30	26830	03273	19806	40 30	19081	11022	37173
11 00	26682	03421	20129	41 00	18968	11135	37432
11 30	26535	03568	20451	41 30	18857	11246	37690
12 00	26389	03714	20771	42 00	18746	11357	37948
12 30	26244	03859	21091	42 30	18635	11468	38204
13 00	26099	04004	21479	43 00	18525	11578	38459
13 30	25955	04148	21725	43 30	18415	11688	38714
14 00	25811	04292	22041	44 00	18306	11797	38968
14 30	25668	04435	22355	44 30	18197	11906	39221
15 00	0.25526	5.04577	4.22668	45 00	0.18089	5.12014	4.39473
15 30	25385	04718	22980	45 30	17981	12122	39725
16 00	25244	04859	23290	46 00	17874	12229	39975
16 30	25104	04999	23599	46 30	17767	12336	40225
17 00	24964	05139	23907	47 00	17660	12443	40474
17 30	24825	05278	24214	47 30	17554	12549	40722
18 00	24687	05416	24520	48 00	17449	12654	40969
18 30	24550	05553	24825	48 30	17344	12759	41215
19 00	24413	05690	25128	49 00	17239	12864	41461
19 30	24276	05827	25430	49 30	17135	12968	41706
20 00	0.24141	5.05962	4.25731	50 00	0.17032	5.13071	4.41950
20 30	24006	06097	26031	50 30	16928	13175	42193
21 00	23871	06232	26330	51 00	16826	13277	42435
21 30	23738	06365	26628	51 30	16724	13379	42677
22 00	23605	06498	26924	52 00	16622	13481	42918
22 30	23472	06631	27220	52 30	16520	13583	43158
23 00	23340	06763	27514	53 00	16419	13684	43398
23 30	23209	06894	27807	53 30	16319	13784	43636
24 00	23078	07025	28099	54 00	16219	13884	43874
24 30	22948	07155	28391	54 30	16119	13984	44111
25 00	0.22819	5.07284	4.28681	55 00	0.16020	5.14083	4.44346
25 30	22690	07413	28969	55 30	15921	14182	44583
26 00	22561	07542	29257	56 00	15823	14280	44816
26 30	22433	07670	29544	56 30	15725	14378	45052
27 00	22306	07797	29830	57 00	15628	14475	45286
27 30	22180	07923	30115	57 30	15530	14573	45519
28 00	22054	08049	30398	58 00	15434	14669	45750
28 30	21928	08175	30681	58 30	15338	14765	45981
29 00	21803	08300	30963	59 00	15242	14861	46212
29 30	21679	08424	31244	59 30	15146	14957	46442

M. S.	¼ Elapf. Time.	Middle Time.	Rifing.	M. S.	¼ Elapf. Time.	Middle Time.	Rifing.
00 00	0.15051	5.15052	4.46671	30 00	0.10053	5.20050	4.59244
00 30	14957	15146	46899	30 30	09981	20122	59436
01 00	14863	15240	47127	31 00	09909	20194	59627
01 30	14769	15334	47354	31 30	09837	20266	59818
02 00	14676	15427	47580	32 00	09765	20338	60008
02 30	14583	15520	47806	32 30	09694	20409	60198
03 00	14490	15613	48031	33 00	09623	20480	60387
03 30	14398	15705	48255	33 30	09552	20551	60576
04 00	14307	15796	48479	34 00	09482	20621	60764
04 30	14215	15888	48701	34 30	09412	20691	60952
05 00	0.14124	5.15979	4.48924	35 00	0.09343	5.20760	4.61139
05 30	14034	16069	49145	35 30	09273	20830	61326
06 00	13944	16159	49366	36 00	09204	20899	61512
06 30	13854	16249	49586	36 30	09136	20967	61698
07 00	13765	16338	49806	37 00	09067	21036	61883
07 30	13676	16427	50025	37 30	08999	21104	62068
08 00	13587	16516	50243	38 00	08931	21172	62252
08 30	13499	16604	50461	38 30	08864	21239	62436
09 00	13411	16692	50677	39 00	08797	21306	62619
09 30	13324	16779	50894	39 30	08730	21373	62802
10 00	0.13237	5.16866	4.51109	40 00	0.08664	5.21439	4.62984
10 30	13150	16953	51324	40 30	08597	21506	63166
11 00	13064	17039	51539	41 00	08531	21572	63347
11 30	12978	17125	51753	41 30	08466	21637	63528
12 00	12893	17210	51966	42 00	08401	21702	63708
12 30	12807	17296	52178	42 30	08336	21767	63888
13 00	12723	17380	52390	43 00	08271	21832	64068
13 30	12638	17465	52601	43 30	08207	21896	64246
14 00	12554	17549	52812	44 00	08143	21960	64425
14 30	12471	17632	53022	44 30	08079	22024	64603
15 00	0.12387	5.17716	4.53231	45 00	0.08015	5.22088	4.64780
15 30	12305	17798	53440	45 30	07952	22151	64957
16 00	12222	17881	53648	46 00	07889	22214	65134
16 30	12140	17963	53856	46 30	07827	22276	65310
17 00	12058	18045	54063	47 00	07765	22338	65486
17 30	11977	18126	54269	47 30	07703	22400	65661
18 00	11895	18208	54475	48 00	07641	22462	65836
18 30	11815	18288	54680	48 30	07579	22524	66010
19 00	11734	18369	54885	49 00	07518	22585	66184
19 30	11654	18449	55089	49 30	07458	22645	66357
20 00	0.11575	5.18528	4.55293	50 00	0.07397	5.22706	4.66530
20 30	11495	18608	55496	50 30	07337	22766	66702
21 00	11416	18687	55698	51 00	07277	22826	66874
21 30	11338	18765	55900	51 30	07217	22886	67046
22 00	11259	18844	56101	52 00	07158	22945	67217
22 30	11181	18922	56301	52 30	07099	23004	67388
23 00	11104	18999	56501	53 00	07040	23063	67558
23 30	11027	19076	56701	53 30	06982	23121	67728
24 00	10950	19153	56900	54 00	06923	23180	67897
24 30	10873	19230	57098	54 30	06865	23238	68066
25 00	0.10797	5.19306	4.57296	55 00	0.06808	5.23295	4.68235
25 30	10721	19382	57494	55 30	06751	23352	68403
26 00	10646	19457	57690	56 00	06693	23410	68571
26 30	10579	19533	57886	56 30	06636	23466	68738
27 00	10495	19608	58082	57 00	06580	23523	68905
27 30	10421	19682	58277	57 30	06524	23579	69071
28 00	10347	19756	58471	58 00	06468	23625	69237
28 30	10272	19831	58665	58 30	06412	23691	69403
29 00	10199	19904	58859	59 00	06357	23746	69568
29 30	10126	19977	59052	59 30	06302	23801	69733

IV HOURS.

M. S.	¼ Elapſ. Time.	Middle Time.	Riſing.	M. S.	¼ Elapſ. Time.	Middle Time.	Riſing.
00 00	0.06247	5.23856	4.69897	30 00	0.03438	5.26665	4.79051
00 30	06192	23911	70061	30 30	03399	26704	79192
01 00	06138	23965	70224	31 00	03360	26743	79334
01 30	06084	24019	70387	31 30	03322	26781	79475
02 00	06030	24073	70550	32 00	03283	26820	79615
02 30	05977	24126	70712	32 30	03245	26858	79756
03 00	05924	24179	70874	33 00	03207	26896	89896
03 30	05871	24232	71036	33 30	03170	26933	80035
04 00	05818	24285	71197	34 00	03132	26971	80175
04 30	05766	24337	71357	34 30	03095	27008	80314
05 00	0.05714	5.24389	4.71518	35 00	0.03058	5.27045	4.80452
05 30	05662	24441	71678	35 30	03021	27082	80591
06 00	05610	24493	71837	36 00	02985	27118	80729
06 30	05559	24544	71996	36 30	02949	27154	80866
07 00	05508	24595	72155	37 00	02913	27190	81004
07 30	05457	24646	72313	37 30	02877	27226	81141
08 00	05406	24697	72471	38 00	02841	27262	81277
08 30	05356	24747	72628	38 30	02806	27297	81414
09 00	05306	24797	72785	39 00	02771	27332	81550
09 30	05257	24846	72942	39 30	02736	27367	81686
10 00	0.05207	5.24896	4.73098	40 00	0.02701	5.27402	4.81821
10 30	05158	24945	73254	40 30	02667	27436	81956
11 00	05109	24994	73410	41 00	02633	27470	82091
11 30	05060	25043	73565	41 30	02599	27504	82226
12 00	05012	25091	73720	42 00	02565	27538	82360
12 30	04964	25139	73874	42 30	02532	27571	82494
13 00	04916	25187	74028	43 00	02499	27604	82628
13 30	04868	25235	74182	43 30	02466	27637	82761
14 00	04821	25282	74335	44 00	02433	27670	82894
14 30	04774	25329	74488	44 30	02400	27703	83026
15 00	0.04727	5.25376	4.74641	45 00	0.02368	5.27735	4.83159
15 30	04680	25423	74793	45 30	02336	27767	83291
16 00	04634	25469	74945	46 00	02304	27799	83423
16 30	04588	25515	75096	46 30	02273	27830	83554
17 00	04542	25561	75247	47 00	02241	27862	83685
17 30	04496	25607	75398	47 30	02210	27893	83816
18 00	04451	25652	75549	48 00	02179	27924	83947
18 30	04406	25697	75699	48 30	02149	27954	84077
19 00	04361	25742	75848	49 00	02118	27985	84207
19 30	04317	25786	75997	49 30	02088	28015	84337
20 00	0.04272	5.25831	4.76146	50 00	0.02058	5.28045	4.84466
20 30	04228	25875	76295	50 30	02028	28075	84595
21 00	04185	25918	76443	51 00	01999	28104	84724
21 30	04141	25962	76591	51 30	01969	28134	84852
22 00	04098	26005	76738	52 00	01940	28163	84981
22 30	04055	26048	76885	52 30	01912	28191	85108
23 00	04012	26091	77032	53 00	01883	28220	85236
23 30	03969	26134	77179	53 30	01854	28249	85363
24 00	03927	26176	77325	54 00	01826	28277	85490
24 30	03885	26218	77470	54 30	01798	28305	85617
25 00	0.03843	5.26260	4.77616	55 00	0.01771	5.28332	4.85744
25 30	03802	26301	77761	55 30	01743	28360	85870
26 00	03760	26343	77906	56 00	01716	28387	85996
26 30	03719	26384	78050	56 30	01689	28414	86121
27 00	03678	26425	78194	57 00	01662	28441	86246
27 30	03638	26465	78338	57 30	01635	28468	86371
28 00	03597	26506	78481	58 00	01609	28494	86496
28 30	03557	26546	78624	58 30	01583	28520	86621
29 00	03517	26586	78767	59 00	01557	28546	86745
29 30	03478	26625	78908	59 30	01531	28572	86869

V HOURS.

M. S.	½ Elapf. Time.	Middle Time.	Rifing.	M. S.	½ Elapf. Time.	Middle Time.	Rifing.
00 00	0.01656	5.28597	4.86992	30 00	0.00373	5.29730	4.93926
00 30	01480	28623	87116	30 30	00361	29742	94034
01 00	01455	28648	87239	31 00	00349	29754	94141
01 30	01430	28673	87362	31 30	00337	29766	94249
02 00	01406	28697	87484	32 00	00325	29778	94356
02 30	01381	28722	87606	32 30	00313	29790	94463
03 00	01357	28746	87728	33 00	00302	29801	94570
03 30	01333	28770	87850	33 30	00291	29812	94676
04 00	01310	28793	87971	34 00	00280	29823	94782
04 30	01286	28817	88093	34 30	00269	29834	94888
05 00	0.01263	5.28840	5.88213	35 00	0.00259	5.29844	4.94994
05 30	01240	28863	88334	35 30	00249	29854	95100
06 00	01217	28886	88454	36 00	00239	29864	95205
06 30	01194	28909	88574	36 30	00229	29874	95310
07 00	01172	28931	88694	37 00	00219	29884	95415
07 30	01150	28953	88814	37 30	00210	29893	95520
08 00	01128	28975	88933	38 00	00200	29903	95624
08 30	01106	28997	89052	38 30	00191	29913	95728
09 00	01084	29019	89171	39 00	00183	29920	95832
09 30	01063	29040	89289	39 30	00174	29929	95936
10 00	0.01042	5.29061	4.89407	40 00	0.00166	5.29937	4.96040
10 30	01021	29082	89525	40 30	00157	29946	96143
11 00	01000	29103	89643	41 00	00149	29954	96246
11 30	00980	29123	89760	41 30	00142	29961	96349
12 00	00960	29143	89877	42 00	00134	29969	96451
12 30	00940	29163	89994	42 30	00127	29976	96554
13 00	00920	29183	90111	43 00	00120	29983	96656
13 30	00900	29203	90227	43 30	00113	29990	96758
14 00	00881	29222	90343	44 00	00106	29997	96860
14 30	00861	29241	90459	44 30	00099	30004	96961
15 00	0.00843	5.29260	5.90575	45 00	0.00093	5.30010	4.97062
15 30	00824	29279	90690	45 30	00087	30016	97163
16 00	00805	29298	90805	46 00	00081	30022	97264
16 30	00787	29316	90920	46 30	00075	30028	97365
17 00	00769	29334	91034	47 00	00070	30033	97465
17 30	00751	29352	91149	47 30	00065	30038	97565
18 00	00733	29370	91263	48 00	00060	30043	97665
18 30	00716	29387	91377	48 30	00055	30048	97765
19 00	00699	29404	91490	49 00	00050	30053	97865
19 30	00682	29421	91603	49 30	00046	30058	97964
20 00	0.00665	5.29438	5.91716	50 00	0.00041	5.30062	4.98063
20 30	00648	29455	91830	50 30	00037	30066	98162
21 00	00632	29471	91942	51 00	00033	30070	98261
21 30	00616	29487	92054	51 30	00030	30073	98359
22 00	00600	29503	92166	52 00	00026	30077	98457
22 30	00584	29519	92278	52 30	00023	30080	98555
23 00	00568	29535	92390	53 00	00020	30083	98653
23 30	00553	29550	92501	53 30	00017	30086	98751
24 00	00538	29565	92612	54 00	00015	30088	98848
24 30	00523	29580	92723	54 30	00013	30090	98945
25 00	0.00508	5.29595	5.92833	55 00	0.00010	5.30092	4.99042
25 30	00494	29609	92944	55 30	00008	30094	99139
26 00	00480	29623	93054	56 00	00007	30096	99235
26 30	00466	29637	93164	56 30	00005	30098	99332
27 00	00452	29651	93273	57 00	00004	30099	99428
27 30	00438	29665	93383	57 30	00003	30100	99524
28 00	00425	29678	93492	58 00	00002	30101	99619
28 30	00412	29691	93600	58 30	00001	30102	99715
29 00	00399	29704	93709	59 00	00000	30103	99810
29 30	00386	29717	93817	59 30	00000	30103	99905

M. S.	VI Hours. Rising.	VII Hours. Rising.	VIII Hours. Rising.	M. S.	VI Hours. Rising.	VII Hours. Rising.	VIII Hours. Rising.
00 00	5.00000	5.09996	5.17607	30 00	5.05327	5.14071	5.20648
00 30	00094	10068	17663	30 30	05410	14134	20695
01 00	00188	10140	17717	31 00	05493	14198	20742
01 30	00282	10212	17772	31 30	05576	14261	20788
02 00	00376	10284	17826	32 00	05659	14324	20835
02 30	00469	10356	17880	32 30	05740	14386	20881
03 00	00563	10429	17934	33 00	05822	14449	20926
03 30	00657	10501	17988	33 30	05904	14511	20972
04 00	00751	10573	18042	34 00	05985	14573	21018
04 30	00844	10645	18095	34 30	06067	14635	21063
05 00	5.00936	5.10714	5.18148	35 00	5.06149	5.14697	5.21109
05 30	00998	10785	18202	35 30	06230	14795	21155
06 00	01121	10856	18255	36 00	06312	14821	21201
06 30	01213	10926	18308	36 30	06392	14882	21245
07 00	01305	10997	18361	37 00	06472	14943	21290
07 30	01398	11068	18414	37 30	06553	15004	21335
08 00	01490	11137	18467	38 00	06633	15065	21379
08 30	01550	11208	18519	38 30	06713	15126	21424
09 00	01671	11278	18571	39 00	06793	15187	21469
09 30	01762	11347	18623	39 30	06873	15248	21513
10 00	5.01851	5.11417	5.18675	40 00	5.06954	5.15309	5.21558
10 30	01943	11486	18727	40 30	07033	15369	21602
11 00	02034	11556	18779	41 00	07111	15428	21645
11 30	02125	11625	18831	41 30	07190	15488	21689
12 00	02215	11694	18883	42 00	07269	15548	21733
12 30	02304	11763	18934	42 30	07348	15608	21777
13 00	02394	11831	18985	43 00	07427	15667	21820
13 30	02483	11899	19035	43 30	07505	15727	21864
14 00	02572	11967	19086	44 00	07584	15787	21908
14 30	02631	12036	19137	44 30	07662	15846	21950
15 00	5.02750	5.12104	5.19188	45 00	5.07739	5.15904	5.21993
15 30	02839	12172	19239	45 30	07816	15963	22036
16 00	02928	12240	19290	46 00	07894	16022	22078
16 30	03016	12307	19340	46 30	07971	16080	22121
17 00	03104	12374	19390	47 00	08049	16139	22164
17 30	03191	12441	19439	47 30	08126	16197	22206
18 00	03279	12508	19489	48 00	08203	16256	22249
18 30	03366	12575	19539	48 30	08280	16314	22291
19 00	03454	12642	19589	49 00	08356	16371	22332
19 30	03542	12709	19639	49 30	08432	16429	22374
20 00	5.03620	5.12776	5.19689	50 00	5.08508	5.16486	5.22416
20 30	03715	12841	19738	50 30	08584	16544	22457
21 00	03801	12907	19786	51 00	08660	16601	22499
21 30	03887	12973	19835	51 30	08736	16659	22541
22 00	03974	13039	19884	52 00	08812	16716	22583
22 30	04060	13104	19933	52 30	08887	16773	22623
23 00	04146	13170	19982	53 00	08961	16829	22664
23 30	04232	13236	20030	53 30	09036	16885	22705
24 00	04318	13302	20079	54 00	09111	16942	22745
24 30	04402	13366	20127	54 30	09185	16998	22786
25 00	5.04487	5.13431	5.20175	55 00	5.09260	5.17054	5.22827
25 30	04571	13495	20222	55 30	09335	17111	22868
26 00	04656	13560	20270	56 00	09409	17167	22908
26 30	04740	13624	20318	56 30	09483	17222	22948
27 00	04825	13689	20366	57 00	09556	17277	22988
27 30	04910	13753	20413	57 30	09629	17333	23027
28 00	04994	13818	20461	58 00	09703	17388	23067
28 30	05077	13881	20508	58 30	09776	17443	23107
29 00	05160	13944	20555	59 00	09850	17498	23146
29 30	05243	14008	20601	59 30	09923	17554	23186

5·905			
9068			
9080			
90926			
91034			
91149			
91263			
91377			
91490			
91603			
5·91716	5		
91830	5.		
91943	5		
92054	5		
92166	52		
92278	52		
92390	53		
92501	53		
92612	54		
92723	54		
5·92833	55		
92944	55		
93054	56		
93164	56		
93273	57		
93383	57		
93492	58		
93600	58		
93709	59		
93817	59		

10 degr.	11 degr.	12 degr.	13 degr.	14 degr.	15 degr.	16 degr.	17 degr.	18 degr.	19 degr.	
17365	19081	20791	22495	24192	25882	27564	29237	30902	32557	60
17393	19109	20820	22523	24220	25910	27592	29265	30929	32584	59
17422	19138	20848	22552	24249	25938	27620	29293	30957	32612	58
17451	19167	20877	22580	24277	25966	27648	29321	30985	32639	57
17479	19195	20905	22608	24305	25994	27676	29348	31012	32667	56
17508	19224	20933	22637	24333	26022	27704	29376	31040	32694	55
17537	19252	20962	22665	24361	26050	27731	29404	31068	32722	54
17565	19281	20990	22693	24390	26079	27759	29432	31095	32749	53
17594	19309	21019	22722	24418	26107	27787	29460	31123	32777	52
17623	19338	21047	22750	24446	26135	27815	29487	31151	32804	51
	19366	21076	22778	24474	26163	27843	29515	31178	32832	50
0	19395	21104	22807	24503	26191	27871	29543	31206	32859	49
	19423	21132	22835	24531	26219	27899	29571	31233	32887	48
	19452	21161	22863	24559	26247	27927	29599	31261	32914	47
	19480	21189	22892	24587	26275	27955	29626	31289	32942	46
	19509	21218	22920	24615	26303	27983	29654	31316	32969	45
	19538	21246	22948	24644	26331	28011	29682	31344	32997	44
	9566	21275	22977	24672	26359	28039	29710	31372	33024	43
	9595	21303	23005	24700	26387	28067	29737	31399	33051	42
	623	21331	23033	24728	26415	28095	29765	31427	33079	41
	552	21360	23062	24756	26443	28113	29793	31454	33106	40
	80	21388	23090	24784	26471	28150	29821	31482	33134	39
	09	21417	23118	24813	26500	28178	29849	31510	33161	38
	17	21445	23146	24841	26528	28206	29876	31537	33189	37
	6	21474	23175	24869	26556	28234	29904	31565	33216	36
	1	21502	23203	24897	26584	28262	29932	31592	33244	35
		21530	23231	24925	26612	28290	29960	31620	33271	34
		21559	23260	24953	26640	28318	29987	31648	33298	33
		21587	23288	24982	26668	28346	30015	31675	33326	32
		21616	23316	25010	26696	28374	30043	31703	33353	31
		1644	23345	25038	26724	28402	30071	31730	33381	30
		1672	23373	25066	26752	28429	30098	31758	33408	29
		1701	23401	25094	26780	28457	30126	31786	33436	28
		729	23429	25122	26808	28485	30154	31813	33463	27
		758	23458	25151	26836	28513	30182	31841	33490	26
		786	23486	25179	26864	28541	30209	31868	33518	25
		814	23514	25207	26892	28569	30237	31896	33545	24
		43	23542	25235	26920	28597	30265	31923	33573	23
		71	23571	25263	26948	28625	30292	31951	33600	22
		99	23599	25291	26976	28652	30320	31979	33627	21
		8	23627	25320	27004	28680	30348	32006	33655	20
		5	23656	25348	27032	28708	30376	32034	33682	19
			23684	25376	27060	28736	30403	32061	33710	18
			23712	25404	27088	28764	30431	32089	33737	17
			23740	25432	27116	28792	30459	32116	33764	16
			23769	25460	27144	28820	30486	32144	33792	15
			23797	25488	27172	28847	30514	32171	33819	14
			23825	25516	27200	28875	30542	32199	33846	13
			23853	25545	27228	28903	30570	32227	33874	12
			23882	25573	27256	28931	30597	32254	33901	11
			910	25601	27284	28959	30625	32282	33929	10
			938	25629	27312	28987	30653	32309	33956	9
			966	25657	27340	29015	30680	32337	33983	8
			995	25685	27368	29042	30708	32364	34011	7
			23	25713	27396	29070	30736	32392	34038	6
			51	25741	27424	29098	30763	32419	34065	5
			79	25769	27452	29126	30791	32447	34093	4
			8	25798	27480	29154	30819	32474	34120	3
			6	25826	27508	29182	30846	32502	34147	2
				25854	27536	29209	30874	32529	34175	1
				25882	27564	29237	30902	32557	34202	0
			75 degr.	74 degr.	73 degr.	72 degr.	71 degr.	70 degr.		M

NATURAL CO-SINES.

M	0 degr.	1 degr.	2 degr.	3 degr.	4 degr.	5 degr.	6 degr.	7 degr.	8 degr.	9 degr.	
0	00	1745	3490	5234	6976	8716	10453	12187	13917	15643	60
1	29	1774	3519	5263	7005	8745	10482	12216	14946	15672	59
2	58	1803	3548	5292	7034	8774	10511	12245	14975	15701	58
3	87	1832	3577	5321	7063	8803	10540	12274	14004	15730	57
4	116	1862	3606	5350	7092	8831	10569	12302	14033	15758	56
5	145	1891	3635	5379	7121	8860	10597	12331	14061	15787	55
6	175	1920	3664	5408	7150	8889	10626	12360	14090	15816	54
7	204	1949	3693	5437	7179	8918	10655	12389	14119	15845	53
8	233	1978	3723	5466	7208	8947	10684	12418	14148	15873	52
9	262	2007	3752	5495	7237	8976	10713	12447	14177	15902	51
10	291	2036	3781	5524	7266	9005	10742	12476	14205	15931	50
11	320	2065	3810	5553	7295	9034	10771	12504	14234	15959	49
12	349	2094	3839	5582	7324	9063	10800	12533	14263	15988	48
13	378	2123	3868	5611	7353	9092	10829	12562	14292	16017	47
14	407	2152	3897	5640	7382	9121	10858	12591	14320	16046	46
15	436	2181	3926	5669	7411	9150	10887	12620	14349	16074	45
16	465	2211	3955	5698	7440	9179	10916	12649	14378	16103	44
17	495	2240	3984	5727	7469	9208	10945	12678	14407	16132	43
18	524	2269	4013	5756	7498	9237	10973	12706	14436	16161	42
19	553	2298	4042	5785	7527	9266	11002	12735	14464	16189	41
20	582	2327	4071	5814	7556	9295	11031	12764	14493	16218	40
21	611	2356	4100	5844	7585	9324	11060	12793	14522	16246	39
22	640	2385	4129	5873	7614	9353	11089	12822	14551	16275	38
23	669	2414	4159	5902	7643	9382	11118	12851	14580	16304	37
24	698	2443	4188	5931	7672	9411	11147	12880	14608	16333	36
25	727	2472	4217	5960	7701	9440	11176	12908	14637	16361	35
26	756	2501	4246	5989	7730	9469	11205	12937	14666	16390	34
27	785	2530	4275	6018	7759	9498	11234	12966	14695	16419	33
28	814	2560	4304	6047	7788	9527	11263	12995	14723	16447	32
29	844	2589	4333	6076	7817	9556	11291	13024	14752	16476	31
30	873	2618	4362	6105	7846	9585	11320	13053	14781	16505	30
31	902	2647	4391	6134	7875	9614	11349	13081	14810	16533	29
32	931	2676	4420	6163	7904	9642	11378	13110	14838	16562	28
33	960	2705	4449	6192	7933	9671	11407	13139	14867	16591	27
34	989	2734	4478	6221	7962	9700	11436	13168	14896	16620	26
35	1018	2763	4507	6250	7991	9729	11465	13197	14925	16648	25
36	1047	2792	4536	6279	8020	9758	11494	13226	14954	16677	24
37	1076	2821	4565	6308	8049	9787	11523	13254	14982	16706	23
38	1105	2850	4594	6337	8078	9816	11552	13283	15011	16734	22
39	1134	2879	4623	6366	8107	9845	11580	13312	15040	16763	21
40	1164	2908	4652	6395	8136	9874	11609	13341	15069	16792	20
41	1193	2938	4682	6424	8165	9903	11638	13370	15097	16820	19
42	1222	2967	4711	6453	8194	9932	11667	13399	15126	16849	18
43	1251	2996	4740	6482	8223	9961	11696	13427	15155	16878	17
44	1280	3025	4769	6511	8252	9990	11725	13456	15184	16906	16
45	1309	3054	4798	6540	8281	10019	11754	13485	15212	16935	15
46	1338	3083	4827	6569	8310	10048	11783	13514	15241	16964	14
47	1367	3112	4856	6598	8339	10077	11812	13543	15270	16992	13
48	1396	3141	4885	6627	8368	10106	11840	13572	15299	17021	12
49	1425	3170	4914	6656	8397	10135	11869	13600	15327	17050	11
50	1454	3199	4943	6685	8426	10164	11898	13629	15356	17078	10
51	1483	3228	4972	6714	8455	10192	11927	13658	15385	17107	9
52	1513	3257	5001	6743	8484	10221	11956	13687	15414	17136	8
53	1542	3286	5030	6773	8513	10250	11985	13716	15442	17164	7
54	1571	3316	5059	6802	8542	10279	12014	13744	15471	17193	6
55	1600	3345	5088	6831	8571	10308	12043	13773	15500	17222	5
56	1629	3374	5117	6860	8600	10337	12071	13802	15529	17250	4
57	1658	3403	5146	6889	8629	10366	12100	13831	15557	17279	3
58	1687	3432	5175	6918	8658	10395	12129	13860	15586	17308	2
59	1716	3461	5205	6947	8687	10424	12158	13889	15615	17336	1
60	1745	3490	5234	6976	8716	10453	12187	13917	15643	17365	0
	89 degr.	88 degr.	87 degr.	86 degr.	85 degr.	84 degr.	83 degr.	82 degr.	81 degr.	80 degr.	M

M.	10 degr.	11 degr.	12 degr.	13 degr.	14 degr.	15 degr.	16 degr.	17 degr.	18 degr.	19 degr.	
0	17365	19081	20791	22495	24192	25882	27564	29237	30902	32557	60
1	17393	19109	20820	22523	24220	25910	27592	29265	30929	32584	59
2	17422	19138	20848	22552	24249	25938	27620	29293	30957	32612	58
3	17451	19167	20877	22580	24277	25966	27648	29321	30985	32639	57
4	17479	19195	20905	22608	24305	25994	27676	29348	31012	32667	56
5	17508	19224	20933	22637	24333	26022	27704	29376	31040	32694	55
6	17537	19252	20962	22665	24361	26050	27731	29404	31068	32722	54
7	17565	19281	20990	22693	24390	26079	27759	29432	31095	32749	53
8	17594	19309	21019	22722	24418	26107	27787	29460	31123	32777	52
9	17623	19338	21047	22750	24446	26135	27815	29487	31151	32804	51
10	17651	19366	21076	22778	24474	26163	27843	29515	31178	32832	50
11	17680	19395	21104	22807	24503	26191	27871	29543	31206	32859	49
12	17708	19423	21132	22835	24531	26219	27899	29571	31233	32887	48
13	17737	19452	21161	22863	24559	26247	27927	29599	31261	32914	47
14	17766	19480	21189	22892	24587	26275	27955	29626	31289	32942	46
15	17794	19509	21218	22920	24615	26303	27983	29654	31316	32969	45
16	17823	19538	21246	22948	24644	26331	28011	29682	31344	32997	44
17	17852	19566	21275	22977	24672	26359	28039	29710	31372	33024	43
18	17880	19595	21303	23005	24700	26387	28067	29737	31399	33051	42
19	17909	19623	21331	23033	24728	26415	28095	29765	31427	33079	41
20	17937	19652	21360	23062	24756	26443	28123	29793	31454	33106	40
21	17966	19680	21388	23090	24784	26471	28150	29821	31482	33134	39
22	17995	19709	21417	23118	24813	26500	28178	29849	31510	33161	38
23	18023	19737	21445	23146	24841	26528	28206	29876	31537	33189	37
24	18052	19766	21474	23175	24869	26556	28234	29904	31565	33216	36
25	18081	19794	21502	23203	24897	26584	28262	29932	31592	33244	35
26	18109	19823	21530	23231	24925	26612	28290	29960	31620	33271	34
27	18138	19851	21559	23260	24953	26640	28318	29987	31648	33298	33
28	18166	19880	21587	23288	24982	26668	28346	30015	31675	33326	32
29	18195	19908	21616	23316	25010	26696	28374	30043	31703	33353	31
30	18224	19937	21644	23345	25038	26724	28402	30071	31730	33381	30
31	18252	19965	21672	23373	25066	26752	28429	30098	31758	33408	29
32	18281	19994	21701	23401	25094	26780	28457	30126	31786	33436	28
33	18309	20022	21729	23429	25122	26808	28485	30154	31813	33463	27
34	18338	20051	21758	23458	25151	26836	28513	30182	31841	33490	26
35	18367	20079	21786	23486	25179	26864	28541	30209	31868	33518	25
36	18395	20108	21814	23514	25207	26892	28569	30237	31896	33545	24
37	18424	20136	21843	23542	25235	26920	28597	30265	31923	33573	23
38	18452	20165	21871	23571	25263	26948	28625	30292	31951	33600	22
39	18481	20193	21899	23599	25291	26976	28652	30320	31979	33627	21
40	18509	20222	21928	23627	25320	27004	28680	30348	32006	33655	20
41	18538	20250	21956	23656	25348	27032	28708	30376	32034	33682	19
42	18567	20279	21985	23684	25376	27060	28736	30403	32061	33710	18
43	18595	20307	22013	23712	25404	27088	28764	30431	32089	33737	17
44	18624	20336	22041	23740	25432	27116	28792	30459	32116	33764	16
45	18652	20364	22070	23769	25460	27144	28820	30486	32144	33792	15
46	18681	20393	22098	23797	25488	27172	28847	30514	32171	33819	14
47	18710	20421	22126	23825	25516	27200	28875	30542	32199	33846	13
48	18738	20450	22155	23853	25545	27228	28903	30570	32227	33874	12
49	18767	20478	22185	23882	25573	27256	28931	30597	32254	33901	11
50	18795	20507	22212	23910	25601	27284	28959	30625	32282	33929	10
51	18824	20535	22240	23938	25629	27312	28987	30653	32309	33956	9
52	18852	20563	22268	23966	25657	27340	29015	30680	32337	33983	8
53	18881	20592	22297	23995	25685	27368	29042	30708	32364	34011	7
54	18910	20620	22325	24023	25713	27396	29070	30736	32392	34038	6
55	18938	20649	22353	24051	25741	27424	29098	30763	32419	34065	5
56	18967	20677	22382	24079	25769	27452	29126	30791	32447	34093	4
57	18995	20706	22410	24108	25798	27480	29154	30819	32474	34120	3
58	19024	20734	22438	24136	25826	27508	29182	30846	32502	34147	2
59	19052	20763	22467	24164	25854	27536	29209	30874	32529	34175	1
60	19081	20791	22495	24192	25882	27564	29237	30902	32557	34202	0
	79 degr.	78 degr.	77 degr.	76 degr.	75 degr.	74 degr.	73 degr.	72 degr.	71 degr.	70 degr.	M

M.	20 degr.	21 degr.	22 degr.	23 degr.	24 degr.	25 degr.	26 degr.	27 degr.	28 degr.	29 degr.	
0	34202	35837	37461	39073	40674	42262	43837	45399	46947	48489	60
1	34229	35864	37488	39100	40700	42288	43863	45425	46973	48506	59
2	34257	35891	37515	39127	40727	42315	43889	45451	46999	48532	58
3	34284	35918	37542	39153	40753	42341	43916	45477	47024	48557	57
4	34311	35945	37569	39180	40780	42367	43942	45503	47050	48583	56
5	34339	35973	37595	39207	40806	42394	43968	45529	47076	48608	55
6	34366	36000	37622	39234	40833	42420	43994	45554	47101	48634	54
7	34393	36027	37649	39260	40860	42446	44020	45580	47127	48659	53
8	34421	36054	37676	39287	40880	42473	44046	45606	47153	48684	52
9	34448	36081	37703	39314	40913	42499	44072	45632	47178	48710	51
10	34475	36108	37730	39341	40939	42525	44098	45058	47204	48735	50
11	34503	36135	37757	39367	40966	42552	44124	45684	47229	48761	49
12	34530	36162	37784	39394	40992	42578	44151	45710	47255	48786	48
13	34557	36190	37811	39421	41019	42604	44177	45736	47281	48811	47
14	34584	36217	37838	39448	41045	42631	44203	45762	47306	48837	46
15	34612	36244	37865	39474	41072	42657	44229	45787	47332	48862	45
16	34639	36271	37892	39501	41098	42683	44255	45813	47358	48888	44
17	34666	36298	37919	39528	41125	42709	44281	45839	47383	48913	43
18	34694	36325	37946	39555	41151	42736	44307	45865	47409	48938	42
19	34721	36352	37973	39581	41178	42762	44333	45891	47434	48964	41
20	34748	36379	37999	39608	41204	42788	44359	45917	47460	48989	40
21	34775	36406	38026	39635	41231	42815	44385	45942	47486	49014	39
22	34803	36433	38053	39661	41257	42841	44411	45968	47511	49040	38
23	34830	36461	38080	39688	41284	42867	44437	45994	47537	49065	37
24	34857	36488	38107	39715	41310	42894	44464	46020	47562	49090	36
25	34884	36515	38134	39741	41337	42920	44490	46046	47588	49116	35
26	34912	36542	38161	39768	41363	42946	44516	46072	47614	49141	34
27	34939	36569	38188	39795	41390	42972	44542	46097	47639	49166	33
28	34966	36596	38215	39822	41416	42999	44568	46123	47665	49192	32
29	34993	36623	38241	39848	41443	43025	44594	46149	47690	49217	31
30	35021	36650	38268	39875	41469	43051	44620	46175	47716	49242	30
31	35048	36677	38295	39902	41496	43077	44646	46201	47741	49268	29
32	35075	36704	38322	39928	41522	43104	44672	46226	47767	49293	28
33	35102	36731	38349	39955	41549	43130	44698	46252	47793	49318	27
34	35130	36758	38376	39982	41575	43156	44724	46278	47818	49344	26
35	35157	36785	38403	40008	41602	43182	44750	46304	47844	49369	25
36	35184	36812	38430	40035	41628	43209	44776	46330	47869	49394	24
37	35211	36839	38456	40062	41655	43235	44802	46355	47895	49419	23
38	35239	36867	38483	40088	41681	43261	44828	46381	47920	49445	22
39	35266	36894	38510	40115	41707	43287	44854	46407	47946	49470	21
40	35293	36921	38537	40141	41734	43313	44880	46433	47972	49495	20
41	35320	36948	38564	40168	41760	43340	44906	46458	47997	49521	19
42	35347	36975	38591	40195	41787	43366	44932	46484	48022	49546	18
43	35375	37002	38617	40221	41813	43392	44958	46510	48048	49571	17
44	35402	37029	38644	40248	41840	43418	44984	46536	48073	49596	16
45	35429	37056	38671	40275	41866	43445	45010	46561	48099	49622	15
46	35456	37083	38698	40301	41892	43471	45036	46587	48124	49647	14
47	35483	37110	38725	40328	41919	43497	45062	46613	48150	49672	13
48	35511	37137	38752	40355	41945	43523	45088	46639	48175	49696	12
49	35538	37164	38778	40381	41972	43549	45114	46664	48201	49723	11
50	35565	37191	38805	40408	41998	43575	45140	46690	48226	49748	10
51	35592	37218	38832	40434	42024	43602	45166	46716	48252	49773	9
52	35619	37245	38859	40461	42051	43628	45192	46742	48277	49798	8
53	35647	37272	38886	40488	42077	43654	45218	46767	48303	49824	7
54	35674	37299	38912	40514	42104	43680	45243	46793	48328	49849	6
55	35701	37326	38939	40541	42130	43706	45269	46819	48354	49874	5
56	35728	37353	38966	40567	42156	43732	45295	46844	48379	49899	4
57	35755	37380	38993	40594	42183	43759	45321	46870	48405	49924	3
58	35782	37407	39020	40621	42209	43785	45347	46896	48430	49950	2
59	35810	37434	39046	40647	42235	43811	45373	46921	48456	49975	1
60	35837	37461	39073	40674	42262	43837	45399	46947	48489	50000	0
	69 degr.	68 degr.	67 degr.	66 degr.	65 degr.	64 degr.	63 degr.	62 degr.	61 degr.	60 degr.	M.

NATURAL CO-SINES,

M.	30 degr.	31 degr.	32 degr.	33 degr.	34 degr.	35 degr.	36 degr.	37 degr.	38 degr.	39 degr.	
0	50000	51504	52992	54464	55919	57358	58779	60181	61566	62932	60
1	50025	51529	53017	54488	55943	57381	58802	60205	61589	62955	59
2	50050	51554	53041	54513	55968	57405	58826	60228	61612	62977	58
3	50076	51579	53066	54537	55992	57429	58849	60251	61635	63000	57
4	50101	51604	53091	54561	56016	57453	58873	60274	61658	63022	56
5	50126	51628	53115	54586	56040	57477	58896	60298	61681	63045	55
6	50151	51653	53140	54610	56064	57501	58920	60321	61704	63068	54
7	50176	51678	53164	54635	56088	57524	58943	60344	61726	63090	53
8	50201	51703	53189	54659	56112	57548	58967	60367	61749	63113	52
9	50227	51728	53214	54683	56136	57572	58990	60390	61772	63135	51
10	50252	51753	53238	54708	56160	57596	59014	60414	61795	63158	50
11	50277	51778	53263	54732	56184	57619	59037	60437	61818	63180	49
12	50302	51803	53288	54756	56208	57643	59061	60460	61841	63203	48
13	50327	51828	53312	54781	56232	57667	59084	60483	61864	63225	47
14	50352	51852	53337	54805	56256	57691	59107	60506	61887	63248	46
15	50377	51877	53361	54829	56280	57715	59131	60529	61909	63271	45
16	50403	51902	53386	54854	56305	57738	59154	60553	61932	63293	44
17	50428	51927	53411	54878	56329	57762	59178	60576	61955	63316	43
18	50453	51952	53435	54902	56358	57786	59201	60599	61978	63338	42
19	50478	51977	53460	54926	56377	57809	59225	60622	62001	63361	41
20	50503	52002	53484	54951	56401	57833	59248	60645	62024	63383	40
21	50528	52026	53509	54975	56425	57857	59272	60668	62046	63406	39
22	50553	52051	53534	54999	56449	57881	59295	60691	62069	63428	38
23	50578	52076	53558	55024	56473	57904	59318	60714	62092	63451	37
24	50603	52101	53583	55048	56497	57929	59342	60738	62115	63473	36
25	50628	52126	53607	55072	56521	57952	59365	60761	62138	63496	35
26	50654	52151	53632	55097	56545	57976	59389	60784	62160	63518	34
27	50679	52175	53656	55121	56569	57999	59412	60807	62183	63540	33
28	50704	52200	53681	55145	56593	58023	59435	60830	62206	63563	32
29	50729	52225	53705	55169	56617	58047	59459	60853	62229	63585	31
30	50754	52250	53730	55194	56641	58070	59482	60876	62251	63608	30
31	50779	52275	53754	55218	56665	58094	59506	60899	62274	63630	29
32	50804	52299	53779	55242	56689	58118	59529	60922	62297	63653	28
33	50829	52324	53804	55266	56713	58141	59552	60945	62320	63675	27
34	50854	52349	53828	55291	56738	58165	59576	60968	62342	63698	26
35	50879	52374	53853	55315	56760	58189	59599	60991	62365	63720	25
36	50904	52398	53877	55339	56784	58212	59622	61015	62388	63742	24
37	50929	52423	53902	55363	56808	58236	59646	61038	62411	63765	23
38	50954	52448	53926	55388	56832	58260	59669	61061	62433	63787	22
39	50979	52473	53951	55412	56856	58283	59693	61084	62456	63810	21
40	51004	52498	53975	55436	56880	58307	59716	61107	62479	63832	20
41	51029	52522	54000	55460	56904	58330	59739	61130	62502	63854	19
42	51054	52547	54024	55484	56928	58354	59763	61153	62524	63877	18
43	51079	52572	54049	55509	56952	58378	59786	61176	62547	63899	17
44	51104	52597	54073	55533	56976	58401	59809	61199	62570	63922	16
45	51129	52621	54097	55557	57000	58425	59832	61222	62592	63944	15
46	51154	52646	54122	55581	57024	58449	59856	61245	62615	63966	14
47	51179	52671	54146	55605	57047	58472	59879	61268	62638	63989	13
48	51204	52696	54171	55630	57071	58496	59902	61291	62660	64011	12
49	51229	52720	54195	55654	57095	58519	59926	61314	62683	64033	11
50	51254	52745	54220	55678	57119	58543	59949	61337	62706	64056	10
51	51279	52770	54244	55702	57143	58567	59972	61360	62728	64078	9
52	51304	52794	54269	55726	57167	58590	59995	61383	62751	64100	8
53	51329	52819	54293	55750	57191	58614	60019	61406	62774	64123	7
54	51354	52844	54317	55775	57215	58637	60042	61429	62796	64145	6
55	51379	52869	54342	55799	57238	58661	60065	61451	62819	64167	5
56	51404	52893	54366	55823	57262	58684	60088	61474	62842	64190	4
57	51429	52918	54391	55847	57286	58708	60112	61497	62864	64212	3
58	51454	52943	54415	55871	57310	58731	60135	61520	62887	64234	2
59	51479	52967	54439	55895	57334	58755	60158	61543	62909	64256	1
60	51504	52992	54464	55919	57358	58779	60181	61566	62932	64279	0
	59 degr.	58 degr.	57 degr.	56 degr.	55 degr.	54 degr.	53 degr.	52 degr.	51 degr.	50 degr.	M

M.	40 degr.	41 degr.	42 degr.	43 degr.	44 degr.	45 degr.	46 degr.	47 degr.	48 degr.	49 degr.	
0	64279	65606	66913	68200	69466	70711	71934	73135	74314	75471	60
1	64301	65628	66935	68221	69487	70731	71954	73155	74334	75490	59
2	64323	65650	66956	68242	69508	70752	71974	73175	74353	75509	58
3	64346	65672	66978	68264	69529	70772	71995	73195	74373	75528	57
4	64368	65694	66999	68285	69549	70793	72015	73215	74392	75547	56
5	64390	65715	67021	68306	69570	70813	72035	73234	74412	75566	55
6	64412	65738	67043	68327	69592	70834	72055	73254	74431	75585	54
7	64435	65759	67064	68349	69612	70855	72075	73274	74451	75604	53
8	64457	65781	67086	68370	69633	70875	72095	73294	74470	75623	52
9	64479	65803	67107	68391	69654	70896	72116	73314	74489	75642	51
10	64501	65825	67129	68412	69675	70916	72136	73333	74509	75661	50
11	64523	65847	67151	68433	69696	70937	72156	73353	74528	75680	49
12	64546	65869	67172	68455	69717	70957	72176	73373	74548	75699	48
13	64568	65891	67194	68476	69737	70978	72196	73393	74567	75719	47
14	64590	65913	67215	68497	69758	70998	72216	73412	74586	75738	46
15	64612	65935	67237	68518	69779	71019	72236	73432	74606	75756	45
16	64635	65956	67258	68539	69800	71039	72257	73452	74625	75775	44
17	64657	65978	67280	68561	69821	71059	72277	73472	74644	75794	43
18	64679	66000	67301	68582	69842	71080	72297	73491	74664	75813	42
19	64701	66022	67323	68603	69862	71100	72317	73511	74683	75832	41
20	64723	66044	67344	68624	69883	71121	72337	73531	74703	75851	40
21	64746	66066	67366	68645	69904	71141	72357	73551	74722	75870	39
22	64768	66088	67387	68666	69925	71162	72377	73570	74741	75889	38
23	64790	66109	67409	68688	69946	71182	72397	73590	74760	75908	37
24	64812	66131	67430	68709	69966	71203	72417	73610	74780	75927	36
25	64834	66153	67452	68730	69987	71223	72437	73629	74799	75946	35
26	64856	66175	67473	68751	70008	71243	72457	73649	74818	75965	34
27	64878	66197	67495	68772	70029	71264	72477	73669	74838	75984	33
28	64901	66218	67516	68793	70049	71284	72497	73688	74857	76003	32
29	64923	66240	67538	68814	70070	71305	72517	73708	74876	76022	31
30	64945	66262	67559	68835	70091	71325	72537	73728	74896	76041	30
31	64967	66284	67580	68857	70112	71345	72557	73747	74915	76059	29
32	64989	66306	67602	68878	70132	71366	72577	73767	74934	76078	28
33	65011	66327	67623	68899	70153	71386	72597	73787	74953	76097	27
34	65033	66349	67645	68920	70174	71407	72617	73806	74973	76116	26
35	65055	66371	67666	68941	70195	71427	72637	73826	74992	76135	25
36	65077	66393	67688	68962	70215	71447	72657	73846	75011	76154	24
37	65099	66414	67709	68983	70236	71468	72677	73865	75030	76173	23
38	65122	66436	67730	69004	70257	71488	72697	73885	75050	76192	22
39	65144	66458	67752	69025	70277	71508	72717	73904	75069	76210	21
40	65166	66480	67773	69046	70298	71529	72737	73924	75088	76229	20
41	65188	66501	67795	69067	70319	71549	72757	73944	75107	76248	19
42	65210	66523	67816	69088	70339	71569	72777	73963	75126	76267	18
43	65232	66545	67837	69109	70360	71590	72797	73983	75146	76286	17
44	65254	66566	67859	69130	70381	71610	72817	74002	75165	76304	16
45	65276	66588	67880	69151	70401	71630	72837	74022	75184	76323	15
46	65298	66610	67901	69172	70422	71650	72857	74041	75203	76342	14
47	65320	66632	67923	69193	70443	71671	72877	74061	75222	76361	13
48	65342	66653	67944	69214	70463	71691	72897	74080	75241	76380	12
49	65364	66675	67965	69235	70484	71711	72917	74100	75261	76398	11
50	65386	66697	67987	69256	70505	71732	72937	74120	75280	76417	10
51	65408	66718	68008	69277	70525	71752	72957	74139	75299	76436	9
52	65430	66740	68029	69298	70546	71772	72976	74159	75318	76455	8
53	65452	66762	68051	69319	70567	71792	72996	74178	75337	76473	7
54	65474	66783	68072	69340	70587	71813	73016	74198	75356	76492	6
55	65496	66805	68093	69361	70608	71833	73036	74217	75375	76511	5
56	65518	66827	68115	69382	70628	71853	73056	74237	75395	76530	4
57	65540	66848	68136	69403	70649	71873	73076	74256	75414	76548	3
58	65562	66870	68157	69424	70670	71894	73096	74276	75433	76567	2
59	65583	66891	68179	69445	70690	71914	73116	74295	75452	76586	1
60	65606	66913	68200	69466	70711	71934	73135	74314	75471	76604	0
	49 degr.	48 degr.	47 degr.	46 degr.	45 degr.	44 degr.	43 degr.	42 degr.	41 degr.	40 degr.	M.

M.	50 degr.	51 degr.	52 degr.	53 degr.	54 degr.	55 degr.	56 degr.	57 degr.	58 degr.	59 degr.	
0	76604	77715	78801	79864	80902	81915	82904	83867	84805	85717	60
1	76623	77733	78819	79881	80919	81932	82920	83883	84820	85732	59
2	76642	77751	78837	79899	80936	81949	82936	83899	84836	85747	58
3	76661	77769	78855	79916	80953	81965	82953	83915	84851	85762	57
4	76679	77788	78873	79934	80970	81982	82969	83930	84866	85777	56
5	76698	77806	78891	79951	80987	81999	82985	83946	84882	85792	55
6	76717	77824	78908	79968	81004	82015	83001	83962	84897	85806	54
7	76734	77843	78926	79976	81021	82032	83017	83978	84913	85821	53
8	76754	77861	78944	80003	81038	82048	83994	83994	84928	85836	52
9	76772	77879	78962	80021	81055	82065	83050	84009	84943	85851	51
10	76791	77897	78980	80038	81072	82082	83066	84025	84959	85866	50
11	76810	77916	78998	80056	81089	82098	83082	84041	84974	85881	49
12	76828	77934	79015	80073	81106	82115	83098	84057	84989	85896	48
13	76847	77952	79033	80091	81123	82132	83115	84073	85005	85911	47
14	76866	77970	79051	80108	81140	82148	83131	84088	85020	85926	46
15	76884	77988	79069	80125	81157	82165	83147	84104	85035	85941	45
16	76903	78007	79086	80143	81174	82181	83163	84120	85051	85956	44
17	76921	78025	79105	80160	81191	82198	83179	84135	85066	85970	43
18	76940	78043	79122	80178	81208	82214	83195	84151	85081	85985	42
19	76959	78061	79140	80195	81225	82231	83212	84167	85096	86000	41
20	76977	78079	79158	80212	81242	82248	83228	84183	85112	86015	40
21	76996	78098	79176	80230	81259	82264	83244	84198	85127	86030	39
22	77014	78116	79193	80247	81276	82281	83260	84214	85142	86045	38
23	77033	78134	79211	80264	81293	82297	83276	84230	85157	86059	37
24	77051	78152	79229	80282	81310	82314	83292	84245	85173	86074	36
25	77070	78170	79247	80299	81327	82330	83308	84261	85188	86089	35
26	77088	78188	79264	80316	81344	82347	83324	84277	85203	86104	34
27	77107	78206	79282	80334	81361	82363	83340	84292	85218	86119	33
28	77125	78225	79300	80351	81379	82380	83356	84308	85234	86133	32
29	77144	78243	79318	80368	81395	82396	83373	84324	85249	86148	31
30	77162	78261	79335	80386	81412	82413	83389	84339	85264	86163	30
31	77181	78279	79353	80403	81428	82429	83405	84355	85276	86178	29
32	77199	78297	79371	80420	81445	82446	83421	84370	85291	86192	28
33	77218	78315	79388	80437	81462	82462	83437	84386	85310	86207	27
34	77236	78333	79406	80455	81479	82478	83453	84402	85325	86222	26
35	77255	78351	79424	80472	81476	82495	83469	84417	85340	86237	25
36	77273	78369	79441	80489	81513	82511	83485	84433	85355	86251	24
37	77292	78387	79459	80507	81530	82528	83501	84448	85370	86266	23
38	77310	78405	79477	80524	81546	82544	83517	84464	85385	86281	22
39	77329	78424	79494	80541	81563	82561	83533	84480	85401	86295	21
40	77347	78442	79512	80558	81580	82577	83549	84495	85416	86310	20
41	77366	78460	79530	80576	81597	82593	83565	84511	85431	86325	19
42	77384	78478	79547	80593	81614	82610	83581	84526	85446	86340	18
43	77402	78496	79565	80610	81631	82626	83597	84542	85461	86354	17
44	77421	78514	79583	80627	81647	82642	83613	84557	85476	86369	16
45	77439	78532	79600	80644	81664	82659	83629	84573	85491	86384	15
46	77458	78550	79618	80661	81681	82675	83645	84588	85506	86398	14
47	77476	78568	79635	80679	81698	82692	83661	84604	85521	86413	13
48	77494	78586	79653	80696	81714	82708	83676	84619	85536	86427	12
49	77513	78604	79671	80713	81731	82724	83692	84635	85551	86442	11
50	77531	78622	79688	80730	81748	82741	83708	84650	85567	86457	10
51	77550	78640	79706	80748	81765	82757	83724	84666	85582	86471	9
52	77568	78658	79723	80765	81781	82773	83740	84681	85597	86486	8
53	77586	78676	79741	80782	81798	82790	83756	84697	85612	86501	7
54	77605	78693	79758	80799	81815	82806	83772	84712	85627	86515	6
55	77623	78711	79776	80816	81832	82822	83788	84728	85642	86530	5
56	77641	78729	79793	80833	81848	82839	83804	84743	85657	86544	4
57	77660	78747	79811	80850	81865	82855	83819	84759	85672	86559	3
58	77678	78765	79829	80867	81882	82871	83835	84774	85687	86573	2
59	77696	78783	79846	80885	81899	82887	83851	84789	85702	86588	1
60	77715	78801	79864	80902	81915	82904	83867	84805	85717	86603	0
	39 degr.	38 degr.	37 degr.	36 degr.	35 degr.	34 degr.	33 degr.	32 degr.	31 degr.	30 degr.	M.

NATURAL COSINES

M.	60 degr.	61 degr.	62 degr.	63 degr.	64 degr.	65 degr.	66 degr.	67 degr.	68 degr.	69 degr.	
0	86003	87462	88295	89101	89787	90631	91355	92050	92718	93358	60
1	86017	87476	88308	89114	89892	90643	91366	92062	92729	93368	59
2	86032	87490	88322	89127	89905	90655	91378	92073	92740	93379	58
3	86046	87504	88336	89140	89918	90668	91390	92085	92751	93389	57
4	86061	87518	88349	89153	89930	90680	91402	92096	92762	93400	56
5	86075	87532	88363	89167	89943	90692	91414	92107	92773	93410	55
6	86790	87546	88377	89180	89956	90704	91425	92119	92784	93420	54
7	86704	87560	88390	89193	89968	90717	91437	92130	92794	93431	53
8	86719	87575	88404	89206	89981	90729	91449	92141	92805	93441	52
9	86733	87589	88417	89219	89994	90741	91461	92152	92816	93452	51
10	86748	87603	88431	89232	90007	90753	91472	92164	92827	93462	50
11	86762	87617	88445	89245	90019	90766	91484	92175	92838	93472	49
12	86777	87631	88458	89259	90032	90778	91496	92186	92849	93483	48
13	86791	87645	88472	89272	90045	90790	91508	92198	92859	93493	47
14	86805	87659	88485	89285	90057	90802	91519	92209	92870	93503	46
15	86820	87673	88499	89298	90070	90814	91531	92220	92881	93514	45
16	86834	87687	88512	89311	90082	90826	91543	92231	92892	93524	44
17	86849	87701	88526	89324	90095	90837	91555	92243	92902	93534	43
18	86863	87715	88539	89337	90107	90851	91566	92254	92913	93544	42
19	86878	87729	88553	89350	90120	90863	91578	92265	92924	93555	41
20	86892	87743	88566	89363	90133	90875	91590	92270	92935	93565	40
21	86906	87756	88580	89376	90146	90887	91601	92287	92945	93575	39
22	86921	87770	88593	89389	90158	90899	91613	92299	92956	93585	38
23	86935	87784	88607	89402	90171	90911	91625	92310	92967	93596	37
24	86949	87798	88620	89415	90183	90924	91636	92321	92978	93606	36
25	86964	87812	88663	89428	90196	90936	91648	92332	92988	93616	35
26	86278	87826	88854	89441	90208	90948	91660	92343	92999	93626	34
27	86993	87840	88661	89454	90221	90960	91671	92355	93010	93637	33
28	87007	87853	88467	89467	90233	90972	91683	92366	93020	93647	32
29	87021	87808	88688	89480	90246	90984	91694	92377	93031	93657	31
30	87036	87882	88701	89493	90258	90996	91706	92388	93042	93667	30
31	87050	87896	88715	89506	90271	91008	91718	92399	93052	93677	29
32	87064	87909	88728	89519	90284	91020	91729	92410	93063	93688	28
33	87079	87923	88741	89532	90296	91032	91741	92421	93074	93698	27
34	87093	87937	88755	89545	90309	91044	91752	92432	93084	93708	26
35	87107	87951	88768	89558	90321	91056	91764	92444	93095	93718	25
36	87121	87965	88782	89571	90334	91068	91775	92455	93106	93728	24
37	87136	87979	88795	89584	90346	91080	91787	92466	93116	93738	23
38	87150	87993	88808	89597	90358	91092	91799	92477	93127	93748	22
39	87164	88006	88822	89610	90371	91104	91810	92488	93137	93759	21
40	87178	88020	88835	89623	90383	91116	91822	92499	93148	93769	20
41	87193	88234	88848	89636	90396	91128	91833	92510	93159	93779	19
42	87207	88048	88862	89649	90408	91140	91845	92521	93169	93789	18
43	87221	88062	88875	89662	90421	91152	91856	92532	93180	93799	17
44	87235	88075	88888	89674	90433	91164	91868	92543	93190	93809	16
45	87250	88089	88901	89687	90446	91176	91879	92554	93201	93819	15
46	87264	88103	88915	89700	90458	91188	91891	92565	93211	93829	14
47	87278	88117	88928	89713	90470	91200	91902	92576	93222	93839	13
48	87292	88130	88942	89725	90483	91212	91914	92587	93232	93849	12
49	87306	88144	88955	89739	90495	91224	91925	92598	93243	93859	11
50	87321	88158	88968	89752	90507	91236	91936	92609	93253	93869	10
51	87335	88172	88981	89764	90520	91248	91948	92620	93264	93879	9
52	87349	88185	88995	89777	90531	91260	91959	92631	93274	93889	8
53	87363	88199	89008	89790	90545	91272	91971	92642	93285	93899	7
54	87377	88213	89021	89803	90557	91283	91982	92653	93295	93909	6
55	87391	88226	89035	89816	90569	91295	91994	92664	93306	93919	5
56	87405	88240	89048	89828	90582	91307	92005	92675	93316	93929	4
57	87420	88254	89061	89841	90594	91319	92016	92686	93327	93939	3
58	87434	88267	89074	89854	90606	91331	92028	92697	93337	93949	2
59	87448	88281	89087	89867	90618	91343	92039	92707	93348	93959	1
60	87462	88295	89101	89879	90631	91355	92050	92718	93358	93669	0
	19 degr.	28 degr.	27 degr.	26 degr.	25 degr.	24 degr.	23 degr.	22 degr.	21 degr.	20 degr.	M

NATURAL CO-SINES

M.	70 degr.	71 degr.	72 degr.	73 degr.	74 degr.	75 degr.	76 degr.	77 degr.	78 degr.	79 degr.	
0	93969	94552	95106	95630	96126	96593	97030	97437	97815	98163	60
1	93979	94561	95115	95639	96134	96600	97037	97444	97821	98168	59
2	93989	94571	95124	95647	96142	96608	97044	97450	97827	98174	58
3	93999	94580	95133	95656	96150	96615	97051	97457	97833	98179	57
4	94009	94590	95142	95664	96158	96623	97058	97463	97839	98185	56
5	94019	94599	95150	95673	96166	96630	97065	97470	97845	98190	55
6	94029	94609	95159	95681	96174	96638	97072	97476	97851	98196	54
7	94039	94618	95168	95690	96182	96645	97079	97483	97857	98201	53
8	94049	94627	95177	95698	96190	96653	97086	97489	97863	98207	52
9	94058	94637	95186	95707	96198	96660	97093	97496	97869	98212	51
10	94068	94646	95195	95715	96206	96667	97100	97502	97875	98218	50
11	94078	94656	95204	95724	96214	96675	97106	97508	97881	98223	49
12	94088	94665	95213	95732	96222	96682	97113	97515	97887	98229	48
13	94098	94674	95222	95740	96230	96690	97120	97521	97893	98234	47
14	94108	94684	95231	95749	96238	96697	97127	97528	97899	98240	46
15	94118	94693	95240	95757	96246	96705	97134	97534	97905	98245	45
16	94127	94702	95248	95766	96253	96712	97141	97541	97910	98250	44
17	94137	94712	95257	95774	96261	96719	97148	97547	97916	98256	43
18	94147	94721	95266	95782	96269	96727	97155	97553	97922	98261	42
19	94157	94730	95275	95791	96277	96734	97162	97560	97928	98267	41
20	94167	94740	95284	95799	96285	96742	97169	97566	97934	98272	40
21	94176	94749	95293	95807	96293	96749	97176	97573	97940	98277	39
22	94186	94758	95301	95816	96301	96756	97182	97579	97946	98283	38
23	94196	94768	95310	95824	96308	96764	97189	97585	97952	98288	37
24	94206	94777	95319	95832	96316	96771	97196	97592	97958	98294	36
25	94216	94786	95328	95841	96324	96778	97203	97598	97963	98299	35
26	94225	94795	95337	95849	96332	96786	97210	97604	97969	98304	34
27	94235	94805	95345	95857	96340	96793	97217	97611	97975	98310	33
28	94245	94814	95354	95865	96347	96800	97223	97617	97981	98315	32
29	94254	94823	95363	95874	96355	96807	97230	97623	97987	98320	31
30	94264	94832	95372	95882	96363	96815	97237	97630	97992	98325	30
31	94274	94842	95380	95890	96371	96822	97244	97636	97998	98331	29
32	94284	94851	95389	95898	96379	96829	97251	97642	98004	98336	28
33	94293	94860	95398	95907	96386	96837	97257	97648	98010	98341	27
34	94303	94869	95407	95915	96394	96844	97264	97655	98016	98347	26
35	94313	94878	95415	95923	96402	96851	97271	97661	98021	98352	25
36	94322	94888	95424	95931	96410	96858	97278	97667	98027	98357	24
37	94332	94897	95433	95940	96417	96866	97284	97673	98033	98362	23
38	94342	94906	95441	95948	96425	96873	97291	97680	98039	98368	22
39	94351	94915	95450	95956	96433	96880	97298	97686	98044	98373	21
40	94361	94924	95459	95964	96440	96887	97304	97692	98050	98378	20
41	94370	94933	95467	95972	96448	96894	97311	97698	98056	98383	19
42	94380	94943	95476	95981	96456	96902	97318	97705	98061	98388	18
43	94390	94952	95485	95989	96463	96909	97325	97711	98067	98394	17
44	94399	94961	95493	95997	96471	96916	97331	97717	98073	98399	16
45	94409	94970	95502	96005	96479	96923	97338	97723	98079	98404	15
46	94418	94979	95511	96013	96486	96930	97345	97729	98084	98409	14
47	94428	94988	95519	96021	96494	96937	97351	97735	98090	98414	13
48	94438	94997	95528	96029	96502	96945	97358	97742	98096	98420	12
49	94447	95006	95536	96037	96509	96952	97365	97748	98101	98425	11
50	94457	95015	95545	96046	96517	96959	97371	97754	98107	98430	10
51	94466	95024	95554	96054	96524	96966	97378	97760	98112	98435	9
52	94476	95033	95562	96062	96532	96973	97384	97766	98118	98440	8
53	94485	95043	95571	96070	96540	96980	97391	97772	98124	98445	7
54	94495	95052	95579	96078	96547	96987	97398	97778	98129	98450	6
55	94504	95061	95588	96086	96555	96994	97404	97784	98135	98455	5
56	94514	95070	95596	96094	96562	97001	97411	97790	98140	98460	4
57	94523	95079	95605	96102	96570	97008	97417	97797	98146	98466	3
58	94533	95088	95613	96110	96578	97015	97424	97803	98152	98471	2
59	94542	95097	95622	96118	96585	97023	97430	97809	98157	98476	1
60	94552	95106	95630	96126	96593	97030	97437	97815	98163	98481	0
	19 degr.	18 degr.	17 degr.	16 degr.	15 degr.	14 degr.	13 degr.	12 degr.	11 degr.	10 degr.	M.

NATURAL CO-SINES.

M.	80 degr.	81 degr.	82 degr.	83 degr.	84 degr.	85 degr.	86 degr.	87 degr.	88 degr.	89 degr.	
0	98481	98769	99027	99255	99452	99619	99756	99863	99939	99985	60
1	98486	98773	99031	99258	99455	99623	99758	99864	99940	99985	59
2	98491	98778	99035	99262	99458	99625	99760	99866	99941	99985	58
3	98497	98782	99039	99265	99461	99627	99762	99867	99942	99986	57
4	98501	98787	99043	99269	99464	99630	99764	99869	99943	99987	56
5	98506	98791	99047	99272	99467	99632	99766	99870	99944	99987	55
6	98511	98796	99051	99276	99470	99635	99768	99872	99945	99988	54
7	98516	98800	99055	99279	99473	99637	99770	99873	99946	99988	53
8	98521	98805	99059	99283	99476	99639	99772	99875	99947	99989	52
9	98526	98809	99063	99286	99479	99642	99774	99876	99948	99989	51
10	98531	98814	99067	99290	99482	99644	99776	99878	99949	99989	50
11	98536	98818	99071	99293	99485	99647	99778	99879	99950	99990	49
12	98541	98823	99075	99297	99488	99649	99780	99881	99951	99990	48
13	98546	98827	99079	99300	99491	99652	99782	99882	99952	99991	47
14	98551	98832	99083	99303	99494	99654	99784	99883	99952	99991	46
15	98556	98836	99088	99307	99497	99657	99786	99885	99953	99991	45
16	98561	98841	99091	99310	99500	99659	99788	99886	99954	99992	44
17	98565	98845	99095	99314	99502	99661	99790	99888	99955	99992	43
18	98570	98849	99099	99317	99505	99664	99792	99889	99956	99993	42
19	98575	98854	99103	99320	99508	99666	99793	99890	99957	99993	41
20	98580	98858	99106	99324	99511	99668	99795	99892	99958	99993	40
21	98585	98863	99110	99327	99514	99671	99797	99893	99959	99994	39
22	98590	98867	99114	99331	99517	99673	99799	99894	99959	99994	38
23	98595	98871	99118	99334	99520	99676	99801	99896	99960	99994	37
24	98600	98876	99122	99337	99523	99678	99803	99897	99961	99995	36
25	98604	98880	99125	99341	99526	99680	99804	99898	99962	99995	35
26	98609	98884	99129	99344	99528	99683	99806	99900	99963	99995	34
27	98614	98889	99133	99347	99531	99685	99808	99901	99963	99995	33
28	98619	98893	99137	99351	99534	99687	99810	99902	99964	99996	32
29	98624	98897	99141	99354	99537	99689	99812	99904	99965	99996	31
30	98629	98902	99144	99357	99540	99692	99813	99905	99966	99996	30
31	98633	98906	99148	99360	99542	99694	99815	99906	99966	99996	29
32	98638	98910	99152	99364	99545	99696	99817	99907	99967	99997	28
33	98643	98914	99156	99367	99548	99699	99819	99909	99968	99997	27
34	98648	98919	99160	99370	99551	99701	99821	99910	99969	99997	26
35	98652	98923	99163	99374	99553	99703	99822	99911	99969	99997	25
36	98657	98927	99167	99377	99556	99705	99824	99912	99970	99998	24
37	98662	98931	99171	99380	99559	99708	99826	99914	99971	99998	23
38	98667	98936	99175	99383	99562	99710	99827	99915	99972	99998	22
39	98671	98940	99178	99386	99564	99712	99829	99916	99972	99998	21
40	98676	98944	99182	99390	99567	99714	99831	99917	99973	99998	20
41	98681	98948	99186	99393	99570	99716	99833	99918	99974	99998	19
42	98686	98953	99189	99396	99572	99719	99834	99919	99974	99999	18
43	98690	98957	99193	99399	99575	99721	99836	99921	99975	99999	17
44	98695	98961	99197	99402	99578	99723	99838	99922	99976	99999	16
45	98700	98965	99200	99406	99580	99725	99839	99923	99976	99999	15
46	98704	98969	99204	99409	99583	99727	99841	99924	99977	99999	14
47	98709	98973	99208	99412	99586	99729	99842	99925	99977	99999	13
48	98714	98978	99211	99415	99588	99731	99844	99926	99978	99999	12
49	98718	98982	99215	99418	99591	99734	99845	99927	99979	99999	11
50	98723	98986	99219	99421	99594	99736	99847	99929	99979	100000	10
51	98728	98990	99222	99424	99596	99736	99849	99930	99980	100000	9
52	98732	98994	99226	99428	99599	99738	99851	99931	99980	100000	8
53	98737	98998	99230	99431	99602	99742	99852	99932	99981	100000	7
54	98741	99002	99233	99434	99604	99744	99854	99933	99982	100000	6
55	98746	99006	99237	99437	99607	99746	99855	99935	99983	100000	5
56	98751	99011	99240	99440	99609	99748	99857	99935	99983	100000	4
57	98755	99015	99244	99443	99612	99750	99858	99936	99983	100000	3
58	98760	99019	99248	99446	99614	99752	99860	99937	99984	100000	2
59	98764	99023	99251	99449	99617	99754	99861	99938	99984	100000	1
60	98769	99027	99255	99452	99619	99756	99863	99939	99985	100000	0
M.	9 degr.	8 degr.	7 degr.	6 degr.	5 degr.	4 degr.	3 degr.	2 degr.	1 degr.	0 degr.	M.

NATURAL CO-SINES

A TABLE

OF

CORRECTION

OF THE

MOON'S ALTITUDE.

Alt. ☽	HORIZONTAL PARALLAX.																			
	53'		54'		55'		56'		57'		58'		59'		60'		61'		62'	
	m.	f.	m.	f.	m.	f.	m.	f.	m.	f.	m.	f.	m.	f.	m.	f.	m.	f.	m.	f.
0	20	0	21	0	22	0	23	0	24	0	25	0	26	0	27	0	28	0	29	0
1	28	31	29	31	30	31	31	31	32	31	33	31	34	31	35	31	36	31	37	31
2	34	23	35	23	36	23	37	23	38	23	39	23	40	23	41	23	42	23	43	23
3	38	20	39	20	40	20	41	20	42	20	43	20	44	20	45	19	46	19	47	19
4	41	1	42	1	43	1	44	1	45	1	46	0	47	0	48	0	49	0	50	0
5	42	54	43	53	44	53	45	53	46	53	47	52	48	52	49	52	50	52	51	52
6	44	15	45	14	46	14	47	14	48	13	49	13	50	13	51	12	52	12	53	12
7	45	16	46	15	47	15	48	14	49	14	50	14	51	13	52	13	53	12	54	12
8	46	0	46	59	47	58	48	58	49	57	50	57	51	56	52	56	53	55	54	54
9	46	32	47	32	48	31	49	30	50	29	51	29	52	28	53	27	54	26	55	26
10	46	57	47	56	48	55	49	54	50	53	51	52	52	51	53	50	54	50	55	49
11	47	15	48	14	49	13	50	12	51	11	52	9	53	8	54	7	55	6	56	5
12	47	27	48	26	49	25	50	23	51	22	52	21	53	19	54	18	55	17	56	16
13	47	35	48	34	49	32	50	31	51	29	52	28	53	26	54	25	55	23	56	22
14	47	40	48	38	49	36	50	35	51	33	52	31	53	29	54	28	55	26	56	24
15	47	42	48	40	49	38	50	36	51	34	52	31	53	29	54	27	55	25	56	23
16	47	40	48	38	49	35	50	33	51	31	52	28	53	26	54	24	55	21	56	19
17	47	36	48	34	49	31	50	29	51	26	52	23	53	21	54	18	55	16	56	13
18	47	31	48	28	49	25	50	22	51	19	52	16	53	13	54	10	55	7	56	4
19	47	23	48	20	49	16	50	13	51	10	52	6	53	3	54	0	54	57	55	53
20	47	13	48	9	49	6	50	2	50	59	51	55	52	51	53	48	54	44	55	40
21	47	2	47	58	48	54	49	50	50	46	51	42	52	38	53	34	54	30	55	26
22	46	48	47	44	48	39	49	35	50	31	51	26	52	22	53	18	54	13	55	9
23	46	33	47	29	48	24	49	19	50	14	51	10	52	5	53	0	53	55	54	51
24	46	18	47	12	48	7	49	2	49	57	50	52	51	47	52	41	53	36	54	31
25	46	0	46	55	47	49	48	44	49	38	50	32	51	27	52	21	53	15	54	10
26	45	42	46	36	47	30	48	24	49	18	50	12	51	5	51	59	52	53	53	47
27	45	22	46	16	47	9	48	3	48	56	49	49	50	43	51	36	52	30	53	23
28	45	1	45	54	46	47	47	40	48	33	49	26	50	19	51	12	52	5	52	58
29	44	39	45	31	46	24	47	16	48	9	49	1	49	54	50	46	51	39	52	31
30	44	15	45	7	45	59	46	51	47	43	48	35	49	27	50	19	51	11	52	3
31	43	51	44	43	45	34	46	25	47	17	48	8	49	0	49	51	50	43	51	34
32	43	26	44	16	45	7	45	58	46	49	47	40	48	31	49	22	50	13	51	4
33	42	59	43	50	44	40	45	30	46	21	47	11	48	1	48	52	49	42	50	32
34	42	32	43	22	44	11	45	1	45	51	46	41	47	30	48	20	49	10	50	0
35	42	3	42	53	43	42	44	31	45	20	46	9	46	58	47	47	48	37	49	26
36	41	34	42	23	43	12	44	0	44	48	45	37	46	25	47	14	48	2	48	51
37	41	4	41	52	42	40	43	28	44	16	45	3	45	51	46	39	47	27	48	15
38	40	33	41	20	42	7	42	55	43	42	44	29	45	16	46	4	46	51	47	39
39	40	1	40	47	41	34	42	21	43	7	43	54	44	41	45	27	46	14	47	1
40	39	28	40	14	41	0	41	46	42	32	43	18	44	4	44	50	45	36	46	22
41	38	54	39	40	40	25	41	10	41	56	42	41	43	26	44	11	44	57	45	42
42	38	20	39	4	39	49	40	34	41	18	42	3	42	47	43	32	44	17	45	1
43	37	44	38	28	39	12	39	56	40	40	41	24	42	8	42	52	43	36	44	19
44	37	8	37	52	38	35	39	18	40	1	40	44	41	27	42	11	42	54	43	37
45	36	32	37	14	37	56	38	39	39	21	40	4	40	46	41	29	42	11	42	53

A TABLE

OF

CORRECTION

OF THE

MOON'S ALTITUDE.

Alt. D	HORIZONTAL PARALLAX									
	53'	54'	55'	56'	57'	58'	59'	60'	61'	62'
	m. f.	m. f.	m. f.	m. f.	m. f.	m. f.	m. f.	m. f.	m. f.	m. f.
46	35 54	36 35	37 17	37 59	38 41	39 22	40 4	40 46	41 27	42 9
47	35 16	35 56	36 37	37 18	37 59	38 40	39 21	40 2	40 43	41 24
48	34 37	35 17	35 57	36 37	37 17	37 57	38 37	39 18	39 58	40 38
49	33 57	34 36	35 16	35 55	36 34	37 14	37 53	38 32	39 12	39 51
50	33 16	33 55	34 34	35 12	35 51	36 29	37 8	37 46	38 25	39 3
51	32 35	33 13	33 51	34 29	35 6	35 44	36 22	37 0	37 37	38 15
52	31 54	32 30	33 7	33 44	34 21	34 58	35 35	36 12	36 49	37 26
53	31 11	31 47	32 23	32 59	33 36	34 12	34 48	35 24	36 0	36 36
54	30 28	31 3	31 39	32 14	32 49	33 24	34 0	34 35	35 10	35 45
55	29 44	30 19	30 53	31 28	32 2	32 36	33 11	33 45	34 20	34 54
56	29 0	29 33	30 7	30 41	31 14	31 48	32 21	32 55	33 28	34 2
57	28 15	28 48	29 20	29 53	30 26	30 58	31 31	32 4	32 36	33 9
58	27 30	28 1	28 33	29 5	29 37	30 9	30 40	31 12	31 44	32 16
59	26 44	27 14	27 45	28 16	28 47	29 18	29 49	30 20	30 51	31 22
60	25 57	26 27	26 57	27 27	27 57	28 27	28 57	29 27	29 57	30 27
61	25 10	25 39	26 8	26 37	27 6	27 35	28 4	28 34	29 3	29 32
62	24 22	24 51	25 19	25 47	26 15	26 43	27 11	27 40	28 8	28 36
63	23 35	24 2	24 29	24 56	25 23	25 51	26 18	26 45	27 12	27 40
64	22 46	23 12	23 39	24 5	24 31	24 58	25 24	25 50	26 17	26 43
65	21 57	22 23	22 48	23 13	23 39	24 4	24 30	24 55	25 20	25 46
66	21 8	21 32	21 57	22 21	22 46	23 10	23 34	23 59	24 23	24 48
67	20 18	20 42	21 5	21 29	21 52	22 16	22 39	23 2	23 26	23 49
68	19 28	19 51	20 13	20 36	20 58	21 21	21 43	22 6	22 28	22 51
69	18 38	18 59	19 21	19 42	20 4	20 25	20 47	21 8	21 30	21 51
70	17 47	18 7	18 28	18 49	19 9	19 30	19 50	20 11	20 31	20 52
71	16 56	17 15	17 35	17 54	18 14	18 33	18 53	19 12	19 32	19 52
72	16 4	16 23	16 41	17 0	17 18	17 37	17 55	18 14	18 33	18 51
73	15 12	15 30	15 47	16 5	16 23	16 40	16 58	17 15	17 33	17 50
74	14 20	14 37	14 53	15 10	15 26	15 43	16 0	16 16	16 33	16 49
75	13 28	13 43	13 59	14 14	14 30	14 46	15 1	15 17	15 32	15 48
76	12 35	12 50	13 4	13 19	13 33	13 48	14 2	14 17	14 31	14 46
77	11 42	11 56	12 9	12 23	12 36	12 50	13 3	13 17	13 30	13 44
78	10 49	11 2	11 14	11 27	11 39	11 51	12 4	12 16	12 29	12 41
79	9 55	10 7	10 19	10 30	10 42	10 53	11 4	11 16	11 27	11 39
80	9 2	9 13	9 23	9 33	9 44	9 54	10 5	10 15	10 25	10 36
81	8 8	8 18	8 27	8 37	8 46	8 55	9 5	9 14	9 24	9 33
82	7 15	7 23	7 31	7 40	7 48	7 56	8 5	8 13	8 21	8 30
83	6 21	6 28	6 35	6 42	6 50	6 57	7 4	7 12	7 19	7 27
84	5 26	5 32	5 39	5 45	5 51	5 58	6 4	6 10	6 17	6 23
85	4 32	4 37	4 43	4 48	4 53	4 58	5 4	5 9	5 14	5 19
86	3 38	3 42	3 46	3 50	3 55	3 59	4 3	4 7	4 11	4 15
87	2 43	2 47	2 50	2 53	2 56	2 59	3 2	3 5	3 9	3 12
88	1 49	1 51	1 53	1 55	1 57	1 59	2 2	2 4	2 6	2 8
89	0 54	0 56	0 57	0 58	0 59	1 0	1 1	1 2	1 3	1 4
90	0 0	0 0	0 0	0 0	0 0	0 0	0 0	0 0	0 0	0 0

A TABLE of the AMOUNT of L. 1
Compound Interest.

Years	3 p.C.	4 p.C.	5 p.C.	Years	3 p.C.	4 p.C.	5 p.C.
1	1.03000	1.04000	1.05000	26	2.15659	2.77247	3.55567
2	1.06090	1.08160	1.10250	27	2.22129	2.88337	3.73346
3	1.09273	1.12486	1.15762	28	2.28793	2.99870	3.92013
4	1.12551	1.16986	1.21551	29	2.35657	3.11865	4.11614
5	1.15927	1.21665	1.27628	30	2.42726	3.24340	4.32194
6	1.19405	1.26532	1.34010	31	2.50008	3.37313	4.53804
7	1.22987	1.31593	1.40710	32	2.57508	3.50806	4.76494
8	1.26677	1.36857	1.47746	33	2.65234	3.64838	5.00319
9	1.30477	1.42331	1.55133	34	2.73191	3.79432	5.25335
10	1.34392	1.48024	1.62895	35	2.81386	3.94609	5.51602
11	1.38423	1.53945	1.71034	36	2.89828	4.10393	5.79182
12	1.42576	1.60103	1.79586	37	2.98523	4.26809	6.08141
13	1.46853	1.66507	1.88565	38	3.07478	4.43881	6.38548
14	1.51259	1.73168	1.97993	39	3.16709	4.61637	6.70475
15	1.55797	1.80094	2.07893	40	3.26204	4.80102	7.03999
16	1.60471	1.87298	2.18287	41	3.35990	4.99306	7.39199
17	1.65285	1.94790	2.29202	42	3.46070	5.19278	7.76159
18	1.70243	2.02582	2.40662	43	3.56452	5.40050	8.14967
19	1.75351	2.10685	2.52695	44	3.67145	5.61652	8.55715
20	1.80611	2.19112	2.65330	45	3.78160	5.84118	8.98501
21	1.86029	2.27877	2.78596	46	3.89504	6.07482	9.43426
22	1.91610	2.36992	2.92526	47	4.01190	6.31782	9.90597
23	1.97359	2.46472	3.07152	48	4.13225	6.57053	10.40127
24	2.03279	2.56330	3.22510	49	4.25622	6.83335	10.92133
25	2.09378	2.66584	3.38635	50	4.38391	7.10668	11.46740

A TABLE of the PRESENT VALUE of L. 1
Compound Interest.

Years	3 p.C.	4 p.C.	5 p.C.	Years	3 p.C.	4 p.C.	5 p.C.
1	.970874	.961538	.952381	26	.463695	.360689	.281241
2	.942596	.924556	.907029	27	.450189	.346817	.267848
3	.915142	.888996	.863838	28	.437077	.333477	.255094
4	.888487	.854804	.822702	29	.424346	.320651	.242946
5	.862609	.821927	.783526	30	.411987	.308319	.231377
6	.837484	.790315	.746215	31	.399987	.296460	.220359
7	.813092	.759918	.710681	32	.388337	.285058	.209866
8	.789409	.730690	.676839	33	.377026	.274094	.199873
9	.766417	.702587	.644609	34	.366045	.263552	.190355
10	.744094	.675564	.613913	35	.355383	.253415	.181290
11	.722421	.649581	.584679	36	.345032	.243669	.172657
12	.701380	.624597	.556837	37	.334983	.234297	.164436
13	.680951	.600574	.530321	38	.325226	.225285	.156605
14	.661118	.577475	.505068	39	.315754	.216621	.149148
15	.641862	.555265	.481017	40	.306557	.208289	.142046
16	.623167	.533908	.458112	41	.297628	.200278	.135282
17	.605016	.513373	.436297	42	.288959	.192575	.128840
18	.587395	.493628	.415521	43	.280543	.185168	.122704
19	.570286	.474642	.395734	44	.272372	.178046	.116864
20	.553676	.456387	.376889	45	.264439	.171198	.111297
21	.537549	.438834	.358942	46	.256737	.164614	.105997
22	.521893	.421955	.341850	47	.249259	.158283	.100949
23	.506692	.405726	.325571	48	.241999	.152195	.096142
24	.491934	.390121	.310068	49	.234950	.146341	.091364
25	.477606	.375117	.295303	50	.228107	.140713	.087204

A TABLE OF THE AMOUNT OF L. 1 ANNUITY
Compound Interest.

Years	3 p.C.	4 p.C.	5 p.C.	Years	3 p.C.	4 p.C.	5 p.C.
1	1.0000	1.0000	1.0000	26	38.5530	44.3117	51.1135
2	2.0300	2.0400	2.0500	27	40.7096	47.0842	54.6691
3	3.0909	3.1216	3.1525	28	42.9309	49.9676	58.4026
4	4.1836	4.2465	4.3101	29	45.2189	52.9663	62.3227
5	5.3091	5.4163	5.5256	30	47.5754	56.0849	66.4388
6	6.4684	6.6330	6.8019	31	50.0027	59.3283	70.7608
7	7.6624	7.8983	8.1420	32	52.5028	62.7015	75.2988
8	8.8923	9.2142	9.5491	33	55.0778	66.2095	80.0638
9	10.1591	10.5828	11.0266	34	57.7302	69.8579	85.0670
10	11.4639	12.0061	12.5779	35	60.4621	73.6522	90.3203
11	12.8078	13.4864	14.2068	36	63.2759	77.5983	95.8363
12	14.1920	15.0258	15.9171	37	63.1742	81.7022	101.6281
13	15.6178	16.6268	17.7130	38	66.1594	85.9703	107.7095
14	17.0863	18.2919	19.5986	39	72.2342	90.4091	114.0950
15	18.5989	20.0236	21.5786	40	75.4013	95.0255	120.7998
16	20.1569	21.8245	23.6575	41	78.6633	99.8265	127.8398
17	21.7616	23.6975	25.8404	42	82.0232	104.8196	135.2318
18	23.4144	25.6454	28.1324	43	85.4839	110.0124	142.9933
19	25.1169	27.6712	30.5390	44	89.0484	115.4128	151.1430
20	26.8704	29.7781	33.0660	45	92.7199	121.0294	159.7002
21	28.6765	31.9692	35.7193	46	96.5014	126.8706	168.6852
22	30.5368	34.2480	38.5052	47	100.3965	132.9453	178.1194
23	32.4529	36.6179	41.4305	48	104.4084	139.2632	188.0254
24	34.4265	39.0826	44.5020	49	108.5406	145.8337	198.4267
25	36.4593	41.6459	47.7271	50	112.7969	152.6671	209.3480

A TABLE OF THE PRESENT VALUE OF L. 1 ANNUITY
Compound Interest.

Years	3 p.C.	4 p.C.	5 p.C.	Years	3 p.C.	4 p.C.	5 p.C.
1	0.9709	0.9615	0.9524	26	17.8768	15.9828	14.3752
2	1.9135	1.8861	1.8594	27	18.3270	16.3296	14.6430
3	2.8286	2.7751	2.7232	28	18.7640	16.6631	14.8981
4	3.7171	3.6299	3.5460	29	19.1885	16.9837	15.1411
5	4.5797	4.4518	4.3295	30	19.6004	17.2920	15.3725
6	5.4172	5.2421	5.0757	31	20.0004	17.5885	15.5928
7	6.2303	6.0021	5.7864	32	20.3888	17.8736	15.8027
8	7.0197	6.7327	6.4632	33	20.7658	18.1476	16.0025
9	7.7861	7.4353	7.1078	34	21.1318	18.4112	16.1929
10	8.5302	8.1109	7.7217	35	21.4872	18.6646	16.3742
11	9.2526	8.7605	8.3064	36	21.8323	18.9083	16.5469
12	9.9540	9.3851	8.8633	37	22.1672	19.1426	16.7113
13	10.6350	9.9856	9.3936	38	22.4925	19.3679	16.8679
14	11.2961	10.5631	9.8986	39	22.8082	19.5845	17.0170
15	11.9379	11.1184	10.3797	40	23.1148	19.7928	17.1591
16	12.5611	11.6523	10.8378	41	23.4124	19.9931	17.2944
17	13.1661	12.1657	11.2741	42	23.7014	20.1856	17.4232
18	13.7535	12.6593	11.6896	43	23.9819	20.3708	17.5460
19	14.3238	13.1340	12.0853	44	24.2543	20.5488	17.6628
20	14.8775	13.5903	12.4622	45	24.5187	20.7200	17.7741
21	15.4150	14.0292	12.8212	46	24.7754	20.8847	17.8801
22	15.9369	14.4511	13.1630	47	25.0247	21.0429	17.9810
23	16.4436	14.8568	13.4886	48	25.2662	21.1951	18.0772
24	16.9355	15.2470	13.7986	49	25.5017	21.3415	18.1687
25	17.4131	15.6221	14.0939	50	25.7298	21.4822	18.2559

A TABLE OF THE PROBABILITIES OF LIFE,

According to the Bills of Mortality at London CORRECTED.

A	Liv.	D.	A	Liv.	D.	A	Liv.	D.	A	Liv.	D.	A	Liv.	D.	A	Liv.	D.
0	1518	486	16	522	7	31	404	9	46	262	10	61	139	7	76	43	5
1	1032	200	17	515	7	32	395	9	47	252	10	62	132	7	77	38	5
2	832	85	18	508	7	33	386	9	48	242	9	63	125	7	78	33	4
3	747	59	19	501	7	34	377	9	49	233	9	64	118	7	79	29	4
4	688	42	20	494	7	35	368	9	50	224	9	65	111	7	80	25	3
5	646	23	21	487	8	36	359	9	51	215	9	66	104	7	81	22	3
6	623	20	22	479	8	37	350	9	52	206	8	67	97	7	82	19	3
7	603	14	23	471	8	38	341	9	53	198	8	68	90	7	83	16	3
8	589	12	24	463	8	39	332	10	54	190	7	69	83	7	84	13	2
9	577	10	25	455	8	40	322	10	55	183	7	70	76	6	85	11	2
10	567	9	26	447	8	41	312	10	56	176	7	71	70	6	86	9	2
11	558	9	27	439	8	42	302	10	57	169	7	72	64	6	87	7	2
12	549	8	28	431	9	43	292	10	58	162	7	73	58	5	88	5	1
13	541	7	29	422	9	44	282	10	59	155	8	74	53	5	89	4	1
14	534	6	30	413	9	45	272	10	60	147	8	75	48	5	90	3	1
15	528	6															

A TABLE OF THE PROBABILITIES OF LIFE,

According to the Bills of Mortality at Northampton.

A	Liv.	D.	A	Liv.	D.	A	Liv.	D.	A	Liv.	D.	A	Liv.	D.	A	Liv.	D.
0	11650	3000	17	5320	58	33	4160	75	49	2936	79	65	1632	80	81	406	60
1	8650	1367	18	5262	63	34	4085	75	50	2857	81	66	1552	80	82	346	57
2	7283	502	19	5199	67	35	4010	75	51	2776	82	67	1472	80	83	289	55
3	6781	335	20	5132	72	36	3935	75	52	2694	82	68	1392	80	84	234	48
4	6446	197	21	5060	75	37	3860	75	53	2612	82	69	1312	80	85	186	41
5	6249	184	22	4985	75	38	3785	75	54	2530	82	70	1232	80	86	145	34
6	6065	140	23	4910	75	39	3710	75	55	2448	82	71	1152	80	87	111	28
7	5925	110	24	4835	75	40	3635	76	56	2366	82	72	1072	80	88	83	21
8	5815	80	25	4760	75	41	3559	77	57	2284	82	73	992	80	89	62	16
9	5735	60	26	4685	75	42	3482	78	58	2202	82	74	912	80	90	46	12
10	5675	52	27	4610	75	43	3404	78	59	2120	82	75	832	80	91	34	10
11	5623	50	28	4535	75	44	3326	78	60	2038	82	76	752	77	92	24	8
12	5573	50	29	4460	75	45	3248	78	61	1956	82	77	675	73	93	16	7
13	5523	50	30	4385	75	46	3170	78	62	1874	81	78	602	68	94	9	5
14	5473	50	31	4310	75	47	3092	78	63	1793	81	79	534	65	95	4	3
15	5423	50	32	4235	75	48	3014	78	64	1712	80	80	469	63	96	1	1
16	5373	53															

A TABLE OF THE EXPECTATION OF LIFE AT NORTHAMPTON.

A	Expect.	A	Expect.	A	Expect.	A	Expect.	A	Expect.	A	Expect.
0	25.18	17	35.20	33	26.72	49	18.49	65	10.88	81	4.41
1	32.74	18	34.58	34	26.20	50	17.99	66	10.42	82	4.09
2	37.79	19	33.99	35	25.68	51	17.50	67	9.96	83	3.80
3	39.55	20	33.43	36	25.16	52	17.02	68	9.50	84	3.58
4	40.58	21	32.90	37	24.64	53	16.54	69	9.05	85	3.37
5	40.84	22	32.39	38	24.12	54	16.06	70	8.60	86	3.19
6	41.07	23	31.88	39	23.60	55	15.58	71	8.17	87	3.01
7	41.03	24	31.36	40	23.08	56	15.10	72	7.74	88	2.86
8	40.79	25	30.85	41	22.56	57	14.63	73	7.33	89	2.66
9	40.36	26	30.33	42	22.04	58	14.15	74	6.92	90	2.41
10	39.78	27	29.82	43	21.54	59	13.68	75	6.54	91	2.09
11	39.14	28	29.30	44	21.03	60	13.21	76	6.18	92	1.75
12	38.49	29	28.79	45	20.52	61	12.75	77	5.83	93	1.37
13	37.83	30	28.27	46	20.02	62	12.28	78	5.48	94	1.05
14	37.17	31	27.76	47	19.51	63	11.81	79	5.11	95	0.75
15	36.51	32	27.24	48	19.00	64	11.35	80	4.75	96	0.50
16	35.85										

A
TABLE

OF THE VALUE OF

An ANNUITY OF L. 1

FOR A SINGLE LIFE,

According to Mr. De Moivre's Hypothesis.

Age	3 Per Cent.	4 Per Cent.	5 Per Cent.	Age	3 Per Cent.	4 Per Cent.	5 Per Cent.
10	19.868	16.882	14.607	48	13.012	11.748	10.679
11	19.736	16.791	14.544	49	12.764	11.548	10.515
12	19.604	16.698	14.480	50	12.511	11.344	10.348
13	19.469	16.604	14.412	51	12.255	11.135	10.176
14	19.331	16.508	14.342	52	11.994	10.921	9.999
15	19.192	16.410	14.271	53	11.729	10.702	9.817
16	19.050	16.311	14.197	54	11.457	10.478	9.630
17	18.905	16.209	14.123	55	11.183	10.248	9.437
18	18.759	16.105	14.047	56	10.902	10.014	9.239
19	18.610	15.999	13.970	57	10.616	9.773	9.036
20	18.458	15.891	13.891	58	10.325	9.527	8.826
21	18.305	15.781	13.810	59	10.029	9.275	8.611
22	18.158	15.669	13.727	60	9.727	9.017	8.389
23	17.990	15.554	13.642	61	9.419	8.753	8.161
24	17.827	15.437	13.555	62	9.107	8.482	7.926
25	17.664	15.318	13.466	63	8.787	8.205	7.684
26	17.497	15.197	13.375	64	8.462	7.921	7.435
27	17.327	15.073	13.282	65	8.132	7.631	7.179
28	17.154	14.946	13.186	66	7.794	7.333	6.915
29	16.979	14.816	13.088	67	7.450	7.027	6.643
30	16.800	14.684	12.988	68	7.099	6.714	6.362
31	16.620	14.549	12.855	69	6.743	6.394	6.073
32	16.436	14.411	12.780	70	6.378	6.065	5.775
33	16.248	14.270	12.673	71	6.008	5.728	5.468
34	16.057	14.126	12.562	72	5.631	5.383	5.152
35	15.864	13.979	12.449	73	5.246	5.029	4.826
36	15.666	13.829	12.333	74	4.854	4.666	4.489
37	15.465	13.676	12.214	75	4.453	4.293	4.143
38	15.260	13.519	12.091	76	4.046	3.912	3.784
39	15.053	13.359	11.966	77	3.632	3.520	3.415
40	14.842	13.196	11.837	78	3.207	3.111	3.034
41	14.626	13.028	11.705	79	2.776	2.707	2.641
42	14.407	12.858	11.570	80	2.334	2.284	2.235
43	14.185	12.683	11.431	81	1.886	1.850	1.816
44	13.958	12.504	11.288	82	1.429	1.406	1.384
45	13.728	12.322	11.142	83	0.961	0.950	0.937
46	13.493	12.135	10.992	84	0.484	0.481	0.476
47	13.254	11.944	10.837	85	0.000	0.000	0.000

A
TABLE
OF THE VALUE OF
AN ANNUITY OF 1 L.
ON A SINGLE LIFE,

According to the Probabilities of Life at Northampton.

Age.	3 Per Cent.	4 Per Cent.	5 Per Cent.	Age.	3 Per Cent.	4 Per Cent.	5 Per Cent.
0	13.802	10.327	8.863	49	12.693	11.475	10.433
1	16.021	13.465	11.563	50	12.436	11.264	10.269
2	18.599	15.633	13.420	51	12.183	11.057	10.097
3	19.575	16.462	14.135	52	11.930	10.849	9.925
4	20.210	17.010	14.613	53	11.674	10.637	9.748
5	20.473	17.248	14.827	54	11.414	10.421	9.567
6	20.727	17.482	15.041	55	11.150	10.201	9.382
7	20.853	17.611	15.166	56	10.826	9.977	9.193
8	20.885	17.662	15.226	57	10.611	9.749	8.999
9	20.812	17.625	15.210	58	10.337	9.516	8.801
10	20.663	17.523	15.139	59	10.058	9.280	8.599
11	20.480	17.393	15.043	60	9.777	9.039	8.392
12	20.283	17.251	14.937	61	9.493	8.795	8.181
13	20.081	17.103	14.826	62	9.205	8.547	7.966
14	19.872	16.950	14.710	63	8.910	8.291	7.742
15	19.657	16.791	14.588	64	8.611	8.030	7.514
16	19.435	16.625	14.460	65	8.304	7.761	7.276
17	19.218	16.462	14.334	66	7.994	7.488	7.034
18	19.013	16.309	14.217	67	7.632	7.211	6.787
19	18.820	16.167	14.108	68	7.367	6.930	6.536
20	18.638	16.033	14.007	69	7.051	6.647	6.281
21	18.470	15.912	13.917	70	6.734	6.361	6023
22	18.311	15.797	13.833	71	6.418	6.075	5.764
23	18.148	15.680	13.746	72	6.103	5.790	5.504
24	17.983	15.560	13.658	73	5.794	5.507	5.245
25	17.814	15.438	13.567	74	5.491	5.230	4.990
26	17.642	15.312	13.473	75	5.198	4.962	4.744
27	17.467	15.184	13.377	76	4.925	4.710	4.511
28	17.289	15.053	13.278	77	4.652	4.457	4.277
29	17.107	14.918	13.177	78	4.372	4.197	4035
30	16.922	14.781	13.072	79	4.077	3.921	3.776
31	16.732	14.639	12.965	80	3.781	3.643	3.515
32	16.540	14.495	12.854	81	3.499	3.377	3.263
33	16.343	14.347	12.740	82	3.229	3.122	3.020
34	16.142	14.195	12.623	83	2.982	2.887	2.797
35	15.938	14.039	12.502	84	2.793	2.708	2.627
36	15.729	13.880	12.377	85	2.620	2.543	2.471
37	15.515	13.716	12.249	86	2.461	2.393	2.328
38	15.298	13.548	12.116	87	2.312	2.251	2.193
39	15.075	13.375	11.979	88	2.185	2.131	2.080
40	14.848	13.197	11.837	89	2.015	1.967	1.924
41	14.620	13.018	11.695	90	1.794	1.758	1.723
42	14.391	12.838	11.551	91	1.501	1.474	1.447
43	14.162	12.657	11.407	92	1.190	1.171	1.153
44	13.929	12.472	11.258	93	0.839	0.827	0.816
45	13.692	12.283	11.105	94	0.536	0.530	0.523
46	13.450	12.089	10.947	95	0.242	0.240	0.238
47	13.203	11.890	10.784	96	0.000	0.000	0.000
48	12.951	11.685	10.616				

A TABLE

OF THE VALUE OF

An ANNUITY of L. 1

ON TWO JOINT LIVES,

According to the Probabilities of Life at Northampton.

Age	Ages	3 Per Cent.	4 Per Cent.	5 Per Cent.
10	10	16.339	14.227	12.665
	15	15.702	13.841	12.302
	20	15.151	13.355	11.906
	25	14.683	12.948	11.627
	30	14.150	12.586	11.304
	35	13.525	12.098	10.916
	40	12.791	11.513	10.442
	45	11.976	10.851	09.900
	50	11.044	10.085	09.260
	55	10.055	09.256	08.560
	60	08.952	08.314	07.750
	65	07.718	07.236	06.830
	70	06.342	06.008	05.700
15	15	15.223	13.411	11.960
	20	14.660	12.961	11.585
	25	14.230	12.630	11.324
	30	13.734	12.246	11.021
	35	13.151	11.787	10.655
	40	12.459	11.234	10.205
	45	11.687	10.607	09.690
	50	10.798	09.872	09.076
	55	09.850	09.077	08.403
	60	08.790	08.170	07.622
	65	07.597	07.117	06.705
	70	06.264	05.933	05.631
20	20	14.133	12.535	11.232
	25	13.741	12.229	10.989
	30	13.286	11.873	10.707
	35	12.744	11.445	10.363
	40	12.096	10.924	09.937
	45	11.367	10.330	09.448
	50	10.522	09.630	08.861
	55	09.616	08.869	08.216
	60	08.596	07.995	07.463
	65	07.443	06.986	06.576
	70	06.149	05.826	05.532
25	25	13.383	11.944	10.764
	30	12.966	11.618	10.499
	35	12.463	11.287	10.175
	40	11.854	10.725	09.771
	45	11.164	10.160	09.304
	50	10.356	09.488	08.759
	55	09.484	08.754	08.116
	60	08.495	07.906	07.383
	65	07.370	06.920	06.515
	70	06.092	05.780	05.489

Age	Ages	3 Per Cent.	4 Per Cent.	5 Per Cent.
30	30	12.589	11.313	10.255
	35	12.131	10.948	09.954
	40	11.568	10.490	09.576
	45	10.923	09.959	09.135
	50	10.160	09.321	08.596
	55	09.329	08.619	07.999
	60	08.378	07.802	07.292
	65	07.286	06.844	06.447
	70	06.043	05.729	05.442
35	35	11.722	10.612	09.680
	40	11.213	10.196	09.331
	45	10.622	09.706	08.921
	50	09.912	09.110	08.415
	55	09.131	08.448	07.849
	60	08.227	07.669	07.114
	65	07.117	06.747	06.360
	70	05.971	05.663	05.382
40	40	10.764	09.820	09.018
	45	10.235	09.381	08.643
	50	09.590	08.834	08.177
	55	08.870	08.221	07.651
	60	08.025	07.490	07.015
	65	07.029	06.614	06.240
	70	05.870	05.571	05.298
45	45	09.776	08.990	08.312
	50	09.204	08.503	07.891
	55	08.557	07.948	07.411
	60	07.781	07.274	06.822
	65	06.850	06.453	06.094
	70	05.749	05.460	05.195
50	50	08.714	08.081	07.522
	55	08.151	07.593	07.098
	60	07.460	06.989	06.568
	65	06.611	06.236	05.897
	70	05.582	05.306	05.054
55	55	07.681	07.179	06.735
	60	07.088	06.659	06.272
	65	06.334	05.986	05.671
	70	05.394	05.132	04.893
60	60	06.606	06.226	05.888
	65	05.970	05.658	05.372
	70	05.149	04.900	04.680
65	65	05.471	05.201	04.960
	70	04.782	04.573	04.378
70	70	04.261	04.087	03.930

CPSIA information can be obtained
at www.ICGtesting.com
Printed in the USA
BVHW041820090222
628519BV00009B/271

9 780343 984106